THE
LANCASHIRE WITCHES
HISTORIES AND STORIES

edited by Robert Poole

MANCHESTER
UNIVERSITY PRESS
Manchester and New York

distributed exclusively in the USA by Palgrave

Published by Manchester University Press
Oxford Road, Manchester M13 9NR, UK
and Room 400, 175 Fifth Avenue, New York, NY 10010, USA
www.manchesteruniversitypress.co.uk

Distributed exclusively in the USA by
Palgrave, 175 Fifth Avenue, New York,
NY 10010, USA

Distributed exclusively in Canada by
UBC Press, University of British Columbia, 2029 West Mall,
Vancouver, BC, Canada V6T 1Z2

British Library Cataloguing-in-Publication Data
A catalogue record for this book is available from the British Library

Library of Congress Cataloging-in-Publication Data applied for

ISBN   0 7190 6203 9 *hardback*
        0 7190 6204 7 *paperback*

First published 2002

10 09 08 07 06 05 04 03 02   10 9 8 7 6 5 4 3 2 1

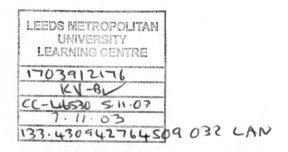
Printed in Great Britain
by Bookcraft (Bath) Ltd, Midsomer Norton

THE
WONDERFVLL
DISCOVERIE OF
WITCHES IN THE COVN-
TIE OF LAN-
CASTER.

With the Arraignement and Triall of
Nineteene notorious WITCHES, at the Assizes and
generall Gaole deliuerie, holden at the Castle of
LANCASTER, vpon Munday, the se-
uenteenth of August last,
1612.

Before Sir IAMES ALTHAM, and
Sir EDWARD BROMLEY, Knights; BARONS of his
Maiesties Court of EXCHEQVER: And Iustices
of Assize, Oyer and Terminor, and generall
Gaole deliuerie in the circuit of the
North Parts.

Together with the Arraignement and Triall of IENNET
PRESTON, at the Assizes holden at the Castle of Yorke,
the seuen and twentieth day of Iulie last past,
with her Execution for the murther
of Master LISTER
by Witchcraft.

Published and set forth by commandement of his Maiesties
Iustices of Assize in the North Parts.

By THOMAS POTTS Esquier.

LONDON,
Printed by W. Stansby for Iohn Barnes, dwelling neare
Holborne Conduit. 1613.

Title page to Thomas Potts, *The Wonderfull Discoverie of
Witches in the Countie of Lancaster* (1613)

Contents

CONTENTS

Notes on contributors

Kirsteen Macpherson Bardell is Lecturer in History at the University of Wolverhampton and the University of Nottingham and is also a holistic therapist. Her Ph.D. thesis, '"Death by divelishe demonstracion": witchcraft beliefs, gender and popular religion in the early modern midlands and north of England' (Nottingham Trent University, 1999) focused on popular witchcraft beliefs in early modern England.

Alison Findlay is Senior Lecturer in English at Lancaster University. She has written extensively on women in Renaissance drama and on Shakespeare. Her publications include *Illegitimate Power: Bastards in Renaissance Drama* (1994), *A Feminist Perspective on Renaissance Drama* (1998) and (as co-author) *Women and Dramatic Production 1550–1700* (2000). She is co-director of a practical research project on early modern women's drama, and an editor of the *Lancastrian Shakespeare* volumes (2003).

Marion Gibson is Lecturer in English at Exeter University and Truro College, Cornwall. Her research interests include Renaissance literature, biography, and British and American representations of the supernatural, including on film. She is the author of *Reading Witchcraft: Stories of Early English Witches* (1999) and *Early Modern Witches: Witchcraft Cases in Contemporary Writing* (2000).

Jonathan Lumby read Theology at Cambridge and subsequently studied at both Oxford and London universities. He has taught in Zimbabwe and England, is a former Vicar of Gisburn, and is now Rector of Eccleston, Chester. He is the author of *The Lancashire Witch-Craze: Jennet Preston and the Lancashire Witches* (1995).

Michael Mullett is Professor of Cultural and Religious History at the University of Lancaster, where he has taught for over thirty years, his current teaching concerns being popular culture and popular protest, the history of the Jews in Europe, and Luther and the European Reformation. His most recent books are *John Bunyan in Context* (1996), *Catholics in Britain and Ireland, 1558–1829* (1998) and *The Catholic Reformation* (1999). He is currently working on a life of Martin Luther.

Joanne Pearson is Lecturer at the Department of Religious and Theological Studies, Cardiff University. She is the author of *A Popular Dictionary of Paganism* (2002), and of *Wicca: Magic, Spirituality and the 'Mystic Other'* (2003), a revised version of her Lancaster University Ph.D. thesis. She was the organiser of a 1996 conference on modern paganism at Lancaster University, whose papers were published as *Nature Religion Today* (1998).

Robert Poole is Reader in History at St Martin's College, Lancaster, where he teaches early modern and modern British history, and was the organiser of the 1999 weekend conference on 'The Lancashire Witches: History, Heritage and Representation 1612–1999' which gave rise to this book. His publications include *Time's Alteration: Calendar Reform in Early Modern England* (1998) and *The Diaries of Samuel Bamford* (with Martin Hewitt) (2000).

Stephen Pumfrey is Senior Lecturer in History at the University of Lancaster. He has written on the history of science and ideas in early modern England, editing and contributing to *Science, Culture and Popular Belief in Renaissance Europe* (1991). His book *Latitude and the Magnetic Earth* was published in 2002.

Jeffrey Richards is Professor of Cultural History at the University of Lancaster and has written and broadcast extensively on both medieval history and nineteenth- and twentieth-century cultural history. He is the author of a number of books, including *The Popes and the Papacy in the Early Middle Ages* (1979), *Sex, Dissidence and Damnation* (1991) and *Imperialism and Music* (2001).

James Sharpe is Professor of History at York University. He has written extensively on the social history of early modern England, particularly crime and witchcraft. His publications include *Early Modern England: A Social History 1550–1750* (1987), *Instruments of Darkness: Witchcraft in England 1550–1750* (1996), *The Bewitching of Anne Gunther: A Horrible and True Story of Football, Witchcraft, Murder, and the King of England* (1999) and *Witchcraft in Early Modern England* (2001).

John Swain teaches history at Nottingham High School. He is author of 'The Lancashire witch trials of 1612 and 1634 and the economics of witchcraft' (*Northern History*, 1994), *Industry Before the Industrial Revolution: North-East Lancashire c. 1500–1640* (1986) and 'Capital formation by clothiers in north-east Lancashire c. 1550–1640' (*Northern History*, 1997).

Richard Wilson is Professor of Renaissance Studies at the University of Lancaster and Visiting Professor of Shakespeare Studies at the Sorbonne University (Paris III). He was co-organiser of the 1999 Lancastrian Shakespeare conference and is Academic Adviser to the planned Hoghton Tower Shakespeare Centre. He has edited volumes on *New Historicism and Renaissance Drama* (1993), *Christopher Marlowe* (1999), *Julius Caesar* (2001) and *Lancastrian Shakespeare* (2003). His publications include *Will Power: Essays on Shakespearean Authority* (1993) and *Secret Shakespeare* (2003).

Preface

> If we want to solve a problem that we have never solved before, we must leave the door to the unknown ajar. (Richard Feynman[1])

Sometimes the Lancashire witches seem very close. The well tower at Lancaster Castle where they were imprisoned, centuries old even then, looms over the city. Inside are rusty iron fittings. Water still drips into hidden wells, and as the ancient studded oak door closes the darkness is that of another age. The cobbled Roman road along which the witches travelled on their final journey to the gallows passes a fine Jacobean residence, used as lodgings for later generations of Assize judges. In front is a memorial to Thomas Covell, the witches' gaoler. Across the city centre the road begins its climb to the moor at the Golden Lion, the site of a pub since 1612 – the year of the witches. The moor itself remains green, occupied now by a playing field, a fine Edwardian park, and St Martin's College. There, generations of history students have learned about the trial of the Lancashire witches, within sight of the castle and close to the spot, now unknown, where those same witches were hanged nearly four centuries before.

In another sense, the Lancashire witches are far away. We (or most of us) no longer believe, as both they and their persecutors believed, that witchcraft is possible. The mental world of the seventeenth century is almost as alien to us as that of the Incas. It was the imaginative study of such alien phenomena as witchcraft that helped fuel the social and cultural history renaissance of the last third of the twentieth century. Many of those scholars have had connections with Lancaster's two higher education institutions, Lancaster University and St Martin's College, although specialist knowledge of the Lancashire witch trials is by no means confined to academics. All this work is underpinned by an unquenchable public interest in this most famous and best-documented of all English witch trials.

Thus it was that a two-day event entitled 'The Lancashire Witches: History, Heritage and Representation 1612–1999' came to be held on 23–24 April 1999. Organised jointly by the Centre for North West Regional Studies, Lancaster University, and St Martin's College, it took place at the College, on what used to be part of the moor, a few hundred yards from an ancient row of cottages whose name preserves the memory of a place of execution: Golgotha. On the first day nearly a hundred participants listened to seven invited speakers – Stephen Pumfrey, Marion Gibson, John Swain, Jonathan Lumby, Kirsteen Macpherson Bardell, Richard Wilson and Sarah Lee – give papers on various aspects of the Lancashire witch trials. After dinner, they reassembled at the King's Arms Hotel, opposite Lancaster Castle, for talks by Ronald Hutton and Joanne Pearson on twentieth-century Wicca and paganism. The next day, a Saturday, two coaches set off to visit the principal sites of the Lancashire witches trail, meeting in Whalley Abbey for a lunchtime paper by Michael Mullett, memorably concluded out of doors in the abbey ruins. Throughout the event there was the exciting sense of a number of different kinds of expertise coming together on the same historical problem to generate new insights. Eight of the ten papers from 1999 are included in this collection. Two further essays have since been added: those by Alison Findlay and Jeffrey Richards. James Sharpe, unable to attend, kindly agreed to read all the papers and to write the introduction.

The result is a book in which experts in a variety of fields bring to bear their expertise on different aspects of the Lancashire witch trials of 1612 and 1633–34: history of science, history of religion, cultural history, social and economic history, English literature, Renaissance studies, religion and theology, and, of course, the specialist history of witchcraft. Seven of them are or have been Lancaster-based, and all have worked extensively on Lancashire sources. Readers will have to assess how successful this book has been in making sense of its subject, and in communicating their findings to those non-specialists who form the vast majority of those interested in the Lancashire witch trials.

This volume, like the 1999 event which gave rise to it, is aimed at academics and general readers alike. The subject of witchcraft appeals to as wide a range of interests as any historical topic, and it is right and necessary that at least some of the literature should address as many of them as possible. I trust that academic readers will understand that the editorial material is intended mainly for non-specialists, and that non-academic readers will understand that the most rewarding papers may be those whose full meaning is not apparent on a first reading. But the ideal is clarity all round, not least because there are so many different kinds of academic specialism; most of the time, we are all non-specialists. In writing up their papers for publication, the authors have been asked to bear in mind the needs of non-specialist readers from other disciplines and from none, and to write clearly, explaining technical terms and allusions. Each was given access to the papers of all the others, and encouraged to make connections. The aim has been to produce a book which can be read with pleasure and profit by people with every kind of interest, and which hangs together as more than the sum of its parts.

This collection is, however, not intended to be one of those tombstone volumes that settle all possible debates. Doubt, not certainty, is the foundation of learning. This volume settles some issues and suggests solutions to many others, but in the end it gives us not less to discuss but more. It does not close off lines of enquiry but opens them up. Its success will be measured by its effect in generating further debates, revelations and new perspectives. The door to the unknown remains open. The Lancashire witches are not dead yet.

Robert Poole
Lancaster

Notes

1 Richard P. Feynman, *The Pleasure of Finding Things Out* (1999; London: Allen Lane, 2000), p. 149.

Acknowledgements

The 1999 event on 'The Lancashire Witches: History, Heritage and Representation 1612–1999' was only one of several academic gatherings in the 1990s which had looked at the Lancashire witches in one way or another. The participants at the 'Reading Witchcraft' conference held at the University of Wales, Swansea, in September 1998 included Marion Gibson and Kirsteen Macpherson Bardell, both of whom had worked on Lancashire material and who were duly conscripted for the Lancaster event.[1] Two years before this, in April 1996, the Religious Studies department at Lancaster University had held a conference on 'Nature Religion Today', which covered twentieth-century paganism and Wicca with papers by Ronald Hutton and Joanne Pearson.[2] Ronald Hutton was to revisit Lancaster for the January 1997 Social History Society conference on 'Time and the Construction of the Past' to talk about his related work on calendar customs. In December 1993, the English department at Lancaster University had held a day conference on 'Law, Literature and Seventeenth-Century Women' which included papers by John Swain, Jonathan Lumby, James Sharpe and Alison Findlay. Three months after the 'Lancashire Witches' event, in July 1999, another, much larger, interdisciplinary event took place in the area, the international 'Lancastrian Shakespeare' conference staged between Lancaster University and Hoghton Tower, seat of the bard's likely Lancastrian residence. Richard Wilson and Alison Findlay were among the organisers.[3] To watch as the sun set on a motley band of black-faced morris dancers and Shakespearean scholars capering in the courtyard of an ancient hall where Catholics were sheltered, where Shakespeare sojourned, and where King James I was entertained by some of the same Lancashire gentry who had prosecuted the Lancashire witches, was to understand that neither the past nor the present can exist without the other.

The 1999 event which gave rise to this book could not have happened without the efforts of Christine Wilkinson and Jean Turnbull at the Centre for

ACKNOWLEDGEMENTS

North West Regional Studies, Lancaster University; the staff of Whalley Abbey, Pendle Heritage Centre, Ribble Valley Tourism and Pendle Borough Tourism; Ron Sands and colleagues at Lancaster City Council tourism service; and Christine Goodier and colleagues at Lancaster Castle. St Martin's College, Lancaster, hosted the conference, notwithstanding the eyebrows raised at the prospect of a Church of England institution assisting the study of witchcraft. At St Martin's I have benefited in various ways from the support and interest of Jan Bolton, Alan Farmer, Pam King, Steve Longstaffe and Andrew Sneddon, from the indispensable administrative support of Justine Bigland, and from the generations of St Martin's undergraduates, both BA and BEd/ QTS, who have followed a social history course so heavily skewed towards the Lancashire witches as to be justified only by their own resourceful and enthusiastic responses. If this book reaches some of them, and encourages schools in Pendle to begin introducing the citizens of the future to the most important historical episode in which their area has figured, it will have achieved something worthwhile.

Notes

1 Papers from the conference have been published in Stuart Clark (ed.), *Languages of Witchcraft: Narrative, Ideology and Meaning in Early Modern Culture* (London: Macmillan, 2001).
2 See Joanne Pearson, Richard H. Roberts and Geoffrey Samuels (eds), *Nature Religion Today: Paganism in the Modern World* (Edinburgh: Edinburgh University Press, 1998).
3 Papers from the conference are being published as Richard Dutton, Alison Findlay and Richard Wilson (eds), *Lancastrian Shakespeare: Religion and Europe* and *Lancastrian Shakespeare: Religion, Region and Patronage* (Manchester: Manchester University Press, forthcoming 2002).

1

Introduction: the Lancashire witches in historical context

James Sharpe

It is probably true to say that a clearer memory remains of the Lancashire witches of 1612 than of any of the other people who were tried and executed for witchcraft in early modern England. To an extent unique for England, the Lancashire witches have been appropriated by the tourist and heritage industries. In Newchurch village, in the heart of the Pendle country, the visitor can call in at 'Witches Galore', a shop easily identifiable by the life-size figures of witches that are placed outside it, and buy model witches, and maps, posters, pottery, or T-shirts bearing witch motifs. The visitor might then like to travel the 45-mile 'Pendle Witch Trail', which begins at the Pendle Heritage Centre at Barrowford and ends, appropriately enough, at Lancaster Castle, where the witches of 1612 were incarcerated before their trials and, in the case of ten of them, executed. Those completing the trail might refresh themselves with a bottle of Moorehouse's excellent 'Pendle Witches Brew' beer, and while away the evening reading either the novel about the witches written by that forgotten giant of the mid-nineteenth-century literary world, William Harrison Ainsworth, or a more recent fictional account, first published in 1951, Robert Neill's *Mist over Pendle*. In 1911 Wallace Notestein, a pioneer scholar of English witchcraft history, commented of the 1612 Lancashire trials that 'no case in the history of the superstition in England gained such wide fame'.[1] Nearly a century later, his sentiments seem to be equally valid.

The celebrated 1612 witch scare began on 21 March of that year when Alizon Device had her fateful encounter with the pedlar John Law, as a result of which, following that refusal of a favour which so often provoked the wrath of a witch, the unfortunate man went instantly into what was identified as a witchcraft-induced illness.[2] Law and his relatives decided to invoke the aid of officialdom, and on 30 March the local Justice of the Peace (JP) Roger Nowell examined and took statements from Alizon Device, her mother Elizabeth and her brother James, and from John Law's son, Abraham. On 2 April Nowell, as further accounts of suspected witchcraft reached him, examined Elizabeth Device's mother, the eighty-year-old Elizabeth Southerns (alias 'Old Demdike'), Anne Whittle (alias 'Chattox'), and three local witnesses. Around 4 April Nowell committed Alizon Device, Demdike, Chattox, and Chattox's daughter Anne Redferne to prison in Lancaster Castle to await trial at the next session of the Assizes. A day or two later, over the county border in York, another woman who was to become involved in the story of the Lancashire witches, Jennet Preston, was tried and acquitted at York for the killing of a child by witchcraft. On 10 April there allegedly occurred a meeting of witches at the Demdikes' home, the Malkin Tower, where the witches discussed their situation, plotted further acts of witchcraft, and planned to blow up Lancaster Castle with gunpowder and release their imprisoned friends. From the point of view of the investigating authorities, the real breakthrough came on 27 April, when in the course of further examinations Elizabeth Device and her children James and Jennet all told of the meeting at the Malkin Tower. This implicated a number of other local people as witches, and convinced Nowell and his fellow JPs that they were confronting a major outbreak of witchcraft. Accordingly, a number of suspects were rapidly committed to Lancaster Castle. The presence of a major witchcraft outbreak was confirmed on 19 May when Chattox and James Device (who confessed to being a witch at this point) made further statements to Thomas Covell, coroner and keeper of Lancaster Castle, William Sandes, the mayor of Lancaster, and the JP James Anderton.

Given more space, it would be possible to trace in detail how the statements of the alleged witches changed as their interrogations proceeded, and how initial denials or guarded statements changed into confessions as official pressure and questioning continued. The evidence of the children Jennet and James Device was vital in initiating the wider allegations of witchcraft, and a reading of the examinations published by Thomas Potts in his account of the trials shows that by this stage suspects were clearly beginning to panic and accuse each other. The investigations had reached critical mass, and neighbours came forward in large numbers to tell the authorities of acts of witchcraft which had occurred sometimes many years before, their statements sometimes revealing how witchcraft suspicions were enmeshed in local feuds and rivalries. Various local JPs were involved in gathering evidence over a period of several months.

On 27 July Jennet Preston was again tried at York Assizes, this time for witchcraft against the Listers, a locally important gentry family, and was found guilty and executed. Evidence against Preston was sent to York, and the two judges who presided there, Sir Edward Bromley and Sir James Altham, were also those in charge of the subsequent Lancaster Assizes. By this point the Lancashire authorities were clearly in close contact with the Assize judges about the forthcoming trials, and the Preston case prepared Bromley and Altham for what they were to find when they came to Lancaster. The trials of the Lancashire witches, presided over by Bromley, were held on 18–19 August. Old Demdike had died in gaol before her case came to court. Chattox, Elizabeth Device, James Device and Anne Redferne were all tried on the first day, and all but Redferne were found guilty. Redferne was tried again on the following day, as were Alizon Device, Alice Nutter, John and Jane Bulcock, Katherine Hewit, Isabel Roby and Margaret Pearson. All of them were found guilty, and in a markedly prompt exercise of justice ten of them were executed on Lancaster Moor on Thursday 20 August. Margaret Pearson, convicted for non-capital witchcraft, was sentenced to stand on the pillory in Lancaster, Clitheroe, Whalley and Padiham on four market days, where she was to make public confession of her offence, followed by a year's imprisonment. Five other individuals, of whom we learn little, were acquitted.

The Lancashire trials, so well remembered subsequently, did, in fact, constitute a remarkable episode in the history of English witchcraft.[3] There was, perhaps, little that was really novel in the matters related to the court, and most of the witnesses' and alleged witches' depositions were formed by standard accounts of witchcraft, with, of course, some interesting variations. What was unusual, apart from Potts's lengthy and apparently officially requested account of the trials, was that so many witches were hanged together, eleven if we count Jennet Preston's execution in York. Current estimates suggest that the witch persecutions in Europe between the early fifteenth and the mid eighteenth centuries resulted in about 40,000 executions, and it is probable that executions in England contributed fewer than 500 to this total.[4] There was, as far as we know, only one really mass witch-craze in England, that associated with the witch-hunter Matthew Hopkins which broke out in East Anglia in 1645 and claimed over a hundred lives.[5] But, in general, England was one of those parts of Europe where witchcraft was an endemic rather than an epidemic problem, where witch trials were sporadic and few, where accusations were usually levelled against individuals or groups of three or four suspects, and where the acquittal rate was high in witchcraft cases. The hanging of ten or eleven witches at one go was, therefore, very unusual: certainly, nothing in the experience of witch trials in England before 1612 had prepared either the population of Lancashire or those sections of the literate public who were to read Potts's *Discoverie* for the Pendle trials.

But concentration on the main series of trials has tended to divert our attention away from the associated trial of 1612, that involving the Samlesbury witches.[6] This resulted not in a clutch of executions, but rather in the acquittal of the three accused women (and it should, of course, be remembered that five of those tried in the main set of 1612 trials were also acquitted). The Samlesbury affair demonstrated just how diverse witchcraft beliefs were becoming in England by the early seventeenth century, and also how officialdom manifested a diversity of reactions to those beliefs. In the main series of trials, those which led to the conviction of Demdike, Chattox, and the rest, the root problem was *maleficium*, that doing of harm by witchcraft which lay at the heart of peasant concern over witches throughout Europe. In the Samlesbury case, we encounter in a very overt form the interface between learned views of witchcraft and those of the peasantry. Young Grace Sowerbutts accused four women (one of whom was not tried) of subjecting her to various physical abuses, of tempting her to commit suicide, of killing a young child and then exhuming and eating its body, and of transporting her over the River Ribble to what was in effect a sabbat, where she and the women danced with 'foure black things', and after the dancing had sexual intercourse with them. The court simply threw these accusations out, and Potts in his account was able both to enhance Judge Bromley's image by relating how he exposed the fraudulent nature of Sowerbutts's accusations, and to score important points against the Catholics by insisting that her accusations had been framed according to the instructions of a Catholic priest named Christopher Southworth, alias Thompson. Again, Sowerbutts's evidence deserves deeper analysis than can be devoted to it here. The incident does, however, remind us that the handling of witchcraft, demonic possession and exorcism was a contested issue between Protestants and Catholics in the decades around 1600, and it also raises the possibility that one way in which learned demonology entered the English popular consciousness was through the input of Catholic priests in cases of demonic possession and witchcraft.[7]

The 1612 trials therefore demonstrated something of the complexities of English witchcraft history. These complexities were illustrated further by the Lancashire scare of 1633–34, an incident which is maddeningly badly documented, but which, as I have contended elsewhere, marked something of a watershed in the history of English witchcraft.[8] By the early 1630s one has a sense that witchcraft, both as an offence tried by the courts and as a matter of intellectual and theological interest, had become something of a dead issue in England. In the five counties covered by the Home Circuit of the Assizes, the only Assize circuit which enjoys anything like a full survival of indictments for the relevant period, surviving documentation furnishes only nineteen accusations of malefic witchcraft, none of which resulted in execution.[9] There had been no pamphlets describing witch trials since that published in 1621 which recounted the story of Elizabeth Sawyer, of Edmonton in Middlesex, who was tried and executed for witchcraft in that year.[10] No major work of demonology had followed that written by the Puritan minister Richard Bernard, first published in 1627 and reprinted in 1629.[11] Among the population at large fear of witches was as strong as ever, as is shown by John Webster's later account of how young Edmund Robinson, the boy whose accusations prompted the 1634 craze, and his father and their associates were able to go out witch-finding.[12] But by this stage officialdom, and perhaps more accurately those Arminian senior churchmen who were flourishing during the reign of Charles I, were happy to discountenance witchcraft, at least as it was understood by the population at large.

The Lancashire scare of 1633–34 could have developed into a major outbreak of witch persecution: one contemporary account refers to sixty persons being suspected of witchcraft, and in August 1636 there were still ten suspected witches held in Lancaster gaol. Yet the reactions of central government in dampening this outbreak down were firm and decisive: the Assize judge confronting the initial prosecutions was worried and invoked central government assistance; the Bishop of Chester, John Bridgeman, was instructed to intervene and examine the suspects; the boy Edmund Robinson and his father were hauled down to London for interrogation; and five of the suspected witches were brought to the capital for examination by a medical team headed by the eminent physician William Harvey. If the 1612 executions can be adduced as a symbol of the more extreme aspects of English witch persecution, the government handling of the 1633–34 accusations demonstrates just how sceptical central authority, the upper reaches of the Church, and possibly educated opinion in general had become about malefic witchcraft by that date.[13]

Giving an outline of what happened in 1612 and 1633–34 is easy enough. Explaining why the witch trials occurred, and in particular providing an explanation for the trials and executions of 1612, is more difficult. There now exists a vast witchcraft historiography, and those seeking to account for any outbreak of witch-hunting in early modern Europe have access to a whole range of interpretations.[14] Perhaps the most widely accepted of these would revolve variously around the impact of the more intense religiosity generated by the Reformation and Counter-Reformation; the processes of state formation; the impact of socio-economic change, and more particularly population pressure and the resultant pressure on resources, in rural communities; and the problem of gender, of why so many of those accused as witches were women. As the chapters in this collection demonstrate, a number of these interpretations are relevant to witchcraft in early Stuart Lancashire.

Since the publication of important works by Alan Macfarlane and Keith Thomas in the early 1970s,[15] the standard interpretation of witchcraft in England has tended to privilege a socio-economic interpretation. Thus witchcraft accusations were seen characteristically as being levelled by richer villagers against poorer ones, with refusals of charity (broadly defined) being the most important trigger for the 'fallings-out' which characteristically preceded an accusation of witchcraft. An old woman would come to the door of a neighbour, ask for food, drink, a little money or the opportunity to do some work, would be denied her request, and would walk away uttering curses. A little later, a misfortune would befall the household of the refuser, and the link would be made between the misfortune and the curses or other expressions of discontent made by the old woman, a connection which would be made all the more readily if the woman already had the reputation of being a witch. As John Swain demonstrates in this volume, the Pendle area, like most rural areas in western and central Europe, was experiencing population pressure, poverty and the reality of scarce resources at the base of society. To these general issues were added the more local problems of occasional disruption in the cloth trade, and, in 1623, crisis mortality following a bad harvest. But as Swain makes clear, it is difficult to link these economic pressures directly to the outbreaks of witch accusations in 1612 and 1633, while there were, of course, innumerable other parts of England which were experiencing similar economic problems but little or no witch accusations. The socio-economic background provides a vital context, but it cannot give us a complete explanation.

Much the same is true of the religious background. The witch-hunts of early modern Europe are inseparable from Christianity, from what the great French religious historian Jean Delumeau has encouraged us to think of as Christianisation,[16] or from that post-Reformation insistence that the believer should adopt a more stringent and more internalised form of Christianity, which in England took the form of Puritanism.[17] In Lancashire, perceived by contemporaries and many later writers as one of the 'dark corners of the realm', where both religious ignorance and popery could flourish, the problems may have been especially acute. The county was one of Catholicism's strongholds in the Elizabethan and Stuart periods, while from the 1590s there obviously existed a self-conscious grouping of Puritan or at least relatively advanced Protestant clergymen and gentry who were anxious to advance right religion and dispel both popery and the ignorance which they thought helped foster it.[18] It is, therefore, hardly surprising that Hugh Trevor-Roper, in his important essay on the European witch-craze, should choose Lancashire as an example of an area where religious strife helped engender witchcraft accusations.[19] This idea is taken further and treated in considerable detail in the present volume by Jonathan Lumby, while Richard Wilson's chapter demonstrates a wider context for the events of 1612 which locates them firmly in the religious strife of the period. Moreover, as Michael Mullett has demonstrated in this volume, the local religious situation in the Pendle area had been complicated by the consequences of the dissolution of Whalley Abbey in the 1530s, and by the incumbency, for the first thirty-three years of Elizabeth's reign, of George Dobson, a 'recalcitrant traditionalist', as the vicar of Whalley.

Lancashire in general, and Whalley parish in particular, may therefore, to use Mullett's phrase, have lain on religious fault lines. Again, however, our current level of knowledge allows us only to interpret this as a contextual rather than a causal factor. As Mullett himself makes clear, that local Protestant manifesto, *The State, Civil and Ecclesiastical, of the County of Lancaster,* makes no mention of witchcraft, and, indeed, recent rethinking on the history of English witchcraft has very much questioned the connection between Puritanism and a desire to prosecute witches.[20] Some advanced English Protestants, notably the great William Perkins,[21] argued violently for the extirpation of witches. Others, while in no way denying the reality of witchcraft or its hatefulness, were very cautious about how to approach the issue. One problem was the degree of power which some of the more avid demonologists afforded to the Devil, the argument being that many misfortunes which were ascribed to the Devil were in fact due to the providence of God, and that the correct response was to maintain a Job-like resignation in the face of adversity rather than attribute it to the Devil's minions and start launching witchcraft accusations against bothersome neighbours. This line of approach fitted in neatly with that great bugbear of reformed ministers, including the authors of *The State ... of Lancashire*: the religious ignorance and superstition in which the bulk of England's population tended to live. Accordingly, some writers tended to marginalise accusations of malefic witchcraft as yet another sign of peasant backwardness. At the very least, among English Puritans, witchcraft was a contested issue, rather than a phenomenon which was likely to engender a persecutory knee-jerk reaction.

This situation, early in the seventeenth century, was very much reflected at the top of the Church establishment, which in turn leads us on to that much discussed issue, the attitudes to witchcraft held by James VI and I. Late in Elizabeth's reign the ascendancy of Whitgift as Archbishop of Canterbury led to the development of a religious style which eschewed both popery and extreme Protestantism. This style was essentially continued by Richard Bancroft, who succeded Whitgift early in 1605 after holding the politically vital see of London. One of the major controversies which the Church establishment had had to face late in Elizabeth's reign lay around the problem of how to treat demonic possession (which was frequently linked to witchcraft in England) and exorcism. A series of well-publicised cases of exorcism by Catholics, notably the Jesuit William Weston, had forced the Church of England to mount a propaganda campaign against what was regarded as an empty piece of popish mummery. The situation was complicated, however, by the activities of what were in effect Puritan exorcists, notably a young minister named John Darrell, which meant that over-enthusiastic dispossessions by Protestant ministers had also to be discouraged. Bancroft and his chaplain Samuel Harsnett (a future Archbishop of York) were heavily involved in developing a sceptical approach to demonic possession and witchcraft, an approach which was forged and publicised in a number of *causes célèbres* which occurred around 1600.[22]

Thus James, a prime mover of the North Berwick trials of 1590–91 and, in 1597, author of the *Daemonologie*, entered his southern kingdom at a point when the upper reaches of the Church of England were very unconvinced about the threat of witchcraft. This suggests that we are urgently in need of a reinterpretation of the 1604 Witchcraft Act. This Act, whose passing has so often been linked simplistically to James's coming to the throne, needs, I would contend, to be analysed in the context of the religio-political faction struggles which accompanied the arrival of the new monarch. And that monarch, of course, was not, at least by 1603, the avid witch-hunter of historical myth. His deployment of scepticism in the 1616 Leicester case, referred to in Stephen Pumfrey's chapter later in this volume, is well known; but as early as 1605, in the case of the alleged bewitchment of a Berkshire girl named Anne Gunter, James was showing that the British Solomon could demonstrate his expertise in matters of witchcraft as effectively by exposing frauds as by finding nests of malefic witches.[23]

So times were hard in Pendle early in the seventeenth century, and the local religious situation was confused and possibly polarised. What initiated the trials of 1612, however, was a desire by the pedlar John Law and his family to prosecute an incident of *maleficium*, and the encouragement given to this prosecution by Roger Nowell. The input of concerned JPs was clearly of great importance in a number of witchcraft cases. In 1582, in a local craze in Essex that could have resulted in as many executions as did the Lancashire episode of 1612 had the Assize judges not been sceptical, a leading role was played by Brian Darcy, not only a JP but also lord of the manor among whose tenants the initial accusations of witchcraft occurred.[24] The conviction of Elizabeth Sawyer of Edmonton in Middlesex in 1621 was largely due to the decisive input of a local JP in the course of her trial.[25] Bouts of prosecution in the West Country later in the century apparently owed much to Robert Hunt, a Somersetshire JP who was involved in witch investigations of 1657–58, 1664 and 1665.[26]

Roger Nowell, aged sixty-two in 1612, was an experienced JP and important local landholder. Jonathan Lumby, who has carried out important research on the Nowell and Lister families, demonstrates in his chapter that Nowell possessed sound Protestant family connections, although this would not necessarily, as Lumby argues, automatically lead to a propensity to hunt witches. Although much could perhaps be inferred from his actions, we have little direct evidence of Nowell's attitude to or knowledge of witchcraft. It is perhaps worth noting that another educated northern gentleman, Edward Fairfax of Fewston in Yorkshire, was able to respond to his daughters' possible affliction by witchcraft in 1621 by deploying a knowledge of the relevant theology, of references to the subject by classical authors, and of recent cases in both England and the continent.[27] He was, however, initially sceptical that his daughters' sufferings were attributable to supernatural causes. Nowell was, certainly, vital in moving the 1612 witch prosecutions along, but it is unclear if he went in as a determined witch-hunter, or if he was a gentleman with very much standard ideas of witchcraft who was sucked into an ever-growing mass of accusations which became all the more convincing as witness after witness came to give evidence, and witch after witch confessed. Nowell at least countenanced the spread of accusations, that escalation from John Law's charges against Demdike to a full-scale witch-craze, but it is unclear how far he actually encouraged it, although, as Lumby points out, he did have family connections which might have provided him with motives for so doing. The conduct of the presiding judge, Sir Edward Bromley, is, as Stephen Pumfrey's chapter suggests, equally problematic. English Assize judges were, for the most part, fairly circumspect over the handling of witchcraft trials, as the 1582 Essex incident to which we have already referred reminds us. Before 1612, no English judge had condemned so many witches at one Assize, and it is noteworthy that Bromley authorised a tract justifying his actions immediately after the trials, almost certainly as a response to general feeling that something very unusual had happened. As the problems surrounding Nowell and Bromley's conduct reminds us, there are still, despite the longevity of the interest in the 1612 Lancashire trials, and despite the value of the chapters collected in this volume, many aspects of what happened in 1612 which have not been, and probably never will be, fully pinned down.

It is, then, difficult to ascertain which of the mix of contributory factors was responsible for precipitating a major witch-panic in Lancashire in 1612. What is certain, however, is that the materials generated by this panic and by the scare of 1633–34 constitute a major source for uncovering popular beliefs about witchcraft in early Stuart England. The major source here is, of course, Thomas Potts's *The Wonderfull Discoverie of Witches*. This, like any other printed account of witchcraft trials, is a problematic source: in Part I of this volume Stephen Pumfrey demonstrates the context within which it was written, while Marion Gibson, benefiting from her established expertise in dealing with this type of material,[28] demonstrates how and why Potts's account was crafted in particular ways. In particular, Gibson leaves us with a sense of how Potts dramatised the trial by relying heavily on witnesses' depositions and accounts of what happened in court, yet at the same time editing and manipulating the materials to give an impression of an unfolding succession of dreadful revelations. The depositions relating to the 1633 cases were, likewise, distorted by being adjusted to the conventions and needs of court documentation, and by the process of rendering what was initially first-hand information into a third-hand statement. Yet, when all due allowance is made for such problems, the records do provide a rich vein for those exploring early modern witchcraft beliefs.

Behind all this there lies the issue of local witchcraft traditions. These are, of course, central to Alison Findlay's discussion of the events of 1633–34, while, as Kirsteen Macpherson Bardell's chapter makes clear, Lancashire was not only the location of important witch trials in 1612 and of an incipiently major witch-scare in 1633–34, but also an area where a variety of witch-beliefs flourished. Macpherson Bardell demonstrates that Lancashire experienced not just large-scale panics, but also, for most of the time, that low level of prosecution which Alan Macfarlane thought typical of Essex. Indeed, the records of the Assizes of the Palatinate of Lancaster were searched thoroughly many years ago by that pioneer student of English witchcraft, C. L'Estrange Ewen, who found, among other things, four alleged witches being hanged in 1633, and a further group of indictments in 1638, although damage to records has made it impossible to be precise about what happened in this latter incident. Other indictments followed, the last occurring in 1681.[29] Lancashire was therefore obviously a county where witchcraft was a recurring problem. Yet it is instructive to compare Lancashire's experience with the neighbouring county of Cheshire. That county, too, had its economic problems, its Catholics, and its Protestant activists. It did not, however, experience much by way of prosecutions for malefic witchcraft. On the evidence of the records of the Court of Great Sessions of Chester, sixty-nine indictments were found, all of them falling within the period 1589–1675, these involving forty-seven alleged witches of whom only eleven were found guilty.[30] If Essex was unusual among south-eastern counties for the intensity of its witch-hunting, so Lancashire, albeit on a much smaller scale than Essex, was clearly peculiar in its region for the frequency with which witches were prosecuted before its courts.

The Lancashire prosecutions of 1612 and 1633 are important in demonstrating how witch-beliefs were developing. As several of the chapters in this collection make clear, there are two initial sets of issues which must be discussed here. The first is the notion that there was a distinctive 'English' witchcraft, which might be contrasted with a more exotic and demonically driven 'continental' witchcraft. This idea, central to much previous writing on English witchcraft, has recently been severely challenged. It is intrinsically implausible to posit the existence of a unified 'continental' witchcraft stretching from the English Channel to the Urals, and it is now customary to see witchcraft and witch prosecutions being affected by a number of variables across Europe, these variables producing a mosaic of regional variations.[31] Secondly, there is the problem of alleged polarity of 'learned' and 'popular' views. Obviously something like this polarity, in the last resort, may well have existed, but the interplay between the popular and the elite views of witchcraft was perhaps more complex than has sometimes been assumed.[32] Many contemporary writers were anxious that a theologically correct view of witchcraft (i.e that the core issue was the demonic pact, not the harm done by *maleficium*) should be spread among the populace, and a close reading of accounts of witch trials between the mid sixteenth and early eighteenth centuries does suggest some progress in such matters. But the process of downward diffusion of learned ideas was not one of docile acceptance by the masses: the ideas they were presented with by the learned were sometimes rejected, and sometimes adapted to popular needs or conflated with popular notions and practices. Conversely, educated demonologists were anxious to find empirical evidence to support their contentions. Hence details from the Lancashire trials were used in an important demonological tract published in 1627 by the Puritan clergyman and religious writer George Bernard,[33] whose writing was in turn incorporated into subsequent editions of an important manual for JPs, Michael Dalton's *Country Justice*.[34]

This interplay of popular and elite beliefs is nowhere more apparent than when the witches of 1612 described their first meetings with the Devil. The notion of a demonic pact, as we have noted, was central to demonological views of witchcraft, and it was undoubtedly a central, and perhaps fairly novel, aspect of the 1612 trials. It should be noted, however, that earlier English witchcraft trials were perhaps not so innocent of the Devil as has sometimes been suggested,[35] and, perhaps more importantly, we as yet know very little about how popular culture viewed the Devil. The Reformation had attacked the old mystery plays in which the Devil featured, and had obliterated the wall-paintings in churches which doubtlessly contained many images of the Christian's chief enemy. Yet it is impossible that folklorised notions of the Devil were not present in English popular culture, and might be adduced readily enough when the notion that the Devil was somehow connected with witchcraft began to become current.[36] And, of course, there was that significant feature of English witchcraft beliefs, the familiar, the half-animal and half-demonic being which was apparently central to English witchcraft, and which, in Lancashire in 1612 as in other parts of Elizabethan and Stuart England, performed the function of the Devil of the demonologist.[37]

Anne Whittle, alias Chattox, confessed on 19 May 1612 (the story was to shift in her later confessions) to making a pact with the Devil, who appeared to her in the likeness of a man, and to whom after some persuasion she agreed to give her soul. The Devil, in the standard style of a familiar, then demanded 'one part of her body for him to sucke upon', the right side of her body 'neere to her ribbes' being selected as an appropriate place. The Devil was immediately complemented by 'a thing in the likenes of a spotted bitch', in other words a normal familiar.[38] On 13 March Alizon Device told Roger Nowell that her grandmother, Elizabeth Southerns, alias Old Demdike, had advised her 'to let a devil or familiar appear to her; and that shee this examinate, would let him sucke at some part of her, and shee might have, and doe what shee would'.[39] Young James Device told Nowell and the other JP examining him how he met 'a thing like unto a browne dogge, who asked this examinate to give him his soule, and he should be revenged of any on whom hee would'.[40] By the time Margaret Johnson was confessing in 1634 matters had become clearer: the Devil appeared to her 'in the similitude or proportion of man apparelled in a suite of blacke tied about with silke points', whereupon they made a pact and had sexual intercourse.[41] In 1612 we are still in a world where the Devil had not dislodged the familiar as the witch's main source of temptation and malefic assistance.

This interplay of popular and elite beliefs, and the resilience of the former, is also vividly demonstrated by the accounts of the sabbat in the depositions of Edmund Robinson and Margaret Johnson in 1633–34. Historians of English witchcraft have generally been in agreement that the sabbat was largely absent in English witch accusations,[42] and both the court records and demonological writings of the period confirm this impression. Conversely, there are some intriguing clues to the existence of a belief in witches' meetings,[43] which sometimes amounted to folkloric versions of the sabbat, among the population at large, a well known example, of course, being the Malkin Tower meeting which figured so prominently in the 1612 Lancashire trials. Margaret Johnson's evidence of 1634 is especially intriguing in this respect. She told how she met the Devil (or at least a 'devil or spirit'), who told her to call him Mamilian (different texts give different spellings) and with whom she entered into the standard pact, giving him her soul in return for the supply of all her wants, and had sexual intercourse with him. She then related how she later rode to a meeting of thirty or forty witches, who rode there 'to consult for the killinge and hurtinge of men and beasts'. They all had their own familiar spirits with them, but there was also present 'one greate or grand devill or spirit more eminent than the rest'. She gave, however, little by way of detail about what happened at such meetings, and it was Robinson who told of the feasting at Hoar Stones, and the way in which witches pulled on ropes and produced 'flesh smokeinge, butter in lumps, and milke as it were syleinge [i.e. being strained]', and how he was offered a glass of some foul liquid to drink.[44] This is not, perhaps, the full-blown sabbat of Catholic demonologists, but obviously something which a peasant boy could fashion from the witch-beliefs current in his culture. As an account of a witches' meeting it has certain similarities with the fullest account of a witches' sabbat that survives in English records, that given by a Northumbrian woman named Anne Armstrong in 1673.[45]

Read as a source for witch-beliefs, our Lancashire materials are therefore a rich seam of evidence. There is much that is found elsewhere: the suddenness with which a witch could strike, as John Law discovered; the way in which witchcraft, on a village level, was very often about power, and in particular a type of power which it was felt most appropriate for women to wield; the way in which, as the case of Anne Whittle demonstrated, a woman who was executed for malefic witchcraft might at an earlier point be asked to assist a neighbour with a problem, in her case at the request of the wife of John Moore 'to helpe drinke that was forspoken or bewitched'.[46] There were, of course, also some peculiarities in the Lancashire trials. The pervasiveness of image magic in Potts's account of the 1612 trials, while not unprecedented, was unusual, and might reflect some regional variation in witch-beliefs. There was evidence of the folklore of popular magical beliefs in, for example, the two prayers which young Jennet Device told the court her mother had taught her, 'the one to cure the bewitched, and the other to get drinke',[47] or in her brother James's mention of his mother's belief in the magical properties of communion bread.[48] And there is also evidence of that most elusive of entities, popular scepticism. John Nutter deposed how, some eighteen or nineteen years previously, he heard his brother Robert tell their father that he thought he was bewitched either by Anne Chattox or by her daughter Anne Redferne. 'Thou art a foolish ladde, it is not so', the father replied, 'it is thy miscarriage [i.e. misfortune].'[49] Evidently, popular beliefs about witchcraft included space for doubt about the reality of specific cases.

One thing which is certain, as Edward Robinson's statement makes clear, is that there were witch-beliefs and stories about witchcraft current in the Pendle region in the early seventeenth century. When he retracted his previous statements in July 1634 while in custody in London, he declared that 'all that tale is false and feigned, and has no truth at all, but only as he has heard tales and reports made by women, so he framed his tale out of his own invention', and (in another deposition) that 'he had heard his neighbours talk of a witch feast that was kept at Mocking [i.e. Malkin] Tower in Pendle Forest about twenty years since'.[50] Robinson's statement provides rare evidence of the persistence of local traditions about witchcraft, and of that telling of tales of witchcraft which must have been so much a part of gossip in this period, and which can occasionally be sensed in some of the better-documented cases. It is interesting, and perhaps significant, that Robinson's statement implies that such tales were most typically current among woman and children, perhaps evidence of how witchcraft was very much something which operated within the culture of women. Notoriously, Hugh Trevor-Roper, in the introduction to his book on the European witch-craze, announced his uninterest in what he termed 'those elementary village credulities which anthropologists discover at all times and in all places'.[51] But as close study of the sources for the Lancashire witches makes clear, 'elementary village credulities' could be surprisingly rich, were constantly evolving, and were malleable enough to be adapted to specific circumstances and specific individuals.

But with early Stuart Lancashire witchcraft, we are not just looking at early modern popular mentalities: we are also confronting a historical phenomenon which, as Potts's *Discoverie* ensured, would be widely read about both by contemporaries and by later generations. As Alison Findlay reminds us, the 1633–34 accusations formed the basis of a semi-documentary play,[52] and the story of the Lancashire trials was to be warmed over again in a later dramatic work, Thomas Shadwell's *The Lancashire-Witches, and Tegue o' Divelly the Irish Priest* of 1681, a work which demonstrated how sophisticated taste had moved on by using witchcraft as a comic theme in what was essentially an anti-Tory and anti-Catholic satire. Not everybody, however, even among the educated, remained quite so distanced. Thomas Dunham Whitaker, the vicar of Whalley, in his history of the parish first published in 1801, printed a version of some of the 1633–34 depositions, and in a remarkable passage animadverted on the possible reality of witchcraft:

> Of the system of witchcraft, the real defect is not in theory but in evidence. A possibility that the bodies of men may sometimes be given up to infernal agency is no more to be denied, than that their souls should be exposed to infernal illusions ... Were I to behold with my own eyes such circumstances as have often been related, or were they to be reported to me by a philosophical observer of perfect integrity on the evidence of *his* senses, I know not upon what principles I could refuse my assent to the conclusion, that they were really the effects of diabolical power.[53]

Such sentiments may have been more widespread in the early nineteenth century than has sometimes been thought.

In any case, within a generation of Whitaker's expressing these sentiments, William Harrison Ainsworth, as Jeffrey Richards reminds us in his chapter, had in effect recreated the Lancashire witches for the reading public. Ainsworth, although writing a work of fiction, did research the subject thoroughly, while he had, of course, from his teens been a close friend and admirer of James Crossley, the gifted Mancunian antiquarian who in 1845 published an edition of Potts's *Discoverie*. Whatever its historical inaccuracies, and whatever the broader problems of the relationship between the output of the historical novelist and that of the academic historian, Ainsworth's rendering of the incidents of 1612 was, and continued to be, widely read. Doubtless the popularity of his book reinvigorated any local traditions about the Lancashire witches among the respectable classes, and close study of local newspapers may well reveal many instances in which the witchcraft images were drawn on for fêtes, fancy dress parties, village celebrations and other events. Joanne Pearson's contribution to this collection raises the question of how historical events of this type are remembered, and how they are created and recreated for religious and political reasons. Her piece reinforces the conclusion that, despite popular belief, there is precious little connection between modern paganism and early modern witchcraft. But whatever the opinions of modern Wiccans about the Lancashire trials, scraps of evidence suggest that the Lancashire witches were well remembered, whether through Ainsworth's influence or not, at the turn of the nineteenth and twentieth centuries. Thus a Lancashire diarist could record attending a wedding at Preston on 24 November 1909, held at Preston parish church 'which was *packed*', and at which the happy couple were attended by '14 bridesmaids, 3 pages & after them walked 20 little girls dressed as Lancashire witches'.[54]

But we will end, not with the *bons bourgeois* of Edwardian Preston, but rather with that world of local early modern plebeian beliefs to which we have already referred. In November 1736, by a happy coincidence a few months after the passing of the Act which repealed the English and Scottish witchcraft statutes, thus ending witchcraft's status as a capital felony, Mary Hartley of Baildon, just over the county boundary in West Yorkshire, was bound over to keep the peace after an incident in which she had accused two other women in the village, Bridget and Margaret Goldsbrough, of being witches and had, together with her son John, threatened to kill them. More specifically, Hartley had declared that Margaret Goldsbrough 'was riding of her son to Pendle Hill the night before and that Margaret brought a saddle & a bridle and wou'd put the bridle into his mouth but that the bitts were too large'.[55] A century after Edmund Robinson made his accusations, and a century and a quarter after ten people were hanged for witchcraft on Lancaster Moor, Pendle Hill in all its brooding splendour was still regarded among the local populace as an appropriate meeting place for witches.

Notes

1 Wallace Notestein, *A History of Witchcraft in England from 1558 to 1718* (Washington, DC: American Historical Association, 1911), p. 121.

2 This account of the 1612 trials is based on Thomas Potts, *The Wonderfull Discoverie of Witches in the Countie of Lancaster: with the Arraignment and Triall of Nineteene Notorious Witches, at the Assizes and Generall Gaol Deliverie, Holden at the Castle of Lancaster, upon Munday, the Seventeenth of August Last, 1612* (London, 1613).

3 For an overview of English witchcraft in this period, see James Sharpe, *Instruments of Darkness: Witchcraft in England 1550–1750* (London: Hamish Hamilton, 1996), and, for a briefer introduction, James Sharpe, *Witchcraft in Early Modern England* (London: Longman, 2001). Keith Thomas, *Religion and the Decline of Magic: Studies in Popular Beliefs in Sixteenth- and Seventeenth-Century England* (1971; London: Penguin, 1973) is a classic study of witchcraft and associated beliefs in England. Alan Macfarlane, *Witchcraft in Tudor and Stuart England: A Regional and Comparative Study* (1970; 2nd edn, with introduction by James Sharpe, London: Routledge, 1999), dealing with the county of Essex, is a major regional study of the phenomenon.

4 For a recent acceptance of the total of 40,000 executions, which refers to other works citing this figure, see Geoffrey Scarre, *Witchcraft and Magic in Sixteenth- and Seventeenth-Century Europe* (1987; 2nd edn, London: Palgrave, 2001), p. 21. The estimate of a maximum of 500 executions for England was put forward by Christina Larner, *Witchcraft and Religion: The Politics of Popular Belief* (Oxford: Blackwell, 1984), pp. 71–2, in a critique of a higher estimate put forward by C. L'Estrange Ewen, *Witch Hunting and Witch Trials: The Indictments for Witchcraft from the Records of 1373 Assizes held for the Home Circuit A.D. 1559–1736* (London: Kegan Paul, 1929), p. 112. More recent research by Sharpe on English sources has suggested that Larner's estimate was in all probability accurate: *Instruments of Darkness*, p. 125.

5 The East Anglian witch-hunts of 1645–47 are in urgent need of full-scale detailed scholarly study. For a brief guide to the subject, see Sharpe, *Instruments of Darkness*, ch. 5, 'England's mass witch-hunt: East Anglia 1645–7'.

6 The Samlesbury case is described in Potts, *Wonderfull Discoverie*, sig. K3–M4.

7 For an initial exploration of the possible influence of seminary priests on English witchcraft beliefs, see Warren J. Karle, 'The devil in the vineyard: the role of seminary priests in the

introduction of continental witchlore into England' (unpublished M.A. thesis, University of York, 1992).

8 Sharpe, *Instruments of Darkness*, pp. 126–7.

9 Ewen, *Witch Hunting and Witch Trials*, pp. 215–20.

10 Henry Goodcole, *The Wonderfull Discoverie of Elizabeth Sawyer a Witch late of Edmonton, her Conviction and Condemnation and Death* (London, 1621).

11 Richard Bernard, *A Guide to Grand Jury Men: Divided into Two Bookes* (London, 1627). For a brief discussion of the significance of this work, see Sharpe, *Instruments of Darkness*, pp. 100–1.

12 John Webster, *The Displaying of Supposed Witchcraft* (London, 1677), pp. 276–8. It should be noted that Webster was an eyewitness of the events he describes at this point.

13 Sources for the 1633–34 Lancashire affair are scattered, and in particular the statements of Edmund Robinson and Margaret Johnson survive in manuscript copies in various collections: the major sources are listed in C. L'Estrange Ewen, *Witchcraft and Demonianism: A Concise Account Derived from Sworn Depositions and Confessions Obtained in the Courts of England and Wales* (London: Heath Cranton, 1933), pp. 244–51. The Lancashire witch-scare of 1633–34 prompted the writing of a play, Thomas Heywood and Richard Brome's *The Late Lancashire Witches: A Well Received Comedy, Lately Acted at the Globe on the Banks-Side, by the Kings Majesties Actors* (London, 1634).

14 Perhaps the most rounded survey is Brian P. Levack, *The Witch-Hunt in Early Modern Europe*, 2nd edn (London: Longman, 1995). For recent brief introductions, see Scarre, *Witchcraft and Magic*, and P. G. Maxwell-Stuart, *Witchcraft in Europe and the New World, 1400–1800* (Basingstoke: Palgrave, 2001).

15 Macfarlane, *Witchcraft in Tudor and Stuart England*; Thomas, *Religion and the Decline of Magic*.

16 Jean Delumeau, *Catholicisme entre Luther et Voltaire* (Paris: Presses universitaires de France, 1971).

17 For the most recent thinking on English Puritanism, see Christopher Durston and Jacqueline Eales (eds), *The Culture of English Puritanism, 1560–1700* (London: Macmillan, 1996). John Bossy, 'Moral arithmetic: seven sins to ten commandments', in E. Leites (ed.), *Conscience and Casuistry in Early Modern Europe* (Cambridge: Cambridge University Press, 1988) provides a short and brilliant analysis of what the new religiosity meant, and makes some very pertinent comments about how this connected with the development of new concerns over witchcraft.

18 Evidence on this point is provided by F. R. Raines (ed.), *The State, Civil and Ecclesiastical, of the County of Lancaster, about the Year 1590* (Manchester: Chetham Society publications xcvi, 1875), pp. 1–48. Christopher Haigh, *Reformation and Resistance in Tudor Lancashire* (Cambridge: Cambridge University Press, 1975) remains the main guide to the county's religious affairs in the sixteenth century.

19 H. R. Trevor-Roper, *The European Witch-Craze of the Sixteenth and Seventeenth Centuries* (London: Penguin, 1969), p. 70.

20 Sharpe, *Instruments of Darkness*, pp. 235–8. The clearest statement on this issue is provided by J. L. Teall, 'Witchcraft and Calvinism in Elizabethan England: divine power and human will', *Journal of the History of Ideas* 23 (1962), pp. 21–36.

21 Notably in one of the major English demonological works, Perkins's *A Discourse of the Damned Art of Witchcraft. So Farre Forth as it is Revealed in the Scriptures, and Manifest by True Experience* (Cambridge, 1608).

22 These controversies are discussed in: Corinne Holt Rickert, *The Case of John Darrell: Minister and Exorcist* (Gainsville, Fla.: University of Florida Monographs, Humanities, 9, Winter 1962); D. P. Walker, *Unclean Spirits: Possession and Exorcism in France and England in the Late Sixteenth and Early Seventeenth Centuries* (London: Scolar Press, 1981); Malcolm

Macdonald, *Witchcraft and Hysteria in Elizabethan London: Edward Jorden and the Mary Glover Case* (London: Routledge, 1991); F. W. Brownlow, *Shakespeare, Harsnett and the Devils of Denham* (Newark: University of Delaware Press, 1993); and James Sharpe, *The Bewitching of Anne Gunter: A Horrible and True Story of Football, Witchcraft, Murder, and the King of England* (London: Profile Books, 1999). Darrell's activities are also discussed, and linked to the Lancashire trials, in Jonathan Lumby, *The Lancashire Witch-Craze: Jennet Preston and the Lancashire Witches* (Preston: Carnegie, 1995), pp. 119–28.

23　Sharpe, *Bewitching of Anne Gunter*, ch. 8, 'Anne meets the King'. For an important early discussion of James VI and I's attitudes to witchcraft, see G. L. Kittredge, *Witchcraft in Old and New England* (Cambridge, Mass.: Harvard University Press, 1929), ch. 17, 'King James the First'. Lawrence Normand and Gareth Roberts, *Witchcraft in Early Modern Scotland: James VI's Demonology and the North Berwick Witches* (Exeter: Exeter University Press, 2000) provides not only a full scholarly edition of the *Daemonologie* but also a sound analysis of James's attitudes to witchcraft before 1603.

24　W. W., *A True and Just Recorde, of the Information, Examination, and Confession of All the Witches, Taken at S. Oses in the Countie of Essex, Whereof Some were Executed, and Some Entreated According to the Determination of the Law* (London, 1582).

25　Goodcole, *Wonderfull Discoverie of Elizabeth Sawyer*, sig. B2.

26　Details of the relevant cases are given in Ewen, *Witchcraft and Demonianism*, pp. 335–6, 341–7, 353–4.

27　William Grainge (ed.), *Daemonologia: A Discourse on Witchcraft as it was Acted in the Family of Mr Edward Fairfax, of Fuston, in the County of York, in the Year 1621* (Harrogate, 1882), pp. 73–5, 96–8.

28　See her *Reading Witchcraft: Stories of Early English Witches* (London: Routledge, 1999), and *Early Modern Witches: Witchcraft Cases in Contemporary Writing* (London: Routledge, 2000).

29　Ewen, *Witchcraft and Demonianism*, pp. 407–13.

30　Ewen, *Witchcraft and Demonianism*, pp. 413–22; Sharpe, *Instruments of Darkness*, pp. 121–2. The best guide to the history of Cheshire in the relevant period is John Morrill, *Cheshire 1630–1660: County Government and Society during the English Revolution* (Oxford: Oxford University Press, 1974).

31　This point is demonstrated in the essays brought together in Bengt Ankarloo and Gustav Henningsen (eds), *Early Modern European Witchcraft: Centres and Peripheries* (Oxford: Oxford University Press, 1990).

32　For an important discussion of this theme, see Clive Holmes, 'Popular culture? Witches, magistrates and divines in early modern England', in Steven L. Kaplan (ed.), *Understanding Popular Culture: Europe from the Middle Ages to the Nineteenth Century* (Berlin: Mouton, 1984).

33　Bernard, *Guide to Grand Jury Men*.

34　Michael Dalton, *The Countrey Justice, Containing the Practice of the Justices of the Peace out of their Sessions* (London, 1630 edn), pp. 338–9. This passage should be compared with the much briefer comments on witchcraft given in the original 1618 edition of *The Countrey Justice*, pp. 242–3.

35　Sharpe, *Instruments of Darkness*, pp. 74–5.

36　Some of the approaches to this problem are suggested in Darren Oldridge, *The Devil in Early Modern England* (Stroud: Sutton, 2000).

37　The familiar has long been recognised as a peculiar aspect of English witchcraft beliefs: see, for example, the discussion in Kittredge, *Witchcraft in Old and New England*, pp. 174–84.

38　Potts, *Wonderfull Discoverie*, B4.

39　Potts, *Wonderfull Discoverie*, R3.

40　Potts, *Wonderfull Discoverie*, H3.

41 British Library Add. Mss. 36,674, fol. 197.

42 For example, Kittredge, *Witchcraft in Old and New England*, p. 25; Ewen, *Witchcraft and Demonianism*, p. 57; Thomas, *Religion and the Decline of Magic*, pp. 444–5.

43 Sharpe, *Instruments of Darkness*, pp. 75–8.

44 British Library Add. Mss. 36,674, fols 197, 192.

45 Public Record Office, Clerks of Assize Records, Northern Circuit Depositions, ASSI 45/10/ 3/34, 36, 40, 43–54.

46 Potts, *Wonderfull Discoverie*, E2.

47 Potts, *Wonderfull Discoverie*, G3.

48 Potts, *Wonderfull Discoverie*, H3.

49 Potts, *Wonderfull Discoverie*, O2.

50 *Calendar of State Papers Domestic*, 1634–35, pp. 141, 152–3.

51 Trevor-Roper, *European Witch-Craze*, p. 9.

52 For another perspective on this work, see Diane Purkiss, *The Witch in History: Early Modern and Twentieth-Century Representations* (London: Routledge, 1996), pp. 235–47.

53 Thomas Dunham Whitaker, *History of the Original Parish of Whalley* (1801; 3rd edn, London, 1818), p. 217.

54 Merseyside Record Office, Diary of Mary Weld, 920 WCD/3, 24 November 1909. It is interesting that the number of little girls mentioned here as being dressed as Lancashire witches, twenty, corresponds to the total of those tried in 1612, i.e. nineteen at Lancaster and one, Jennet Preston, at York. I am grateful to Krista Cowman for this reference.

55 West Yorkshire Record Office, Wakefield, Quarter Sessions Rolls, QS1/76/2/File 3.

PART I

THE TRIALS OF 1612

That the trial of the Lancashire witches is so well known is largely because we have unusually good evidence for it, in the form of Thomas Potts's 1613 book *The Wonderfull Discoverie of Witches in the Countie of Lancaster.* The three chapters in this first section re-examine the events of 1612, which have been often summarised but rarely analysed. They all combine a close reading of Potts's text with evidence from other areas to place it in a particular context: the politics of witch-hunting and royal patronage (Pumfrey); the literary genre of witchcraft stories and their relationship with actual trials (Gibson); and the network of relationships and motivations among the accusers and accused in the Pendle area (Lumby). In doing so they shed light not only on how the trials were constructed but also on how the evidence itself came into being.

Stephen Pumfrey's chapter explores the political context of the trials. Ever since James Crossley produced the first modern edition of *The Wonderfull Discoverie* in the 1840s, writers have noticed Potts's allusions to King James I and his writings on witchcraft. Was James involved? There is no evidence that he was, but the trial does seem to have been, in part, an attempt to curry favour with the King. Although it eventually met with some success, to bid for royal favour by prosecuting witches was a risky strategy, for cases of witch-craft and demonic possession were by now being disputed, in Lancashire and elsewhere, and James himself had been showing clear signs of scepticism. Potts therefore aimed high, basing his own account of the methods and find-ings of the Lancashire witch trial on the principles set out by the King in the 1590s, as Pumfrey is able to document in convincing detail. James's ideas in turn were taken from the fantasies of satanic conspiracy developed by the continental demonologists of the past, which had until then made little impact in England. It seems, then, that the demonic pacts and witches' sabbats which make their first English appearance in the Lancashire trials of 1612 owe more to the desire of Potts and the judges to vindicate their actions by appealing to royal authority than to any actual activities of the Lancashire witches.

Marion Gibson's chapter, too, demonstrates that (as Pumfrey puts it) '*The Wonderfull Discoverie* is not an innocent text'. It is, she finds, 'the clearest example of an account obviously published to display the shining efficiency and justice of the legal system'. By comparing Potts's account with what is known of Jacobean judicial procedures, she is able to show how Potts arranged the evidence in a kind of 'mock trial', designed to convey the impression of a transparent courtroom reconstruction at the same time as subtly manipulating the evidence. Potts's exceptional craft appears still more clearly from Gibson's systematic reading of all the surviving accounts of witchcraft from the period. *The Wonderfull Discoverie* turns out to be an unusually late and detailed example of a genre which had been disused in England for some twenty years: the evidence-based account of witchcraft. This analysis of the text seems to take us further away than ever from the actual events of 1612, until we remember that witchcraft itself is not a fact but (as Gibson puts it) an 'impossible crime', which had itself to be constructed in the minds of all those concerned, victims and accusers alike. There is no dead body, no smoking gun, just a collection of competing claims about an event that may or may not have happened at all. In understanding the construction of Potts's account we also come to understand the construction of the trial, of the evidence, and of the crime itself.

With the next chapter we move from the judges and their clerk to the prosecuting gentry and magistrates. The importance of Jonathan Lumby's work lies in the light it sheds on something not previously recognised as important: the related trial of Jennet Preston of Gisburn. Historians have been at a loss to explain why Thomas Potts added an account of this trial in distant York to that of the Lancaster one. The simplistic assumption has been that the Pendle investigation threw up evidence relating to the Yorkshire events, which was duly forwarded and acted upon. Closer investigation reveals the interdependence of the two trials. The Yorkshire events took place only just across the county border, a few miles up the Ribble Valley from the Pendle area. The gentry accusers and magistrates in both cases were part of the same Protestant social network, and both had family experience of suffering at the alleged hands of witches. The breakthrough in both cases came when Roger Nowell, the Pendle magistrate, extracted from the two child witnesses, James and Jennet Device, a string of allegations, and it was this evidence above all that hanged both Jennet Preston and the Lancashire witches. Young Jennet Device's canny observation that the recently hanged Jennet Preston was missing from the ranks of the Lancashire accused provided one of the climactic moments of the Lancaster trial, but also in a sense of the York trial. It had a powerful impact on the courtroom audience and appeared to validate both convictions. Indeed, it may even be that the York trial helped to bring about the Lancaster one, for Jennet Preston had earlier that year been tried unsuccessfully for witchcraft at York Lent Assizes. The news of this was still fresh as Nowell received the first reports of witchcraft in Lancashire and reacted with such unusual vigour.

Lumby's close attention to the parish registers of Gisburn (where he was minister at the time of his researches) and neighbouring Bracewell, and to other time-consuming local sources of a kind which academic historians often neglect to follow up, uncovers a whole web of connections, with numerous suggestions of family intrigue and manipulation. The issue of whether Lister senior really did die on the day of his son's wedding is obscured by a smudge in a 400-year-old parish register, but the argument does not depend on it: insights at this level of detail into cases of witchcraft are rare indeed. To these perhaps dramatic events Lumby brings an individual perspective on family breakdown, persecution and victimisation, reminding us that historians (fortunately) do not have a monopoly on interpretations of the past.

Taken together, the three chapters in this section show us the full range of forces coming to bear on the case of a few miserable witches in a remote corner of England, from royal policy down to family feuds. At the centre is Thomas Potts, the Clerk of Arraigns, busily organising both trial and text, accusers and victims, evidence and record. The three authors' expertise ranges widely, but at the core of each chapter is a close reading of Potts's account of the trial, not as a mere record of events (although it is in part that) but as both creation and creator of the very events it purports to record. At our closest possible approach to these events, hard facts disappear; it turns out that our evidence is stories and the stories are evidence. Historical texts have to be approached as a kind of narrative claim, rather than as a window on the truth. But far from undermining the possibility of historical knowledge, this approach leads us towards an awareness of witchcraft as an aspect of the past constructed from a mixture of events and imagination. We cannot separate the history from the stories, and our understanding of both is the richer because of it.

2

Potts, plots and politics:
James I's *Daemonologie* and
The Wonderfull Discoverie of Witches

Stephen Pumfrey

Thomas Potts's first season as an associate clerk on the Northern Circuit witnessed extraordinary events, and the judges instructed him to record them in a book.[1] *The Wonderfull Discoverie of Witches in the Countie of Lancaster*, published in London in 1613, told Jacobean readers of a new chapter in the history of England's war against heresy. Satanic witchcraft had at last been proven in a court of law to exist in James VI and I's southern kingdom. For the first time an English jury heard sworn evidence, including four confessions, of pacts made with the Devil and of witches' sabbats. These depositions had been taken by the local magistrate, Roger Nowell, before the judges arrived. Of the witches from Pendle, Elizabeth Southerns (alias Old Demdike) had confessed to Nowell and died in Lancaster Castle before the trials began. Margaret Pearson was convicted but was spared the death penalty. Ten others, including Anne Whittle (alias Chattox), the gentlewoman Alice Nutter, and one man, were found guilty and hanged, nine of them on the evidence of the young girl Jennet Device. A further five people were acquitted. A separate case against three other accused, the 'witches of Samlesbury', collapsed spectacularly when the chief witness, once again a young girl, Grace Sowerbutts, was exposed by the judge, Edward Bromley, as the perjuring tool of a Catholic priest. Of course, confessions of satanic pacts and rituals had become the common currency of inquisitorial trials in the witch-hunting regions of continental Europe. It was during the Assizes held at Lancaster Castle in August 1612 that an English court put aside any Euro-scepticism about these phenomena.

Potts's book is almost as remarkable as the trials it presents. Because it consists largely of official court records, until the 1980s historians read it as a uniquely transparent window on to the process of an English witch trial. But, as Marion Gibson shows in this volume, Potts was an active and selective reporter. He omitted important aspects of trial procedure, reordered the documents, represented prior written depositions as *viva voce* testimony, and may have 'improved' Judge Bromley's speeches. Gibson does not dispute that *The Wonderfull Discoverie* 'is apparently honestly meant', but concludes that it 'is the clearest example of an account obviously published to display the shining efficiency and justice of the legal system'.[2] In this chapter I offer an explanation of why and how the judges charged Potts to defend their justice. The verdicts provoked damaging controversy both in Lancashire and, with more severe consequences for the law officers, in Jacobean London. We will see that Potts's text was carefully crafted to secure James I's favour by showing that the judges had perfectly executed his policy on witchcraft, and also on Catholic conspirators. Given that James's policies at the time were so unclear that historians remain unsure what they were, such a reading of Potts can advance our understanding of this important issue in the history of English witchcraft.

James Stuart was the only monarch to publish a treatise on witchcraft. Proclaimed James VI of Scotland at the age of one in 1567, his *Daemonologie* was first printed in Edinburgh in 1597.[3] It was reprinted in London shortly after he also acceded to the English throne in 1603. James was a product of the strict Scottish Reformation, and took an intense scholarly interest in Protestant theology, including the theology of witchcraft. In the early 1590s he became convinced that he was the object of plots by Scottish witches. He acquainted himself with continental theories of satanic witchcraft (and other occultist fashions), helped by his marital ties with the Danish court. His reputation as a witch-hunter came with him to England: Shakespeare's *Macbeth* was performed before him in 1606, as Richard Wilson discusses elsewhere in this volume.

    James's demonology, literally the science of demons, reproduced the 'continental' discourse of witchcraft as the ultimate, satanic heresy. Some historians have assumed that the accession to the throne of a monarch with a paranoiac fear of attack by witches, readily displayed in the book which Wallace Notestein said 'offered a textbook to officials', altered English legal attitudes and made an event like the Lancaster witch trials inevitable. They have accused James of personally initiating credulous witch-hunting in England. Some have reproduced the (understandable) misconception that James actually instigated the ground-breaking Lancaster trials. Notestein more cautiously asserted that they 'were clearly the outcome of James's writings and policies', but he was unable to produce any direct evidence of the influence of the *Daemonologie*.[4] In fact, Potts's *Wonderfull Discoverie* was constructed around it.

    But by the time Potts was writing, James I's policies and attitudes towards witchcraft were not clear, simple or consistent. He now manifested considerable scepticism and was concerned about trumped-up and incredible accusations which were nevertheless believed by the superstitious. He had already personally detected fraud in the celebrated case of Anne Gunter,[5] and did so again, four years after the Lancaster trials, at the Leicester summer Assizes of 1616. Like Bromley (and his senior, Justice Altham) in Lancaster, the circuit judge Crew (and his colleague Winch) were faced with multiple cases of witchcraft. As in the Lancaster trials, a child was a crucial witness. As in the Lancaster trials, the child's evidence was accepted, and the accused were convicted. But there was immediate unease about the convictions. Five were reprieved and James I himself initiated an investigation into the 'fraud'. The gossipy diarist John Chamberlain recorded that '[Winch and Crew] are somewhat discountenanced for hanging certain witches in the circuit at Leicester; whereas the King, coming that way, found out the juggling and imposture of the boy, that counterfeited the bewitching'. Chamberlain appears to have exaggerated the King's direct intervention and disapproval of the judges, but the currency in London of the story shows the dangers that faced credulous judges.[6]

Stuart Clark is surely right that James developed his 'continental' views on witchcraft as a diabolic compact and conspiracy of great extent and danger to Christian monarchies some time after 1590. James's demonology, Clark argues, was responsible for the intense Scottish witch-hunt, which only ceased in 1597, when his *Daemonologie* was published. But what happened during his reign in England's less fevered, more sceptical territories from 1603 to 1625? The argument that by the 1610s James had undergone a radical change of views towards the sceptical stance he exhibited in the Leicester case is discussed by Clark, who concludes that 'the King was not significantly more shrewd in the 1610s than in the 1590s'.[7] The fact is that the evidence is contradictory and circumstantial: we cannot be certain.

This uncertainty is perplexing for historians, but we should try to imagine what it meant to Justices Altham and Bromley as they and Potts bumped along the trans-Pennine tracks from the York to the Lancaster Assizes in the summer of 1612. Altham's anxiety would have been particularly acute because, as we shall see, he had just been accused of engineering a miscarriage of justice at the York Assize by hanging one woman for witchcraft. Bromley knew that he would take the criminal cases, which included the arraignments for witchcraft. While Altham was towards the end of his career (he died in 1617), Bromley expected promotion. The remote Northern Circuit, encompassing 'dark corners of the land' such as Lancashire, was a low rung on the judicial ladder, and court patronage was needed for promotion to a circuit nearer London. But how was he to ensure courtly favour when dealing with witchcraft accusations? What was royal policy in 1612? Was favour to be gained by encouraging convictions or, as Crew found out in Leicester, by sceptically testing the witnesses to destruction?

Judges were briefed on Whitehall policy before riding out, and sometimes were 'charged' by James himself. These charges were vital instruments for communicating London policy to the regions, but we do not know what, if anything, the 1612 charges had to say about witchcraft. Judges opened each Assize with the 'charge', augmented with their own opinions. In Cockburn's view, Jacobean charges 'often degenerated into a vehicle for prejudice and intimidation', and exposed political tensions between court and country.[8] As sophisticated London courtiers, Altham and Bromley would have shared the common metropolitan view of north Lancashire as a region mired in stubborn popery, attempted witchery, superstitious credulity and other heterodoxies. Since James now insisted upon religious conformity, their Lancaster charge could safely have included some diatribes against heresy. But to be the first judge to hang a coven of people accused of making diabolic compacts was a risky career move.

Sure enough, the trials rapidly achieved fame and added to Lancashire's reputation for credulity. Ben Jonson had it in mind in *The Divell is an Asse*, his play of 1616 in which the protagonist is persuaded to simulate demonic possession so that he can accuse his wife of witchcraft. As with his other works, Jonson used the play to communicate to the London court the views of his royal patron James, in this case the need to guard against credulity in witchcraft cases. In a revealing opening passage, Jonson has Satan address his laughable minor demons in this way: 'The state of Hell must care whom it imploves, in point of reputation, heere about London. You would make, I thinke, an Agent, to be sent, for Lancashire, proper enough.' Jonson also reminded his audience of 'little Darrels tricks, / With the boy o' Burton and the 7. In Lancashire'.[9] John Darrell was a highly controversial Puritan minister who had (in-)famously been invited in 1597 to exorcise demons from seven members of Nicholas Starkie's household in Tyldesley, Lancashire. The next year he was imprisoned as a fraud by the Commission for Ecclesiastical Causes. A pamphlet war ensued which exposed divisions in the Anglican Church. Moderates tended to treat possession and exorcism as false phenomena, and witchcraft accusations with scepticism. Puritans were readier to believe in all three. Jonson (and, we can presume, James) backed the moderate, sceptical view in 1616. Clearly, in 1612, the Lancaster magistrate Roger Nowell did not. Nowell was already pursuing the Pendle witches, and he was a close relative of Nicholas Starkie.[10]

Sophisticated London circles would surely have treated news of the Lancashire convictions with scepticism. Was this not the kind of nonsense to be expected in Lancashire? Had not Bromley and Altham themselves been guilty of credulity or worse, as Chamberlain was later to imply of Crew in 1616? There is clear evidence that Bromley and Altham returned from the Northern Circuit under clouds of suspicion. Problems began in York on 27 July, when Altham heard the case of Jennet Preston, accused of murdering one Thomas Lister in 1607 by diabolic witchcraft. Preston lived in Gisburn, at that time (just) in Yorkshire but only a few miles from Pendle. Indeed, Preston was hanged primarily because the York jury heard the recent depositions of the

Lancaster accused, and of little Jennet Device, that Preston had attended their 'sabbat'.

In his admirable book, and in his chapter elsewhere in this volume, Jonathan Lumby suggests that Preston's true crime was to have been the mistress of Thomas Lister, and thus to have provoked the enmity of his son, Thomas Lister junior. Some explanation is certainly needed of the suspicious case. Just three months earlier at the York Easter Assize Preston had been tried and acquitted of using witchcraft to kill a boy. On her release she made the mistake of visiting the Pendle witches, already under Nowell's surveillance. Only when the case failed did Thomas Lister junior accuse her of his father's murder five years earlier. The prosecuting magistrate who prepared the case, Thomas Heaber, was Lister junior's father-in-law.[11]

Preston's friends were convinced that she had been outrageously framed. This is evident from the small pamphlet *The Arraignement and Triall of Jennet Preston*. Potts reproduced it in 1613 as the concluding section of *The Wonderfull Discoverie*, although his printer had published it separately in 1612. Despite some differences in style from *The Wonderfull Discoverie* itself, Potts is the most likely author. In *The Arraignement* he began with a rebuke:

> You that were husband to this *Jennet Preston*; her friends and kinsfolkes ... have not beene sparing to devise so scandalous a slander out of the malice of your hearts, as that shee was maliciously prosecuted by Master *Lister* and others; Her life unjustly taken away by practise [i.e. deceit]; and that (even at the Gallowes where shee died impenitent and void of all feare or grace) she died an Innocent woman, because she would confesse nothing: You I say may not hold it strange, though at this time, being not only moved in conscience, but directed, for example sake, with that which I have to report of her, I suffer you not to wander any further; but with this short discourse oppose your idle conceipts able to seduce others: And by Charmes of Imputations and slander, laid upon the Justice of the Land, to cleare her that was justly condemned and executed for her offence.[12]

With seductive slanders against them already, Altham and Bromley must have worried about the credibility of their handling of the Lancaster cases. Neither those proceedings nor *The Arraignement* quelled the doubts. Potts wrote that his judges had requested him to publish *The Wonderfull Discoverie* because 'there doe passe divers uncertaine reportes and relations of such Evidences, as was publiquely given'.[13]

The judges' decision to commission the much longer *Wonderfull Discoverie* was a very high risk strategy. It confidently called attention to convictions that could have been adjudged in London as a miscarriage of justice. It seems likely that all those associated with *The Wonderfull Discoverie*, Bromley, Altham, Potts and Baron Thomas Knyvet, the book's dedicatee, were confident that it would stop criticism and even advance their careers. Their confidence rested upon their belief that they knew James's policy on witchcraft in 1612, and transformed the Lancashire witches to fit it. If so, although we cannot extract James's policy from *The Wonderfull Discoverie*, we can analyse the reaction to it of some very interested and informed contemporaries.

The Wonderfull Discoverie is not an innocent text, and not just because of Potts's selective representation of the judicial process. It was carefully crafted to confirm James's *Daemonologie*. In doing so, it transformed the Lancashire witches in two ways, the first well known, the second overlooked. The first transformation took the witches out of their local context of English popular culture, in which the Devil played a small part, and re-presented them in the discourse of continental demonology as servants of Satan. James's treatise provided a perfect but not unique model. The second transformation read and used the *Daemonologie* in a more subtle way, which we can only recover with knowledge of the political micro-context within which the law officers worked. They read it with inside knowledge of James's concerns and policies in 1612, and artfully fashioned both the witches and the judicial process to fit them. In reproducing testimony of compacts between witches and the Devil, and even more sensationally of witches' sabbats, Potts bequeathed us the first English trial records employing the 'continental' discourse of witchcraft. On the continent, following the theory of witchcraft developed by the Dominican inquisitors Heinrich Kramer and Jacob Sprenger in their *Malleus Maleficarum* of 1486, investigating magistrates had routinely taken the initiative to look for and find evidence that accused witches were the willing servants of Satan. For the elite lawyers, theologians and other scholars of demonology who propagated this theory, the crime of witchcraft was the crime of diabolism.

Diabolism meant devil worship – it was the extreme apostasy of turning away from God to his arch-enemy, and of furthering Satan's goal of destroying Christendom. European fears of diabolism grew with an increasing emphasis in Christian theology, from the late Middle Ages onwards, upon Satan as a real, powerful spiritual being. As Stuart Clark shows in his magisterial work *Thinking with Demons*, diabolism fitted well with the contemporary belief that the world was constructed around opposites: hot versus cold, male versus female, heaven versus earth. The existence of God, angels, saintly believers and sacred rituals almost required a belief in the contrary reality of Satan, legions of demons, human agents and blasphemous inversions of Christian devotion such as black masses.[14] Satan therefore gave (or seemed to give) witches wonderful powers in order to attract new followers and to harm the godly. But Renaissance demonologists turned the essence of witchcraft into a thought crime – that of belief in Satan as lord. Given the power of torture to obtain confessions of allegiance, the difficulty of refuting witnesses' allegations, and the lack of necessity to prove any criminal act on the part of the witch, the elite model of diabolic witchcraft produced in sixteenth- and early-seventeenth-century Europe explosions of cases that were indeed witch-hunts.[15]

By contrast, English courts had continued to work with a more traditional model of witchcraft, which accorded with that of popular culture. Unlike the continental inquisitorial system, English law required members of a community to make an accusation against their neighbours, and required juries drawn from the community to reach the verdict. English witch trials therefore revolved around popular beliefs, according to which the crime of witchcraft was one of *maleficium*, Latin for evil-doing. Until Parliament amended English statutes in 1604, courts required tangible evidence of evil-doing, such as killing and maiming, or harming livestock or crops, and punished such malefactors in ways not dissimilar to other, less mysterious murderers.[16] But in 1604 English law adopted a crime from the repertoire of elite demonology and made the mere conjuring of spirits a capital offence.[17] Whatever James's scepticism about particular cases, throughout his reign in England he promoted the continental view, increasingly shared by English intellectuals, that witchcraft represented a diabolic threat to the social order. Through Potts's record, the Lancaster trials provided the first legal proof that James was right.

Late-twentieth-century historians such as Carlo Ginsberg, Keith Thomas and Brian Levack have shown that trial records such as those accurately reproduced by Potts are the result of complex interactions between the elite culture of demonology and the popular one of instrumental *maleficium*. In his book *The Night Battles*, Ginsberg convincingly showed how popular non-diabolic beliefs could be transformed by elite inquisitors into stories of satanism that could even come to be accepted by the accused themselves.[18] There is no reason to assume that the testimony concerning Chattox, Demdike, Alice Nutter and the rest was not fashioned in this way. *The Wonderfull Discoverie* therefore represents the first successful intrusion of elite demonology into an English trial. But, as Clive Holmes has noted, the shaping of discourses was not all one way. Local, popular beliefs shaped local versions of elite witchcraft discourse. English elites accepted the popular (English) belief that witches kept familiars, or companion animals.[19] Continental demonology and trials had no place for familiars. This difference provided Potts and Bromley with a reason to acquit the Samlesbury witches. It was entirely credible that the Pendle witches kept familiars, but incredible that the Samlesbury women apparently did not.

Whether convicted people like Chattox and Demdike really kept familiars, were really witches, or really made pacts with the Devil are questions that I, like many modern historians of witchcraft, do not want to address. As Clark argues, the power of the elite discourse of demonology was to construct a reality of Satan and his agents that was coherent and utterly believable to many of those involved.[20] Let us leave this discussion with the conclusion that *The Wonderfull Discoverie* is England's first example of the intrusion into popular testimony of a widespread elite ideology of witchcraft, one strongly promoted by the Jacobean administration. That conclusion leaves *The Wonderfull Discoverie* remarkable, but only as England's first example of a very general transformation that was common elsewhere in Europe.

There is a second, more revealing transformation, in which Potts turned the process of the witches' discovery and trial into an ideal example of mid-Jacobean justice, modelled on the example set by the King himself. Tracts from the preceding decades, such as those catalogued by Wallace Notestein in the early part of the twentieth century or published and discussed by Marion Gibson at its end,[21] fall into three broad genres. First, there was sensational popular journalism: Assizes were excellent sources of scandal of every kind, and tales of witchcraft can be found bound indiscriminately with other horrid murders turned into racy narratives. One such is the anonymous *Witches of Northamptonshire*, published almost contemporaneously with *The Wonderfull Discoverie* in 1612.[22] The publication contains no references to diabolism, although this would have ensured good sales.

A second genre was religious controversy, in which court cases and evidence were mobilised by self-styled learned authors to support their contentions about what witchcraft 'really was', how serious a threat it represented, and how religious and judicial authorities should respond to it. One example is the *Dialogue Concerning Witches and Witchcraftes*, published in 1593 by the famous divine George Gifford. Like many English authors of this genre, Gifford promoted demonological theory well before Potts but did not support it with documents from the trials he knew. These authors instead justified their demonology with a plethora of references to the Bible, and theological and classical sources. It is noteworthy that Potts nowhere deploys these typical resources of Christian humanism.

This leaves a third group of tracts, those that reproduced legal documents in order to secure the reputation of the law officers.[23] As Gibson notes, examples of this genre 'abruptly ceased' just after 1590,[24] and it is interesting that Potts revived and produced the lengthiest instance of it. A significant precursor with parallels to *The Wonderfull Discoverie* is *The Most Strange and Admirable Discoverie of the Three Witches of Warboys*, compiled anonymously and presented to the presiding judge, Edward Fenner, in 1593.[25] Fenner's career was dogged by talk of his stupidity and unsound religion, and he was sacked in 1606. He had just been moved in the winter of 1592–93 from the Midland to the Norfolk Circuit, which included Huntingdon, when he was faced with the difficult Warboys or 'Throckmorton' case. The difficulty was that the Throckmorton girls, like Alice Nutter in the Pendle case, were unusual in being genteel. In consequence the case 'received wide currency', and may even have inspired the trickery that faced the Leicester judges in 1616. The convictions were based on slender evidence, but one of the accused, Alice Samuel, conveniently confessed just before her execution.[26]

Fenner surely commissioned this account of the trial and its aftermath to protect his reputation on his new circuit. Just as Potts later wrote of 'divers uncertaine reportes and relations', so the anonymous author mentioned 'your worships care, as well for the furthering of the truth of the malefactors, [but] also the crossing of whatsoever Pamphlets should have beene preferred, respecting either the matter partly or confusedly'. Fenner was as involved in this compilation as Bromley was in *The Wonderfull Discoverie*. His chosen tool was able to 'prefer the patronage here of to Your Worship [because Fenner had] taken extraordinary paines in perfecting this work for the printing to others example'.[27] *The Wonderfull Discoverie* remains the first tract overtly commissioned by the presiding judge, but *The Three Witches of Warboys* provides an important precedent of a judge using the publication of trial documents in order to defend his competence.

Let us now examine the evidence for *The Wonderfull Discoverie* being an especially artful attempt to defend the reputation of the law officers. Although there were precursors, *The Wonderfull Discoverie* is unprecedented in several ways besides its focus on diabolism. First, Potts's authorship is declared, not concealed like 'Anon' or 'W. W.'. Secondly, the fiction of the work being offered to a grateful judge is dispensed with; Potts declared that it 'hath *pleased [the judges] out of their respect to mee to impose this worke upon mee*'.[28] Thirdly, no other work reproduces such rich detail, including the Assize calendar, and this makes it especially useful to historians. Fourthly, the work is dedicated to a very powerful, and significant, patron at James's court, Sir Thomas Knyvet (and his wife). Fifthly, *The Wonderfull Discoverie* is an explicit appeal to James I himself. This last point explains the others, and merits closer attention.

There is a very profound connection, indeed considerable intertextuality, between James's *Daemonologie* and *The Wonderfull Discoverie*. We can go well beyond Potts's general observation, to which Notestein drew attention: 'What hath the Kings Majestie written and published in his *Daemonologie*, by way of praemonition and prevention, which hath not here by the first or last beene executed, put in practise or discovered?'[29] But we can build on the connection with the *Daemonologie* to argue that *The Wonderfull Discoverie* is very carefully constructed to accord with what the protagonists believed was James's policy in 1612.

A major piece of evidence here is the way that Potts's account emphasises its departure from the expected order, and has evidence from the Samlesbury acquittals 'placed amongst the Witches, by special order and commandement'. As Potts put it, Almighty God 'in his providence had provided meanes for [the Samlesbury women's acquittal because he] ... had prepared and placed in the Seate of Justice, an upright Judge to sit in judgement upon their lives'.[30] It was indeed providential that Bromley was led to 'expose' the Catholic priest, Christopher Southworth, as Grace Sowerbutts's coach. The Lancaster trials now combined the two big threats to Jacobean order in Lancashire, witchery and popery. The political complexities were likewise doubled.

We have seen how James's witchcraft policy now encompassed the conflicting needs of taking diabolic witchcraft seriously while at the same time countering superstitious credulity through a vigilant scepticism. But James's policy on Catholic recusancy was equally ambivalent. Elizabethan policy had tended to proceed firmly against the heterodoxies of witchcraft and Catholic superstition together, as a twin effort to impose conformity. James's policy tended to separate them, aiming at his vision of bringing Catholics within the Protestant fold. His faith in the tractability of Catholics was occasionally shaken, notably, and significantly for the Lancaster trials, by the Gunpowder Plot of 1605. Indeed, James's sensibilities were heightened by warnings of another Catholic plot in 1612. He resolved the tension by deciding that the majority of Catholics were law-abiding, loyal subjects who could be won over. To win them they had to be isolated from a rotten core of Jesuit-led agents, who were dedicated to the destruction not only of Protestantism but, in accordance with his earlier fear of witches, with the destruction of his own body also. Judicial charges of the period confirm that judges were expected to show moderation towards ordinary Catholics, but militancy against the nests of treacherous activists.[31]

Given that witchcraft was believed to flourish amid the superstitious and papist resistance for which Lancashire was renowned, we can imagine Bromley and Altham's ideal judicial result as they contemplated the cases. Diabolic witchcraft would be detected, but not in every case. Popery would be shown to be at work, but in fanatics not ordinary subjects. The judges would be presented as shrewd discriminators between credible and incredible testimony, according to the standards not of a northern jury but 'heere about London'. The brilliant achievement of the law officers and of *The Wonderfull Discoverie* is that they achieved all of these things. Since elite investigators could transform raw popular testimony into line with their presuppositions, it seems safe to assume that the Lancaster cases did not fit the judges' ideal outcome by a lucky chance, but because the law officers made them fit. A question arises as to whether the fit was the outcome of unconscious projection, or conscious manipulation. I suggest that it was both.

Certainly Potts could do little but add commentary, sometimes extensive, to the examinations and depositions, most of which had been taken by the local magistrate Roger Nowell before Potts and the judges arrived for the summer Assizes. These were unmanipulable 'docile records'. Nowell had been working with Bromley since they were both appointed in 1610. It is likely that

Nowell had had prior discussions with the judges about the longstanding rumours of Pendle witchery and how he should investigate them. Moreover, it was probably Nowell's local knowledge that suggested to Bromley that the Catholic priest Christopher Southworth had manufactured evidence against the Samlesbury accused. The Protestant Nowells and Catholic Southworths had been contesting power in the region for decades. Nowell surely knew that Robert Holden, the magistrate who led the Samlesbury prosecutions, was a marked Catholic from a family of recusants.[32] Lumby is sure that Nowell read James and other leading demonologists.[33] But my interpretation requires only that Nowell was broadly familiar with James's *Daemonologie*, and autonomously exacted the first English confessions of a suitably diabolic kind. I do, however, believe that Bromley and Altham worked very closely with Potts to manipulate the extraordinary records into an account that would protect and advance their careers. As Potts confidently declared: 'GOD graunt us the long and prosperous continuance of these Honourable and Reverend Judges, under whose Government we live in these North parts: for we may say, that GOD Almightie hath singled them out, and set them on his Seat, for the defence of Justice'.[34]

Potts's *Wonderfull Discoverie* is unique among the genres of witchcraft tracts mentioned above in that it legitimated its model of witchcraft without reference to the Bible, or classical and theological authorities. The sole appeal is to James's *Daemonologie*. There are six features of witchcraft for which there are explicit parallels. Some are remarkably singular. Others are standard features, but are described in James's own words.

First, James divided witches into two classes, poor and rich, whom the Devil tempted in different ways:

> These two degrees now of persones, that practises this craft, answers to the passions in them, which ... the Devil used as means to intyse them to his service, for such of them as are in great miserie and povertie, he allures to follow him, by promising unto them greate riches, and worldlie commoditie. Such as though riche, yet burnes in a desperat desire of revenge, hee allures them by promises, to get their turne satisfied to their hartes contentment.[35]

The Pendle witches were all poor, except Alice Nutter. From a family of the middling sort, 'she was [noted Potts] a rich woman; had a great estate, and children of good hope: in the common opinion of the world, of good temper, free from envy or malice'.[36] As Fenner had found with the Throckmorton case, public scepticism could surround the conviction of 'respectable' suspects.

Nevertheless, Nutter was hanged, and Potts went to some lengths to defend the verdict. He displayed a full knowledge of James's analysis, with this extensive, unacknowledged reference, largely word for word, to the *Daemonologie*:

The two degrees of persons which chiefly practise Witchcraft, are such, as are in great miserie and povertie, for such the Devill allures to follow him, by promising great riches, and worldly commoditie; Others, though rich, yet burne in a desperate desire of Revenge; Hee allures them by promises, to get their turne satisfied to their hearts contentment.[37]

Potts drew attention to Nutter's anomalous prosperity: 'to attempt this woman in that sort, the Divel had small meanes'. Consequently, Potts emphasised Bromley's particular caution in Nutter's case. 'Great was the care and paines of his Lordship, to make triall of the Innocencie of this woman, as shall appear unto you ... by an extraordinary meanes of Triall, to marke her out from the rest'.[38] This was an identity parade made up of witches, other prisoners and 'some other strange women'. Under cross examination, the child witness Jennet Device 'in the presence of this great Audience, in open Court, she went and tooke Alice Nutter, this prisoner, by the hand, and accused her'. When Jennet subsequently declined to incriminate a name invented by Bromley, Potts concluded, with a nod to the forthcoming evidence of Grace Sowerbutts, that '[t]his could be no forged or false Accusation, but the very Act of GOD to discover her'.[39]

The second parallel between the *Daemonologie* and *The Wonderfull Discoverie* is the process by which the Devil discloses himself to his targets. James described three stages. Satan first insinuates himself 'either by a voice, or in a likeness of a man' when they are alone. At the second meeting he concludes the pact and places 'his marke upon some secreit place of their bodie'. At the third meeting he begins to satisfy their needs.[40] The four confessions, of Demdike, Chattox, James and Alizon Device, fit James's pattern very closely.[41] This is extraordinary given that diabolism and pacts were not part of Pendle popular beliefs.

A third parallel can be seen in the treatment of sabbats, described by James at some length. Of course, sabbats loomed large in elite demonological discourse, even if evidence of them had not previously been given in an English court. But Potts's evidence is made to fit James's description in two ways that are remarkable. First, James reasoned that, since only witches attended sabbats, then only witches, unreliable witnesses as they were, could give credible evidence of sabbats. When the Pendle witch James Device attested to being present at a sabbat at Malkin Tower, Potts quoted exactly, without acknowledgement, from the *Daemonologie*: 'who but Witches can be proofes, and so witnesses of the doings of Witches? since all their Meetings, Conspiracies, Practises, and Murthers, are the Workes of Darknesse'.[42] Secondly, there is Potts's handling of the alleged sabbat attended by the Samlesbury witches. The examination of Grace Sowerbutts described an archetypically satanic black mass, including the ritual murder and eating of a baby, and sexual abuse by the Devil. However, Bromley threw out this evidence as a papist fabrication. Potts's text uniquely goes back over Sowerbutts's evidence, highlighting its incredibility. As Stuart Clark has emphasised, demonologists placed limits upon what demons, and witches with demonic assistance, could do. These limits provided criteria against which to judge the credibility of extraordinary tales of witchery. Most demonologists, including James, agreed that God did not give demons the power to break the laws of nature. Demons could work impressive *mirabila* (wonders), but only God could perform supernatural *miracula*.[43] Of course, demonologists disagreed about what was naturally possible. For example, could Satan actually animate the corpse of a dead person? Or could he transform himself or witches into the likeness of other beings? Most demonologists held that he could merely simulate appearances, or simply implant images in a subject's mind. James made his own choice of criteria of the unnaturally impossible, and these were used by Potts. In describing the attendance of witches at sabbats, James denied that they travelled either by flying or by being 'transformed into the likeness of a little beast or foule'. Flying and shape-shifting were naturally impossible, and therefore literally incredible.[44] Potts accordingly emphasised Bromley's incredulity concerning 'what impossibilities are in this accusation brought to this perfection by the great care and pains of this officious doctor [Southworth]'. The impossibilities include Jennet Bierley's 'transformation in to the likeness of a black dog', falling from a height without pain, and a baby being impaled without crying. In other respects, however, this Catholic confection of a continental sabbat was not impossible enough, or at least not English enough: 'the Seminarie forgot to devise a Spirit [i.e. an animal familiar] for [the witches]'.[45]

The fourth and fifth parallels are more circumstantial. Fourthly, James described the supposedly widespread technique of making doll-like wax or clay images of the victim.[46] This turned out to be the Pendle witches' method of choice. Southerns was induced to describe her method using details very reminiscent of the *Daemonologie*. Her use of image magic underlined Potts's contention that nothing described by his king 'hath not here by the first or last beene executed, put in practise or discovered'.[47]

Fifthly, James reasoned that the extraordinarily heinous crime of witchcraft permitted extraordinary legal measures. These included admitting evidence from witches and children, which Potts duly noted. But 'God hath appointed (for a supernaturall signe of the monstrous impietie of the witches)' an extraordinary proof of guilt: the ducking or floating of witches. This godly miracle was 'just as', James continued, 'in a secret murther, if the deade carcase be at any time handled by the murtherer, it wil gush out of bloud'.[48] The Pendle witches were not ducked, but Potts highlighted the fact that 'the said *Jennet Preston* comming to touch the dead corpes, they bled fresh bloud presently, in the presence of all that were there present: Which hath ever beene held a great argument to induce a Jurie to hold him guiltie that shall be accused of Murther'. This was indeed the case until later in the century, but few legal records of its use have survived.[49]

The sixth and perhaps strongest parallel concerns *The Wonderfull Discoverie*'s presentation of the acquittal of the three Samlesbury witches. Here Potts moves from making the most out of Nowell's prior depositions to emphasising Bromley's impeccable actions in court on Wednesday 19 August 1612. There is no doubt that *The Wonderfull Discoverie* appeals to a clever reading of the *Daemonologie*.

Even in 1597, James had cautioned against judicial credulity in witchcraft cases. Indeed, the *Daemonologie* may have been intended to damp down the Scottish witch-hunts of the 1590s. James wrote: 'it is as great a crime (as SALOMON [Solomon] sayeth,) to condemne the innocent as to let the guiltie escape free'.[50] Bromley must have been anxious to clear himself from charges of having credulously or corruptly condemned the innocent. His problem was that, having dispensed on Tuesday with the four Pendle witches who had confessed, he now had to deal with the eight who maintained their innocence. They would be convicted on the slender testimony of young Jennet Device that they had once attended a meeting that was allegedly a sabbat.

The Wonderfull Discoverie rhetorically protected Bromley's reputation against charges of credulity by the order in which it recounted the cases. Following Potts's reconstruction of the gaol calendar, those Pendle witches who confessed came first. But when it came to the disputable 'not guilty' pleas, it made a point of departing from the expected order. 'Thus', wrote Potts, 'have we left for a time the Graund Witches of the Forrest of Pendle, to the good consideration of a very sufficient jury'. Instead 'the discourse of these three women of Samlesbury ... is placed here amongst the witches, by special order and commandment'.[51] We can assume that the commandment came from the judges who oversaw the text.

The sequence gave Potts the opportunity to present Bromley's masterful exposure of Father Christopher Southworth as the coach behind Grace Sowerbutts's lurid, continental-style testimony. Potts tells us that the three Samlesbury accused, who included Christopher's niece Jane, were Anglican converts, 'once obstinate Papists, and now came to Church'.[52] Their acquittals showed that Bromley was alert to all the dangers of witchcraft cases that were coming to preoccupy James: the use of trumped-up evidence; the caution needed in dealing with evidence from witches; the particular problem of child witnesses; the danger of credulity; and the injustice of convicting the innocent. Indeed, by bringing a sceptical perspective to Lancashire witchery, Bromley simultaneously showed himself to be alert to James's new public enemy – conspiratorial Catholic priests. Lancashire had been infected with, but judicially purged of, both satanic and popish plotters. Bromley also enacted James's leniency and belief that recusants could be won over to Protestantism. At his direction Sowerbutts was asked 'whether shee ever was at the Church, shee saith, shee was not, but promised hereafter to goe to the Church, and that very willingly'.[53]

With Bromley's competence and credibility thus enhanced, Potts went back to the Pendle witches, whose convictions on the similarly uncorroborated evidence of a child now looked much safer. If one remains unconvinced of the artifice of *The Wonderfull Discoverie*, one should read the final page. Potts recalled Bromley's warning, which was itself James's warning in the *Daemonologie*, that one cannot expect 'such apparent proof' in witch trials as in other crimes. But, Potts continued, '[n]either do I urge this any further, then with this, that I would alwaies intreat you to remember, that it is as great a crime (as *Salomon* [Solomon] sayeth, *Prov.* 17) to condemne the innocent, as to let the guiltie escape free'.[54] This is Potts's only biblical reference and, needless to say, he quoted directly and without acknowledgement from the *Daemonologie*.

The power and influence of Nowell the magistrate, Bromley the judge and Potts the author, all with James's *Daemonologie* in their minds, transformed the events of 1612 into England's first example of the diabolism described by European demonologists. That much is obvious. But the evidence allows us to go further, from a general to a micro-contextual transformation: *The Wonderfull Discoverie* was specifically fashioned to exemplify what Justices Bromley and Altham believed was Jacobean policy at the time of the Lancaster trials. We can now infer that policy from *The Wonderfull Discoverie*. The inference is that James was still very receptive to stories of satanic pacts and sabbats, but that he was concerned about judicial credulity well before his involvement with Crew's 1616 cases. Moreover, he was equally if not more worried about Catholic conspiracies as about demonic ones.

Of course, the argument in this chapter depends upon the possibility that the authors' artifice and manoeuvring could bring them courtly favour. Given more space, we might examine how *The Wonderfull Discoverie* worked as a ploy for patronage within the complex patron–client system that underpinned the Jacobean court and the judicial system. Limited space allows exploration of just one strand of evidence that places Potts's work within the Jacobean system of patronage and promotion. He compiled *The Wonderfull Discoverie* at the command and direction of Bromley and Altham. They could have insisted upon being Potts's dedicatees: by virtue of his position as clerk, they were his patrons. But Potts was also the client of the powerful courtier Sir Thomas Knyvet, Baron of Escrick and Privy Councillor. The lowly Potts paid tribute in his dedicatory epistle to Knyvet's patronage of his learning and legal career.[55] If Potts and the judges were seeking James's approval, Knyvet's access to the King made him a more effective channel, and *The Wonderfull Discoverie* was indeed dedicated to him. It was conventional to secure in advance the approval of the dedicatee. Given that Knyvet's client was offering him a sensational defence of impugned judges, we can be doubly confident that Knyvet judged that *The Wonderfull Discoverie* would bring favour to

Potts, to the judges and, by association, to himself.

Knyvet's career made him a very appropriate patron for *The Wonderfull Discoverie*. Under Elizabeth, his connections with the Cecil family had brought him a position in the Privy Chamber. With a female monarch this conferred only limited access to the royal face, although he had responsibilities in the Jewel House. Changes of monarch usually brought changes in patronage networks. On James's accession, Knyvet retained his Jewel House duties, and seems to have flourished because of James's extraordinary appetite for jewels. But James revived the importance of the Bedchamber, staffing it with Scots and reducing the Privy Chamber to unimportant shifts of attendance upon the King. It was in this minor capacity that, providentially, Knyvet was despatched on 4 November 1605 to make a follow-up search of the Parliament cellars, where he found and arrested the Catholic conspirator and gunpowder plotter Guy Fawkes.[56]

Knyvet now became a favourite of James. He was made a knight, guardian of James's daughter Mary, Privy Councillor and Warden of the Mint. He was made Baron of Escrick in 1607 despite having 'lost' thousands of pounds of royal funds. But thereafter his fortunes stalled. As Warden of the Mint he was ineffectual in developing a sound money supply for the cash-strapped administration, and in 1612 he suffered the nightmare of every courtier, the death of his major patron Salisbury.[57] To revive his fortunes he seems to have played upon his reputation as a defender of the King's person from Catholic traitors. In the 1610 parliament one of only two speeches by him concerned a bill on the 'King's Safety'. In the aftermath of the assassination of Henry IV of France by a Catholic fanatic, the brutal measure of executing the descendants of known Catholic 'traitors' was discussed. Knyvet said that he could 'like it very well to have this punishment inflicted upon papists'.[58]

The Wonderfull Discoverie was well suited to remind James of Knyvet's reputation. His client Potts had played a part in, and was now publicising, the vindication of James's *Daemonologie* and the skilful '*Wonderfull Discoverie*' of James's two nightmares, satanic witches and Catholic agents. But there is another, most extraordinary parallel between Knyvet and the Lancaster witches.

If *The Wonderfull Discoverie* is evidence of the power of law officers to transform popular beliefs and testimony to fit the discourse and concerns of the elite, then surely its most singular example is the alleged plot to free the Pendle witches. James Device deposed that the Pendle witches convened their sabbat for several purposes. The first was spirit conjuring. 'The second was, for the delivery of [the imprisoned witches]; killing the Gaoler at Lancaster; and before the next Assises to blow up the Castle there: and to that end the aforesaid prisoners might by that time make an escape, and get away.'[59]

It is possible that the suspects considered how to free their neighbours. But did they discuss the use of gunpowder? Where would they have procured it? How would they have got it into the castle? Lancaster Castle would certainly have required a hefty and skilfully set charge to breach its walls! It is surely more reasonable that the preposterous scheme was invented or embellished by magistrates Nowell and Bannister and agreed to by James Device during his interrogations as a witch. Wherever the scheme originated, the echoes of the Gunpowder Plot in *The Wonderfull Discoverie* matched Knyvet's own noises concerning plotters. It was certainly a timely gift to give, if not directly to the King, then, in the first instance, to Knyvet, for James was being warned of a second Catholic plot in the summer of 1612. As *The Wonderfull Discoverie*'s nineteenth-century editor observed (one hopes drily), 'who so fit to have the book dedicated to him as one who had acted so conspicuous a part on the memorable occasion at Westminster'.[60]

The extent to which *The Wonderfull Discoverie* was a deliberate patronage ploy for turning potential metropolitan scepticism into royal favour remains conjectural. There is no direct evidence that Knyvet used it, or that James approved or disapproved of it. Knyvet's fortunes underwent no quantum leap at this time, although he received valuable gifts, grants and positions.[61] However, the judges did well, at a time when the judicial pole was especially greasy, notably because of the confrontation between Lord Chief Justice Edward Coke and James over the question of the royal prerogative. Altham successfully distanced himself from Coke, survived an allegation of corruption in May 1612 and, despite or because of the Lancaster trials, pursued a successful career until his death in 1617.[62] Bromley, the younger and more ambitious of the two, was clearly not harmed by the publicity. Indeed, in 1616 he was promoted to the Midlands Circuit to replace Crew in the aftermath of the Leicester trials. No doubt regarded as a safe pair of hands, he was still hanging witches in 1618.[63]

And what of Potts, our notional author? The normal aspiration for a humble clerk of the court without university training would have been slow promotion to Clerk of the Assize. But Potts soon received considerable royal favour, most likely mediated by Knyvet. In 1615 'the keepership of Skalme Park [was given] to Thomas Potts the Kings servant, for the breeding and training of hounds', a keen interest of James. In 1618 he was granted 'the office of collecting the forfeitures on the laws concerning sewers, for twenty-one years'. *The Wonderfull Discoverie*'s author was now a minor patron himself, with the power to appoint collectors.[64]

The evidence is circumstantial, but it points to the success of the judges' bold decision to publicise the extraordinary Lancaster trials at such confident length. Potts's audacious use and interpretation of James's treatise must have chimed with Whitehall policy in 1612–13. That Potts could use James's 1597 text so effectively gives some support to Clark's view that James had not become more shrewd by the 1610s. But that conclusion overlooks Potts's expansion of James's brief warning against condemning the innocent into a key part

38

of his defence. Four years before James's personal investigation of the Leicester fraud, Potts, Bromley and Altham had judged James to favour stories of judicial scepticism, exposure of superstition, extreme caution with child witnesses, and the pursuit of Catholic as much as diabolic enemies. These aspects must be balanced against Potts's more sensational confirmation that Satan's servants had at last been caught on English soil, and had confessed to all the diabolic deeds that James had warned about.

We must therefore be doubly wary of using *The Wonderfull Discoverie* as an innocent text. But the loss, in terms of a window onto Lancashire witchcraft, is compensated. The chain of personal and textual connections that links the Lancaster witches, via Nowell, Bromley, Potts and Knyvet, to the royal author of *Daemonologie* opens a unique window onto Jacobean witchcraft policy.

Notes

I am grateful to Clive Holmes and Robert Poole for reading a draft version and providing additional information.

1 *Dictionary of National Biography* (hereafter *DNB*), s.v. 'Potts, Thomas'.

2 See Gibson's chapter in this volume.

3 James VI and I, *Daemonologie, in Forme of a Dialogue, Divided into Three Bookes* (Edinburgh, 1597; facsimile edn, Edinburgh: Edinburgh University Press, 1966), hereafter *Daemonologie*. The most recent edition appears in Lawrence Normand and Gareth Roberts (eds), *Witchcraft in Early Modern Scotland: James VI's Demonology and the North Berwick Witches* (Exeter: Exeter University Press, 2000). See also Julian Goodare (ed.), *The Scottish Witch Hunt in Context* (Manchester: Manchester University Press, 2002).

4 Wallace Notestein, *History of Witchcraft in England from 1558 to 1718* (Washington, DC: American Historical Association, 1911; reprint edn, 1965), pp. 101, 130.

5 D. P. Walker, *Unclean Spirits: Possession and Exorcism in France and England in the Late Sixteenth and Early Seventeenth Centuries* (London: Scolar Press, 1981), ch. 4, pp. 77–84.

6 Quoted and discussed in D. H. Willson, *King James VI and I* (London: Cape, 1956), p. 311.

7 Stuart Clark, 'King James's *Daemonologie*: witchcraft and kingship', in Sydney Anglo (ed.), *The Damned Art: Essays in the Literature of Witchcraft* (London: Routledge, 1977), pp. 156–81, at p. 163. James's views on witchcraft have recently been extensively discussed in Normand and Roberts (eds), *Witchcraft in Early Modern Scotland* and in Goodare (ed.), *The Scottish Witch Hunt in Context*.

8 J. S. Cockburn, *A History of the English Assizes 1558–1714* (Cambridge: Cambridge University Press, 1972), pp. 183–4, 226, 68.

9 Ben Jonson, *The Divell is an Asse*, in Ben Jonson, *Works*, ed. C. H. Herford (Oxford: Oxford University Press, 1938), vi, pp. 155–270. For Darrell and exorcism see pp. 254–69. Quotation from I, i, esp. ll. 31–3. For Eitherside, see V, viii. The play was first performed late in 1616, but publication was deferred until 1631, possibly because it was offensive to London mercantile interests. The message to the London audience receives impressive analysis in Leah S. Marcus, *The Politics of Mirth* (Chicago and London: Chicago University Press, 1986), ch. 3.

10 For connections between Darrell and Lancashire witchcraft see Jonathan Lumby, *The Lancashire Witch-Craze: Jennet Preston and the Lancashire Witches* (Preston: Carnegie, 1995), chs 22, 23.

11 Lumby, *Lancashire Witch-Craze*, ch. 2 and *passim*.

12 Thomas Potts, *The Wonderfull Discoverie of Witches in the Countie of Lancaster* (London, 1613), X4.

13 Potts, *Wonderfull Discoverie*, B.

14 Stuart Clark, *Thinking with Demons: The Idea of Witchcraft in Early Modern Europe* (Oxford: Clarendon Press, 1997).

15 For a good general introduction, see Brian P. Levack, *The Witch-hunt in Early Modern Europe*, 2nd edn (London: Longman, 1995).

16 The best recent survey of English witchcraft is James Sharpe, *Instruments of Darkness: Witchcraft in England 1550–1750* (London: Hamish Hamilton, 1996).

17 The 1604 statute is analysed in G. L. Kittredge, *Witchcraft in Old and New England* (Cambridge, Mass.: Harvard University Press, 1929; reprinted, New York, 1958), pp. 276–328.

18 Keith Thomas, *Religion and the Decline of Magic: Studies in Popular Beliefs in Sixteenth- and Seventeenth-Century England* (1971; London: Penguin, 1973), pp. 535–69; Levack, *Witch-Hunt in Early Modern Europe*; Carlo Ginzburg, *Night Battles: Witchcraft and Agrarian Cults in the Sixteenth and Seventeenth Centuries*, trans. J. and A. Tedeschi (London: Routledge, 1983) is the classic study of how popular testimony (of the benandanti agrarian cult) was forced into inquisitorial notions of demonic witchcraft.

19 Clive Holmes, 'Popular culture? Witches, magistrates and divines in early modern England', in S. L. Kaplan (ed.), *Understanding Popular Culture: Europe from the Middle Ages to the Nineteenth Century* (Berlin: Mouton, 1984), pp. 85–110. See especially p. 97.

20 Clark, *Thinking with Demons*, p. 8.

21 Notestein, *History of Witchcraft*; Marion Gibson, *Early Modern Witches: Witchcraft Cases in Contemporary Writing* (London: Routledge, 2000).

22 Anon., *The Witches of Northamptonshire* (London, 1612).

23 An early example is W. W., *A True and Just Recorde, of the Information, Examination, and Confession of all the Witches, Taken at S. Oses in the Countie of Essex* (London, 1582).

24 Gibson's chapter in this volume.

25 Anon., *The Most Strange and Admirable Discoverie of the Three Witches of Warboys, (Arraigned, Convicted and Executed at the Last Assizes at Huntington)* (London, 1593).

26 Cockburn, *History of the English Assizes*, pp. 51, 125, 222–6, 267–8; Kittredge, *Witchcraft in Old and New England*, p. 6.

27 Anon., *Witches of Warboys*, A2; Potts, *Wonderfull Discoverie*, B.

28 Potts, *Wonderfull Discoverie*, 'Epistle Dedicatorie'.

29 Potts, *Wonderfull Discoverie*, T2.

30 Potts, *Wonderfull Discoverie*, N3, M3.

31 Willson, *James I*, ch. 13 *passim*. For warnings of plots in 1611 and 1612 see *Calendar of State Papers Domestic* (hereafter *CSPD*), 1611–18, pp. 138, 142, 146, 152, 164.

32 Lumby, *Lancashire Witch-Craze*, pp. 115–18, 136–42.

33 Lumby, *Lancashire Witch-Craze*, p. 23.

34 Potts, *Wonderfull Discoverie*, Z3.

35 James VI and I, *Daemonologie*, p. 32.

36 Potts, *Wonderfull Discoverie*, O3.

37 Potts, *Wonderfull Discoverie*, O3.

38 Potts, *Wonderfull Discoverie*, O3.

39 Potts, *Wonderfull Discoverie*, P2.

40 James VI and I, *Daemonologie*, pp. 32–3, 51–2.

41 Potts, *Wonderfull Discoverie*. For Southerns see B; for Whittle, B4; for James Device, C2; for Alizon Device, C.

42 Potts, *Wonderfull Discoverie*, P3. Compare with James VI and I, *Daemonologie*, p. 79.

43 On the Devil's confinement to natural powers see Stuart Clark, 'The rational witchfinder: conscience, demonological naturalism and popular superstitions', in S. Pumfrey *et al.* (eds),

Science, Culture and Popular Belief in Renaissance Europe (Manchester: Manchester University Press, 1991), pp. 222–48.

44 James VI and I, *Daemonologie*, pp. 38–41.

45 Potts, *Wonderfull Discoverie*, M–M4.

46 James VI and I, *Daemonologie*, pp. 44–6.

47 Potts, *Wonderfull Discoverie*, B and T2. For the general use of images see Thomas, *Religion and the Decline of Magic*, pp. 437–8.

48 James VI and I, *Daemonologie*, pp. 80–1.

49 Potts, *Wonderfull Discoverie*, Y3. Thomas, *Religion and the Decline of Magic* (p. 220, n. 11) lists only ten instances, Jennet Preston's being one. For a recent discussion of corpse bleeding and its fortune as a form of proof see Malcolm Gaskill, 'The displacement of providence', *Continuity and Change* 11 (1996), pp. 341–74, especially p. 354.

50 James VI and I, *Daemonologie*, pp. 78–9.

51 Potts, *Wonderfull Discoverie*, K3, N3.

52 Potts, *Wonderfull Discoverie*, M4.

53 Potts, *Wonderfull Discoverie*, N.

54 Potts, *Wonderfull Discoverie*, Z3.

55 Potts, *Wonderfull Discoverie*, 'Epistle Dedicatorie'.

56 See articles by Pam Wright and Neil Cuddy in D. Starkey *et al.* (eds), *The English Court from the Wars of the Roses to the Civil War* (London: Longman, 1987). See especially pp. 155, 156, 161, 164, 183. For Knyvet in the Jewel House see *CSPD*, 1598–1601, p. 476; *CSPD*, 1603–1610, I, 89; VI, 29, 54. For James's extravagant purchases of jewels see Frederick C. Dietz, *English Public Finance 1558–1641* (1932; 2nd edn, London: Frank Cass, 1964), p. 105. The various accounts of Fawkes's arrest are compared in the apologetic John Gerard, S.J., *What was the Gunpowder Plot? The Traditional Story Tested by Original Evidence* (London: Osgood and McIlvaine, 1897), pp. 124–6.

57 *DNB*, s.v. 'Knyvet, Thomas, Lord Knyvet of Escrick'. For the financial scandal, see Historical Manuscripts Commission, *Salisbury* Series 9 (reprinted London, 1970), part 18, pp. 246, 248–9; J. Paynes Collier (ed.), *The Egerton Papers* (London, 1840), pp. 409–10, 432–4; Linda Levy Peck, *Northampton: Patronage and Policy at the Court of James I* (London: Allen and Unwin, 1982), p. 88; Dietz, *English Public Finance* p. 149; *Acts of the Privy Council 1615–1616*, 23 July 1615. In this letter James was impatient with the failure of previous consultations.

58 Elizabeth Read Foster (ed.), *Proceedings in Parliament 1610* (New Haven and London: Yale University Press, 1966), p. 148. Knyvet dismissed any moral objections, but did not think the policy would be effective.

59 Potts, *Wonderfull Discoverie*, P.

60 Crossley, notes to edition of Potts, *Wonderfull Discoverie* (ed. James Crossley, Manchester: Chetham Society publications vi, 1845), p. 1.

61 *CSPD*, 1611–18, pp. 20, 25, 75, 111, 198. The money was to be paid from the profits of the Mint. Ironically, given that Knyvet was Warden, the profits were found to be 'decayed and not sufficing therefor'. He was nonetheless to be paid 'from the Exchequer'. *DNB*, s.v. 'Knyvet, Sir Thomas'; *Acts of the Privy Council*, 1 May 1613.

62 *DNB*, s.v. 'Altham, Sir James'.

63 Cockburn, *History of the English Assizes*, pp. 269–70; C. L'Estrange Ewen, *Witchcraft and Demonianism: A Concise Account Derived from Sworn Depositions and Confessions Obtained in the Courts of England and Wales* (London: Heath Cranton, 1933), pp. 232–3.

64 *CSPD*, 1611–18, pp. 315, 535. For Potts's office collecting forfeitures and appointing deputies (granted together with Patrick Murray), see Public Record Office (London), C66/2176, Chancery and Supreme Court of Judicature: Patent Rolls. For James and hunting see Willson, *James VI and I*, pp. 178–82.

3

Thomas Potts's 'dusty memory': reconstructing justice in *The Wonderfull Discoverie of Witches*

Marion Gibson

On 16 November 1612 Thomas Potts, a court clerk at that summer's Lancashire witch trials, sat in his lodgings in London's Chancery Lane putting the finishing, and slightly desperate, touches to the enormous work *The Wonderfull Discoverie of Witches*, which he had been put in charge of compiling and editing. Potts said that he had 'taken paines' over the account of the Lancashire witches, reconstructing from memory their activities and their trials, at the behest of their judges and 'for the benefit of my Countrie' (a3). He was to say later in his text that it 'was a worke imposed upon me ... in respect I was so wel instructed in every particular', that 'I wanted libertie to write what I would' and, heartrendingly, that 'I have undertaken to finish it in a busie Tearme amongst my other imploiments ... it is no part of my profession to publish any thing in print' (X–X2). But what benefit did Potts hope to bring to his countrymen and women by publishing his painstaking memorial reconstruction, which, as the novelist Robert Neill touchingly pointed out, became his dusty memorial in a literal sense?[1] What were his patrons' restrictive instructions to him as reluctant editor? What traces are left in his text of the straightforward difficulties and less obvious evasions of representing this legal process against witches? How much did Potts clean up his memory of the witchcraft trials with tidying, editing and sweeping under the carpet, and how much did that other dust of forgetfulness, mistaking and prejudice blur the account he has left us? This chapter looks at what Potts's witchcraft pamphlet can tell us about how the Lancashire witches were tried, and what it cannot tell us, as well as considering more widely how stories of witchcraft were used both at trials and by pamphleteers.[2]

It is important to analyse not just the content of the story of the Lancashire witches, but also how that story has been transmitted to us, by whom and why, and whether that process can straightforwardly give us access to the actual personalities and events of the early seventeenth century. The creation of the Lancashire witches story is seen in this chapter to be as much a process of mythologising as it is of documentary reportage, but the lines between actuality and creative writing are inevitably and severely blurred by the fact that we can never know precisely what happened four hundred years ago. It is now a commonplace to say that in attempting to reconstruct events we must rely on relatively unreliable strategies: decoding bias and rhetorical sleights of hand by 'recorders' of events, overcoming our own and others' culturally conditioned assumptions about past (and present) societies, and dissecting bodies of hotly disputed and often contradictory evidence about a crime most people would now define as impossible.

The legal historian J. S. Cockburn has summed up views about how early modern news pamphlets represent witchcraft trials with this delicately balanced admission of the complex and contradictory nature of the sources: 'some of the pamphlet evidence is persuasive ... on the other hand, doubt about the reliability of the pamphlet evidence persists'.[3] What Cockburn is partially persuaded by, yet remains to be fully persuaded of, is that pamphlets such as *The Wonderfull Discoverie of Witches* represent, to use Barbara Rosen's phrase, 'what really happened' at witchcraft trials.[4] Yet Cockburn's own phraseology, careful and tentative as it is, still suggests that there is some agreed criterion for judgement of what is 'plausible' or 'reliable'. In fact, we might ask how we can possibly make a judgement on the truth when faced only by a mass of anecdotes from early modern trials, and a mass of commentators to help us interpret them? Which accounts might we consider authoritative? Do we believe those who seem educated and expert, or distrust their motives as biased by class, gender or investment in the accepted (and now questionable) ideologies of their time? Do we trust accounts which agree, or see them as coloured by mass delusion or mutual incomprehension? Suppose accounts agree on something we now find incredible?

David Cressy has recently suggested that in looking at contested events in early modern England, we might 'posit a double set of negotiations, a nested epistemology, involving past and present'. If we look not just at the negotiations between (in this case) witches, their questioners and recorders in deciding what had occurred and why, but also at our own attempts to untangle events, we can admit that 'the telling takes precedence to the tale' and look at the tellers, their strategies and our own expectations as readers – potentially a much richer exploration of events than a simple desire to know 'what really happened'.[5] By looking at a selection of early modern trial pamphlets, this chapter contextualises Potts's heroic efforts to represent the trials in whose particulars he was so well instructed and asks how his work compares with that of other writers in representing 'wonderful discoveries' of witches. It also raises questions of how we might assess reliability of representation. If we are to bring Thomas Potts to the bar as a witness to witchcraft, or even as a defendant of his version of what it was thought to be, then how shall we rightly judge him and his work?

The charge against Potts might be worded as follows: Thomas Potts, Associate Clerk on the Northern Circuit, used formulaic legal documents in his *Wonderfull Discoverie* as a substitute for what was actually said at the witch trial. He omitted many details of procedure and added distorting comment. But in his defence, it will be argued here that provided that these editorial choices are recognised and allowed for, *The Wonderfull Discoverie of Witches* is still supremely interesting to those who wish to know more about early modern society, legal processes and especially the history of witchcraft. Potts's account is apparently honestly meant (which still counts for something in an age where sensational stories were, as now, sometimes manufactured simply for entertainment and financial gain) and it is certainly meticulous.

Potts wrote *The Wonderfull Discoverie* from an unrivalled position of expertise. As an Associate Clerk, he was possibly the Clerk of Arraigns on the Northern Circuit in summer 1612, judging from the judges' description of him as 'a Clerke at that time in Court imploied in the Arraignement and Triall of them [the witches]' (A2). If so, he would have been involved with drafting indictments and producing examinations and informations (witness statements) at appropriate moments.[6] He recreates the legal process for his readers, in 'a Particular Declaration of the proceedings of Justice in those partes'. 'Here shall you behold the Justice of this Land, truely administered', he says proudly, making us wary, however, that he will idealise his account (a3).[7]

Potts begins his trial account by describing the JP Roger Nowell preparing evidence, committing the witches for trial at Lancaster, and sending some examinations to the Assizes at York (C2–C3). In preparing for such a trial, the magistrate, having taken examinations of the suspects, informations of the witnesses and recognisances (documents binding them all to appear), would carry the documents to the Assizes or send them with his clerk or others if he was unable to attend. The Clerk of Assize would number and organise all documents for the prosecution. He worked with the Associate Clerks, here Potts, organising the cases. Because the two judges divided to hear Crown (criminal) and civil cases separately, the clerks were also empowered to act as one of the 'judges', as two were theoretically required in each type of trial.[8] Another pamphlet describing a witchcraft trial, *The Most Strange and Admirable Discoverie of the Three Witches of Warboys* (London, 1593), describes Edward Fenner as 'for that time ... Judge alone' (N3), a representation of common practice as if it were exceptional, because it was not legally defensible. This careful presentation of reality, framed within an ideal which did not exist in practice, warns us again that in reading Potts's work, we may be reading an account that is economical with the truth: justice is always represented as infallible in pamphlets.

As soon as they arrived in the Assize town from the last place on the circuit, the judges were given the gaol calendar (list of persons in gaol) and the clerks drew up indictments.[9] Potts relates:

> The Circuite of the North partes being now almost ended.
> The 16. of August.
> Upon Sunday in the afternoone, my honorable Lords the Judges of Assise, came from Kendall to Lancaster. Whereupon M. Covell [the gaoler at Lancaster Castle] presented unto their Lordships a Calender, conteyning the Names of the Prisoners committed to his charge, which were to receive their Tryall at the Assises; Out of which, we are onely to deale with the proceedings against Witches, which were as followeth. (C3)

This is presented almost like an official document, headed and dated, and Potts also includes, equally formally laid out, a list of the witches, looking like the gaol calendar which listed prisoners to be tried. He apparently intends to represent for us visually the orderliness and official rectitude which he perceived in the conduct of the trial. The printer displays the documents with flair, wasting pages of space, apparently for the visual effect of authority and recorded truth.

But whilst Potts's concern for clarity and thoroughness is complemented by a sense of the grandeur of justice and the authority and aura of any official document, he misrepresents these in his concern for 'reproducing' them. This list is probably only an excerpt from the gaol calendar, or an imaginative recreation of it – not necessarily corresponding to any existing separate record of witches. One of Potts's favourite reminders to the reader is that these matters 'are upon Record', and 'amongst the Recordes of the Crowne at Lancaster', but we have to treat his reassurances with care.[10] Original readers may have believed that these 'reproductions' were proof of the truth of the account, and infused with the authority of the original, but we would now think of the reproduction as having lost the 'aura' of the actual document.[11] The way Potts, the publisher (William Stansby) and the printer (John Barnes) exhibit them suggests they hoped to convince readers that what they saw was an exact copy, as good as seeing the document itself. But we should not mistake representation for reality in the same way, because we can also see that Potts wants us to read in awe of the justice of the legal system and the truth of its records – and of his account. To some extent, Master Covell presents the gaol calendar to us too: we are the judges, sitting through the trial forming opinions based on the evidence represented to us. For example, Potts speaks to the reader to 'commend to your examination and judgement' his interpretation of Grace Sowerbutts's evidence (M). But we are not judges of the fact, only of Potts's representation – which must be carefully examined for deliberate misrepresentation or confusion, and examined alongside other representations to gain an impression of what it foregrounds, omits or downplays as compared with other sources.

When we do this, we see at once that Potts tries to dazzle us with ceremony, and silently edits out sections of more convoluted procedure against the Lancashire witches – procedure not focused on the heroised judges. He mimics on paper the pomp of the opening of the Assizes, impressing us by heading his account in capital-lettered Latin ('*PLACITA CORONAE, Apud Lancasterium. Deliberatio Gaole Domini Regis Castri sui Lancastrii ...*'), and he recreates for us Judge Bromley's entry into the hall and the issuing of his proclamation:

> that all Justices of Peace that had taken any Recognisaunces, or Examinations of Prisoners, should make returne of them: And all such as were bound to prosecute Indictmentes, and give Evidence against Witches, shoulde proceede, and give attendance: for hee now intended to proceed with the Arraignement and Tryall of Witches. (C4)

But then he misses out several stages in procedure, evidence of selectivity common to all trial pamphleteers, and in each case differently motivated. Potts does not tell us that indictments were next submitted to the grand jury,[12] who examined indictments to decide whether the Crown had a *prima facie* case[13] (in which case they endorsed the indictment '*billa vera*', a true bill), and to do this they heard oral evidence from the victim and witnesses, and read the suspect's examination.[14] Potts omits all these stages of grand jury procedure from his account, saying 'Heere you may not expect the exact order of the Assises, with the Proclamations, and other solemnities belonging to so great a Court of Justice' (D). He may omit them due to lack of space, or see them as tedious and unrelated to the real judicial business of the court which concerned his illustrious patrons. But equally he may regard them as sacred mysteries which should be of no concern to the implied lay reader. Such is his pamphlet's dangerous reverence for due legal process, however, that he represents even this incomplete version as unquestionably infallible.

As soon as the grand jury 'found' the first batch of indictments the prisoners were brought in to the main courtroom for the central experience of the Assize – the consideration of cases in open court by the petty jury. The petty jury was the ancestor of the modern trial jury – twelve men who judged the prisoners guilty or not on the evidence which they heard.[15] Potts enjoys the drama of the jury trial, returning to his suspenseful and detailed account with: 'Whereupon, the first of all these, Anne Whittle, alias Chattox, was brought to the Barre: against whom wee are now ready to proceed' (D). This intimate phrasing (we) and present tense (now) makes it feel as though the reader is actually present at the trial: but we need to ask how correct an impression this is. Is Potts really showing us what he saw in 1612? He certainly seems reliable, echoing other accounts of the legal process, when he reports the procedure for the arraignment of each prisoner, giving the text of the indictment translated.

According to other contemporary sources, the accused had the translated indictment read to him or her, and if s/he pleaded not guilty, was asked how s/he wished to be tried, replying formally, as Potts (apparently accurately, therefore) reports, that they put themselves on God and their country (D2). Other prisoners were arraigned until there were enough for a jury to try. But, crucially, Potts's representation of trial alters this in appearance, showing each person's arraignment with the records of his or her trial, giving an impression of individual attention to witches (and other felons) which was far from what contemporaries and historians perceived as the truth. Some pamphleteers suggest similarly individual attention given to witches (Henry Goodcole's *The Wonderfull Discoverie of Elizabeth Sawyer, a Witch* (London, 1621) for example) but most represent witches as being tried in groups (three witches in *The Examination and Confession of Certaine Wytches* (London, 1566), three or four by implication in *The Apprehension and Confession of Three Notorious Witches* (London, 1589)).

Presumably Potts's separating out of cases was done for narrative coherence: in his account in particular this would have been a matter of great importance, given the number of cases, and it would be good to know if someone (who?) had suggested this solution to the problem of reader confusion. But although the device of listing cases separately is a matter of stylistic choice, it is also a matter of substance, obscuring the amply documented reality of the early modern legal process. The courts were in fact so overworked that juries had to assess too many prisoners to remember the facts of each case. J. S. Cockburn shows conclusively that most Home Circuit cases (i.e. those tried in the counties surrounding London) took 15–20 minutes including time for the jury to deliberate or at least decide a verdict.[16] Some prisoners saved the court time by pleading guilty.[17] This meant they were set aside and not tried by the jury.[18] Potts's account of Alizon Device shows her doing this (R3), but adds that Bromley still wished to hear the evidence against her (R4). This highly unusual proceeding suggests the desire to show a very high priority given to the cases of the witches, as in the 1593 pamphlet *The Most Strange and Admirable Discoverie* where the case of three witches is reported to have taken five hours to be tried.[19] Bromley and Potts would no doubt also see advantage in hearing and reporting the evidence of one who, by admitting her guilt, would also incriminate others of her family and provide a firm foundation of confessed crime for the whole series of convictions. Pleas made, a petty jury was impanelled, which Potts again omits, cutting out the all-important yet unimportant middling men who would decide the prisoners' fates.[20] The suspect's examination was read to these men and they and the court were given as much evidence as was thought necessary to prove the felony.

With astonishing mimetic zeal, Potts chose that the trial of the Lancashire witches should be represented by a reconstruction of this process. Or perhaps his patrons (the judges Bromley and Altham and his dedicatees Thomas and

Elizabeth Knyvet) chose for him: justice must be seen being done in a case involving suspected gunpowder treason, plotted assassination and mass murder on an unprecedented scale, and Knyvet had been closely involved in apprehending the gunpowder plotters of 1605, giving him a great interest in rightful representation of the wickedness of treason.[21] In pursuit, therefore, of thoroughness, Potts even went so far as to reconstruct before opening his mock-trial the way the documents and the testimony they represented *would have* been used to try Elizabeth Southerns (Old Demdike), who had died in prison. Proof of the thoroughness and correctness of justice seems so important in the pamphlet that Potts not only gives us documentary evidence in vast quantities, but also, in a belt and braces approach, frames events by commenting on the witches' characters in each case before he introduces their trial, with phrases such as 'a dangerous Witch of very long continuance' or 'this wicked and miserable Wretch' (D2, H). He is keen to stress the witches' sinfulness – especially the motiveless or disproportionate fury of their 'revenges' on those who had more or less innocently displeased them. But in doing so he is revealing a persuasive intent and showing the danger of taking his proofs as facts, for there is often disagreement over witches' motives and indeed their actual actions.

For example, Alizon Device, grand-daughter of Old Demdike, pleaded guilty to laming pensioner John Law because he would not sell her any pins. John Law himself said that Alizon had *begged* pins and he had refused her – whereupon he fell ill. But the pedlar's son told the court that not only had Alizon no money to pay for the pins but that his father *had* given her some. Potts, without comment, chooses to endorse the archetypal story of the witch being refused neighbourly help and retaliating, a story that provides the reader with a motive for the crime of which Alizon was convicted: 'behold', he says, '… what punishment [Law] endured for a small offence'. Yet he reserves the right in other cases to avoid looking for a motive: Alice Nutter is denied even the motive of poverty, just as, later in the pamphlet, Jennet Preston stands accused of ingratitude.[22] Clashing theories of witchcraft and contradictory stories are of no importance to his account and this is probably because in court the clashes were either not heard or not emphasised.

Although in printing indictments (translated and paraphrased) and in reporting pleas and other set phrases, Potts is reflecting what happened, he is not writing a verbatim court report of what everyone really said. Pamphlets often claim to be doing this. Stories might have changed, and become more harmonious, since pre-trial informations were given, and witnesses might subconsciously or deliberately omit or edit material which contradicted evidence given in court by other accusers or the witch. *The Examination and Confession of Certayne Wytches* states that it gives an account from the 'Sise' (Assize) 'verbatum', whilst *A True and Just Recorde* claims to be 'written orderly, as the cases were tryed by evidence'.[23] In fact, both are based on pre-trial documents, and although the first pamphlet later contains a report from the Assize court, its account of procedure is confused and what it initially describes as the Assize trial is in fact the preliminary hearing before local magistrates. Like other pamphleteers, then, Potts is using those documents which he has, in a way which suggests one witness after another orally giving evidence. But in fact we are reading what they said well before the trial, probably even in those cases where Potts *says* that the witness gave the evidence orally.

For example, Jennet Device, he says, gave evidence 'against Elizabeth Device her Mother, Prisoner at the Barre upon her Arraignement and Triall' (F4). This implies it was given orally on 18 August 1612. All Jennet's evidence is reported like this. But her testimony (like that of James and Elizabeth Device) consists mostly of repetitions of her story of a 'sabbat' at Pendle. Each time the evidence of these three is used, it is slightly altered – the same basic description of the sabbat plus that part of the testimony concerning the witch presently on trial. For example:

> The said *Jennet Device* saith, That upon Good Friday last there was about twentie persons (whereof onely two were men, to this Examinates remembrance) at her said Grandmothers house, called Malking-Tower aforesaid, about twelve of the clocke: all which persons this Examinates said mother told her, were Witches, and that they came to give a name to *Alizon Device* Spirit, or Familiar, sister to this Examinate, and now prisoner at Lancaster. And also this Examinate saith, That the persons aforesaid had to their dinners Beefe, Bacon, and roasted Mutton; which Mutton (as this Examinates said brother said) was of a Wether of *Christopher Swyers* of Barley: which Wether was brought in the night before into this Examinates mothers house by the said *James Device*, this Examinates said brother: and in this Examinates sight killed and eaten, as foresaid. And she further saith, That shee knoweth the names of sixe of the said Witches, *viz.* the wife of *Hugh Hargraves* under Pendle, *Christopher Howgate* of Pendle, unckle to this Examinate, and *Elizabeth* his wife, and *Dick Miles* his wife of the Rough-Lee; *Christopher Jackes* of Thorny-holme, and his wife: and the names of the residue shee this Examinate doth not know, saving that this Examinates mother and brother were both there. And lastly, she this Examinate confesseth and saith, That her mother hath taught her two prayers: the one to cure the bewitched, and the other to get drinke; both of which particularly appeare. (G3–G4)[24]

This highly formal ('the said .., this Examinates said brother ... as aforesaid'), almost word-for-word repetition is clearly based on documents, not near-flawlessly repeated oral testimony. A subtly different story might have been told in court, with different events, motivations and outcomes. Given what we have read of the court's and Potts's blindness to inconsistencies in the evidence against Alizon Device, do we really think anyone would have noticed the implications of this inadequate representation of reality?

In similar confusion, Grace Sowerbutts's evidence is apparently oral, with

Potts reporting she 'said as followeth', but in fact it is dated in April (L). Alizon Device's confession, when 'shee humbly upon her knees at the Barre with weeping teares, prayed the court to hear her' and Bromley encouraged her (R3), is actually partly composed from her examination *cum* information against her grandmother (C). Potts acknowledges this, saying it 'agreeth *verbatim* with her owne examination taken at Reade ... the thirtieth day of March' (R4) – that verbatim word again.[25] But how much is this *'verbatim'* agreement simply reproduction – with or without alteration? Informations (witness statements) are treated in a similar way. It might be that the information was actually written out many times with just the relevant evidence included for each arraignment. Or the editing may be subsequent. But all the apparently unmediated verbal description of events that we have is textual, not oral. This means that not only was it not spoken in the Lancaster courtroom exactly as Potts reports, but that it is the product of very complex question and answer procedures at the pre-trial stage several months before the trial – a process in which questions were not recorded and answers were noted down as bald statements rather than the changeable and tentative attempts to quantify the truth which many of them undoubtedly were.[26] The material so problematically assembled has then been edited heavily by our pamphleteer Potts. None of this is immediately obvious, but it is vitally important to an understanding of the Lancashire witches and their trials because it alters the order and context of witch and witness evidence in examinations and informations. We have no idea what is missing, what was confessed first, who echoed whom, and how the informant's story was originally structured.

Potts and other pamphleteers have a different understanding of truthful reporting from modern scholars, subjugating what really happened to what ought to have happened. Philip Sidney, in his 1595 *Apology for Poetry*, was typical of his time in stating that 'a feigned example hath as much force to teach as a true example'. He argued that for the purposes of instructing a readership it was far better to ignore the 'bare *was*' of the historian and construct an event or character 'as it should be'.[27] Whatever Potts's philosophy of the role of the legal historian, if he had one, his attempt to represent as spoken *verbatim* those of the above texts which are clearly examinations is by modern standards inaccurate, because they, according to the consensus of other contemporary accounts, would have been *read*. Also, more complexly, his reporting of the evidence of witnesses and conduct of the courtroom examinations, whilst accurately reported as spoken, is in practice limited only to what was *documented*, with the exception of reports of a few striking moments. It is still valuable, however, as an insight into a lost interaction between members of a community and their magistracy, and a record of perceptions of a vanished world. Perhaps the best way of reading these accounts is as records of a kind of oral history – the magistrate and his clerk acting as partial and selective recorders of conflicting and unfixed stories circulating in the community, which come to be retold and reused as evidence of crime.

Although we can see Potts blurring the status of the documents he has collected, conversely his care and fundamental regard for accurate detail is suggested by his very use of these documents as the basis for his pamphlet. He believes the documents contain the most truthful account of events, as 'matters upon Record'. To his credit, he does not deny us access to these complex tale-tellings by writing a narrative account, as all other witchcraft pamphleteers were doing by 1612; however, his comment that 'I wanted libertie to write what I could, and am limited to set forth nothing against them, but matter upon Record, even in their owne Countrie tearmes, which may seeme strange' suggests that his openness may have been forced upon him by his patrons (X). Nevertheless, *The Wonderfull Discoverie* bucks a trend: just after 1590, the documentary use of pre-trial materials in witchcraft pamphlets (such as those described above) had abruptly ceased, and with them the role of the clerkly or journalistic author basing his account primarily on evidence taken from the legal process. If Potts had any models in mind for his account, the most likely would have been the thirty-year-old *A True and Just Recorde* (London, 1582), which at over one hundred pages is second only to Potts's work in its length and obsessive detailing of events by the use of examinations and informations. By 1612 Potts's fellow pamphleteers had resorted to ill-informed snippets from trials, heavily glossed and intercut with confused reportage of dreams and visions, and materials based on gossip such as those in *The Witches of Northamptonshire* (London, 1612), which rambles through 'I had almost forgotten to tell you before ...' to 'it was credibly reported that ...'.[28] But Potts returned to an older and much more labour-intensive way of representing witch trials.

Potts knows his material and procedures well, and seems to give a generally trustworthy, though not comprehensive, account of an Assize witchcraft trial, provided that the reader is constantly aware of his use of written material instead of verbatim reports – use which variably reflects actual practice, and is situated by Potts with varying degrees of clarity or honesty. His account, in other words, is reasonably 'accurate' in so far as we can define accuracy in these circumstances. But his methodology of representation, where documents represent speech and bitter invective is interspersed with heavily edited text, is extremely suspect. Edgar Peel and Pat Southern sum up: 'it is often impossible to decide what evidence given in Potts's book is that read from statements, what was given verbally in court, and what he copied from documents available to him'.[29] It is impossible also to know how much he idealised. Thus it is difficult to comment authoritatively on issues of interest to witchcraft scholars, such as the atmosphere of the witchcraft trial, the justness of procedure, or lack of it, and the attitude to proof in witchcraft trials. Potts gives us a detailed and highly fascinating representation, which tallies on the whole with other representations, both by experts and observers – but no more. Like Edward Bromley we must judge as well as we can from the 'facts' laid before us.

When all the requisite evidence had been heard, the judge did not need to sum up, as he had already commented as statements were made.[30] He would tell the jury that they had heard the evidence against the prisoner and what s/he could say for himself or herself, and must reach a verdict remembering God, their consciences and what had been said. None of this appears in pamphlets, which without exception rush to judgement.[31] Potts is careful to describe, however, how in the 1612 case the prisoners' examinations were given to the jury, by the judge's direction, 'for the better satisfaction of their consciences'. He splits up the giving of verdicts, revealing incidentally the groups in which the prisoners were being tried: Anne Whittle alias Chattox, Elizabeth Device and James Device; Anne Redferne, Alice Nutter and Katherine Hewit; John and Jane Bulcock and Alizon Device; Isabel Roby and Margaret Pearson; and Jennet Bierley, Ellen Bierley and Jane Southworth (the Samlesbury accused). 'After due consideration', says Potts, the jury delivered up their verdict in each case (for example, K2, Q and S3). Elsewhere, he says the jury 'having spent the most part of the day in due consideration of their offences, returned into the Court' to do so (Q and S2). Does Potts's description include time spent listening in court, or are witch trials as a class, or Northern Circuit trials, different from those of the Home Circuit where Cockburn found fifteen minutes spent on each case without the jury necessarily retiring at all? Or is Potts idealising again? Perhaps not, this time. He does record the verdicts as they would have been returned, in batches, officially presenting them under the heading 'The verdict of life and death' (K2, Q). Most other pamphlets simply record the verdicts in the text.

The verdict itself, however, might not be the end of the matter: judges were not obliged to accept verdicts and sometimes imprisoned the acquitted if they thought them guilty.[32] In *The Wonderfull Discoverie* we see the judge telling the acquitted that 'without question there are amongst you, that are as deepe in this Action, as any of them that are condemned to die for their offences' and ordering them to appear at the next Assizes and be of good behaviour, forsaking the Devil. Only those he had himself found to be victims of a Catholic plot were truly 'delivered',[33] and Bromley then proceeded to sentence. One would expect pamphleteers to get at least the sentence right, because of their interest in crime and just punishment. But even W. W. in his *A True and Just Recorde* failed to attribute correctly the word 'condemned' which litters his text. Some of those whom he describes as being condemned were, according to their own indictments, reprieved, whilst others were imprisoned. Some of those described as 'continued in prison' were discharged by proclamation or acquitted.[34] Likewise, Thomas Potts reports (more tragically) that John and Jane Bulcock were acquitted when they were in fact condemned; but the printer blames himself for this mistake in the 1613 corri-genda to the pamphlet (A4). This reminds us that serious and uncheckable mistakes may be made at any level of the representation, even down to a misreading or compositor's error – Potts's own attempts at accuracy, such as they are, are subject to more erosion further down the line. As the trial ended in the noisy courtroom, crucial mistakes might be made and reporters often omitted vast amounts of incidental material in their *post hoc* rationalisation of a guilty verdict.

Before sentence, for example, prisoners who were about to be condemned were asked whether there were any circumstances preventing sentence of death being passed. There is none of this in Potts, although there is an unusual record of a sentence less than the death penalty for a witch. Those who had not killed anyone by witchcraft were sentenced to pillory and imprisonment, and Potts is the only pamphleteer to record at length such a sentence, on Margaret Pearson (V4). Potts is unlike other pamphleteers, too, in that he includes long speeches by the judge to the convicted and the acquitted as part of his sentencing. These may be later accounts, possibly written by Bromley (who supervised the pamphlet), as it is unlikely that Potts took them down verbatim in court even if they were uttered at such length and so elegantly. The final part of the speech to the condemned is the traditional form of the death sentence, and must have been spoken, but the rest may be simply an ideal speech, given Potts's tendencies to stress the grandeur and solemnity of justice (V4). Possibly Bromley wrote down what he would like to have said. Again Potts represents the trial of witches as decorous, just, painstaking, perfect. Sentencing over, the condemned were returned to the gaol, and many of the pamphlets contain an account of the executions, as being of far more intelligible significance than the court proceedings. Potts does not: his interest is, commendably, in justice, not in the horrors of punishment.

Potts's *Wonderfull Discoverie* is the clearest example of an account obviously published to display the shining efficiency and justice of the legal system. He wants us to understand and revere its processes:

> Here shall you behold the Justice of this Land, truely administered, Proemium & Poenam, Mercie and Judgement, freely and indifferently bestowed and inflicted; And above all thinges to bee remembered, the excellent care of these Judges in the Triall of offendors. (a3)

This is a clear statement of why the pamphlet was published. Its dedication to Thomas Knyvet, who helped foil the Gunpowder Plot, also suggests a concern with local Catholicism: the plan to blow up Lancaster Castle described by some of the witches, as well as the collapse of the prosecution instigated by Grace Sowerbutts and, allegedly, her Catholic adviser, confirms the suspicion that questions were asked about treacherous plots.[35] But the main thrust of the presentation of evidence seems to be to inspire confidence in the judiciary, the systems of justice and the rightness of sentencing – perhaps particularly in the north of England, represented here as both remote and prone to sectarianism, and perhaps particularly in witch trials.

This is certainly the main aim of the passages at the pamphlet's end, describing the trial of Jennet Preston in York – an aim which is all the more striking because this section may have been written by another author. It feels tacked-on after Potts's peroration; its choppy sentences are unlike Potts's usual lengthy style, and it contains harsh, personalised and incisive attacks on the survivors of the episode which lash the unfortunate in a way that Potts never achieves in all his denunciations.[36] But whoever the writer is, he clearly shares Potts's interests in promoting confidence in local justice, sharpening our attention to this concern in Potts's main text:

> GOD graunt us the long and prosperous continuance of these Honorable and Reverend Judges, under whose Government we live in these North parts: for we may say, that GOD Almightie hath singled them out, and set them on his Seat, for the defence of Justice. (Z3)

He is also troubled by accusations that his subject, Jennet Preston, was wrongly convicted of witchcraft, a matter of secondary but important concern for Potts in describing the Pendle and Samlesbury cases:

> I find such apparant matter to satisfie the World, how dangerous and malitious a Witch this *Jennet Preston* was, How unfit to live, having once so great mercie extended to her: And againe to exercise her practises, and returne to her former course of life, that I thinke it necessarie not to let the memorie of her life and death die with her ... You that were husband to this *Jennet Preston*; her friends and kinsfolkes, who have not beene sparing to devise so scandalous a slander out of the malice of your hearts, as that shee was maliciously prosecuted by Master *Lister* and others; Her life unjustly taken away by practise, and that (even at the Gallowes where shee died impenitent and void of all feare and grace) she died an Innocent woman, because she would confesse nothing: You I say may not hold it strange, though at this time, being not only moved in conscience, but directed, for example sake, with that which I have to report of her, I suffer you not to wander any further; but with this short discourse oppose your idle conceipts able to seduce others: And by Charmes of Imputations and slander, laid upon the Justice of the Land, to cleare her that was justly condemned and executed for her offence. (X4)

Potts's vicious attack on the incredibility of evidence in Grace Sowerbutts's priest-inspired testimony immediately springs to mind – charms, seduction and attacks on justice are all trigger-words which in Elizabethan England suggest fears of Catholic subtlety, and here imply a wider assault on northern justice than could be mounted by a single family. Potts's articulation of such fears throws up as an afterthought a defence of evidence in the other, 'real' witchcraft cases:

> Now was the time for the Seminarie [priest] to instruct, accuse, and call into question these poore women: for the wrinckles of an old wives face is good evidence to the Jurie against a Witch. And how often will the common people say *(Her eyes are sunke in her head,* GOD *blesse us from her.)* But old *Chattox* had *Fancie* besides her withered face, to accuse her. (M2)

Because Chattox was accused by her spirit, Fancy, she must truly have been a witch – and in the light of this certainty the witchmongering fancies of northern Catholics can be set aside. Potts shows his hand in this discrimination between cases.

Concerns with credibility, propaganda and the prevention of subversive comment on the judicial system shape *The Wonderfull Discoverie of Witches*, from dictating what questions were (unknowably) asked of suspects to determining the presentation of evidence, the tone of authorial comment, and the omission or addition of significant details. It is important to understand the context of Potts's work, and this can in part be (to coin a phrase) 'discovered' by close reading of the text. Potts has anticipated us in this, and his work concludes with a plea for understanding in the difficulties of producing a lengthy and controversial work for demanding readers: 'If I have omitted any thing materiall, or published any thing imperfect, excuse me for that I have done … But if this discoverie may serve for your instruction, I shall thinke my selfe very happie in this Service' (X–X2). Potts's *Discoverie* is certainly instructive, for its omissions and imperfections (both deliberate and naïve) teach a harsh lesson about blind trust in authority, reliance on official accounts and the infallibility of the written word in history. Potts cannot tell us what witchcraft 'really' was, for his accounts conflict and his glosses do not disguise this fact. He cannot tell us all that we need to know about witch trials, for he refuses to be open about the nature of his sources or full in his account of procedure. But he can tell us what he believed early modern readers wanted to read about witchcraft, what his patrons wanted him to produce, and something of what a reasonably well-educated legal official thought of the job he was doing in trying witches, rooting out conspirators, and writing accounts of their crimes. Describing himself as unable to 'paint in extraordinary terms' (X2), he can nevertheless sketch for us a picture of the Lancashire witches, although some of his lines are uncertain and smudged and an understanding of the perspective is all-important in evaluating the picture's worth. Like all works of art, *The Wonderfull Discoverie* merits a careful inspection of its origins and techniques, the skills and biases of its creator, and the genre from which it comes if we are to begin to understand the reasons why its images were, and will continue to be, so compelling.

Notes

1 Robert Neill dedicates his novel *Mist over Pendle* to 'the dusty memory of Thomas Potts' (London: Hutchinson, 1951).

2 For editions of the various witchcraft texts mentioned in this essay, including Potts, see Marion Gibson, *Early Modern Witches: Witchcraft Cases in Contemporary Writing* (London: Routledge, 2000). See also Robert Poole (ed.), *The Wonderfull Discoverie of Witches in the Countie of Lancaster, and Other Sources* (forthcoming).

3 J. S. Cockburn, *Calendar of Assize Records: Home Circuit: Elizabeth I and James I: Introduction* (London: HMSO, 1985), pp. 97–8, 14, 97.

4 Barbara Rosen, *Witchcraft in England 1558–1618* (Amherst: University of Massachusetts Press, 1991), p. 43.

5 David Cressy, *Agnes Bowker's Cat: Travesties and Transgressions in Tudor and Stuart England* (Oxford: Oxford University Press, 2000), p. 26. See also Marion Gibson, *Reading Witchcraft: Stories of Early English Witches* (London: Routledge, 1999) for a similar argument relating particularly to witchcraft cases.

6 Cockburn's description of the work of the Clerk of Arraigns fits Potts's selection of documents for his pamphlet, which he was ordered to produce by the judges (Sir James Altham and Sir Edward Bromley). He was ideally situated to understand and have access to the 'gaol book' or calendar of prisoners, pleas and case records, the 'hanging book' of verdicts, and the order book and recognisances. J. S. Cockburn, *A History of English Assizes 1558–1714* (Cambridge: Cambridge University Press, 1972), pp. 82–3 and *Calendar ... Introduction*, pp. 5–8.

7 Thomas Potts, *The Wonderfull Discoverie of Witches in the Countie of Lancaster* (London, 1613). Potts, like other contemporary books, is numbered not in pages but in signatures of eight pages, with each pair of pages numbered 'A, A2, A3 A4', etc. The first signature, carrying the introductory material, is not numbered, and is here referred to as 'a, a2, a3 a4'.

8 Cockburn, *Calendar ... Introduction*, pp. 95, 96, 102–3, 20.

9 Cockburn, *Calendar ... Introduction*, p. 33.

10 For example on B2, D2, G2, N4, S2, etc.

11 See for example W. Benjamin, 'The work of art in the age of mechanical reproduction', in *Illuminations* (1936; London: Fontana, 1992), pp. 211–44. Benjamin's strictures could just as well apply to Potts's seventeenth-century manuscript and its 'copy' here.

12 Cockburn, *Calendar ... Introduction*, pp. 44–5, 47, 52; T. W., *The Clerk of Assize* (London, 1682), pp. 19, 34.

13 Only indictments drawn up at the Quarter Sessions, and already considered by a grand jury there, escaped their scrutiny: Cockburn, *Calendar ... Introduction*, p. 73. Examples of this related to the pamphlets are given in Cockburn, *Calendar of Assize Records: Home Circuit: Essex: Elizabeth I* (London: HMSO, 1978), record 669 (Alice Chaundeler, mother of Elleine Smithe), record 1024 (Elizabeth Frauncis), and records 1063 and 1055 (Margery Stanton), all witches whose cases are detailed in the pamphlet *A Detection of Damnable Driftes* (London, 1579).

14 Cockburn, *Calendar ... Introduction*, pp. 52, 103–4. Testimonials of neighbours' suspicions, possibly like that prepared by Thomas Prat in *Detection* A7, could also be considered.

15 See J. S. Cockburn and T. A. Green (eds), *Twelve Good Men and True: The Criminal Trial Jury in England 1200–1800* (Princeton: Princeton University Press, 1988), pp. 214–53.

16 Cockburn, *Calendar ... Introduction*, pp. 64–5 and 110–11.

17 For example, Elizabeth Frauncis (Anon., *The Examination and Confession of Certaine Wytches* (London, 1566)) and Elizabeth Bennet (W. W., *A True and Just Recorde, of the Information, Examination and Confession of all the Witches, Taken at S. Oses in the Countie of Essex* (London, 1582)) both did so: Cockburn, *Calendar ... Essex ... Elizabeth I*, records 273 and 1316.

18 Cockburn, *Calendar ... Introduction*, p. 65; T. W., *Clerk of Assize*, p. 40.

19 Anon., *The Most Strange and Admirable Discoverie of the Three Witches of Warboys, (Arraigned, Convicted and Executed at the Last Assizes at Huntingdon)* (London, 1593), O.

20 Cockburn, *Calendar ... Introduction*, p. 105. Potts shows the sheriff preparing the petty jury (C4).

21 See Rosen, *Witchcraft in England*, p. 357, Stephen Pumfrey's chapter elsewhere in this volume, and more generally Jonathan Lumby, *The Lancashire Witch-Craze: Jennet Preston and the Lancashire Witches 1612* (Preston: Carnegie, 1995), for discussion of anti-Catholicism, fears of sectarian rebellion in the 1612 trials, and Thomas Knyvet's connection to the Gunpowder Plot of 1605.

22 Potts, *Wonderfull Discoverie*, R3–S, O3, Y.

23 *The Examination and Confession of Certaine Wytches*, A6, and *A True and Just Recorde*, title page.

24 Repeated against Alice Nutter (P, up to 'the names of the residue, she this examinate doth not know'); against Katherine Hewit (Q, up to 'shee knoweth the names of sixe of the said Witches'); and against the Bulcocks (R, as with Hewit). Similar repetitions of evidence appear against James Device (H4, I, introductory piece repeated, followed by two different stories). James's own examinations are repeated – some, like all of Jennet's, are dated as if given on the trial day, others are dated 27 April.

25 In fact the examination was said (C) to have been taken on 13 March. See Edgar Peel and Pat Southern, *The Trials of the Lancashire Witches: A Study in Seventeenth-Century Witchcraft* (Nelson: Hendon, 1994), p. 92. Is this a mistake? Or is Potts referring to a document now lost? The offence did not, apparently, occur until *after* 13 March. See Gibson, *Early Modern Witches*, p. 244, n. 180.

26 See Gibson, *Reading Witchcraft* for further discussion of the process of creating pre-trial documents.

27 Philip Sidney, *An Apology for Poetry* (London, 1595; Manchester: Manchester University Press, 1973), pp. 100, 109–12.

28 Anon., *The Witches of Northamptonshire* (London, 1612), B4v, C.

29 Peel and Southern, *Trials of the Lancashire Witches*, p. 58.

30 Cockburn, *Calendar ... Introduction*, p. 109; Thomas Smith, *De Republica Anglorum* (London, 1583; ed. Mary Dewar, Cambridge: Cambridge University Press, 1982), p. 114.

31 Cockburn, *Calendar ... Introduction*, p. 110; Smith, *De Republica Anglorum*, p. 114; T. W., *Clerk of Assize*, p. 48.

32 Cockburn, *Calendar ... Introduction*, p. 115.

33 Potts, *Wonderfull Discoverie*, X.

34 See Stephen Pumfrey's chapter in this volume.

35 Compare Jonathan Lumby's chapter in this volume.

36 See Gibson, *Early Modern Witches* for an annotated edition of *A True and Just Recorde* commenting on individual sentences.

4

'Those to whom evil is done':
family dynamics in the Pendle witch trials

Jonathan Lumby

What disposed gentry and magistrates in the Lancashire and Yorkshire borderland to promote the destruction of the Pendle witches in 1612? Why did persecution erupt there? Two men of considerable standing in the society of those parts instigated the persecution. The first was Roger Nowell of Read Hall, to the south-west of Pendle. Formerly High Sheriff of Lancashire, he was sixty-four years old in 1612. He was the magistrate who led the investigation. The second was Thomas Lister, a young man who had succeeded to the demesne of Westby or Arnoldsbiggin, a moated manor-house in Gisburn to the north of Pendle, just over the border in Yorkshire.[1] In 1612 Thomas Lister was aged but twenty-two. These two, Nowell and Lister, rather than the accused inhabitants of the hills, are the focus of this account. Their book-taught notion that witchcraft was a Faustian compact with the Devil differed, with tragic consequences, from some of their victims' simpler understanding of themselves as wise women. The account reveals domestic traumas, in both the extended family of Roger Nowell and the family of Thomas Lister. Each family disaster, interpreted within the categories of seventeenth-century Puritanism, was attributed to witchcraft, though the events would have been interpreted differently had they occurred in the context of, say, religious revivalism or modern psychology. As it was, Nowell's and Lister's domestic embarrassments, and their desire later to justify the stance they had adopted, impelled them to accuse others of witchcraft in 1612.

We shall begin with Lister, though Nowell's story stretches farther back. Thomas Lister, the young man, pursued to the gallows one Jennet Preston, like him of Gisburn, a woman about eighteen year his senior. Our main source is the account of Jennet's trial at the York Assizes of 20 July 1612 penned that same year by Thomas Potts, the Clerk to the Court, and printed as an appendix to *The Wonderfull Discoverie of Witches*, Potts's account of the slightly later Lancashire trials. Potts wrote *The Arraignement and Triall of Jennet Preston of Gisborne in Craven in the Countie of Yorke* at the judges' behest, for they wished to quell the indignation of her husband, friends and relations. Potts addresses Jennet's supporters directly:

> You that were husband to this *Jennet Preston*; her friends and kinsfolkes, who have not beene sparing to devise so scandalous a slander out of the malice of your hearts, as that shee was maliciously prosecuted by Master *Lister* and others; Her life unjustly taken away by practise; and that (even at the Gallowes where shee died impenitent and void of all feare or grace) she died an Innocent woman, because she would confesse nothing... I suffer you not to wander any further; but with this short discourse oppose your idle conceipts able to seduce others.

The style of Potts's two-page introduction is majestic in language, but its meaning is sometimes obscure.[2] Modern commentators have been confused as they have sought, as we must, to order the sequence of events.

Jennet Preston's trial in York of July 1612 concerned the death in 1608 of Thomas Lister's father, also called Thomas, master of Westby Hall and its estates. Jennet was accused of bewitching him to death. The court received evidence concerning old Thomas Lister's dying words and the peculiar motions of his corpse. A certain Anne Robinson, probably a servant of the Listers, testified that 'When Master Lister lay upon his death-bedde, hee cried out in great extremitie; Jennet Preston lays heavy upon me, Preston's wife lays heavy upon me; helpe me, help me: and so departed crying out against her'. Young Lister joined with Anne Robinson to give other details of his father's death. They claimed that the elder Lister had been agitated about Jennet Preston, that:

> Master Lister lying in great extremitie, upon his death bedde, cried out to them that stood about him; that Jennet Preston was in the House, look where she is, take holde of her; for God's sake shut the doors, and take her, shee cannot escape away. Look about for her, and lay hold of her, for she is in the house: and so cried very often in his great paines, to them that came to visit him during his sicknesse.

The two also testified that 'after he was dead, and layed out to be wound up in his winding-sheet, the said Jennet Preston comming to touch the dead corpse, they bled fresh bloud presently, in the presence of all'. Potts comments that the bleeding of a corpse 'hath ever been held a great argument to induce a Jurie to hold him guiltie that shall be accused of murther and hath seldome or never fayled in the Tryall'. King James in his *Daemonologie* had called the gushing of blood from a dead carcase which a murderer had touched 'a secret supernaturall signe, for tryall of that secrete unnaturall crime'.[3] That belief was general. Even Reginald Scot and Francis Bacon, writers in general sceptical about witchcraft, held that a corpse would bleed if its murderer touched it.[4]

The court considered these allegations about Thomas Lister's death, and further evidence sent by Roger Nowell from Lancashire. It condemned her to death. That trial was in July of 1612. Potts reveals that this was Jennet's second trial. She had also been arraigned at the Lent Assize of 1612 on a different charge of witchcraft or murder, but had then been acquitted.

If events from the beginning are placed in the order in which they occurred, this is the story that Potts unfolds. Jennet had lived 'neare Master Lister of Westbie'. (In fact she is almost certainly that Jennet Balderston who married William Preston in Gisburn parish church on 10 May 1587.[5]) She had been treated with special generosity by Lister senior, the main landowner of Gisburn. Potts says she 'had access to his house, kind respect and entertainment; nothing denied her that she stood in need of'. Old Thomas Lister's kindness to Jennet was well-known: 'which of you that dwelleth near them in Craven but can and will witness it?'. However, despite 'the grace and goodness bestowed upon her', Jennet began, Potts asserts, to bewitch her benefactor. By witchcraft she had murdered him 'four years since' – that would be in 1608.

After Thomas Lister senior's death, his son, the new master of Westby, at first showed Jennet many kindnesses, but Jennet, ungrateful, bewitched (Potts states) the property of this young Thomas Lister, 'who in a short time received great losse in his goods and Cattel by her meanes'. So Jennet was brought by Thomas Lister before the Lent Assizes at York in 1612, arraigned on a charge (surprisingly irrelevant to the death of Thomas Lister senior) of murdering 'a child of one Dodg-sonnes'. She was acquitted. We know nothing more of this episode.

Four days after this acquittal on 6 April Jennet, it was alleged, attended a great assembly of witches on Good Friday at Malkin Tower to seek malign aid in a vengeful plan to murder Thomas Lister junior. The evidence for this had been collected by Roger Nowell as part of the Pendle investigation and was forwarded to York by him. James Device's statement, sworn before Roger Nowell and a fellow JP on 27 April, contains this passage:

> a woman dwelling in Gisburne Parish ... came into this Examinates said Grand-mothers house ... and craved assistance of the rest of them that were then there, for the killing of Master *Lister* of Westby: because, as she then said, he had borne malice unto her, and had thought to have put her away at the last Assizes at Yorke; but could not. And then this Examinat heard the said woman say, that her power was not strong enough to doe it her selfe, being now lesse then before-time it had beene.
>
> ... they all appointed to meete at the said *Prestons* wifes house that day twelve-month; at which time the said *Prestons* wife promised to make them a great feast; and if they had occasion to meet in the meane time, then should warning bee given that they all should meete upon Romles Moore. And this Examinate further saith, That at the said feast at Malking-Tower, this

Examinat heard them all give their consents to put the said Master *Thomas
Lister* of Westby to death: and after Master *Lister* should be made away by
Witchcraft, then al the said Witches gave their consents to joyne altogether to
hancke Master *Leonard Lister*, when he should come to dwell at the Sowgill,
and so put him to death.

About a week later, on 8 May, Nowell and two other magistrates took the
evidence of one Henry Hargreives, a yeoman of Goldshey-booth in Pendle,
who stated:

That *Anne Whittle*, alias *Chattox*, confessed unto him, that she knoweth one
Prestons wife neere Gisburne, and that the said *Prestons* wife should have
beene at the said feast, upon the said Good-Friday, and that shee was an ill
woman, and had done Master *Lister* of Westby great hurt.

Hargreives then took James Device to Gisburn, where he duly identified
Jennet Preston as the woman at Malkin Tower.[6] Informed of Jennet's attendance at Malkin Tower, Lister returned her to the July Assizes in York. Thomas
Heaber of Marton, near Gisburn, was the prosecuting magistrate. Jennet
now faced the charge of having murdered Thomas Lister senior those four
years before. The death-bed evidence was crucial. Jennet, found guilty, was
hanged.

Any witchcraft allegation must be treated with scepticism. The allegations against Jennet Preston particularly awaken our suspicions. Whatever
seventeenth-century opinions on the matter may have been, a corpse will not
bleed at a touch, yet Lister testified that his father's corpse did just that. Why
did he make this claim? Again, if Jennet was believed to have murdered
Lister's father four years before, why was she first brought to court on a
different charge, that of murdering Dodgeson's child? Had Lister junior at
that stage sought to be rid of Jennet without revealing an embarrassing family
tale?

An inspection of the parish registers of Gisburn and neighbouring
Bracewell increases our unease with Potts's account. The death-bed scene, as
told to the court, implied that Thomas Lister died at home, at Westby: 'Lay
hold on her, for she is in the house'. The court was told nothing to the contrary. Yet Gisburn's burial register for 1607/8 has this entry: 'Thomas Lister,
Ar: de Westbie Mort apud Braswell Octavo die Februarii'. Thomas Lister senior was buried on 8 February. He did not die at home, records the register, but
in Bracewell, a parish that lies to the east, between Gisburn and Marton. Why
was Thomas Lister in Bracewell? Amazingly, Bracewell's marriage register of
1607/8 provides the answer: 'Feby [date illegible] Thomas Lyster Sonn of Tho
Lyster gent was married with Jane daughter of Mr heaber of Marton'.[7] The
next entry was made on 8 February. So in the village of Bracewell in the same
first week of February 1608, Thomas Lister the father died and Thomas Lister
the son was married. The young Thomas Lister was only just seventeen at

the time of his wedding. His bride happened to be the daughter of Thomas Heaber, Lister's close neighbour among the Yorkshire gentry, who on Lister's behalf four years later would, as a magistrate, prosecute Jennet for witchcraft.

The church records suggest a dramatic scenario, one which would traumatise young Lister, the bridegroom. Let us try to recreate it. The gentry families of Craven and Pendle assemble at Bracewell church for the marriage of the heir of the Listers to the daughter of Thomas Heaber, the lord of the manor of Marton. The ritual proceeds, then there is consternation. Either in church or in the festivities which follow, the bridegroom's father, Thomas Lister the elder, owner of great estates, suffers a seizure. He is lifted to a couch. Laughter turns to tears. Lister, dying, cries out repeatedly: 'Jennet Preston lies heavy upon me', or something similar. This much is clear: the name on his lips is not that of his wife but that of Jennet Preston, she whom he had entertained at Westby. Confusion surrounds Lister as his life ebbs away. He is but thirty-eight years old.

Consider the predicament of the wedding guests. The bridegroom's father, their host, has died. Celebration turns to grief and wild surmise. Young Lister and his bride, for their part, would realise that every guest would reflect that within hours, perhaps within minutes, of Heaber's daughter sealing a marriage contract with the heir to the Listers, that heir had inherited. In that same instant the Heaber girl was now mistress of the Lister estate; her home could be Westby itself. Had there been poison in the cup? Would anyone dare ask? Whether Lister senior's death occurred in the day or two before his son's wedding, while he was in Bracewell preparing for it (though would the ceremony not then have been postponed?) or (as in our scenario) on the day itself, or even the day after, suspicion would weigh upon the young bridegroom and his wife's family. We have no guest-list, but it is not unlikely that those invited would include the neighbouring Protestant gentleman Roger Nowell of Read, the magistrate whose evidence would later help to hang Jennet Preston, and his nephew Nicholas Starkie of Huntroyd, whose own experience of family suffering at the hands of witches was already well-known (of whom, more anon). In the whisperings of shocked guests trying to account for this tragic accident would be spawned the rumours of witchcraft.

Why was Jennet Preston accused? If Jennet was not the murderer but the mistress of the dying man, or at any rate a favoured servant who shared some intimacy, then an uncoordinated tale falls into place. Jennet had enjoyed, even Potts admits, 'access to his house, kind respect and entertainment; nothing denied her'. If the dying Lister called Jennet's name and used physical images – 'Jennet Preston lays heavily upon me' – this may express the closeness that they enjoyed or that he desired, or his guilt over the relationship. Jennet gained access to and touched the dead body. Her status as one favoured by the dead man may have allowed her this privilege, or alternatively her touching may be evidence that suspicion of her was generated at an early stage. In Somerset in 1613, for instance, a murderer fled rather than touch a corpse.[8] Again, in 1636 it was alleged that a certain Joan Elderson of Newton-in-Makerfield in Lancashire, a suspected witch, had absented herself from the funeral of two children for fear that if she was made to touch the corpses her murder would be revealed.[9] Thomas Lister's shouts *in extremis* about Jennet Preston, endearments even, would have humiliated his wife, now a widow. To preserve some dignity (she was the daughter of a Member of Parliament)[10] she would welcome the suggestion that her husband had called Jennet's name for some other reason than love, namely, because Jennet had been bewitching him.

Can we piece together a process of victimisation? Now that Thomas senior was dead, Jennet was unprotected. The widow's resentment could be unleashed in the remaining year of her also short life. Thomas Lister junior, under his mother's influence, would cease to provide at Westby a welcome to Jennet. His guilt about offending Jennet by this rebuff might cause young Thomas little by little to justify his harshness by shunning Jennet the more, by attributing malignity to her, by demonising her, by naming her as a witch. If Jennet were as bad as that his unkindness would be amply vindicated. Thus it was that he could have come to accuse Jennet of killing his cattle and of killing the Dodgeson child. By some such process Lister came to defame the one to whom his father had shown surpassing kindness. In the trial at York it was not revealed, at least from the evidence that survives, that the prosecuting magistrate Thomas Heaber was the father-in-law of the dead man's son.[11] The Lister family trauma, concealed in court evidence, is revealed fortuitously by parish records of a burial in Gisburn and a marriage in Bracewell.

Young Lister's will of 1619 is prefaced in Protestant fashion.[12] In Pendle and Craven Lister was allying himself to the other gentry members of the established Church, the Heabers, the Nowells, the Asshetons of Whalley and those of Downham, and the Starkies. Elsewhere in Lancashire, the most Catholic of counties, and in the Yorkshire borderlands, many of the gentry adhered to the old faith. Townleys, Southworths, Sherburns and Tempests paid heavy fines, built priest-holes, were imprisoned at times, sent their sons to the Catholic seminary at Douai, and entertained priests of the illegal Catholic mission. The Protestantism of young Lister cannot have been without anguish, for his grandmother, Alice (née Houghton), was a Catholic recusant; she had paid heavy fines of '£20 per annum in lands'[13] and was always vulnerable to the eruption of horror that being a Catholic might involve. Moreover the elder Thomas Lister's great uncle, born at Westby, had been Cardinal William Allen, the leader in exile of the English Catholics, supporter of the Spanish Armada and promoter of the execrated bull of excommunication of 1571 issued against Queen Elizabeth. Thomas Lister junior conformed to the established faith but probably suffered the pain of guilt for betraying a

Catholic family tradition. One surmises that in his co-operation with Nowell he had the Protestant passion of an anxious convert.

We now turn to Roger Nowell, who pre-eminently promoted the trial of the Pendle witches. Nowell, acting as magistrate, questioned the emotional Alizon Device, old Demdike and Chattox, cross-eyed Elizabeth Device, the unpredictable James Device and the nine-year-old Jennet Device. All that was in 1612. Had anything in his life prepared this landowner to become a witch-hunter?

Roger Nowell of Read Hall was connected through his family with leaders of rigorous Protestantism. The half-brother of his grandfather was the redoubtable, long-lived Alexander Nowell, exiled in Strasbourg and Frankfurt in Mary's reign, Dean of St Paul's throughout Elizabeth's reign. Amongst Roger's second cousins were John Wolton, Bishop of Exeter, also a former exile, and Dr William Whittaker, of a Pendle family, Regius Professor of Divinity at Cambridge and an inflexible Calvinist. Hence Nowell was well-placed to retail to Lancashire the theology which on the continent had inflamed and inspired those crazes of witch persecution of which the exiles were well aware. On Nowell's desk may well have been the *Discourse of the Damned Art of Witches*, published in 1608 by William Perkins, a Cambridge colleague and friend of William Whittaker and the leading Puritan writer of his day. Within the cool idiom of Calvinism, Perkins expressed the notion of witchcraft which a century earlier had been engendered by Catholic inquisitors in the Holy Roman Empire. Witchcraft, in Perkins's view, was no simple playing with occult powers. Perkins wrote:

> The ground of all witchcraft is a league or covenant made between the witch and the devil, wherein they do mutually bind themselves the one to the other ... The devil ... for his part promises to be ready to his vassals command, to appear at any time in the likeness of any creature, to consult with him, to aid and help him.[14]

Witchcraft was the Faustian compact with the prince of darkness, the ultimate, unforgivable heresy of those who had enlisted in the Devil's secret army. Perkins, admired for his Puritan wisdom and goodness, advocated death for all witches. In the pages of Perkins and (as Stephen Pumfrey's chapter elsewhere in this volume shows) in King James's *Daemonologie*, Nowell found his interpretative model, and in the spring of 1612 he conveyed it to Lister and to other gentry around Pendle.

Nowell's family too had suffered a commotion. His mother, before he was born, had first been married to Laurence Starkie of Huntroyd, who had died. So their son, Edmond Starkie of Huntroyd, was Roger Nowell's older half-brother, and Edmond's son, Nicholas Starkie, his half-nephew, though close in age. Neighbours and blood relations, the Nowells and the Starkies were a close family group. We can follow the nephew's strange family life.

Nicholas Starkie in 1577 married Anne Parr, who inherited Cleworth Hall in south Lancashire. At Cleworth, near Leigh, they lived until Nicholas inherited Huntroyd, and at Cleworth they raised a young family, the fame of whose turmoils reached London where society discussed them and playwrights wrote of them.

The events began in 1595, just thirteen years before the strange death of Thomas Lister, seventeen before the trials of the Lancashire witches. Uncle Roger Nowell would be about forty-three years old, an anxious observer. In that year at Cleworth Nicholas Starkie's two children, John and Ann, aged about twelve and ten, began to convulse. Their father, alarmed, spent £200 on the fees of doctors. Desperate, he consulted a Catholic priest, who, alas, claimed not to be carrying his book of exorcism. Starkie, convinced that the children were possessed by the Devil, then engaged a wise man, Edmund Hartley, to cure the children. For about a year Hartley had some success, using 'certain popish charms and herbs'. Then things fell awry. Hartley believed he was underpaid at £2 per year, the children's fits became more furious, and three other girls in the Starkie house acted with similar abandon. So did a maid aged thirty, and a spinster relation aged thirty-three. The house became bedlam. The children romped, screamed, howled, and held their breath until they were blue in the face. They delighted in 'filthy and unsavourie speeches', especially during sermons in church. Perhaps there was method in their madness, for as a result they were rarely taken there. John Starkie, now aged nearly fourteen, himself began to deliver wild, apocalyptic addresses. The parents believed them all to be bewitched, but we can see indications of sexual hysteria like that which ignited the accusations at Salem eighty years later. Hartley bewitched the girls by kissing them, it was alleged later, and lay on the maid's bed. Freudian imagery abounded in the girls' tittering talk about the furry devil which entered little holes. Hartley now was denounced by Nicholas Starkie and brought by him to the Lancaster Assizes in March 1597. Poor Edmund Hartley, who had come to Cleworth to cure, was himself found guilty of witchcraft. Like his trial, his execution was muddled. The rope broke. Hartley, amazed to be alive, 'penitentlie confessed'. He was then hanged successfully.

Starkie now consulted Dr John Dee, the famed master of the occult, then Warden of Manchester College, and on his advice invited to Cleworth two Puritan ministers from Derbyshire, John Darrel from Ashby-de-la-Zouche and George More from Caulk. At Cleworth Darrel spent the night in prayer, then assembled the troubled household. According to Darrel's published account, widely read, he and More, armed with the word of the scripture, confronted the demons. The seven possessed bellowed, blasphemed and convulsed, lay unconscious for a long time, and then rose freed from their possession; all of them except the maid continued in good health thereafter.[15]

There the matter might have rested had not John Darrel, the exorcist, previously exorcised in Burton on Trent Thomas Darling, the 'Boy of Burton' who like a ventriloquist had spouted out conversations between his angelic self and devils; and had Darrel not subsequently in Nottingham exorcised at great public displays the musician's apprentice William Sommers who suffered from contortions, who had an egg-shaped lump that moved around his body, who vomited extraordinarily, and who acted with gross obscenity. After controversies in Nottingham and the confession of 'pretense' by those exorcised, Darrel was tried by the Commission for Ecclesiastical Affairs and imprisoned for deceit and counterfeiting.

Darrel's Puritan supporters did not desert their imprisoned champion. A pamphlet war ensued. Opposing Darrel's claims were Bishop Bancroft of London, soon to be Archbishop of Canterbury, and Bancroft's chaplain Samuel Harsnett, later Archbishop of York, who wrote ironically and intelligently. They, of the Anglican party, were not inclined to believe in magical or devilish agencies nor, as a consequence, in purported exorcisms. In the inflamed atmosphere when parties of the civil war were beginning to coalesce, to believe in the reality of possession and exorcism became a shibboleth for the emerging Puritan party (just as it is for some charismatic Christians today), while the liberal Anglican party could be identified by scepticism about witchcraft. The issue became political and would not subside. 'The Seven in Lancashire', the Starkie household, are mentioned in Ben Jonson's play *The Divell is an Asse* years later in 1616. A character in the play is urged to pretend to be bewitched. It is easy, he is told:

> Did you ne'er read, Sir, little Darrels tricks
> With the boy o' Burton, and the 7 in Lancashire,
> Sommers at Nottingham? All these do teach it,
> And we'll give out, Sir, that your wife has bewitched you.[16]

By 1612 Nicholas Starkie's family were living in Huntroyd, close by Roger Nowell. Nowell, by his discovery of witches in 1612, by giving evidence of their malign activity, and by pursuing them to the gallows, aligned himself with the Starkies in the public debate, championed the Puritan stance, and followed the line of John Darrell who was perhaps his role-model.

It is natural to consider the sufferings of the victims of persecution. Yet when we view closely the lives of the persecutors we see within them also periods of anguish and wounding traumas, distorting experiences, which make us reflect on the tragedy more deeply. As W. H. Auden wrote:

> I and the public know
> What all schoolchildren learn,
> Those to whom evil is done
> Do evil in return.[17]

Nowell's wider appreciation of witchcraft issues will have been of value to Lister when the two collaborated to prepare depositions for Jennet Preston's second trial. In turn Lister's wedding traumas and his growing antipathy to Jennet Preston were the catalyst that unleashed the energy of Nowell, already well-prepared, both intellectually and by his Starkie connection, to fulfil the role of witch-hunter. It was during the unsuccessful first trial of Jennet Preston in York at Lent 1612 that Nowell received at Read Hall Abraham Law of Halifax, who attributed his pedlar father's sudden stroke to bewitching by Alizon Device, to whom his father had refused his wares. Nowell, alert to this issue, listened and acted with vigour. He interviewed. He enlisted other magistrates. The hunt was on.

It happened that many of those whom Nowell's investigations uncovered did consider themselves witches. The depositions reveal that the family groups headed by Demdike and by Chattox – the Devices and the Whittles – were village healers who practised magic. They healed animals, perhaps they healed people, they healed casks of ale, and they cursed them, probably for money. They made potions and fashioned clay images, and crumbled them. They told fortunes. They were affectionately disposed to dogs and cats and hares. They were poor, and scoured the country begging or, occasionally, got day-work carding wool. Traditional village witchcraft was to them something of a family occupation, a cottage industry.[18] They were like those traditional gypsies once common in the English countryside who dabbled a little in the occult but had no grand theory of it. Witches of this sort were common throughout England. Reginald Scot in 1584 wrote that every parish had its miracle-worker, and that some had seventeen or eighteen. Robert Burton, in *The Anatomy of Melancholy*, concurred; there was a cunning man in every village, he said.[19] Throughout the land there were as many of these wise men or wise women as there were parochial clergy and doctors, perhaps many more. They were part of accepted village economy.

Roger Nowell's concept of witchcraft was not so simple; he did have a grand theory. Nowell was learned; he had read King James and William Perkins, and probably recent accounts of English witch trials. He may well have known the *Malleus Maleficarum*, the baleful encyclopaedia of the demonic written in 1486 by the Dominican inquisitors Jacob Sprenger and Heinrich Kramer and endorsed by papal bull.[20] The paradigms in Nowell's mind were those anecdotes about witches which had swirled round the northern foothills of the Alps in the late fifteenth century and which, under the influence of Dominican inquisitors, had crystallised into the doctrine of witchcraft as the ultimate heresy. These doctrines had strangely overleapt the confessional divides of Europe and were now embraced by Puritan intellectuals in England.

Nowell's questions to the Devices and the Whittles show that he thirsted to learn about a Faustian compact with the Devil, about a girl's selling of her soul, about the erotic enormities of the witches' sabbat, and about the sensual intimacies of animal familiars. The villagers, intimidated by the grandeur of Nowell's mansion, were meanwhile trying to tell of the friendships and misunderstandings of village life, about bits of sympathetic magic here and there which might have worked – who knows? – and which won one person or another a reputation as a wise man or woman. Alizon, Demdike, Chattox and James were involved in a simpler notion of witchcraft that did not answer to Nowell's stereotypes. From this mismatch too evolved the tragedy. The families from the hill-country were crushed between the mill-stones of two different perceptions of the nature of witchcraft, mill-stones set on their dire motion by traumas in the families of Roger Nowell and Thomas Lister.

Notes

1 Gisburn was transferred from Yorkshire to Lancashire in the boundary changes of 1974.

2 *The Arraignement and Triall of Jennet Preston*, issued with Potts, *The Wonderfull Discoverie of Witches in the Countie of Lancaster* (London, 1613), X3–Z4 (at X4), and reprinted in Jonathan Lumby, *The Lancashire Witch-Craze: Jennet Preston and the Lancashire Witches* (Preston: Carnegie, 1995), pp. 169–74. Marion Gibson, *Early Modern Witches: Witchcraft Cases in Contemporary Writing* (London: Routledge, 2000), p. 174, notices that the editorial introduction to *The Arraignement and Triall of Jennet Preston* is more assertive in style than Potts's editorial insertions in *The Wonderfull Discoverie*, and suggests that 'it may be by another author'. I am not persuaded of this.

3 James VI and I, *Daemonologie* (Edinburgh, 1597; ed. G. B. Harrison, London: Bodley Head, 1924), p. 80.

4 Reginald Scot, *The Discoverie of Witchcraft* (London, 1584), XIII, ix; Francis Bacon, *Works*, ii, p. 660, both cited in Keith Thomas, *Religion and the Decline of Magic: Studies in Popular Beliefs in Sixteenth- and Seventeenth-Century England* (1971; London: Penguin, 1973), p. 261.

5 Register of Gisburn parish church, Lancashire Record Office (hereafter LRO).

6 Potts, *Wonderfull Discoverie*, Y3–Z.

7 Registers of Gisburn parish church and Bracewell parish church, LRO.

8 *The Autobiography and Correspondence of Sir Simonds D'Ewes*, ed. J. O. Halliwell (1845), i, pp. 59–60, cited in Thomas, *Religion and the Decline of Magic*, p. 262.

9 LRO, QSB 1/170/55–60.

10 The wife of Thomas Lister senior was Jane, daughter and heiress of John Greenacres of Worston, Member of Parliament for the borough of Clitheroe. She died just a year later in February 1608/9. Thomas Dunham Whitaker, *History of the Original Parish of Whalley* (Blackburn, 1801).

11 *The Arraignement and Triall of Jennet Preston*, Y3–Z1, reprinted in Lumby, *Lancashire Witch-Craze*, pp. 169–72.

12 Borthwick Institute, York, V35 fol. 465r.

13 James J. Cartwright, *Chapters in the History of Yorkshire* (Wakefield: B. W. Allen, 1872), p. 149.

14 William Perkins, *A Discourse of the Damned Art of Witchcraft* (Cambridge, 1608), pp. 31, 41, 48.

15 The sources for the Starkie and Darrel episode are: Samuel Harsnett, *A Discovery of the Fraudulent Practices of John Darrel* (London, 1599); John Darrel, *A True Narration of the Strange and Grevous Vexation by the Devil of 7 Persons in Lancashire, and William Somers*

of Nottingham (London, 1600); George More, *A True Discourse Concerning the Certaine Possession and Dispossession of 7 Persons in One Familie in Lancashire* (London, 1600); Samuel Harsnett, *A Declaration of Egregious Popish Impostures* (London, 1603); Anon., *The Triall of Maist. Dorrell: A Collection of Defences* (London, 1599). See also D. P. Walker, *Unclean Spirits: Possession and Exorcism in France and England in the Late Sixteenth and Early Seventeenth Centuries* (London: Scolar Press, 1981).

16 Ben Jonson, *Works*, ed. C. H. Herford (Oxford: Oxford University Press, 1938), pp. 254–69.

17 In the poem '1st September 1939'.

18 See John Swain's chapter in this volume.

19 Scot, *Discoverie of Witchcraft*, I, ii; Robert Burton, *The Anatomy of Melancholy* (1621), ii, p. 6, both cited in Thomas, *Religion and the Decline of Magic*, pp. 291–2.

20 J. Sprenger and H. Kramer, *Malleus Maleficarum* (1486; ed. Montague Summers, London: John Rodker, 1928). This work was supported by the papal bull 'Summis Desiderantes Affectibus' of Innocent VIII in 1484.

PART II

CONTEXTS: SOCIETY, ECONOMY, RELIGION AND MAGIC

In this section, attention shifts from the prosecutors to the prosecuted, and from the trials to their context. The areas in which wider explanations for early modern witchcraft have been sought include society and economy, religion, popular magical beliefs and practices, and the vulnerable position of women. These factors cannot be clearly divided off, but taken together these three chapters address them all.

Perhaps the most influential modern explanation of witchcraft has been the 'village tensions' approach, developed during the 1960s and 1970s social and economic history boom. In this model, which focuses upon the grassroots generation of witchcraft accusations rather than on the prosecution process, the profound social and economic pressures of the later sixteenth and early seventeenth centuries tended to divide the members of parish communities against each other. Bitter and guilty disputes between rich and poor neighbours over property and poor relief became endemic, and these in turn generated threats and accusations of witchcraft. John Swain's research into the economic and social history of this part of early modern Lancashire makes him well-placed to investigate this idea for the Pendle area. Here, he combines an account of the pressures on Pendle's upland 'cattle and cloth economy' with a detailed analysis of the individual accusations in the 1612 trial. He shows that a high proportion of the witchcraft cases in Pendle involved disputes over money and property or misfortunes involving milk and cattle, arguing that social and economic pressures influenced but did not determine the events of 1612. He goes on to suggest that magical powers, offered or threatened, were themselves part of the local economy – what we might call a black economy of witchcraft.

More recently, historians have looked more to religion and ideas for explanations of witch trials. Long ago, as Michael Mullett reminds us, Hugh Trevor-Roper in an influential essay suggested that witchcraft trials were concentrated in areas where there were clashes between strong Roman Catholicism and vigorous reforming Protestantism, and singled out Lancashire as an example. The county was certainly notable at this period for both of these religious tendencies, and this is clearly something to be explored. Michael Mullett's chapter here focuses on the enormous and impoverished parish of Whalley, of which Pendle formed a part. He stresses the 'spiritual vacuum' left by the destructive dissolution of Whalley Abbey in the reign of Henry VIII, the continuing attachment of the population to the older forms of religious belief, and the rise of a determined, reforming Puritanism in the generation or so preceding the trials of 1612. The Reformation proceeded slowly in Whalley, and as Swain and (elsewhere) Lumby show, unreformed religious ideas remained entrenched. But when the godly crusade against sin did finally get underway, it was magistrates such as Roger Nowell and his colleagues among the Protestant gentry of the area who were in the forefront of the campaign to eradicate what they saw as the related phenomena of Catholicism, superstition and witchcraft.

But when godly magistrates took action against witchcraft, what (if anything) were they proceeding against? Thomas Potts is anxious to show that the accused were involved in a dark conspiracy, and had all at some time made pacts with the Devil, but we saw in the work of Gibson and Pumfrey in the first section that these were relatively new, imported ideas, imposed upon the evidence by the prosecution. Kirsteen Macpherson Bardell confirms this sceptical approach to the charge of organised satanism. She casts the net beyond Pendle and 1612 and comes up with evidence of nearly a hundred other cases of witchcraft and magic from the records of the lower courts, the Lancashire Quarter Sessions. Here, we find magic accepted as a familiar part of life, with witchcraft merging into the activities of village healers and 'cunning folk', and indeed with the counter-magic used by ordinary people. It would be surprising if the witches of 1612 were an exception to all this, and indeed the Pendle evidence does suggest that Demdike and Chattox were involved in 'white' magic and counter-magic on behalf of clients, as well as *maleficium* (or harmful magic). This in turn supports the argument of Swain that at least some of the Pendle witches were involved in magic as a living. Further, the fact that they used spells and charms based on garbled versions of old Catholic prayers indicates that the witches – and, by implication, their clients – remained untouched by Puritan campaigns of reformation, carrying down the generations elements of the old popular religious culture of Catholic Lancashire.

All in all, the chapters in this section suggest various fault lines – social and economic, religious, and cultural – opening up within the society of early modern Lancashire, with the accused witches on the wrong side of all of them. Their position was by no means unique in England, or even in Lancashire, but it was their particular misfortune to come to the attention of godly magistrates intent on rooting out 'popery' and witchcraft.

5

Witchcraft, economy and society
in the forest of Pendle

John Swain

It is natural to unnatural people, and peculiar unto witchmongers, to pursue the poor, to accuse the simple, and to kill the innocent.[1]

This assertion, that those in poverty were particularly vulnerable to accusations of witchcraft, was the view in 1584 of the Kentish JP and witchcraft sceptic Reginald Scot. If he was correct to link witchcraft and the poor, it might be assumed that the Lancashire witch trials of 1612 and 1634 were only to be expected, given that they followed more than a century of unfavourable economic changes for those on the margin of subsistence, not least with inflation outpacing wage rises. Keith Thomas and Alan Macfarlane put forward a hypothesis, derived substantially from Scot, that many accusations of witchcraft originated when a beggar, often an old woman, would be refused charity by a wealthier neighbour, would depart muttering curses and would subsequently get the blame for any immediate misfortune. Thomas claimed: 'The overwhelming majority of fully documented witch cases fall into this simple pattern. The witch is sent away empty-handed, perhaps mumbling a malediction; and in due course something goes wrong with the household, for which she is immediately held responsible.'[2]

Thomas and Macfarlane went much further than Scot, ingeniously suggesting that the uncharitable victim realised that he had failed in his social obligations towards the beggar and wished to exonerate himself by transferring this guilt onto the beggar through an accusation of witchcraft. Macfarlane (but, significantly, not Thomas) later repudiated his original ideas, asserting instead that the individualistic characteristics of the English, which might have conflicted with communal values leading to guilt and hence witchcraft accusations, had been present since medieval times; they had not surfaced in the sixteenth century alongside the pronounced increase in witchcraft trials.[3] Nevertheless, Macfarlane's original ideas are still widely quoted whilst his later ideas have not been received with complete acclaim.

It is the aim of this investigation to test empirically the Thomas/ Macfarlane hypothesis, but also to assess more broadly how far the Lancashire witch trials arose from economic pressures and village tensions. It will be shown that there were economic aspects to many of the episodes in 1612 described by Potts, and to the events of 1633–34, but that these do not directly explain the trials and operated indirectly through a variety of social situations.

At the time of the two witch trials, Pendle was a typical upland pastoral economy, far removed from the more prosperous arable villages of southern England. Two economic activities predominated: cattle rearing and woollen cloth making, often in the same household. There was some arable farming, mainly oats, and other important types of craft and industry, such as coal mining, tanning, brewing and quarrying of slate and lime, but 'cattle and cloth country' is a fair summary of how most people made a living.[4]

Probate inventories, lists of movable goods drawn up shortly after death, are testimony to the importance of cattle in Pendle Forest. The median herd size of seventy-five Pendle inventories drawn up between 1558 and 1640 was a dozen head. Sales were often destined for the Colne cattle fairs, held on 24 February, 1 May and 29 September.[5] Pastoral farming is far less labour-intensive than arable cultivation (where labour is required all the year round). Perhaps it is no accident that the two outbreaks of Pendle witchcraft occurred approaching spring, on 18 March 1612 and on 10 February 1634, well away from the haymaking and harvesting seasons, giving people more time to allow petty arguments to get out of hand. Perhaps the Devil does indeed find work for idle hands.

Inventories also reveal that most households were involved in both cattle rearing and making rough woollen cloth called kersey. No less than 70 per cent of Pendle inventories list the tools necessary for cloth production, such as cards, combs, spinning wheels or looms. Just over half of the households owned cards or combs, 56 per cent had spinning wheels, and nearly two-fifths possessed looms. This involved all the family – the women and children carded and spun whilst the menfolk wove the kersey cloth on narrow looms. Four or five people were required to card and spin to produce sufficient yarn to keep one weaver in work, underlining the importance of children and adult females in the household economy. This was an activity which could dovetail well with the fluctuating demands of the agricultural year and provide useful or essential supplementary income.[6]

Several of those involved in the trials of 1612 and 1634 are known to have made a living from cattle and cloth. Thus the star of the second trial of 1634, Edmund Robinson junior, aged ten or eleven, said that his mother had brought him up to spin wool and fetch home her cattle. However, Edmund played with other children when he should have been bringing home the family's cows, and, fearing a beating, he fabricated the story that he had been abducted by witches.[7] One of the leading witches in the first trial in 1612, Anne Whittle alias Old Chattox, was hired about 1606 to card wool for the wife of James Robinson, despite being in her seventies and almost blind and apparently with eight years experience in witchcraft. All went well until the third day when she was accused of souring the ale after drinking from it – what did she do with it or in it? Katherine Hewit, alias Mouldheels, also one of those executed in 1612, was the wife of a Colne clothier, John Hewit.[8]

Cattle as well as humans were targets for disgruntled witches. For example, Alizon Device suggested that Hugh Moore believed on his death-bed that his illness was Old Chattox's revenge for accusing her of bewitching his cattle. Old Chattox was also alleged to have killed one cow belonging to a gentleman, John Moore of Higham, because Moore's wife had nagged her after she had cured his bewitched drink; another belonging to Anthony Nutter because he had favoured her great rival Old Demdike rather than her; and a third belonging to John Nutter of Bull Hole. In this last case, Elizabeth, a daughter of Old Chattox, begged a dish of milk from John Nutter's house in about 1606; she put it into a can, but Nutter's son disliked what Old Chattox was doing with it and so kicked it over; and a cow died three or four days later. This may have been the same cow that John Nutter had asked Old Demdike to cure.[9] Cows were very valuable, nearly £3 each at this time or about thirty weeks net wages for a slater.[10]

The emphasis on cattle and cloth as a means of making a living dates from the medieval period. Pendle Forest was originally designated as a chase for deer hunting, but eleven vaccaries (cattle farms) with over 900 head were in evidence by 1295–96 during Edward I's reign. The de Lacy landlords farmed these ranches themselves at this time, but during the fourteenth century landlords tended to lease them to individual farmers. Cloth making was also important at this time. At the end of Edward II's reign in 1327, there were at least four water-driven fulling mills for finishing cloth in Lancashire, and the fact that two, at Colne and Burnley, were adjacent to Pendle Forest is testimony to the early development and importance of the cloth trade in this area. Both of these fulling mills predate 1295–96. The area passed into Crown ownership in 1399 when Henry, Duke of Lancaster, usurped the throne as Henry IV. Leasing of the vaccaries continued throughout the fifteenth century and was formalised towards the end of Henry VII's reign in 1507 when the forests of the Honor of Clitheroe, of which Pendle was one, were disafforested and granted by copy of court roll according to the custom of the adjacent manors such as Colne and Ightenhill, with fixed rents and entry fines, payable on inheritance, restricted to just one year's rent. Although rents in Pendle rose by 39 per cent, the Crown only benefited in the short term since it surrendered its ability to revise rents and entry fines in line with market forces. Price inflation during the sixteenth century meant that the Pendle copyholders were in real terms increasingly better off, in contrast to those on other estates who experienced rising entry fines and rents or arbitrary eviction by landlords anxious to enclose their lands. On the other hand, those who chose to lease land from the copyholders as their subtenants enjoyed no such restrictions on the rent they paid, and consequently faced the full force of the unfavourable local and national market forces.[11]

The pressures at work during the sixteenth and early seventeenth centuries centred around the rapid rise in population. There had been just twenty-four tenants in Pendle Forest in 1443, but the number had grown to exactly a hundred by 1527. This might suggest that the Pendle population by this time was approaching 500, assuming that average household size was between four and five, but such a calculation ignores the families who were subtenants, squatters or landless, so the true population size was probably greater. The opening up of nearly 7,300 acres in 1507 on such favourable terms, which gave the tenants every incentive to improve their holdings, must have contributed to this population growth. Local facilities had to be built to accommodate this, and the church of Newchurch was consecrated in 1544, two years after a lease to build a new corn mill at New Carr was granted to Lawrence Towneley Esquire of Barnside in Pendle. More accurate figures may be gleaned from the communicants' returns of 1563 and 1650, which suggest that the Pendle population more than doubled, from between 580 and 725 in 1563 to about 1,620 in 1650. A further grant was made in 1598 to Henry Towneley Esquire of Barnside to build a corn mill in Roughlee to satisfy this rising demand.[12]

However, problems were evident even for the copyholders by the early seventeenth century. By legal chicanery, the Duchy of Lancaster lawyers called into question the validity of the copyholders' estates in 1607, exactly a century after the original disafforestation. This was, in reality, a ploy designed to ease James I's financial problems by extracting a cash composition from the copyholders to have confirmed what they believed they already enjoyed. The copyholders petitioned the Duchy in 1608, making the following claims about their and their ancestors' lifestyles since the disafforestation in 1507:

> not only in the enclosure of the same copyholds and the continual manuring and tilling thereof, being before that time in respect both of the nature of the country and the soil thereabouts extremely barren and unprofitable and as yet capable of no other corn but oats and that but only in dry years and not without the continual charge of every third year's new manuring, but also in the building of their houses and habitations thereon having no timber there nor within many miles thereof and having from time to time ever since enjoyed the same and therefore paid a rent and fine at the first as much or more and now very near the value thereof, have nearly disposed, employed and placed all the fruit and increase of their ancestors and their own labours and

industries and the estates and maintenance of themselves, their families and posterities upon the same copyholds.[13]

The copyholders portrayed a very marginal economy in which they lived on the brink of subsistence, and, by implication, their subtenants must have been below the poverty line. If this were true, tensions and feuds in a climate of limited resources must have abounded, making the sort of quarrels leading up to the 1612 trial only to be expected. However, it is clear that the tenants were exaggerating; for example, probate inventories record crops other than oats, such as wheat and barley. They painted a very bleak picture in order to try to persuade the Duchy that they were too poor to purchase the freehold of their estates. Eventually, a settlement was reached whereby the rights of the copyholders were confirmed in return for a lump sum of twelve years' rent, paid by the end of 1609. Such a large amount must have caused resentment, but the real value of the land was far more than this, as the subtenants realised all too well, and there was no sudden upsurge in the number of copyholders forced to mortgage or sell part of their holding.[14] Furthermore, the chain of events which triggered off the 1612 trial began more than two years later, which is probably too long a time lag for us to argue that escalating social tensions created by the composition were the *principal* factor leading to the 1612 trials. Nevertheless, it may have contributed to some extent; some of the witches seem to have lived partly by begging and extortion, and the accusations of acts of witchcraft sometimes centred on a curse following refusal of charity by a wealthier neighbour, who presumably had less to spare after the composition payment.

The real value of the land may be seen from the level of rents paid to the copyholders by their subtenants. Subtenants were paying rents on average over twenty-five times what the copyholders had to pay to the Duchy of Lancaster in the 1600s and 1610s, and this rose to nearly forty-three times the copyhold rent in the 1620s and 1630s.[15] It is clear that at least some of the Pendle witches of 1612 were subtenants. Old Chattox's daughter Anne Redferne was a tenant of the Nutters of Greenhead in New Laund and eighteen or nineteen years earlier Robert Nutter junior had made unwelcome sexual advances and on being rebuffed yelled 'if ever the ground came to him she should never dwell upon his land'. The alleged upshot of this failed attempt to exercise a version of *droit de seigneur* was that Old Chattox procured Robert's death a few months later with the help of her spirit, rather ironically called 'Fancy'.[16] This incident neatly illustrates the insecurity of tenure of the subtenants, in contrast to that enjoyed by the copyholders themselves, the copyhold dispute of 1607–9 excepted. Some of these subtenants had a lease for a period of less than a year and a day, the time limit above which transactions had to be recorded in the rolls of the halmotes (i.e. the forest courts), with an appropriate entry fine of a year's rent paid to the Duchy.

There seems to have been a number of families forced to rent or squat on very small holdings. An Act of 1589 prohibited the use of a cottage for habitation if it had less than four acres attached to it, or taking in more than one family in a cottage as inmates. Landlords could command attractive rents from these minuscule farms and so were prepared to ignore the Act. The local halmotes brought several cases in the 1590s and 1620s; no less than thirty-one were presented for this offence by the Pendle jurors in October 1621, for example, but were not a prominent feature of court business in 1612 and 1634.[17] It may well be that the Malkin Tower was such a cottage, for the names of the Southerns/Device family are mentioned neither in the rentals nor in the court rolls as copyholders or subtenants, so they must have held a lease for less than a year and a day, or, as illegal squatters, held no lease at all.

There was a far greater problem than witchcraft for the Pendle population in the early 1620s and this was crisis mortality. Burials more than doubled in the Colne, Burnley and Padiham area in 1623, as did cereal prices. High bread prices would have been a particular problem because the cloth trade had been in depression since 1614 due to the failure of the Cockayne Project and the disruption of trade following the outbreak of the Thirty Years War in Europe in 1618, and there was therefore less work available. At a time of high bread prices, the demand for non-essentials such as textiles inevitably fell further and thus the harvest failure made the problems in the cloth trade worse. The cause of this crisis mortality was probably famine: the wide geographical spread across isolated hamlets, villages and market towns, the absence of a strongly seasonal pattern to the mortality which would have been apparent if a single epidemic disease had been responsible (plague usually strikes in the summer and autumn and typhus in the winter, for example), and the inverse movement of burials and conceptions, a classic sign of the presence of famine amenorrhoea – all are highly suggestive of a subsistence crisis.[18] Yet the early 1620s did not produce a major witch trial – it is not the case that desperate conditions *for all* drove people to search for a scapegoat. Rather it seems that people stoically accepted their lot when they could see that the whole community was affected, including presumably those with a reputation for witchcraft; it was only when individuals or particular families suffered some inexplicable misfortune that accusations of witchcraft surfaced.

What was the attitude of the mass of the Pendle population to religion? It does not seem that the area was affected by religious strife or tension which might tie in with witchcraft accusations. In October 1608, the only problem identified by the Visitation (a church court, usually presided over by an archdeacon) in relation to Newchurch in Pendle was that a widow called Jane Whalley was a non-communicant (not taking communion in an Anglican church). In October 1611, two matters were reported to the Visitation: first, Henry Standen kept two obstinate recusants (Catholics who refused to attend Anglican services) in his house; secondly, the minister, Christopher Nuttall, had married a couple in an alehouse when the bride was contracted to marry another man. Nuttall, or Nutter as he is described in some sources, had also married a couple without licence in 1592, yet in a survey of Lancashire clergy in 1604 he was described as being in charge of the well-affected parochial chapelry of Pendle. Nutter's occasional indiscretions were little in comparison with those of the Newchurch curate in 1640, John Horrocks, who apparently had

> been much given to excessive drinking of ale, wine and strong beer ... and have lived ... in an alehouse of one Elizabeth Hargreaves of Fence Gate in Pendle and have made several affrays with several men and have oftentimes ... beaten the said Elizabeth and one Henry Robinson son of John Robinson churchwarden of Newchurch aforesaid because he would not pay a drinking shot ... in the said alehouse.

This was only one of several charges which Horrocks had to answer; others included taking bribes for baptising illegitimate children without inquiring into the father's identity or punishing the parents, conducting a marriage in a private house, slander, and having sexual relations with Elizabeth Hargreaves.[19]

If some of the clergy failed to lead by example, perhaps we should not be altogether surprised if some of their flock strayed from the paths of righteousness. Occasionally individuals were presented for expressing extremely unchristian ideas, such as Richard Moore of Newchurch, charged at the Visitation of 1626 for 'saying that God where he did one good turn did two bad and that if God were there he would cut off his head'. The constable of Colne chapelry, whose area of responsibility included the Pendle area of Barrowford, was presented at the Visitation of 1622 for wandering in the streets at the time of divine service and refusing to go to church, 'saying he was about greater business'.[20] However, the infrequent examples cited make the witch accusations of 1612 and 1634 all the more startling and significant, providing as they do an invaluable insight into the attitudes of many ordinary people, both accused and witnesses.

Belief in witchcraft was certainly common in this area in the early seventeenth century. Edmund Robinson junior finally admitted to inventing his story in 1634 but the idea about those accused came to him naturally 'because he heard the neighbours repute them for witches'.[21] The son-in-law of Old Demdike, John Device, was according to his daughter Alizon so afraid of the spells of the other leading witch, Old Chattox, that he agreed to pay her a measure of meal annually in return for an undertaking that she would not harm him or his goods. Apparently, he did not trust the magical powers of his mother-in-law to protect him. For some reason, the meal was not paid one year and John became terminally ill; on his death-bed, he attributed his sad condition to Old Chattox's doing, because of the non-payment of the meal.

There are several other death-bed claims of witchcraft recorded by Potts; Alizon Device also claimed that the dying Hugh Moore believed that he had been bewitched by Old Chattox because he had accused her of bewitching his cattle, and Margaret Crook made the same assertion about the final moments of her brother Robert Nutter (who blamed Anne Redferne and her associates) and her father Christopher Nutter (who did not name the witch responsible). Margaret's and Robert's brother, John Nutter, a yeoman of Higham Booth, said that his father had told him not to be silly when he claimed to have been bewitched by Old Chattox and Anne Redferne: 'Thou art a foolish lad, it is not so, it is thy miscarriage'. It seems, however, that the subsequent death of his son Robert and his own illness had undermined his scepticism.[22]

Many of the accusations of witchcraft in 1612 spring from the family of Old Demdike blaming that of Old Chattox, or vice versa. We do not know what promises of clemency Roger Nowell or other interrogators had made if the accused gave evidence against each other, or whether they had given the impression that the whole story had already emerged from others and that anything less than a full confession would surely condemn them. Nevertheless, whilst there are some inconsistencies, it does seem that there was bad blood between the two families, which seems to have arisen about 1601 when the Device house was apparently burgled and goods worth £1 stolen, a crime which the Device clan attributed to Old Chattox's family. Potts commented on the rivalry between the two families, writing that Old Chattox was 'always opposite to Old Demdike, for whom the one favoured, the other hated deadly, and how they envy and accuse one another in their examinations may appear'.[23]

It is possible that the two families were bitter enemies for reasons other than the break-in, because they were competing against each other for a limited market, making a living by healing, begging and extortion. Alizon Device said that although she did not have the power to cure the pedlar John Law, her grandmother, Old Demdike, could have done if she had lived. John Nutter had apparently asked Demdike to cure a sick cow, but it died. Some of those indicted were probably wise women or men, practitioners of herbal or folk medicine, and inevitably sometimes things went wrong and they got the blame.[24] They certainly obtained some income from begging. Alizon Device said that she had been on several begging expeditions with her grandmother, Old Demdike, and Demdike had told the JP, Roger Nowell, that the Devil first appeared to her twenty years before 'as she was coming homeward from begging'.[25] Old Demdike, according to her daughter Elizabeth and grandson James, had apparently been refused a penny by Henry Mitton of Roughlee; Demdike then consorted with her daughter Elizabeth Device and, rather peculiarly, a rich woman, Alice Nutter of Roughlee, and bewitched Mitton to death. It may seem strange that contemporaries found it credible that a man might be killed for refusal of such a small amount, but it makes sense if people regarded it as an attempt by Old Demdike to maintain her reputation as someone who should not be offended, whose magical powers were greater than her rivals, and to whom it was dangerous to refuse charity when requested. The confession by Old Chattox at Fence, that she had bewitched to death a cow belonging to Anthony Nutter because he favoured Old Demdike rather than her, makes sense if it is seen in the light of a wish to assert magical superiority over her main rival and therefore protect her future income. A reputation for witchcraft, and being more successful than rivals, was therefore all-important. Potts wrote of Old Demdike that 'no man escaped her, or her Furies, that ever gave them any occasion of offence, or denied them anything they stood in need of'.[26] This is very reminiscent of the remarks of Reginald Scot, who wrote in 1584 that witches were 'so odious unto all their neighbours and so feared, as few dare offend them, or deny them anything they ask'. Similarly, Edward Fairfax claimed that one of the Yorkshire witches tormenting his children in 1621 'had so powerful a hand over the wealthiest neighbours about her that none of them refused to do anything she required; yea unbesought they provided her with fire, and meat from their own tables, and did what else they thought to please her'. Robin Briggs, in his study of the French province of Lorraine, has also uncovered examples of people cultivating a reputation as witches in order to secure charity, and Sally Scully has shown that some in seventeenth-century Venice saw witchcraft as a business.[27]

It seems that the local community had tolerated the witches' activities for many years before the 1612 trial, even after the draconian 1604 Act against witchcraft was passed, and that it was only when *outsiders*, the Law family of Halifax, instigated the complaint and brought it to the attention of Roger Nowell that their activities were brought to an end. Was the local community terrified of the witches or did it find their services largely beneficial?[28]

The sources from the second outbreak of Pendle witchcraft in 1633–34 provide further evidence that economic factors featured in the series of accusations which emanated from the Robinson family. Edmund junior should have been looking after his mother's cows but played truant with his friends instead and then invented a story about witches abducting him to cover his tracks. The key questions are why his parents believed him, and why it took three months to report the incident to the local JPs. The local clergyman, John Webster, published his account of the whole affair in 1677 and provides us with a very credible explanation. The Robinsons had attempted to unmask witches in Webster's own congregation at Kildwick in Craven and elsewhere: 'The boy, his father and some others did make a practice to go from church to church that the boy might reveal and discover witches ... and by that means they got a good living, that in a short space the father bought a cow or two, when he had none before'.[29]

Clearly, the Robinsons had owned cattle before this episode so Webster is wrong in this regard, but probably correct in his overall assertion that the Robinsons made a living out of witch-finding. The Bishop of Chester had reported to Secretaries Coke and Windebank on 15 June 1634 that the Robinsons were accused of blackmail:

> Conceit and malice are so powerful with many in those parts that they will easily afford an oath to work revenge upon their neighbour, and it was offered to be deposed by Mary Fisher, widow (where the parties dieted in the assize week) that if Dicconson would have given the accuser Robinson 40s before the arraignment, neither he nor his son (the boy that first set the business on foot) would have said anything against her; but when she advised her husband to give nothing, Robinson said he had no malice to any but her. The like will be testified by others, but such evidence being, as lawyers speak, against the King, the Bishop thought it not meet without further authority to examine.[30]

Frances Dicconson also made this allegation on 13 June, adding further detail about the animosity against her and her husband:

> The boy who accused her has much wronged her. His father, Edmund Rough alias Robinson, bought a cow of her husband, but he would not let her go without surety, whereupon he has ever since maliced her and her husband. The other witness against her, Edmund Stevenson of Stainskow in Pendle, is lately accused of felony, and maliced her upon bargain of butter ... Edmund Robinson offered to have freed her if her husband would have given 40s, and for that end dealt with Richard Hooker of Pendle Forest.[31]

Once his son had owned up in London on 10 July 1634 to fabricating the story, Edmund senior claimed two days later that the initiative for commencing the prosecution came from the JPs Richard Shuttleworth and John Starkie, who had issued a warrant to bring Edmund junior to them; he claimed that he had rebuked his son for his witchcraft story and had refused to believe him. He maintained that the Dicconsons were 'very honest, harmless people' and that there was no previous history of bad blood between him and them; rather, he had bought a cow from John Dicconson for 53s 4d without any problem arising. He denied that he had involved Richard Hooker as an intermediary in his blackmailing machinations regarding Frances Dicconson.[32] It is not unreasonable to conclude that Edmund senior was desperately trying to exonerate himself after his attempt to profit from his son's tale had turned sour. He was not the only one making a profit at the expense of the four unfortunate accused witches in London, Frances Dicconson, Jennet Hargreaves, Margaret Johnson and Mary Spencer. According to Webster, there were 'great sums gotten at the Fleet [prison] to show them and public plays acted thereupon'. These plays included a comedy called *The Late Lancashire Witches* by Thomas Heywood and Richard Brome which was being performed at London's Globe Theatre by October.[33]

It seems that an important theme running through both outbreaks of Pendle witchcraft is the extent to which people could make a living, in part at least, by posing as a witch or by accusing or threatening to accuse others of witchcraft. That is not to say that witchcraft accusations can be reduced to crude economic determinism, or that people could not ascribe non-economic motives to alleged bewitchings. For example, Elizabeth Device claimed in 1612 that her spirit, Ball, told her to make a clay model of John Robinson alias Swyer of Barley; she dried it so that it crumbled and he died about a week later. She did this because he had insulted her by saying that she had an illegitimate child. Old Chattox had allegedly bewitched to death Anne Nutter for laughing at her. The case of Robert Nutter's death allegedly at the hands of Old Chattox for making unwelcome sexual advances to her daughter Anne Redferne has already been quoted.[34]

However, in contrast to these three motives for witchcraft taken from the 1612 evidence, all of which may be categorised as of a non-economic nature, the other nine cases where a motive can be clearly seen all relate to quarrels relating to money, animals or possessions. We have already described the death of Henry Mitton for refusing to give Old Demdike a penny, the death-bed claim by John Device that his imminent demise was due to non-payment of meal to Old Chattox, and Old Chattox's claim that she killed Anthony Nutter's cow because he favoured Old Demdike rather than her. The chain of witchcraft accusations began when Alizon Device demanded to have some pins from the pedlar John Law's pack; she claimed that she wanted to buy them but Law refused to undo his pack. John's son Abraham stated that Alizon had no money but his father still gave her some pins. John said that Alizon 'was very earnest with him for pins, but he would give her none'. Whatever the truth, whether John could not be bothered to undo his pack for such a small transaction or whether Alizon was begging, John then suffered a stroke, which he attributed to Alizon.[35]

The remaining five cases cover a variety of different quarrels about property. John Duckworth of the Laund was apparently killed by Dandy, James Device's spirit, because Duckworth had promised him a shirt but subsequently refused to hand it over. He also said that Mistress Anne Towneley of Carr Hall had been killed by crumbling away a clay effigy because she had accused James and his mother of stealing her turves, and because she had hit James. Old Chattox stated that she had killed a cow belonging to a gentleman, John Moore of Higham, because despite curing his bewitched drink, Moore's wife had nagged her. Alizon Device claimed that Old Chattox had bewitched to death Hugh Moore for accusing her of bewitching his cattle, and a cow belonging to John Nutter because John's son disliked what she was doing with a can of milk which had been begged from his family.[36]

It therefore does not appear that the evidence from the 1612 outbreak of witchcraft provides strong support for the hypothesis put forward by Keith

Thomas and Alan Macfarlane that conflicts over begging were a key factor in witch trials. Only three of the twelve cases from 1612 refer to refusal of charity, and that assumes, perhaps wrongly, that John Law's disagreement with Alizon Device can be properly classified as a refusal of charity. If we are correct to assert that, for some of the witches in 1612, witchcraft was a business combining healing with extortion and blackmail, those wealthy enough to be preyed on by the witches would certainly not feel guilty about denying them charity, but would feel apprehensive about possible retaliation, angry if misfortune occurred, and relieved if the witch was successfully put out of harm's way. The events of 1633–34 also illustrate how people could make a living by threatening to expose others as witches. Evidence from other seventeenth-century English witch trials from the north (Yorkshire), the midlands (Belvoir and Northamptonshire) and the south (Royston and Milton) similarly fails to provide Thomas and Macfarlane with support.[37] The findings of this study do however accord with those of Malcolm Gaskill, who has shown how 'witchcraft accusations might be explained in terms of developing social and economic competition, without tying the dynamic to any particular aspect of this change'.[38]

In conclusion, it is apparent that substantial population growth in the Pendle area in the sixteenth and early seventeenth centuries put severe pressure on limited resources in this upland pastoral economy, and those who were compelled to sublet from the copyholders were in a particularly vulnerable position. The situation was made worse, even for the copyholders, by the legal dispute and composition payment in 1609. It is therefore not surprising that many chose to make a living by having two or more activities, often cattle rearing and cloth making. However, for some of the very poorest in society, essential extra income could be obtained by cultivating a reputation for witchcraft, for good or ill, albeit with the risks involved. Therefore *long- and medium-term* economic factors help to explain the events behind the 1612 trial, even though no *short-term* economic crisis appears to have been present in early 1612. The same may be said of 1633–34, except here the immediate cause was the opportunism and greed of the Robinsons, who saw how they could make a good living by posing as witch-finders.

It might appear that it is easier to raise questions about the Lancashire witches than it is to provide firm answers. Despite the existence of Thomas Potts's version of the 1612 trial, and the state papers of 1634, we lack not just the Assize records but also many crucial sources which might shed light on the two trials. For example, the records of the overseers of the poor have not survived – would their pages have been dominated with payments to those accused, Alice Nutter excepted? It would be surprising not to find payments to a blind woman such as Old Demdike or a virtually blind Old Chattox authorised under the Poor Law Act of 1601.

There is an assumption in much of the writing on witchcraft that those accused or convicted of witchcraft were tragic victims, typically mentally or physically abnormal or economically marginalised, who in a more enlightened and later age would have been either acquitted or not accused in the first place. This is a form of Whig history, looking back and down on an age when people were supposedly ignorant, credulous and superstitious. No doubt many of those accused of witchcraft were innocent, but it may well be that, for some, witchcraft was a business, albeit a very risky one, for which several paid the ultimate price.

Notes

I am very grateful to Robert Poole for his comments and for his initial invitation to speak at the conference on the Lancashire witches at St Martin's College, Lancaster, in April 1999. I am also very grateful to John Hatcher, who has long been a source of support and helpful advice. Final responsibility for any errors naturally rests with the author.

Spelling has been modernised in all quotations, except for the names of the witches.

1 Reginald Scot, *The Discovery of Witchcraft* (London, 1584; ed. Brinsley Nicholson, London, 1886), p. vii.
2 Scot, *Discovery of Witchcraft*, pp. 5–6; Keith Thomas, *Religion and the Decline of Magic: Studies in Popular Beliefs in Sixteenth- and Seventeenth-Century England* (1971; London: Penguin, 1973), p. 661; Alan Macfarlane, *Witchcraft in Tudor and Stuart England: A Regional and Comparative Study* (1970; 2nd edn, London: Routledge, 1999), pp. 172–6, 196–8.
3 Alan Macfarlane, *The Origins of English Individualism: The Family, Property and Social Transition* (Oxford: Basil Blackwell, 1978), pp. 1–2, 59–60.
4 John T. Swain, *Industry before the Industrial Revolution: North-East Lancashire c.1500–1640* (Manchester: Manchester University Press / Chetham Society publications, third series xxxii, 1986). More detailed references to material discussed here may be found in this and other works by the author cited below.
5 Swain, *Industry before the Industrial Revolution*, pp. 43, 47.
6 Swain, *Industry before the Industrial Revolution*, pp. 108–62; John T. Swain, 'The Lancashire witch trials of 1612 and 1634 and the economics of witchcraft', *Northern History* 30 (1994), p. 72.
7 *Calendar of State Papers Domestic* (hereafter *CSPD*), 1634–35, p. 141.
8 Thomas Potts, *The Wonderfull Discoverie of Witches in the Countie of Lancaster* (London, 1613; ed. James Crossley, Manchester: Chetham Society publications vi, 1845), E–E2, P3.
9 Potts, *Wonderfull Discoverie*, E2–E3, F, C.
10 Excluding his allowance for food, i.e. 6d 'for his table' plus 4d wage. John T. Swain 'Industry and economy in north east Lancashire circa 1500–1640' (unpublished Ph.D. thesis, Cambridge University, 1983), table A.3, p. 340; table A.4, p. 342.
11 Swain, *Industry before the Industrial Revolution*, pp. 4–6, 8–9, 56–7.
12 Swain, *Industry before the Industrial Revolution*, pp. 19, 37–8, 58, 70–1; Swain, 'Lancashire witch trials', pp. 70–1.
13 The petition may be found in Lancashire Record Office DDTa 216 fol. 3; further copies are in Manchester Central Library L1/38/3/1 and in Wigan Record Office D/DZ. A4, Towneley MSS, fol. 58.
14 Swain, *Industry before the Industrial Revolution*, pp. 37–8, 60–1; Swain, 'Lancashire witch trials', pp. 73–4.

15 Swain, 'Industry and economy', table 5.6, p. 146, amalgamating the data from Pendle Forest.
16 Potts, *Wonderfull Discoverie*, D3.
17 Swain, *Industry before the Industrial Revolution*, p. 89; Swain, 'Lancashire witch trials', pp. 75–6.
18 Swain, *Industry before the Industrial Revolution*, pp. 22–5, 137–8, 142–4; Swain, 'Lancashire witch trials', p. 73.
19 Cheshire Record Office, EDC 5 (1639), fol. 127; Swain, 'Lancashire witch trials', pp. 77–9.
20 Swain, 'Lancashire witch trials', pp. 78–9.
21 *CSPD*, 1634–35, p. 152.
22 Potts, *Wonderfull Discoverie*, E4, F, O, O2.
23 Potts, *Wonderfull Discoverie*, E4, D4.
24 Potts, *Wonderfull Discoverie*, S, C. For further details of Lancashire witches working beneficial magic as healers, see the chapter by Kirsteen Macpherson Bardell in this volume.
25 Potts, *Wonderfull Discoverie*, C, B2.
26 Potts, *Wonderfull Discoverie*, O4, B2.
27 Scot, *Discovery of Witchcraft*, p. 5; Edward Fairfax, *Daemonologia: A Discourse on Witchcraft as it was Acted in the Family of Mr Edward Fairfax of Fuyston, in the County of York in the Year 1621*, ed. William Grainge (Harrogate, 1882), p. 34; Robin Briggs, *Witches and Neighbours: The Social and Cultural Context of European Witchcraft* (London: Harper Collins, 1996), pp. 91, 155–7; Sally Scully, 'Marriage or a career? Witchcraft as an alternative in seventeenth-century Venice', *Journal of Social History* 28 (1995), pp. 857–76. Brian Levack, *The Witch-Hunt in Early Modern Europe*, 2nd edn (London: Longman, 1995), p. 151, also makes the point that with poverty becoming more widespread in the early modern period, people were more prepared to regard witchcraft as a solution to their financial problems.
28 Clive Holmes, 'Women: witnesses and witches', *Past and Present* 140 (1993), pp. 52–3, argues that communities might treat witches with 'elaborate if cautious deference', tolerating some anti-social behaviour and also employing them as healers and in industry, and paying blackmail or using counter-magic against malevolent witchcraft. He also argues that the 1612 Pendle outbreak began due to elite intervention (Roger Nowell) responding to local rumours, yet it is clear that it was the Laws who initiated proceedings. For further details of Roger Nowell's role in the events of 1612, see the chapter by Jonathan Lumby in this volume.
29 Swain, 'Lancashire witch trials', pp. 67–8; John Webster, *The Displaying of Supposed Witchcraft* (London, 1677), p. 277.
30 *CSPD*, 1634–35, p. 78.
31 *CSPD*, 1634–35, p. 79.
32 *CSPD*, 1634–35, pp. 141, 144.
33 Webster, *Displaying of Supposed Witchcraft*, p. 346; Swain, 'Lancashire witch trials', pp. 65, 68. Further details of this play may be found in the chapter by Alison Findlay in this volume.
34 Potts, *Wonderfull Discoverie*, F4, E4, D3.
35 Potts, *Wonderfull Discoverie*, O4, E4, E3, R3–S.
36 Potts, *Wonderfull Discoverie*, H3–4, H3, E3, F.
37 For Yorkshire, see J. A. Sharpe, 'Witchcraft and women in seventeenth-century England: some northern evidence', *Continuity and Change* 6 (1991), pp. 186–7, and *Witchcraft in Seventeenth-Century Yorkshire: Accusations and Counter-Measures* (York: Borthwick Institute, 1992), p. 8. For the midlands and southern examples, which relate to the period from 1606 to 1619, failure to provide appropriate charity was mentioned only once out of nine cases where the motive for witchcraft was clearly stated, and even this was a case of giving insufficiently generous charity rather than refusal; see Barbara Rosen (ed.) *Witchcraft* (Lon-

don: Edward Arnold, 1969), pp. 323–56, 369–84, and Swain, 'Lancashire witch trials', pp. 83–4. Other criticism of the Thomas/Macfarlane model may be found in Christina Larner, *Witchcraft and Religion: The Politics of Popular Belief* (Oxford: Basil Blackwell, 1984), pp. 50–3; Joseph Klaits, *Servants of Satan: The Age of Witch Hunts* (Bloomington: Indiana University Press, 1985), pp. 89–94; G. R. Quaife, *Godly Zeal and Furious Rage: The Witch in Early Modern Europe* (London: Croom Helm, 1987), pp. 181, 189–90; Geoffrey Scarre, *Witchcraft and Magic in Sixteenth- and Seventeenth-Century Europe* (London: Macmillan, 1987), pp. 40–3; James A. Sharpe, *Instruments of Darkness: Witchcraft in England 1550–1750* (London: Hamish Hamilton, 1996), pp. 60–3; Jonathan Barry, 'Introduction: Keith Thomas and the problem of witchcraft', in Jonathan Barry, Marianne Hester and Gareth Roberts (eds), *Witchcraft in Early Modern Europe: Studies in Culture and Belief* (Cambridge: Cambridge University Press, 1996), pp. 1–28, and, in the same volume, Wolfgang Behringer, 'Witchcraft studies in Austria, Germany and Switzerland', p. 91; James A. Sharpe, 'Introduction', in Macfarlane, *Witchcraft in Tudor and Stuart England*, p. xviii.

38 Malcolm Gaskill, 'Witchcraft and power in early modern England: the case of Margaret Moore', in Jenny Kermode and Garthine Walker (eds), *Women, Crime and the Courts in Early Modern England* (London: UCL Press, 1994), pp. 125–45; Gaskill, 'Witchcraft in early modern Kent: stereotypes and the background to accusations', in Barry *et al.* (eds), *Witchcraft in Early Modern Europe*, p. 259.

6

The Reformation in the parish of Whalley

Michael Mullett

The parish of Whalley in east Lancashire is undoubtedly ancient. Even though we have to discard the old tradition that it was founded by St Augustine in AD 596, we can acknowledge, on the basis of the three preaching crosses in the churchyard, that its foundation dates from the first half of the seventh century. The parish was also of vast extent, covering 180 square miles, and by the time of the Reformation it was supposed to cater for the religious needs of about 10,000 people. By then Whalley parish had jurisdiction over, and pastoral responsibility for, thirty separate townships, including Whalley itself and the chapelries of Padiham, Colne, Clitheroe, Downham, Burnley, Holme and Whitewell. Whalley's dependent chapelry of Newchurch in Pendle, taking in Pendle Forest, included the district from which the Pendle witches of 1612 hailed. Like other northern parishes such as Kendal and Ulverston, Whalley parish was simply too big to be effective in its basic tasks of preaching and teaching Christian doctrine, even though dependent chapels of ease were set up throughout the immense parish to eke out its stretched resources. Catholic survivals in Lancashire after the introduction of the Protestant Reformation by Queen Elizabeth and her Parliament in 1559, and the apparent upsurge of witchcraft in the sixteenth and seventeenth centuries, were both widely attributed to the deficiencies of this kind of over-grown parochial system.[1] A report that we shall examine later in this chapter, *The State, Civil and Ecclesiastical, of the County of Lancaster, about the Year 1590*, specifically charged that the chapel of ease system, assembled on the cheap over the course of time, was responsible for widespread ignorance of Christianity. The 'godly, or 'Puritan', element within the Church of England saw much of Lancashire, with its inadequate parochial and preaching provisions, as a classic 'dark corner of the land', where ignorance prevailed, fostering 'popery', chronic superstition, and a proneness to accept the claims of witches.

During the medieval period an essential supplement to those over-extended parochial resources was provided by the great Cistercian abbey of Whalley, the next-door-neighbour of the parish church. Whalley Abbey was, indeed, almost a kind of bishopric within its division of the north-west. The region was without a cathedral or a bishop until both were set up at Chester in 1541 by Henry VIII, funded out of some of the proceeds of the Dissolution of the Monasteries which had been carried out by the King through his leading minister Thomas Cromwell between 1536 and 1540. But Whalley Abbey itself was to fall a spectacular victim to the Dissolution, and its centuries-old role as provider of welfare, religious worship and education was lost in a matter of months, depleting further the already strained facilities of organised religion in that area. As we shall see later, by examining the judicial proceedings of the Abbey court (the Act Book), the Abbey did indeed exercise a kind of episcopal pastoral oversight over its hinterland in the extensive domain covered by the royal forests of Pendle, Trawden, Rossendale and the Blackburn district, and it used its jurisdiction 'in spirituals' to impose a moral oversight of the district's lay people. The Abbey's court sought to impose a code of behaviour throughout the monastery's extensive sphere of influence and control. Its dissolution left not just a moral vacuum but deprived the community of a great institution, employer and welfare provider.

Into the space left by the Abbey's destruction, from the Elizabethan period (1558–1603) and into the reign of James I (1603–25), a group of Lancashire Puritan clergy, with their allies amongst the 'godly' gentry of the area, set up new disciplinary controls over the laity – the system of oversight that was to lead on to the 1612 trials. We will also investigate the agenda for social, moral and religious reform outlined in the text entitled *The State ... of Lancashire*. This, we shall see, was intended to be applied not only in the Whalley area, where one of the report's authors was minister, but throughout Lancashire. By aligning this manifesto for change with the earlier Abbey court proceedings, we shall seek to trace the long-term impact of the Reformation on the lives of the laity, showing how by the end of the Reformation century a collective Protestant clerical attitude had been assembled with regard to the behaviour of the laity. This group outlook had serious implications for the way that activities such as alleged witchcraft were to be confronted and assailed in the future. We shall conclude with a brief inspection of the way in which some Lancashire clerics in the early 1590s assembled a kind of casebook on witchcraft, a treatise which was to form part of the theoretical base of the 1612 Pendle witch case. That legal action was itself a direct outcome of the Protestant clerical impulse to reform the lives of the laity, in close collaboration with like-minded magistrates of the kind who took the 1612 case to the Lancaster Assizes.

One of a chain of Cistercian monastic foundations set up under aristocratic patronage in post-Conquest England, Whalley, like its Cistercian sister

Furness Abbey in Lancashire north of the sands of Morecambe Bay, soon established itself as a princely presence in its zone. Abandoning its first, flood-prone site at Stanlaw in Cheshire – but retaining its lovely name, *locus benedictus*, 'the blessed place' – the house moved to Whalley in east Lancashire, where its patron was Henry Lacey, Earl of Lincoln. Building work began in 1296 and most of it was completed between 1310 and 1425.[2]

The primary impression we receive of Whalley Abbey and its relations with its district is one of immense and ramified social and economic power. The removal of such a mighty force from the local economic system would have had an enormous impact. We shall also need to give some thought to the magnitude of economic and accompanying social and political power conferred on the local gentry families who acquired the Abbey's estates, above all the Asshetons of Downham and Whalley. For our assessment of the extent of the Abbey's economic force within its sphere of influence and control, we are fortunate in that surveys of Whalley Abbey's economic substance abound. As a kind of audit prior to the Dissolution, the 1535 *Valor Ecclesiasticus*[3] provides an impression of a financial magnet that drew in varying sums in annual tributes from the country roundabout. These could be substantial amounts (£20 from Whalley itself, £10 from nearby Clitheroe) or they might come to lesser dues (15s from Downham, 13s 4d from Chatburn), and they came from as far afield as Preston (2s), and Stanlaw (a hefty £20). Whalley Abbey's claims to levy financial contributions were recognised over a wide area. Further and detailed information on Whalley's economic range and supply system is provided in two lists, each termed a *compotus*. These date from 1478 and 1521 and cover a period in which the Abbey's receipts from the religious payments classed as *in spiritualibus* approximately doubled.[4] The geographical spread of these payments indicate, for one thing, Whalley Abbey's extensive authority as a kind of diocesan in its area of oversight and control. It drew in such dues from its dependent Whalley parish (with Padiham), and from that parish's chapelries of Clitheroe, Downham, Colne, Burnley, Altham and Haslingdon, sums which amounted in total to £129 4s 4d; from Blackburn came £79 16s 9d; from Rochdale, £64; and from Eccles church with Dean chapel, £73 17s 5½d. The total of these receipts *in spiritualibus* was £356 17s 5½d in 1478, which had risen to £592 3s 1½d in 1521. There were also some non-spiritual receipts from dependent farms. The overall impression we should carry away from a study of these accounts, as from other aspects of the Abbey's activities in the decades leading up to the Dissolution, is far from that of a moribund institution, ready for its own *quietus*, but rather of a vibrant and expansionist enterprise, a glittering prize for a hostile takeover.

Whalley Abbey was a big spender of these incomes, a generous paternalistic agribusiness which consolidated its hold on its environment through charity, clientage, job-creating programmes of building and repairs, and massive expenditure on provisions, including a perhaps literally staggering wine bill. The *Valor Ecclesiasticus* further hinted at the power that was consolidated through the disposal of the charity that the inflow of wealth made possible – the large doles of cloth and grain and, on Maundy Thursdays, of money to the local poor.[5] However, the late-eighteenth-century historian of the Abbey and the parish, Thomas Dunham Whitaker, with characteristic vividness, pictured a situation, like a picturesque tableau from *The Lady of Shalott*, in which the Abbey bound fast to itself the varied social strata of its region through tight cords of gift-giving. The monks' 'liberality in money was … great. The nobility and gentry of the county had corrodies [residence rights in the Abbey] or pensions; the poor friars, the minstrels, the officers of the Ecclesiastical Court in their visitation, and even the servants of ordinary visitants, partook liberally of their bounty.'[6]

The documentation in the *compotus* papers amply supports Whitaker's contention. The Abbey paid pensions to some of the highest in the region in 1478: to Thomas Lord Stanley, to two members of a local gentry family, and to two other unnamed noblemen or gentry ('*duobus Generosis*'), as well as to an unnamed student at the Premonstratensian house at Cockersands on the Lancashire coast, while another student was maintained at university at a cost of £5 a year. In the same year a group of pilgrims to Jerusalem received 16d, and a hermit the same sum. In 1521 disbursements included 2s to a servant of the Bishop of Sodor and Man and 6s 8d to a servant of the King. In that year, too, the claim of 3s 4d from a doctor who had travelled from Lancaster was met, and £2 was awarded as an annual donation to the poor. Additional outlays were made on building work and repairs, so that at least some of the money flowing in from the Abbey's various dependencies flowed out again on the costs of improvements. Investments were made in the 'estates elsewhere' ('*firmis exterioribus*'): 9s was paid out to the Abbey at Chester and 11s for certain work on the castle in Liverpool, and in 1478 £1 9s 4d was paid for work at Downham chapelry and £1 0s 4d for the chancel in Rochdale church. It was the last abbot, John Paslew (1507–36), who in 1521 commenced a major project, not completed until 1533, of adding on to the north aisle of the dependent church in Burnley.[7]

Pre-Reformation Whalley Abbey, then, should be seen as a vibrant economic generator in its region, holding a busy portfolio of accounts that moved sums of silver around what might well otherwise have been a sluggish local economy. Whitaker perceived that the monks kept back little for themselves: 'not more than a fourth part of their large income was consumed in their own personal expenses'.[8] It was not that these late medieval Cistercians were always inspired by the austere spirit of Cîteaux – though, as we shall see, they read, or listened to readings from, St Bernard. Payment of 16s was made for specially manufactured hair-shirt fabric in 1478 – arguably something of an extravagance for an austerity – but perhaps more typical of a lifestyle now evidently cultivating gentlemanly comforts was the expenditure of 2s for an iron grate in 1478, and money for sea coal in 1521, perhaps to feed the little luxury. Red wine was the largest indulgence, barrelled French sunshine in that damp climate, in the impressive quantity of 8,064 pints per annum for twenty monks, an abbot and a prior. However, we must not assume that all those thousands of jugs of *vin rouge* were poured down the throats of monastics. Rather, we should try to view Whalley Abbey as a residence on the analogy of a large modern country hotel, taking delivery of large quantities of provender, liquid and solid, for guests both thirsty and hungry. From a massive 1521 beef bill of £72 19s, Whitaker worked out that '162 persons ... must have been constantly fed at the abbot's table' and he wrote, rightly, of 'boundless hospitality' there.[9]

Munificence, the expenditure of income, and lavish hospitality were the characteristics of an institution enmeshed in the social life of its neighbourhood, and, as with other late medieval English abbeys, the local surnames of monks and abbots suggest recruitment from that same area. None of this is to say that the Abbey was always a popular institution amongst its neighbours. Indeed, its very integration in regional life also implicated Whalley Abbey into local habits of fighting and feuding. Thus at some point before 1480 Abbey servants, led by the bursar, took part in a raid to drive cattle off local lands, the ownership of whose tithes was disputed between the Abbey and the parish church; the rector duly incited a mob to attack the Abbey's gang, making the local tenants swear to pay their tithes only to him. The case was serious enough to be referred to Edward IV, whose adjudication in the Abbey's favour was confirmed by Richard III.[10]

More edifyingly, Whalley Abbey provided within its neighbourhood a range of liturgical splendour. Robert Aske, the leader of the Pilgrimage of Grace (the 1536–37 northern rising directed against the suppression of the abbeys), might have had Whalley in mind when he recalled the monasteries' provision of 'the devyn service of almightie God ... great nombre of messes ... the blissed consecracion of the sacrement'.[11] A detailed depiction of one liturgical occasion, in 1425, provides at least one insight into the drama, colour and musical wonder of the Abbey's late medieval liturgical regime: it described in full detail the opening and blessing of a new dormitory, in a ceremony presided over by the abbot himself and comprising the solemn intoning of *Te Deum*, in December darkness, after compline, the abbot blessing the beds with holy water, followed by further chant.[12] The majesty of the ceremonial round was enhanced by the visual splendour of the Abbey's regalia, which included:

> a large crosse of silver and gilte wth ii images of Mary and John ... another crose with the iiii Evangelistes gilte ... a large holy-water fatt with a sprinkelle of silver parcell gilte ... a miter of silver and gilte, sett with safours [saphires], emerodes, balas [rubies], and turkesses [turqoises], as evil [heavy] as can be ... one cope [of] Venise gold with Lord Mount Egle's armes ... other

copes old of grene bawdekyne [baldachin, a rich brocade] with **M** of gold imbroydred on the brest of eyther of them ... one vestment of red clothe of gold with an image in a crosse on the bak with tynnacles [tunicles, or dalmatics] for a deacon and sub-deacon belonging to the same ... a vestment of blak velvett wth a posie of lettres of gold imbroidered, with things there-unto belonging for deacon and sub-deacon ... another vestment of grene velvett with an image of Seinte Michell imbroidered on the bak ...[13]

A further inventory listed sixteen gold chalices, a silver vessel for chrism, silver candlesticks, a gold crucifix, a silver *pax* (the peace symbol passed around at holy communion), and a mitre decorated with lapis lazuli and pearl on silver.[14]

As well as honouring the most important family of the county nobility, the Stanleys, through its liturgical paraphernalia (there were two cloth of gold copes 'with Lord Mount Egle's armes'[15]), Whalley Abbey also celebrated a royal religious cult: the Abbey accounts for 1521 recorded an offering of 1s 6d made 'to Our Lady and St Henry at the chapel' ('*P Stipite beate marie et Sči Henr ad capellam*'). The identity of this sainted Henry is made clearer by a further entry, in the *compotus* accounts of 1510, for an offering 'of [or to] King Henry' ('*Pro Stip Regis Henri*'). The devotion to Henry VI, not an offi-cially canonised saint, yet a recipient of considerable popular veneration in late medieval England, was appropriate in as much as the 'royal saint' had endowed a chantry (a chapel set aside for masses for the dead) at Whalley, and Whitaker justifiably speculated that this Lancastrian cultus, probably sup-pressed or discouraged by the Yorkist kings, was revived by Henry VII, giving the Abbey a devotional link with the Tudor dynasty – which, of course, in no way impeded the Abbey's abrupt suppression by the second Tudor monarch, Henry VIII.[16] In addition to what was clearly a magnetic ceremonial regime and rich cultic life, the Abbey mounted a programme of readings for delivery throughout the year in the refectory or infirmary, including the New Testament, Church fathers and leading medieval monastic writers, the whole making up a learned, diverse and uplifting syllabus.[17]

All this was to come to a violent end between 1536 and 1540 as the religious houses of England and Wales paid with total extirpation for their involvement in the Pilgrimage of Grace, an act of resistance to the first, selective instalment of closures in 1536.[18] In his examination in the Tower in the spring of 1537 the rebel leader Robert Aske poignantly drew attention to the loss of the kind of religious and communal services which abbeys such as Whalley had pro-vided. They offered, he said, 'almons [alms] to poor men and laudable servd God'; they extended plentiful 'hospitalitie'; and their glorious buildings were amongst 'the bewties of this realme'.[19] As Geoffrey Baskerville concluded, the way that the Dissolution impacted on Whalley and its neighbouring sisters Sawley and Jervaulx 'showed how justified was Robert Aske's claim for their value' within their zone.[20]

Whalley's entirely understandable, and entirely disastrous, involvement in the rising at the behest of its last abbot, John Paslew, brought down upon it an abrupt, drastic and vindictive closure. In this process the issue of alleged monastic moral decadence, which had been to the fore as a propaganda justification for condemnations of the monks preceding the first phase of dissolution, now made way for emphasis on the political sin of treason, calling for an obliteration of all traces of the monastic presence in the area:

> for as moche as it apperethe that the house of Whalley hathe been so sore corrupt ... that it shuld seme there remaynethe very few therin that were mete to remayne and contynue in such an incorporation, we thinke it shalbe mete that some ordre be taken for the remotion of the monkes nowe being in the same, and that we shall take the hole house in our oune handes ... and so devise for such *a newe establishment therof* [my emphasis] as shalbe thought mete for the onnour of God, our suretye, and the benefit of the cuntrey.[21]

Whalley Abbey, then, was implicated in rebellion, in the person of its abbot, who was arraigned and convicted of high treason in the 1537 spring Assizes in Lancaster and executed in March, as were two others monks. As a result and a punishment, the Abbey was directly and entirely taken into the King's hands 'by reason of the attainder of John, lately abbot of the same place'.[22] For their 'grievous offences towardes us' the monks were to be scattered to the four winds – 'to go to other houses of their cote [order]'. There was even something of the flavour of an occupation, the Abbey becoming the base for the emergency operations of 'the Kynges counsell within the said countie' dealing with the crisis of the Pilgrimage. There was no mistaking the process by which Whalley, for so long itself a territorial lordship with its own population of subjects, had become in the fullest sense the property and lordship of 'our lord the king'. Thus the most important effect of the first phase of the Reformation under the Tudors as far as Whalley people were concerned was that they were incorporated into a new and vastly more extensive royal subjecthood. The price of survival was an entire subjection, and the penalty for resisting it death, not just for Paslew and the two other attainted monks but even for an old man who had served the King once in the Scottish wars but who was 'at the last ... corrupted against us' and so made 'an example more worthye to suffer [death] thenne the rest'. The passage to survival and worldly success was now to be docility to the Crown's presence. This presence was no longer remote for royal might had supplanted the Abbey to become, virtually overnight, the unrivalled dispenser of patronage thereabouts as a new parochial order emerged out of the ruins of the monastic system. When one of the two priests customarily provided by the Abbey to the parish church needed to be installed, it was the Earl of Sussex and the other royal commissioners who wrote to the King to put in a favourable reference on behalf of the politically safe former prior of the monastery, Christopher Smith.[23]

As elsewhere, the Dissolution in Whalley was, of course, largely motivated by the institution's wealth. Much of this was contained in a dazzling, glittering trove of bullion and jewels, flashy, gorgeous and immediately realisable in value: 'ii large stondinge cuppes with covers of silver and gilte', 'ii stondinge pottes of silver', 'another stondinge cuppe parcill gilte with a cover and a pellican on the toppe'.[24] In addition to the fabulous stores of liturgical regalia described earlier, all this hoard represented a wonderful acquisition for its new owner, the King. However, a more durable asset lay in the estates of the Abbey, whose immense extent was set out in a survey of *c.* 1537 of 'The Demene lands of the late dissolved ... attainted Monasterie of Whalleye'.[25] This survey, evidently compiled shortly after the Dissolution, gives an indication of the sheer wealth in real estate that it records, with cash values carefully entered: pastures, meadows, closes, woodland, arable, crofts, orchards, garths, stables, a henhouse, an 'oxhouse', several houses, a corn mill, barns and so on. The total annual ' letten by the yeare' was £65 12s 10d from the leased demesne, with profits from woodland of £12 per annum. Though few of the sums came to much individually, the overall income from these sixty-three payments from the Abbey's demesne property alone would have been enough to place a member of the gentry within the upper reaches of his status group, especially in Lancashire.[26]

The property, though, did not immediately fall into the hands of any member of the gentry. It was the King's – all the more so on account of the attainder of the last abbot – and a further survey conducted in 1539 made it plain that the knight Sir Thomas Southworke, 'appointed to have the ordering and ruling of the tenants their', was 'yealding accompt theirof to the Kings use'.[27] However, by letters patent issued on 12 April 1539 the demesne property was entrusted into the stewardship ('bailiwick') of John Bradyll of Bradyll and Brockhole. Over the course of the next fourteen years Bradyll was able to turn this tenure to lucrative account with his partner Richard Assheton of Whalley (father of the Richard Assheton reputed to have been bewitched to death in 1597 and of Nicholas Assheton, 1590–1625, heir of the Whalley estate following his elder brother Richard's death and the compiler of a celebrated journal). By the end of the reign of Edward VI in 1553, they were in a position to pay the treasurer for the sale of the King's lands the following sums: 'to his Highness use ... for the ful clere and absolute purchas of the manour of Whalley wth the membres and appurtenaunces in the county of Lancastr. pcell of the late mony of Whalley atteynted the some of two thowsand one hundrethe tharty two powndes three shyllynge nene pence'. This huge sum may be compared with the £5 annual cost of keeping a student at Oxford and ex-prior Smith's stipend of about £6 per annum for serving the parish church. Within days of this transaction Assheton moved into the former abbot's house and Bradyll took possession of the lands.[28]

The full Latin letters patent of 1553 simply amplify the extent and value of this transfer. In return for their massive payment, Bradyll and Assheton won outright ownership 'of all that lordship and manor of ours of Whalley in Lancashire and all our park and all the lands of tenancies called Whalley Park in the said county with all and singular its rights, portions and appurtenances'. Rich bucolic detail was provided of 'meadows, pastures, gardens, orchards, barns, stables', along with a full local toponymy of the gift. Within fifteen years a triple revolution in the ownership of a great estate, from religious order, to Crown, to gentry, had been completed. Before 1553 was out, a two-man gentry consortium was in full possession, and the Abbey was no more: the phrase 'the former monastery' (*nuper monasterio*) was reiterated three times in nine lines of text. Although it took a while, in the following century a markedly Protestant proprietor of the estate, Ralph Assheton of Whalley, Bart. (who was gifted the property by his childless second cousin Richard Assheton, son of the journal compiler), levelled the site of the Abbey church to its present horizontality – surely as much an eradication of 'reliques of popery' as a building-safety precaution.[29] The new occupation at the Abbey and its lands symbolised and summed up a transfer of economic and political power in the locality in favour of the landed gentry. It was members of this class who, as wielders of authority and specifically as magistrates, would steer the prosecution of the Pendle witches in 1612.

In Whalley's parish church, meanwhile, the Reformation made less of a dramatic impact than the Dissolution did on the Abbey, as it unfolded from Henry VIII's nationalisation of religion to a fully fledged Protestant Reformation under Edward VI (1547–53) and Elizabeth I (1558–1603). As part of the local transfer of power, the advowson (right of presentation to a benefice) of the parish church was transferred first to the Crown and then to the Archbishop of Canterbury. However, for much of the reign of Elizabeth the incumbent was one of those half-way-house clerical conformists or crypto-Catholics whose unreconstructed ways licensed the retention of traditionalist religious habits and beliefs, especially amongst Lancashire people.[30] For over twenty years from his appointment by Cranmer in 1537 the parish had had a learned preaching minister, Edward Pedley, a theology graduate and an outright Protestant. However, during the last year of Catholic Queen Mary's reign, 1558, the church acquired as its vicar, and retained for the following thirty-three years, a recalcitrant traditionalist, George Dobson. Dobson, who also held the rural deanery of Blackburn, used the platform and liturgy of the Church of England to subvert its doctrines, worship and sacraments. He taught the Catholic doctrine of seven sacraments and administered the eucharist in the Catholic way, in one 'species' which he called, again in the Catholic fashion (albeit amended to Lancashire dialect), 'Oasts' (Hosts), and which he assured a traditionalist clique of his parishioners guaranteed their salvation. To the 'godly', his unreconstructed Falstaffian lifestyle would have provided a perfect confirmation of the wrong-headedness of his religious views:

> A common drunkard, and such an ale-knight as the like is not in our parish, and in the night when most men be in bed at their rest then is he in the ale-house with a company like to himself, but not one of them can match him in ale-house tricks, for he will, when he cannot discern black from blue, dance with a full cup on his head, surpassing all the rest.[31]

Dobson would no more have passed muster by the new standards of the Catholic renewal or 'Counter-Reformation' of the sixteenth century than he could conform himself to Protestant norms of correct clerical behaviour. Yet with the clerical authority he possessed, and doubtless with his evident genial sociability, he had the capacity to pass on an entrenched Catholic-oriented popular piety and popular culture to the generation of the alleged witches Chattox and Demdike. Godly Lancashire Protestant clerics, including Dobson's successor in Whalley, complained of the persistence of this culture in 1590, just a few years after the close of Dobson's tenure in the parish. Incumbents of his Whalley parish church were in fact expressly debarred from ministering in the chapelry set up in 1544 in Newchurch in Pendle, in the heart of the 'witch country' of 1612. However, though his direct influence in that district was limited, Dobson maintained in the mother church of the immense parish that took in Pendle a stubborn adherence to old ways and to what Protestant innovators were decrying as old superstitions. He could be convincingly seen as standing for a whole world of traditional attitudes and assumptions, attitudes embedded in the word 'popery' and arguably expressed also in the witchcraft 'discovered' within the boundaries of Whalley parish in 1612. Dobson also antagonised a Protestant constituency amongst his own parishioners – those who presented him in 1575 on the charges outlined above.[32] In a pioneering study of witchcraft in early modern Europe, Hugh Trevor-Roper argued that it was likely to be found along lines of discord between the rival Christianities of the post-Reformation period in Europe and in areas where the conflicting Catholic and Protestant faiths overlapped and collided.[33] Whalley parish, with its Protestant gentry – Asshetons, Bradylls and the rest – and its confessionally divided layfolk, lay on just such a fault line.

In the year that Squire Bradyll took up his stewardship of the Crown's properties, the former prior Christopher Smith died: a symbolic figure, the old order changing to accommodate the new. In his later years Smith presided over the ecclesiastical court which gave visible expression to the imposing power of Whalley Abbey over its hinterland. Now by examining the Abbey court's proceedings[34] in some detail, and by aligning them with the c. 1590 manifesto, *The State, Civil and Ecclesiastical, of Lancashire*,[35] we shall attempt to compare two behavioural codes, one pre-Reformation Catholic, the other Calvinist-inspired Protestant, and to assess what they each implied for general social conduct. Obviously, in comparing our two texts, we are not comparing like with like: one source is a minute book of judicial proceeding effected by an ecclesiastical court, the other a set of proposals for change in public behaviour that would in the future, beyond the compilation of the recommendations themselves, *require* legislative and juridical actions. Within these differences of formal institutional provenance of our documents, we shall trace in them an overall discrepancy of goals and assumptions about human beings and their changeability. Broadly speaking our monastic documents will be seen to be generally accepting of the frailties of men and women, or specifically of lay men and women. The *c.* 1590 Lancashire godly manifesto, on the other hand, has a tone that is dynamic and intensely reformist, rather than passive and tolerant, and shows a relentless insistence on transforming people out of their old ways. In that sense, the refusal current throughout *The State … of Lancashire* to accept human raw material for what it is betokened the assailant mentality against witchcraft that was to drive the 1612 trial forward.

A further point, though, to be made about the priorities of clerics as revealed in the Whalley Abbey court proceedings and in the reform manifesto *The State … of Lancashire* is how similar these could be in key respects. In both texts, for example, we read a deeply censorious attitude towards usury: while the Abbey court indicted a 'common usurer', made to pay a fine of 6d for making an usurious charge of 10s, *The State … of Lancashire* headed a list of five 'Sundrie notoriowse vises abowndinge' with 'Unlawfull and unresonable usurie in no Cuntrie more Common'.[36] Again there was considerable anxiety in both texts over the laity's behaviour in church: four cases of talking in church were recorded in the Abbey's Act Book in the period 1517–18.[37] Continuing that concern, the authors of *The State … of Lancashire* denounced those parishioners who were given over to 'talkinge, or otherwise misspendinge the time' and they went on to condemn the 'disturbance of the divine Service most offensive to everie good Conscience … By the walkinge and Talkinge of some'.[38] A further area of concern to Lancashire and Whalley clerical disciplinarians on either side of the Reformation divide in their urgency to control the speech habits of the laity had to do not only with the regulation of *where* layfolk spoke – outside church, but not in it – but also of *how* they spoke, and specifically of how they were required to speak unprofanely. So, while the Abbey Act Book would record proceedings against a woman who, as well as being 'a chatterer in the church', was 'a common swearer',[39] the composers of *The State … of Lancashire* thundered out against 'Continual sweringe and Blaspheming the name of god in the mouthe of owld and young, Riche and poore; no way punished or punishable'.[40]

Further evidence of shared anxiety expressed both in the Abbey Act Book and in the late Elizabethan and Puritan-inspired *State … of Lancashire* over public morals comes to light in expressions of desire to control the laity's time, or at least those segments of it that could plausibly be claimed as the Church's due – holy time, as it were. However, it is in this sphere that differences of underlying philosophy begin to appear. Broadly speaking, while we may recognise that the Abbey's law-makers were likely to uphold reverence for Sundays and holy days by forbidding work on those occasions, the Lancashire reformist writers of 1590 aimed to sanctify Sunday as the Sabbath – and to preclude pleasure-making on it. As far as Sunday was concerned, the early Tudor Act Book's legislation had the effect of extending ecclesiastical claims to exercise power over time by pushing backwards on to Saturday the notion of Sunday as a work-free zone, with the later hours of Saturday being treated as a kind of vigil, devoid of labour. Thus two brothers stood condemned for working too late on Saturday, while a woman was found guilty of doing her laundry on Saturday evening.[41] Further, the Abbey extended its claims over the disposal of time by intervening in the running of the numerous weekdays of the year set aside as feast days – the festivals of major saints, the several days marking events in the life of the Virgin, celebrations of Christ in His Nativity, Passion, Resurrection and Eucharist, and so on. Here the tendency to enlarge prohibitory control was evident in an ongoing move to drag out the aftermath of the great feasts – or at least of Easter – into a period of enforced idleness on the days following. This obviously created problems of enforcement of the Church's and the Abbey's ban on labour, because those April days were essential for agricultural and horticultural preparation. That is why, then, the same two industrious – or irreligious – brothers who had illicitly worked into a Saturday evening were arraigned for making a plough and cutting their hedges on the Wednesday of Easter week, and why others were condemned for ploughing on that forbidden Wednesday, which another woman further defiled by carrying manure and spreading it on her garden.[42] What we may term a kind of sabbatarian attitude to festivals also characterised the Abbey court's censures of the man who both carried wood on a holy day and made a shirt on All Saints' Day, of the woman who made bread on Whitsunday, and the inhabitants of Trawden and Wycoller who carried grain on a feast day.[43]

The reformist clergy who submitted their criticisms and recommendation in 1590 showed no concern whatever, in their single-minded drive to purify the Sabbath, for reverencing festivals. Far from it, they took umbrage at 'Popish ffastes and ffestivalles (now abrogated in the Church of England) duely observed in all these partes, and that with greater devotion then the Sabboth against which daies Crosses in streetes and high waies ar in many places ofte devowtly garnished and wax Candelles duely prepared'.[44] However, if the authors of the Lancashire reform manifesto of 1590 were prepared to surrender control even of those several festivals *not* 'abrogated in the Church of England', they seemed to be doing so, as it were, in exchange for extending ecclesiastical direction of Sunday as the 'sole red-letter day of the Puritan calendar'.[45] They demanded, in short, possession of the whole of that day, morning, afternoon and evening (though they laid no claim, as the Abbey's discipline had, to the Saturday vigil). First, they wanted the suppression of

Sunday trading, since by its means 'ffaires and markets in most Townes ar usually kepte uppon the Sabboth: by occasion whereof divine Service in the fforenoon is greatly neglected'.[46] Having thus laid claim to ownership of Sunday morning, the authors of *The State ... of Lancashire* proceeded to propose their possession of the afternoon of that day, so that 'the youthe will be brought to attend the Exercise of Catechizing'; it only remained to take over the evening, 'the people to be presentt at the Eveninge Service'.[47]

We may see, so far, then, that the pre-Reformation monks and the post-Reformation godly clergy both showed a strong desire to manage the way the laity spent their time on those days conventionally designated religious. There was a tendency to enlarge the hours dedicated to pious pursuits, the monks pushing Sunday back into a Saturday vigil and extending the Easter festival forwards into the week following, and the Puritan clergy impelling holy time forward to embrace the whole of the 'Lord's day'. A further distinction was that whereas the monastic regime insisted on the excision of work from the sacred calendar, the reform-minded Lancashire ministers setting out their proposals in *c.* 1590 foresaw the obliteration of pleasure from consecrated time – the elimination of 'Wackes [Wakes], Ales, Greenes, Maigames, Rushbearinge, Bearebaites, Doveales, Bonfiers, all maner [of] unalwfull Gaming, Pipinge and Daunsinge, and such like ... in all places frely exercised uppon the Sabboth'.[48]

It is, further, clear from the proposals made that the author of *The State ... of Lancashire* had in mind a social agenda of reform that was concerned with the moral tone and quality of the commonwealth. This agenda was to be implemented with the aid of the forces of law and order, whether the magistracy, the Court of High Commission or the Privy Council itself: the tribunal referred to in the peroration of the 1590s draft as 'your worships', those whose 'godly and wise consideration' was sought by the authors in indispensable support of their proposals.[49] The 1590 writers were utterly convinced that change must come about in the collective character of the dismal human raw material with which they were confronted. Though they found Lancastrians usurious, adulterous, drunken, popishly affected and consequently seditious, blasphemous and profane, they did not intend to leave them in that condition but insisted on having them transformed. Common offences such as swearing were 'no way punished or punishable'[50] but had been unchecked because ecclesiastical discipline was inadequate – excommunication, for example, being regarded with contempt. A tougher disciplinary regime, one perhaps combining state-and-church authority in a Genevan way, would need to be introduced to achieve the goals of reforming public morals. This sense of the need to act, with support as necessary from the civil authorities so as to rectify the moral condition of the 'state civil', formed an essential aspect of the set of assumptions that guided the trials of the Lancashire witches in 1612. These assumptions were that the evil in people must be driven out, severely, punitively and with the aid or initiative of the godly civil magistrate.

No such transformative ambitions characterised the proceedings of the Whalley Act Book, and that is partly because that document is the record of the proceedings of a court, while *The State... of Lancashire* was a conscious manifesto of socio-moral ameliorism. That said, it is possible to argue that the minutes of the Abbey court and the tenor of *The State ... of Lancashire* embody two irreconcilable concepts of human nature, and of its potential for change. The Act Book of Whalley Abbey contributed little in the way of a plan of campaign for altering people. For one thing, it was insouciant about 'structures', in ways that *The State ... of Lancashire*, with its acute diagnosis of the urgently reformable institutional arrangements of too few parish churches and too many dependent chapelries (Whalley's particular burden), was not.[51] More generally, the tenor of the Act Book's proceedings with regard to the various fallibilities and peccabilities of human nature was relaxed, whereas *The State ... of Lancashire* was often shrill in its insistence that the plasticity of humankind be remodelled.

Take, for example, the matter of the godly reformers' drive, aided by the civil authorities, to abolish within their moral manor the drunkenness that was 'maintayned by the multitude of Alehouses, and unresonable strength of Ale soulde with owte sise of Statute'.[52] On this issue the Abbey court's proceedings are silent – perhaps because the drunkenness of Lancastrians did increase in the course of the Tudor century, or perhaps because it ill-became an institution with such quaffing power as the Abbey possessed to censure drink in others, or (most likely) because the Abbey's overall approach to human sin was that of relatively calm acceptance of the fact that it existed. Such an attitude may perhaps have arisen from the personality of the presiding judge over much of that period, Prior Christopher Smith, flexible enough to accommodate himself to the Dissolution and therefore perhaps a man of detachment and tolerance. Indeed, the perceptive Edwardian editor of the Act Book detected a certain worldly-wise tolerance in its proceedings – 'a kindly, even paternal, jurisdiction, intimate and gossipy in its range and working, but orderly, beneficent, and wise in its quiescence as in its activity'.[53] 'Quiescence', indeed, seems to sum up the outlook and policy breathed in the Act Book proceedings.

The personal inclinations of the presiding judge at any one time notwithstanding, as with other medieval 'courts Christian', the jurisdictional presuppositions revealed in these transactions may well have been shaped by underlying views that the medieval Church had of sin and forgiveness. Central in this regard was the Church's Sacrament of Penance, a rite whose own vital assumption was and is that men and women sin and need from time to time to be rescued, absolved and penanced. The Abbey court of Whalley, unlike the Lancashire godly and radical social and moral reformers in about 1590, did not set out to eradicate sin's effects, but rather to limit its damage, penancing sin's committers with rites of repentance which were above all formal – and splendid. One rather spectacular adulterer, for example, was the central player in his own drama of penitence in a magnificent ceremony ordered to be played out in Clitheroe church and involving much kneeling, walking barefoot, presenting of candles and so on.[54] It was not of course that such penitential rituals could be everlastingly repeated, though they did provide certain mechanisms for tolerance lacking to the activists reformers of 1590 – Calvinists to whom devices of penance, absolution and satisfaction were theologically denied. To the latter's way of thinking, sin was not to be absolved, repeated and re-absolved: it was to be eradicated, as we have seen. And so the godly crusaders waged war on sin, relying on the collaboration of equally godly magistrates as appropriate. When this kind of coalition turned its attention to sin as witchcraft and to witchcraft as sin, the witch trial of 1612 was the outcome.

Although the 1590 reformist survey made no explicit mention of witchcraft – though it had plenty to say about popish superstition – in 1594 an outbreak of bewitching at the household of Nicholas Starkie of Huntroyd in Whalley parish gave rise to a debate on necromancy amongst godly and preaching ministers. This in turn led to the publication of the Puritan George More's A Discourse Concerning the Possession and Dispossession of 7 Persons of one Family in Lancashire (1600), which explained how godly ministers had succeeded in driving out the Devil from one afflicted household. Supplemented by James VI's Daemonologie (1597), this work assembled the theoretical framework on demonic possession within which the 1612 legal action could commence.[55] The English Reformation, opening with the obliteration of the monastic institution which had for centuries governed so many aspects of the lives of people within its extensive area of jurisdiction and control, removed a vital social agency from the Whalley region and replaced it with the power of the lay gentry families. Included amongst these were the Asshetons, who moved into possession of the Abbey lands, and the Nowells of Read, one of whose members, Alexander, went on to become a celebrated Dean of St Paul's, while Roger of that family was the leading spirit in the prosecution of the Lancashire witches in 1612, as Jonathan Lumby shows in his chapter in this collection. As far as ecclesiastical discipline was concerned, a relaxed and formal set of expectations held by monastic moral magistrates was replaced by new Protestant clerical demands for the intensive policing of public conduct, a line of interventionist approach that culminated in the Pendle dragnet of 1612.

Notes

1 For the size and history of the parish, see S. T. Taylor-Taswell, *Whalley Church and Abbey* (Blackburn: Blackburn Times, n.d.), part I, and Christopher Haigh, *Reformation and Resistance in Tudor Lancashire* (Cambridge: Cambridge University Press, 1975), pp. xii–xiii, 31,

148. For the area's economy, see Swain's chapter in this collection. For the later development of the parish, see Michael Snape, '"Oh happy reformation": Anglicanism and society in a northern parish, 1689–1789' (unpublished Ph.D. thesis, University of Birmingham, 1994).

2 Sir William Dugdale, *Monasticon Anglicanum: A History of the Abbies and Other Monasteries, Hospitals, Frieries, and Cathedral and Collegiate Churches, with their Dependencies in England and Wales* (London, 1655–73; London: James Bohn, 6 vols, 1846), i, p. 639.

3 *Valor Ecclesiasticus*, in Dugdale, *Monasticon*, v, p. 649.

4 The *compotus* lists in Thomas Dunham Whitaker, *History of the Original Parish of Whalley* (1801; 4th edn, ed. J. G. Nichols and P. A. Lyons, London: Routledge, 2 vols, 1872–76), i, p. 116.

5 *Valor Ecclesiasticus*, in Dugdale, *Monasticon*, v, p. 650.

6 Whitaker, *Whalley*, i, p. 101.

7 Whitaker, *Whalley*, i, pp. 121–2, 126 (reproducing the *compotus* lists), 106.

8 Whitaker, *Whalley*, i, p. 101.

9 Whitaker, *Whalley*, i, pp. 126–7, 130–1. My calculation of the Abbey's total red wine consumption is made on the basis of Whitaker's reckoning of the cost of a pipe (usually 105 gallons) of wine in 1504.

10 Whitaker, *Whalley*, i, p. 104.

11 The Examination of Robert Aske 1537, in Anthony Fletcher, *Tudor Rebellions* (London: Longman, 1968), p. 133.

12 Whitaker, *Whalley*, i, p. 99.

13 Whitaker, *Whalley*, i, p. 187.

14 Whitaker, *Whalley*, i, p. 189.

15 Whitaker, *Whalley*, i, p. 187.

16 Whitaker, *Whalley*, i, p. 119, and n. 1.

17 Whitaker, *Whalley*, i, pp. 193–9.

18 See, for example, Joyce Youings, *The Dissolution of the Monasteries* (London: Allen and Unwin / New York: Barnes and Noble, 1971), pp. 53–4.

19 Aske, in Fletcher, *Tudor Rebellions*, pp. 133–4.

20 Geoffrey Baskerville, *English Monks and the Suppression of the Monasteries* (London: Jonathan Cape, 1965), p. 29. Whalley certainly provided the banking facilities to which Aske alluded 'and also ther evidenses and mony left to the usses of infantes in abbeys handes': Fletcher, *Tudor Rebellions*, p. 134. Sir John Husee in 1524 deposited with the Abbey the vast sum of £300 tied up with the wardship and marriage of Lord Monteagle's son: Baskerville, *English Monks*, p. 34.

21 Whitaker, *Whalley*, i, p. 110.

22 Whitaker, *Whalley*, i, pp. 134, 110, 111. The Latin phrase is '*ratio attincturae Johannis nuper abb. ibm*'.

23 Smith secured the position for which Sussex had recommended him: in *c.* 1537 the demesne accounts registered an annual payment of £6 14s 4d in two instalments to the chantry priest in Whalley parish church 'Chris. Smith, clearke, proctor of the late monestery of Whaley': W. A. Hulton (ed.), *The Coucher Book or Chartulary of Whalley Abbey*, iv (Manchester: Chetham Society publications xx, 1849), p. 1190.

24 In Whitaker, *Whalley*, i, p. 185.

25 Hulton, *Coucher Book of Whalley Abbey*, iv, pp. 1184–90 (there are certain extra memoranda of assorted payments (p. 1190) but they add less than £1 to the overall accounts).

26 R. S. Schofield, 'The geographical distribution of wealth in England, 1334–1649', *Economic History Review*, 2nd series, 18 (1965), pp. 483–510.

27 Hulton, *Coucher Book of Whalley Abbey*, iv, p. 1197.

28 Whitaker, *Whalley* i, pp. 134–5; Hulton (ed.), *Coucher Book of Whalley Abbey*, iv, p. 1183.

29 Hulton (ed.), *Coucher Book of Whalley Abbey*, iv, p. 1176; Whitaker, *Whalley*, i, p. 1176.

30 For crypto-Catholicism, and outright Catholic recusancy, in Elizabethan Lancashire, see, *inter alia*, Christopher Haigh, 'The continuity of Catholicism in the English Reformation', *Past and Present* 93 (1981), pp. 37–69; J. A. Hilton, *Catholic Lancashire from Reformation to Renewal 1559–1991* (Chichester: Phillimore, 1994), ch. 1; J. S. Leatherbarrow, *The Lancashire Elizabethan Recusants* (Manchester: Chetham Society publications, new series lxxxx, 1947); Michael A. Mullett, *Catholics in Britain and Ireland, 1558–1829* (Basingstoke: Macmillan, 1998), ch. 1; and Anne C. Parkinson, *A History of Catholicism in the Furness Peninsula 1127–1997* (Lancaster: Lancaster University Centre for North West Regional Studies, 1998), ch. 2.

31 Whitaker, *Whalley*, i, pp. 209, 213, 213; Haigh, *Reformation and Resistance*, pp. 240–1.

32 Whitaker, *Whalley*, i, p. 13, n. 1

33 H. R. Trevor-Roper, *The European Witch-Craze of the Sixteenth and Seventeenth Centuries* (London: Penguin, 1969), pp. 67ff.

34 Alice M. Cook (ed.), *Act Book of the Ecclesiastical Court of Whalley 1510–1538* (Manchester: Chetham Society publications, new series xliv, 1901).

35 F. R. Raines (ed.), *The State, Civil and Ecclesiastical, of the County of Lancaster, about the Year 1590* (Manchester: Chetham Society publications xcvi, 1875), pp. 1–48.

36 Raines, *The State ... of Lancashire*, p. 12; Cook, *Act Book*, p. 16.

37 Cook, *Act Book*, pp. 54, 55, 59.

38 Raines, *The State ... of Lancashire*, p. 12.

39 Cook, *Act Book*, pp. 90, 55.

40 Raines, *The State ... of Lancashire*, p. 12.

41 Cook, *Act Book*, pp. 90–1.

42 Cook, *Act Book*, pp. 54, 16.

43 Cook, *Act Book*, p. 16.

44 Raines, *The State ... of Lancashire*, p. 2.

45 A. G. Matthews, cited in Michael Watts, *The Dissenters: From the Reformation to the French Revolution* (Oxford: Clarendon Press, 1978), p. 313.

46 Raines, *The State ... of Lancashire*, p. 2.

47 Raines, *The State ... of Lancashire*, p. 2.

48 Raines, *The State ... of Lancashire*, p. 2. 'Doveales' may mean drinking at Whitsun.

49 Raines, *The State ... of Lancashire*, p. 13.

50 Raines, *The State ... of Lancashire*, p. 12.

51 Raines, *The State ... of Lancashire*, p. 10, deplored, for example, 'The Chappelles of ease (which ar three times as many as the Parishe Churches, and more), through the backwardnes of the evil affected people in conferringe due maintenance to a minister'.

52 Raines, *The State ... of Lancashire*, p. 12.

53 Cook, *Act Book*, intro., p. xxiii.

54 Cook, *Act Book*, p. 8.

55 Edward Baines, *The History of the County Palatine of Lancaster*, 2 vols (London: Fisher, Son and Jackson, 1836), i, pp. 590–3. See also Jonathan Lumby, *The Lancashire Witch-Craze: Jennet Preston and the Lancashire Witches* (Preston: Carnegie, 1995), chs 22–23.

7

Beyond Pendle: the 'lost' Lancashire witches

Kirsteen Macpherson Bardell

In 1638 Thomas Hope, a blacksmith from Aspull, was formally accused of witchcraft and healing. In his statement, dated 11 May, he claimed that when he was ten years old his uncle took him to Rome where 'he was washed in a chamber with water by vertue of which water he hath helped horses, beasts, and sondrie children'. Christopher Leigh, a physician from Rumworth, complained to the authorities about Thomas after discovering that he had visited Christopher's patient Margery Mullineux and suspected that he had been up to no good.[1] This is just one example of a kind of magic which has been absent from the majority of texts on witchcraft beliefs: the practice of beneficial magic.

This chapter aims to address two areas which have been relatively neglected to a certain extent not only in studies of witchcraft in Lancashire, but in studies of early modern witchcraft beliefs across Europe. First, studies of witchcraft beliefs focus overwhelmingly upon malicious witchcraft or *maleficium*, neglecting to discuss the practices of those seen as good witches: cunning folk or wise people as they were known.[2] Secondly, many analyses of early modern witchcraft, including the most recent gender approaches, have tended to focus upon pamphlet literature or early modern drama.[3] This can give a distorted image of witchcraft beliefs, since these forms of literature also tend to concentrate upon acts of *maleficium*. Practitioners of beneficial or 'white' magic, then, are the 'lost' witches of this chapter.

Work on the witches of Lancashire has largely followed these two trends of focusing upon malicious witches and on pamphlet material, mainly due to the accessibility of the extremely readable *Wonderfull Discoverie of Witches* by Thomas Potts.[4] While this document is undoubtedly an important resource for learning about witchcraft beliefs in early modern Lancashire, discussion of witchcraft beliefs needs to be widened to involve popular belief in beneficial magic across the county. An examination of local Quarter Session court records as well as pamphlet sources is essential to learn more about these neglected practitioners of magical remedies.[5] Thomas Potts's work, like many other witchcraft pamphlets, provides a distorted image of witchcraft beliefs if considered alone. That is not to say that the information he presented was either deliberately inaccurate or sensationalised.[6] However, pamphlets did tend to focus on the more extreme cases which involved stereotypical elements such as wicked women suckling demon spirits and presenting a danger to neighbours' households and children.[7] These were clearly perceived to be more interesting stories for their public.

Potts discusses the cases of twenty-one accused witches in his work, but at least another hundred cases of witchcraft accusations can be found in the various court records of Lancashire. Other accounts may have been lost through the non-survival of many records; also it should be remembered that many more individuals might have been suspected but never formally accused. Potts's *Wonderfull Discoverie of Witches* provides relatively little information on the practices or use of cunning folk. This is not altogether surprising since court officials were only obliged to consider factors which would lead to a prosecution. Various accusations and confessions in the Lancashire Quarter Session court records reveal information about the popular reliance upon cunning folk, and also some detail about popular remedies and practices, both of which are rarely mentioned in pamphlet sources. Thus, examining endemic cases of witchcraft accusations in the court records provides a wider picture of popular witchcraft beliefs.

When we think of Lancashire witches we usually think of Demdike, Chattox and the Pendle witches of 1612, and they have to a certain extent been turned into a stereotype of the Lancashire witch. This discussion will highlight the practitioners of good, or white, magic who have been neglected in this stereotype, and thus lost to history, although it is part of the argument of this chapter that 'good' and 'bad' magic, like orthodox and popular religion, were inseparable and have to be understood together. This chapter will focus on three main, interlocking points: first, the importance of considering cunning folk; secondly, cunning folk and their practices; and finally, the practice of magic by the ordinary populace – a practice that later centuries came to see as 'folk magic'.

The lack of research into the practice of beneficial magic, which the mass of early modern people believed in and used widely, is detrimental to our understanding of witchcraft beliefs, since focusing solely on malicious witchcraft only gives us a very narrow image of popular beliefs in magic at this time. As Willem de Blecourt states, 'cunning folk are not deemed important enough to figure prominently in syntheses and introductions, which consequently points to their marginal place in ... historical works'. Cunning folk are typically ignored, neglected or placed in the context of the myth of their persecution in the witch trials. As de Blecourt argues, it is necessary to examine cunning folk to find out more about who they were, their practices, and why people continued to consult them.[8] Cunning folk were regarded as experts in dealing with the problem of witchcraft at the time, which makes their neglect by modern historians a very serious oversight. To ignore the role of those considered to be experts is to neglect a crucial element of witchcraft beliefs.

Issues surrounding popular belief and culture allow us not only to discover more about witchcraft beliefs in the community, but also to highlight factors pertinent to a gendered reading of the English witch trials. One theory, popular with feminist scholars of the 1970s, claimed that the witch trials constituted a direct attack on female healing by the male medical establishment.[9] Much of this surrounded what is now seen as the myth of the midwife-witch or female herbal healer which has been vigorously contested.[10] For instance, Rachel Hasted has used the Thomas Potts text to argue that there is no evidence of successful healing and no mention of medicinal herbs in the 1612 Pendle trial in particular.[11] However, many cases in the court records do highlight concerns with popular healing. Thus one of the questions which need to be addressed is whether we have been too quick to dismiss links between witchcraft and healing.

Material relating to witchcraft trials can be examined to highlight evidence of community beliefs in popular religion and these sources are also indicative of the confusion suffered by the common people over religious doctrine in the years following the Protestant Reformation. Witchcraft trial records reveal much about popular beliefs in early modern society, and the ways in which people made sense of their world, but to focus solely upon malicious witchcraft provides a narrow, and distorted, picture. It is necessary to consider the wider framework of popular religion and magic in order to understand the context in which witchcraft beliefs operated.

At this time, Europe was still recovering from the disruption of the Protestant and Catholic Reformations which had left the masses confused about the correct form of religious observance that would ensure their salvation and entrance to heaven. Importantly, in Protestant countries such as England, the Reformation had involved the destruction or removal of various quasi-magical props which the people could rely on in times of need – such as praying to certain saints, using holy water and relics, and going on pilgrimages to holy shrines. Thus the late medieval Catholic Church had cared for its flock both spiritually and physically, providing what many saw as magical remedies for their misfortunes. As Gamini Salgado puts it, 'the Church of England almost literally took the magic out of Christianity'.[12]

Despite the Protestant Reformation, there appears to have been much continuity of traditional religious practices across England into the seventeenth century and beyond. Traditional Catholic religious practices arguably appealed to the populace more because they were highly visual and ritualised, appearing almost magical. The people were familiar with these rituals, even if they did not fully understand them.[13] It could even be argued that the quasi-magical elements of traditional orthodox religion made more sense to an early modern mentality which perceived a world in which good and evil were personified as God and the Devil. Such a world could continue to be inhabited by witches, fairies, pixies and ghosts, and the services of cunning folk continued to be relevant. Significantly, most historical accounts of the witch trials ignore the fact that witchcraft was a reality in early modern perceptions, a reality which would have been shared by both accusers and accused.[14]

Many cases involving folk magic or petty sorcery were connected with forms of popular belief and religion. Keith Thomas's work indicated how the populace continued both to rely on cunning people in the community and to distinguish between white and black magic. This was despite the insistence of the elite groups, particularly Puritan writers, that, if anything, white magic was actually worse than black magic. They argued that since all magic was derived from the Devil, the practice of good magic ensnared the innocent as well as the wicked. Thomas argued that not only was there a continuing reliance on cunning people after the Reformation, but that it actually increased because the magical elements of Catholicism had been swept away leaving the people defenceless.[15] Changes in religious doctrine could also intensify the vulnerability of the populace in the face of events over which they had no control. As well as no longer having recourse to the quasi-magical rituals of Catholicism, the newer Protestant religious beliefs frowned on displays of grief and saw misfortune as punishment from God for sins committed.[16] Recourse to cunning folk and folk magic may thus have been a way of coping with, or adapting to, the Protestant Reformation.

Practitioners of white magic were referred to by several terms: cunning or wise folk, blessers, healers, charmers, and wizards. For the purposes of this chapter, these people have been grouped under the term 'cunning folk'. Many learned writers despised the appeal to 'cunning folk', and the use of counter-magic and folk magic by the populace. The author of a witchcraft pamphlet entitled *A True and Just Recorde*, which documented a large trial in St Osyth, Essex, in 1582, stressed that cunning folk were as ungodly as witches. He wished that 'sorcerers, wizards (or rather dizzards), witches, wise women … [should be] rigorously punished'. In 1608, the Puritan writer William Perkins claimed that the injuries caused by evil witches merely led their victims to seek help from white witches who did 'a thousandfold more harm then the former' by luring the innocent to sin. He stated that 'Of bad and good witches … the more horrible and detestable is the good witch … it were a thousand times better for the land if all witches, but specifically the blessing witch, might suffer death'. John Stearne noted in 1648 that 'all witches be bad, and ought to suffer alike, being both in league with the Devill'.[17]

Again, in 1680 John Brinley wrote bemoaning the tendency of 'ignorant and Narrow-sould' people to resort to cunning people and witches, claiming that 'these sort of abused people have as many Followers as the greatest Divines'. His purpose in writing his book *A Discovery of the Impostures of Witches and Astrologers* was 'to undeceive the people, and to shew them that it is altogether Unlawful to have recourse to such men, who practise unlawful Arts; that is in all Trials, Crosses, and Afflictions whatever, God alone is to be sought after'. He deplored the fact that common people attributed their misfortunes to witchcraft, which led them either to seek a blessing from the cunning man or to accuse 'the next Old-woman'. He continued, stating that:

> These are such as we usually call White Witches, a sort of Sots who being Gull'd, and having their understandings Debauch'd by Superstition, do evil that good may come of it, that is use Charms, Spells and Incantations (all of which are of no force without the Cooperation of the Devil) to remove Dis-tempers, and do certain Feats in some measure useful to mankind yet of pernicious consequence to themselves.[18]

These are just a few examples of the more learned view at this time that all magic was evil, whether used for harm or good, since all magical power was demonic in origin. Significantly, the majority of these learned writers were radical Protestants or Puritans, so they had a vested interest in condemning cunning folk who could be seen as challenging the Church's authority by serv-icing the people's needs.

There was no clear-cut distinction between an elite view and a popular view of this issue; in general, however, the common people continued to rely on cunning people in the community, and continued to distinguish between white and black magic. The only times when the two belief systems converged was in cases where healers became suspected of using their powers to harm, which supported elite discourse about the ultimate evil source of all magic.[19] Moreover, even the more learned sections of society were not unanimous in condemning cunning folk or healers. This emphasises the complexity of beliefs about magic across the social spectrum.

Recourse to cunning folk appears to have been a frequent, and accept-able, reaction to illness and misfortune in the community, although resorting to any kind of witch or sorcerer was against the law. Relatively few people were punished for consulting with sorcerers. Those who were punished were usually ordered to do penance, a humiliating punishment which involved making a public apology for one's sins. Most were dismissed with a warning. Moreover, justices appear to have been reluctant to prosecute cunning folk, perhaps because they were popular and well thought of in the community.[20] Cunning folk tended to be prosecuted mostly when they were suspected of using their powers to harm, or when they were believed to be swindling people out of money.

Very few cunning folk appear to have been prosecuted as witches, probably due to their reputation for doing good, and because their clients often appeared unwilling or unable to name them. In various cases the person resorted to was not named, perhaps to protect their identity in an acknowledgement of the court's mistrust of these people, or to avoid prosecution of the client. John Willson, a freemason from Ellel near Lancaster, who believed himself to have been bewitched by Jennett Wilkinson, deposed on 20 August 1629 that 'suspectinge hee was bewitched hee sent his wyfe twoe severall tymes to a woman whose name hee knoweth not who dwelleth in Forton, which was holden to be a skillfull woman'. John may have genuinely not known her name, or could have been protecting her identity, but he certainly knew where to turn for help in this situation. The woman apparently told John's wife that he was indeed forspoken, or bewitched, and that she would heal him. However, she herself refused to reveal the identity of the guilty witch, saying the 'shee would not tell for a thousand pounds'.[21]

From the evidence that survives, it appears that cunning folk in Lancashire were predominantly consulted either as a source of information or for healing services. Cases involving fortune-tellers are more apparent in the records of other English counties, but there is very little evidence of such practices in Lancashire apart from reports in John Harland and T. T. Wilkinson's *Lancashire Folk-lore*, published in 1882.[22] It is difficult to find out about cunning folk since they generally left no records of their activities, so we have to use diaries, court records, treatises and pamphlets. These were usually written by their critics, so it is difficult to establish a balanced view.[23]

There seems to have been a common knowledge of who had magical skills, and this was evidently based upon reputation of their activities and their outcome. People relied on cunning folk for help when they believed that they were bewitched. The cunning person might then help them to find out who it was that had bewitched them, and might employ some counter-magic to attempt to counteract the bad magic. Thus, cunning folk were experts who people could turn to if they believed that they had become the target of malicious witchcraft. The recourse to cunning folk for their expertise in cases of suspected witchcraft can be seen in Potts's *Wonderfull Discoverie of Witches*, in the information given by Peter Chaddock of Windle against Isabel Roby, his wife's godmother, on 12 July 1612. Peter consulted 'one *James*, a Glover' of the same town four years previously when he got pains in his neck after his wife argued with Isabel, whom they suspected to be a witch. James said that he would pray for him, and in four or five days Peter recovered. Peter called for James again when he found that he was unable to drink, when James repeated the following charm: 'take that drinke, and in the name of the *Father*, the *Sonne*, and the *Holy Ghost*, drinke it, saying; The Devill and Witches are not able to prevaile against GOD and his Word'. Peter again recovered, although he claimed to have fallen sick again since.[24] Significantly, this indicates the frequent adoption of religious phraseology into popular religion and folk magic, which appears to have been a common way of adding legitimacy and a sense of ritual to popular remedies. Peter Chaddock's wife also consulted a wise man, named Hasleworth, who reassured her that Isabel was not a witch. However, she continued to believe that Peter would not recover until he had asked for Isabel's forgiveness.[25]

In a further example, in May 1638 the healer Thomas Hope of Aspull confessed to advising Margery Mullineux not to lend Isabell Hyton anything 'but that she should first put salt into itt', the inference being that Isabell was a suspicious person and that all items would have to be protected before she handled them.[26] These cases underline the popular reliance on cunning folk in cases where malevolent witchcraft was suspected, supporting the argument that cunning folk were more prevalent in helping to identify witches than as actual victims of the trials.

People also visited cunning folk to find out information about lost and stolen items. They might be able to identify the thief, perhaps using local gossip or the victim's existing suspicions, or suggest where the items might be found. Thomas Horrocks, the vicar of Broughton, in Craven, was reported to the authorities in the 1570s for claiming to discover the whereabouts of stolen goods using magical means, and was reputed to be a wizard.[27] On 21 August 1634, Lewis and William Rigby of Upholland petitioned the JPs claiming that they had been wrongfully accused of the murder of Humphrey Morecroft of Scarisbrook. Humphrey's friends had consulted John Garnet, then being held on suspicion of witchcraft at Lancaster, 'to knowe what was becomen of him', and Garnet had alleged that Morecroft had been killed and thrown into the marl-pits in Upholland, where the Rigbys worked.[28]

Many of those associated with benevolent forms of magic were particularly known for their skill in healing or blessing. There were a number of people acting as unofficial healers who appear to have been well known in the community for healing both animals and people. Local healers were necessary, as trained practitioners, doctors, apothecaries and barber-surgeons were relatively scarce in rural areas, and were too expensive for most people. Doctors could charge between £1 and £30 at a time when the average yearly income of labourers, schoolmasters and carpenters was between £4 and £20. Therefore, only the wealthiest 5–10 per cent of the population could afford to seek their help.[29] There was no clear-cut distinction between techniques used by professional and lay healers. A 1542 Act conceded that there were 'divers honest persons, as well men as women, whom God hath endowed with the knowledg of the nature kind and operation of certain herbs, roots and waters, and the using and ministering to them to such as be pained with customable disease'.[30]

Evidence of the range of herbal remedies that were used in the home can be seen in the rising numbers of herbals and medical books produced in English, and in diaries, household accounts and recipe books.[31] A variety of herbs thought 'to have a vertue to dispell the power of witch-craft' were in popular use across Europe. One herb thought to be very useful in repelling the power of evil was St John's Wort, now widely used as a herbal anti-depressant; others used were vervain and mugwort.[32] This highlights how the belief in witchcraft was a part of early modern life, another matter to deal with in the best way possible using a range of remedies.[33]

When self-help proved ineffective, people frequently turned to local healers and cunning folk who used a mixture of herbal remedies, charms and spells. Cunning folk often charged little or nothing for their services and were readily accessible. Where healing really upset the authorities was when those healing appeared to be using magical means to cure the patient, whether human or animal. Those known as healers often used religious terminology in their cures and this could result in them being brought before the ecclesiastical courts for challenging the church's position. The local church authorities mistrusted recourse to these popular practitioners. That people were believed to have healing talents, and that others were prepared to pay for them, presented a danger to orthodoxy and uniformity which the authorities were keen to eradicate.

The two main protagonists in the 1612 Pendle trial, Anne Whittle and Elizabeth Southerns, alias Chattox and Demdike, were associated with healing or blessing activities, but these stories were still framed in such a way as to portray the women in a bad light. Alizon Device deposed on 23 March 1612 that John Nutter asked her grandmother, Elizabeth Southerns, to heal his sick cow, but that she believed Elizabeth had bewitched it to death instead.[34] Anne Whittle confessed on 2 April 1612 to healing and counter-magic activities. She claimed that when she was asked to help the wife of John Moore whose drink was apparently bewitched, she used the following charm:

Three Biters hast thou bitten,
The Hart, ill Eye, ill tonge:
Three bitter shall be thy Boote,
Father, Sonne, and Holy Ghost
a Gods name.
Five Pater-nosters, five Avies,
and a Creede,
In worship of five wounds
of our Lord.

However, Mrs Moore subsequently became 'grieved at her', so Anne sent her demon familiar Fancy to bite one of her cows in the head, which subsequently went mad and died six weeks later.[35] These accounts indicate Elizabeth and Anne's reputations as healers in the community, but that accordingly they were also believed to be able to use this power to kill. Again, this case provides further evidence of the use of religious terms in healing. The trial documents of the 1612 Pendle case also refer to the use of two other charms, notably to get drink and to cure the bewitched. Both of these charms incorporated traditional religious terminology, the former referring to the sign of the crucifix (*'Crucifixus hoc signum vitam Eternam. Amen'* or 'This cross is the sign of eternal life. Amen'), the second also in the form of a prayer.[36]

Those at a higher level of society sometimes used cunning folk as well as doctors, indicating the recourse to several types of treatments in times of illness or misfortune. Accounts of the last illness of Ferdinando, the Earl of Derby, at Latham in early April 1594 referred to his use of remedies such as 'Bezars stone, and Unicornes horne' and mentioned four physicians attending to him. Furthermore, the account refers to 'a homely woman, about the age of fifty yeeres ... mumbling in a corner of his honoures chamber, but what God knoweth. This woman ... seemed often to ease his honor, both of his vomiting and hickocke.' Despite her apparent effectiveness, she left after being caught blessing herbs by one of the physicians.[37] This description of the woman mumbling is very similar to Potts's description of Anne Whittle, or Chattox, 'her lippes ever chattering and walking: but no man knew what'.[38] As with the case involving Thomas Hope of Aspull at the beginning of this chapter, it is clear that many physicians did not look too kindly upon cunning folk and their practices since they were regarded as competition. Ferdinando's mother, Margaret, had herself previously written of her use of cures prepared by cunning folk in 1580, for which she was apparently criticised.[39]

In several cases, people appear to have resorted to cunning folk and witches when recourse to other means, including physicians and clerics, had failed. For instance, it was only after spending around £200 in doctors' fees, and consulting a variety of doctors and priests for advice, that Mr Starkie of Leigh, Lancashire, called on Edmund Hartley, known as a conjuror and white witch, for help in curing his sick children in 1596. Hartley was said to have 'used certaine popish charmes and hearbes' to heal the children, but was later hung for witchcraft when the children failed to recover.[40]

The Quarter Sessions court records of Lancashire highlight several cases involving healing and magic. Mary Shawe of Crofte was presented on 22 July 1630 for healing. Anne Urmeston deposed that Mary told her 'that shee might gyve god thankes for her amendment, for shee hadd not amended but for other helpe'. Mary's claim to have personal knowledge of another's health and well-being would itself have been perceived as suspicious, as it showed inappropriate over-interest in other people's affairs. Apparently, Mary further told Anne that she had cured Nicholas Hadfield's pig, claiming that 'she hadd done good, and never did any Hurt, but that shee could doe some litle thinges, but never tooke any money, but what they would geve her of good will'. Anne reported that Mary was 'very sicke' after healing the pig. Robert Gaskell deposed that he had seen Mary 'helpe upp a Cow of the said Nicholas Hadfeilds, but did not see her ... use any Charme to his knowledge, but further saith that shee ys generallie suspected to bee a blesser'. Nicholas Hadfield himself reported that she healed his pig with 'some swyne grasse ... in sweete milke'.[41] This case demonstrates that Mary's healing activities were well-known by her neighbours, and also that she was quick to insist that she was not making any monetary gain out of these actions. This seems to have been a device which people used, when presented before the courts, to make it clear that they were not merely extorting money through their activities but were acting for good.[42]

In a similar case, Henry Baggilie of Oldham was examined by the authorities on 26 May 1634, when he confessed to healing people and animals. He too appears to have had a widespread reputation for his activities. Henry claimed to have been taught a charm by his father, who was himself taught the charm by a Dutchman. This charm, like many others surviving from Lancashire, referred to the Holy Trinity (Father, Son and Holy Ghost), the Lord's Prayer and the Creed. Henry stated that 'frequently for theese two yeares last paste ... people have come to him ... to bless there freindes or cattell', and that 'what hee hath blessed hath recovered and that he hath onely receaved Meale, or sheep, or comodities of that nature but never did take silver or anie other [payment]'. A note written at the bottom of this deposition states 'witchcrafte'. Like Mary Shawe above, Henry was thus at pains to stress that he made little financial gain from his talents, and that furthermore during his blessing activities he 'hath alwaies beene suddenlie taken with sicknes ... alwaies in the same manner that the man or beasts that hee blessed was trobled withall'.[43] Again, the evidence indicates that healers had a widespread reputation in the community but that this ambiguous connection with magic could turn into suspicion of something more malevolent.

The mother of Richard Nuttall, of Great Bolton, also appears to have been connected with healing or knowledge of counter-magic. When brought to the house of William Chisnall in 1634, whom she was suspected of bewitching after he insulted her, she said that she would help him but that 'she could not tell when she could come because that she was very busy for that a man had ridden his horse six dayes about to get some body to helpe his wife beinge overwrought [bewitched]'.[44] This indicates both her widespread reputation for aiding the bewitched, and that she was believed to have the power to bewitch in the first instance. Thus the ambiguous, and vulnerable, reputation which healers cultivated is clear. These examples indicate that in some cases a reputation for healing could lead to suspicion of harmful magic; however it is evidently not the case, as some feminists have argued, that female healers as a group were targeted in the witch trials. Many other cunning folk undoubtedly practised without suspicion, but unfortunately often the only evidence we have is of those who became suspected of evil deeds.

It was not just the cunning folk who practised magic; the ordinary populace also practised counter-magic. Using methods of counter-magic to counteract malicious witchcraft was regarded as problematic by learned writers, since the use of counter-magic, in effect, reduced the distinction between witches and their victims, turning the victims into witches too. As well as a popular knowledge of whom to turn to for help of this kind, there also appears to have been a popular knowledge of techniques to use if witchcraft was suspected in the neighbourhood. There were various types of counter-magic carried out by both cunning folk and ordinary people. Popular methods included burning or boiling afflicted items that were bewitched (such as household goods), or burning items belonging to the suspected witch (such as hair, nails, pieces of clothing). It was believed that if items belonging to a witch were burned she would appear; this could be used as evidence in court.

A common technique of counter-magic was scratching the suspected witch above the mouth to break the bad magic. This resulted in a number of such attacks being included as evidence in court cases, particularly if the scratching was successful and the bewitched person appeared to recover.[45] A petition exists in the Lancashire Quarter Sessions records from October 1661 which involves a complaint about a suspected witch, referring to the mother of a sick child who was 'tought to get blud ... to cure the child and shee did go and the child recovered well'.[46] This provides a clear image of the obvious fear felt both by suspected witches and their victims. It is just one example, but there were undoubtedly many vigilante attacks such as this which were not formally reported to the courts. This demonstrates how knowledge of counter-magic, as well as where to find help from cunning folk, was widespread in the community.

A popular form of magic practised across England, and also in Europe, was the finding of lost or stolen goods through divination, often through use of the 'sieve and shears', during which the sieve was balanced on top of the shears and was believed to spin if the correct name or place was mentioned. Various religious terms were adopted in this ritual, which explains why the ecclesiastical authorities deplored it.[47] Practising magic of this kind was strongly disliked by the authorities, and could be directly linked to accusations of witchcraft. On 11 August 1641, Alice Scholfield of Castleton, near Rochdale, confessed before the Quarter Sessions court to divining to test for pregnancy and to discover the whereabouts of stolen goods by 'the devellish practiseing with a sive & a paire of sheeres', stating that:

> she did learne to set the sive and a pare of sheeres of Jane Brearly alias Ogden. And that together with the sayd Jane did practise to know whether Mary Feilden ... were with child. And whether the said Jane Brearley ... were with Child. And who stole James Newbold his sheepe – and who stole John Feilden his hen. And that the sive did turne about when John Chadwicke of Belfield, and Samuell Greene alias Nichaltie his servant were named.

Jane Brearley claimed that during this ritual 'Alis Scholfeild did use many strang words, which this Examinant did not nowe nor understand', and Mary

Fielden of Belfield deposed that 'the syd Ales did say divers words wch were to this effect. That if Samuel Greane al[ias] Nichaltie stoule the hen Saint Peter sayd soe, St Paule sayd noe.'[48] This case demonstrates the authorities' mistrust of these types of activities associated with popular belief, and which, in some cases, seemed suspiciously like remnants of Catholicism. There seems to have been widespread knowledge of these types of magic; the use of the sieve and shears for divination purposes is mentioned in the court records of several English counties.

The use of religious terms in magic has been noted in many of the cases discussed above. This highlights the continuity of traditional religion through attempts to adopt, translate or assimilate orthodox religious terms into people's lives. In several cases this could be seen as latent Catholicism, particularly so in a county such as Lancashire which was notable for the survival of more traditional belief. People engaged in healing appear to have used these religious terms in an attempt to add some legitimacy to their actions, or to add to the magical feel of their rituals. Clive Holmes has argued that the apparent ability of cunning people to use these religious symbols added to their efficacy in the eyes of the people, while Robin Briggs notes that religious language was seen as a vehicle of power.[49] For instance, Henry Baggilie of Oldham deposed on 26 May 1634 that his father had taught him to use the following words to heal: 'I tell thou forspoken Toothe and Tonge: Hearte and Heart Aike: Three thinges thee Boote moste the father, Sonne, and Holighoste with the Lordes praier and the Beleeve three tymes over'. He also stated that he 'pronounced the wordes and praiers aforesd in utteringe of wch wordes and duringe all the tyme of his blessinge'.[50] This charm is of course very similar to the charm Anne Whittle used to cure bewitched drink in 1612, mentioned earlier. Thomas Hope of Aspull, Lancashire, was possibly attempting to protect his reputation when he told Margery Mullineux in 1638 that he healed 'by the name of Jesus'.[51]

Remnants of healing remedies from around 1750 also involve religious terms. A remedy to stop bleeding in people or animals states that the following words should be recited:

> There was a Man Born in Bethlem of Judea whose name was called Christ Baptized in the River Jordan In the Water of the flood and this Child also was Meak and good and as the Watter Stood so I Desire thee the Blood of Such a person or Beast to stand in their Bodie in the name of the Father Son and Holy Ghost.

This charm aimed to turn powder into blood in a rag to stop bleeding in the victim, and was accompanied by a cure for burns or scalds.[52] Several charms dating from the eighteenth century have been discovered across Lancashire for such uses as curing cows and protecting the occupant against evil spirits.[53] Evidently the use of magical charms for healing and counter-magic, many adopting religious terms, continued not only through the seventeenth century but also well into the eighteenth.

People continued to visit cunning folk up well into the nineteenth century. As well as local healers and practitioners, there were a number of travelling practitioners known as charlatans, mountebanks, quacks, conjurors, and tooth drawers who would travel from place to place, often with markets and fairs, and offer a range of medicines and cures with varying degrees of success.[54] People continued to use cunning folk for help in identifying suspected witches, and used methods of counter-magic well into the nineteenth century. John Harland and T. T. Wilkinson reported in 1882 that 'the wise man and woman (the white witches of our ancestors) still continue their investigations of truth, undisturbed by the rural police or the progress of the schoolmaster'.[55] The 1736 Witchcraft Act repealed the old witchcraft legislation of 1604, so that people could no longer be prosecuted for malevolent witchcraft; instead it became an offence to deceive others by pretending to have magical powers. Despite this, people continued to believe in witchcraft, good and bad, and increasingly had to rely on self-help since the suspect could no longer be prosecuted through the courts. This sometimes led to vigilante activities against suspected witches.[56]

There are examples of cunning folk practising right up until the early twentieth century. Although they may not have been referred to explicitly as cunning people, they were offering similar types of advice and herbal remedies, though perhaps not so many magical charms. Folk medicine (as it was now thought of) really declined in the nineteenth century as a more rational scientific approach spread, as medical science improved, and as people increasingly turned to doctors for help. Methods of folk medicine and magic were increasingly seen as superstitious and ignorant, and cunning folk were more rigorously punished by the local authorities, which saw them as exploiting and duping the people.[57] After the Second World War and the development of a National Health Service folk medicine all but disappeared, particularly in urban areas.

This chapter has demonstrated that research into the practices of cunning folk and the use of folk magic is necessary for a fuller understanding of witchcraft beliefs in early modern England. To focus solely upon witch trials and crimes of *maleficium* provides only a narrow view of what constituted witchcraft in this period. Furthermore, to ignore the role of those considered as experts in dealing with witchcraft in the community is to neglect a crucial element of witchcraft beliefs. Cunning folk were seen as one of a range of sources of useful help and advice, and even the more learned sections of the populace were not unanimous in condemning them. Recourse to cunning folk was evidently seen to be a common, acceptable and legitimate reaction to lingering illnesses and misfortunes for which there appeared to be no normal explanation. This demonstrates that people in the community clearly continued to differentiate between black and white magic, despite the efforts of many Puritan clerics to convince them otherwise.

As has been demonstrated, cunning folk were clearly popular, which is another reason why they were so disliked by the authorities besides the argument that all magic was demonic at source. The majority of the people involved in these cases do not appear to have been using these practices to challenge the Church or the medical profession directly, although there were clearly times when the authority of the Church or orthodox medicine was found lacking. This appears to support Keith Thomas's assertion that people increasingly turned to cunning people after the Protestant Reformation swept away recourse to other 'magical' remedies offered by the Catholic Church, and that these practices increased, paradoxically, as a result of the Protestant Reformation. As well as practices carried out by cunning people, the Lancashire court records have been shown to be a valuable source of evidence about various kinds of magic carried out by amateurs as well as cunning people on a wide scale.

Thus what we see in these cases is a continuation of older traditional magical practices in the face of, or perhaps in direct response to, religious change. Certainly, the frequent use of Catholic religious terms and symbols used in the practices of cunning folk demonstrates a continuing popular desire for religious or quasi-magical remedies. This is especially prevalent in Lancashire cases, since, as has been noted, Catholicism remained entrenched in the county long after its decline in other parts of England.[58] The cases discussed here also provide evidence of people's concern for knowledge and order in their lives. Not only does this not appear to have been addressed by the newer Protestant religion, but the need for it actually increased due to the confusion inherent in the process of major religious change.

Evidence has been provided of the popular reliance upon, and trust in, popular healers in the community, who could be turned to in order to provide remedies for witchcraft. Healers were essential practitioners of both human and animal health in the community. It is indisputable that in a number of Lancashire cases an ambiguous reputation and connection with magic could provoke suspicion of wrongdoing. However, to concentrate solely on these cases could give a distorted image since we have no method of determining how many cunning folk or healers practised without ever falling under suspicion. The frequent references to the reliance upon cunning folk and healers suggest that the practitioners who appear in these records constitute a small minority of those who existed, and whose services were widely valued. Thus it is not the case that healers as a group were deliberately targeted in the witch trials. The common people were undoubtedly more concerned with the danger of *maleficium*, from which the cunning folk provided some reassurance and hope of remedy.

This chapter has demonstrated the complexity of early modern witchcraft beliefs, and the necessity of looking beyond the Pendle trials to examine the practice of beneficial magic which has been neglected in studies of the witch trials not only in Lancashire, but across Europe. This underlines the necessity of considering non-pamphlet as well as pamphlet evidence, as the former provides much more evidence on the practices of cunning folk and popular magic. Further research into beneficial magic in other counties will enable us to understand better the range of early modern popular magical beliefs and practices, to explain why they survived for so long after the decline of the witch trials, and to put the belief in demonic witchcraft into context. For the moment they remain an elusive, but necessary component of understanding magical beliefs in the early modern mental world.

Notes

Many thanks to Ray Bardell, and to colleagues at the University of Wolverhampton and Notting-ham Trent University who have commented on earlier versions of this chapter.

1 Lancashire Record Office (hereafter LRO), QSB 1/202/89, 1/202/33, 38.
2 Notable exceptions being Keith Thomas, *Religion and the Decline of Magic: Studies in Popular Beliefs in Sixteenth- and Seventeenth-Century England* (1971; London: Penguin, 1973), especially ch. 8; Alan Macfarlane, *Witchcraft in Tudor and Stuart England: A Regional and Comparative Study* (1970; 2nd edn, London: Routledge, 1999), especially ch. 8; E. Rothenberg, 'The cunning folk in witchcraft trials, 1560–1700' (unpublished M.Stud. dissertation, University of Oxford, 1999).
3 Marianne Hester, *Lewd Women and Wicked Witches: A Study of the Dynamics of Male Domination* (London: Routledge, 1992); Deborah Willis, *Malevolent Nurture: Witch-Hunting and Maternal Power in Early Modern England* (Ithaca and London: Cornell University Press, 1995); F. E. Dolan, *Dangerous Familiars: Representations of Domestic Crime in England 1550–1700* (London: Cornell University Press, 1995); Diane Purkiss, *The Witch in History: Early Modern and Twentieth-Century Interpretations* (London: Routledge, 1996).
4 With the exception of Jonathan Lumby, *The Lancashire Witch-Craze: Jennet Preston and the Lancashire Witches* (Preston: Carnegie, 1995), ch. 20.
5 This argument, in fuller form, is presented in K. Macpherson Bardell, '"Death by divelishe demonstracion": witchcraft beliefs, gender and popular religion in the early modern midlands and north of England' (unpublished Ph.D. thesis, Nottingham Trent University, 1999), ch. 6 in particular.
6 For further discussion of whether pamphlets can be seen as sensational, see Marion Gibson, *Reading Witchcraft: Stories of Early English Witches* (London: Routledge, 1999); Barbara Rosen, *Witchcraft* (London: Edward Arnold, 1969), pp. 20–1; M. J. Gaskill, 'Attitudes to crime in early modern England, with special reference to witchcraft, coining and murder' (unpublished Ph.D. thesis, University of Cambridge, 1994), pp. 46–7.
7 Macpherson Bardell, '"Death by divelishe demonstracion"', chs 3–4.
8 W. de Blecourt, 'Witch doctors, soothsayers and priests: on cunning folk in European historiography and tradition', *Social History* 19: 3 (Oct. 1994), pp. 285–303.
9 Feminist and gendered approaches focus on explaining why around 90 per cent of those accused of witchcraft were women. B. Ehrenreich and D. English, *Witches, Midwives and Nurses: A History of Women Healers* (New York: Feminist Press, 1973), p. 13; R. A. Horsley, 'Who were the witches? The social roles of the accused in the European witch

trials', *Journal of Interdisciplinary History* 9 (1979), pp. 689–715; T. S. Szasz, *The Manufacture of Madness: A Comparative Study of the Inquisition and the Mental Health Movement* (London: Routledge, 1971), pp. 82–94; J. Ussher, *Women's Madness: Misogyny or Mental Illness?* (Hemel Hempstead: Harvester Wheatsheaf, 1991), pp. 56–8; G. Heinsohn and O. Steiger, 'The elimination of medieval birth control and the witch trials of modern times', *International Journal of Women's Studies* 3 (May/June 1982), p. 204; Andrea Dworkin, *Woman Hating* (New York: E. P. Dutton, 1975), p. 140; A. Barstow, *Witchcraze: A New History of the European Witch Hunts* (London: Harper Collins, 1995), pp. 109–27; T. R. Forbes, 'Midwifery and witchcraft', *Journal of the History of Medicine and Allied Sciences* 17 (1962), p. 280.

10 M. Green, 'Women's medical practice and health care in medieval Europe', *Signs* 14: 2 (1989), pp. 434, 449–51, 454; David Harley, 'Historians as demonologists: the myth of the midwife witch', *Journal of the Society for the Social History of Medicine* 3 (1990), p. 1; E. H. Ackernecht, 'Midwives as experts in court', *Bulletin of the New York Academy of Medicine* 3 (1976), pp. 1224–8; T. R. Forbes, 'A jury of matrons', *Medical History* 32: 1 (1988), pp. 23–33; Lucinda M. Beier, *Sufferers and Healers: The Experience of Illness in Seventeenth-Century England* (London: Routledge, 1987), pp. 15–19, 44, 211–17.

11 Rachel Hasted, 'The new myth of the witch', *Trouble and Strife* 2 (Spring 1982), pp. 9–17; Rachel Hasted, 'Mothers of invention', *Trouble and Strife*, 7 (Winter 1985), pp. 22–5.

12 Gamini Salgado, *The Elizabethan Underworld* (Stroud: Sutton, 1997), p. 73.

13 Christopher Haigh, *Reformation and Resistance in Tudor Lancashire* (Cambridge: Cambridge University Press, 1975); C. Haigh, *English Reformations: Religion, Politics and Society Under the Tudors* (Oxford: Clarendon Press, 1993); and C. Haigh, 'The continuity of Catholicism in the English Reformation', Ronald Hutton, 'The local impact of the Tudor Reformations', and David Palliser, 'Popular reactions to the Reformation during the years of uncertainty 1530–70', all in C. Haigh (ed.), *The English Reformation Revised* (Cambridge: Cambridge University Press, 1987); J. J. Scarisbrick, *The Reformation and the English People* (Oxford: Blackwell, 1994). Hutton has indicated the survival of various 'traditional' practices into the nineteenth century in his 'The English Reformation and the evidence of folklore', *Past and Present* 148 (1995), pp. 89–116.

14 Exceptions are A. L. Rowse, *The Elizabethan Renaissance: The Life of the Society* (London: Sphere Books, 1974), chs 8–9; Thomas, *Religion and the Decline of Magic*, chs 2–6; Patricia Crawford, *Women and Religion in England 1500–1720* (London: Routledge, 1993), pp. 98–102; Robin Briggs, *Witches and Neighbours: The Social and Cultural Context of European Witchcraft* (London: Harper Collins, 1996), pp. 102–4; Purkiss, *The Witch in History*, pp. 154–5; Gaskill, 'Attitudes to crime', pp. 35, 73; James Sharpe, *Instruments of Darkness: Witchcraft in England 1550–1750* (London: Hamish Hamilton, 1996), pp. 37, 58–9, 66–70, 250, 282.

15 Thomas, *Religion and the Decline of Magic*, pp. 493–501; Macfarlane, *Witchcraft in Tudor and Stuart England*, p. 204.

16 Willis, *Malevolent Nurture*, pp. 60–3.

17 W. W., *A True and Just Recorde, of the Information, Examination and Confession of all the Witches, Taken at S. Oses in the Countie of Essex* (London, 1582); Perkins, cited in Rowse, *The Elizabethan Renaissance*, p. 302; J. Stearne, *A Confirmation and Discovery of Witch Craft* (London, 1648), pp. 7–8. Perkins's views on cunning folk are discussed further in Lumby, *The Lancashire Witch-Craze*, pp. 110–14.

18 J. Brinley, *A Discovery of the Impostures of Witches and Astrologers* (London, 1680), pp. 4–5, 15, 45.

19 Thomas claims that cunning folk were treated relatively leniently by the courts: *Religion and the Decline of Magic*, pp. 291–5, 306; Willis, *Malevolent Nurture*, pp. 27–8; Briggs, *Witches and Neighbours*, pp. 121–30, 171–86; de Blecourt, 'Witch doctors, soothsayers and priests',

p. 297; C. Holmes, 'Popular Culture? Witches, magistrates, and divines in early modern England', in S. L. Kaplan (ed.), *Understanding Popular Culture: Europe from the Middle Ages to the Nineteenth Century* (Berlin: Mouton, 1984), pp. 102–3; Briggs, *Witches and Neighbours*, p. 116.

20 Macfarlane, *Witchcraft in Tudor and Stuart England*, found sixty-one possible cunning folk in Essex, while Rothenberg, 'Cunning folk', discovered just seventeen cases of cunning folk involved in witch trials across the Home Assize Circuit, Northern Assize Circuit and reported in sixty-six witchcraft pamphlets.

21 LRO, QSB 1/64/21.

22 J. Harland and T. T. Wilkinson, *Lancashire Folk-lore* (1882; reprinted Wakefield: S. R. Publishers, 1972), pp. 121–6, 165.

23 Macfarlane, *Witchcraft in Tudor and Stuart England*, p. 120.

24 Thomas Potts, *The Wonderfull Discoverie of Witches in the Countie of Lancaster* (London, 1613), T3.

25 Potts, *Wonderfull Discoverie*, T4. Asking for forgiveness, or appeasement, was believed to be an effective way of dealing with malicious witchcraft.

26 LRO, QSB 1/202/89.

27 Lumby, *The Lancashire Witch-Craze*, p. 110; Thomas, *Religion and the Decline of Magic*, pp. 329–30. Connections made between the clergy and magic may have been understandable to contemporaries, since the clergy fulfilled an almost magic role in people's lives. Catholic priests in particular were thought to have curing abilities. For further discussion of the proportion of 'cunning clergy', see de Blecourt, 'Witches, soothsayers and priests', pp. 299–300.

28 LRO, QSB 1/138/59.

29 A. Allen, *A Dictionary of Sussex Folk Medicine* (Newbury: Countryside Books, 1995), pp. 7, 52–6, 60–2; D. E. Nagy, *Popular Medicine in Seventeenth-Century England* (Ohio: Bowling Green State University Press, 1988), chs 1–2.

30 Quoted in A. Sim, *The Tudor Housewife* (Stroud: Sutton, 1996), p. 86. Paracelsus claimed that physicians could learn much from wise women: Paracelsus, *The Archidoxes of Magic* (London, 1656), p. 88.

31 Sim, *Tudor Housewife*, pp. 86, 91; A. Plowden, *Tudor Women: Queens and Commoners* (Stroud: Sutton, 1979), p. 166; C. Larner, *Witchcraft and Religion: The Politics of Popular Belief* (Oxford: Blackwell, 1984), pp. 141–58; Beier, *Sufferers and Healers*, pp. 19–32, 211–41; Nagy, *Popular Medicine*, ch. 5; J. Smith and T. Randall (eds), *Kill or Cure: Medical Remedies of the Sixteenth and Seventeenth Centuries from the Staffordshire Record Office* (Stafford: Staffordshire Record Office, 1996), pp. i–iv.

32 Allen, *Sussex Folk Medicine*, pp. 33–5. Other methods of popular protection against witchcraft included the pimpernel plant, the mountain ash tree, hagstones (stones with a hole running through them), horseshoes and crosses. Harland and Wilkinson, *Lancashire Folk-lore*, pp. 71–2, 76, 209.

33 See John Swain's chapter in this volume for further comments on the place of witchcraft in the local community.

34 Potts, *Wonderfull Discoverie*, C.

35 Potts, *Wonderfull Discoverie*, E2–E3.

36 Potts, *Wonderfull Discoverie*, K, translated and discussed in Hasted, 'New myth of the witch', p. 15. The Catholicised nature of the Pendle charms is discussed further in R. Hasted, *The Pendle Witch-Trial 1612* (Preston: Lancashire County Books, 1987), pp. 48–50.

37 J. Stow, *Annales, or a General Chronicle of England*, ed. E. Howes (London, 1631), p. 768.

38 Potts, *Wonderfull Discoverie*, D2.

39 Lumby, *Lancashire Witch-Craze*, p. 109.

40 G. More, *A True Discourse Concerning the Certaine Possession and Dispossessio[n] of 7*

Persons in One Familie in Lancashire (London, 1600), pp. 12–13; J. Darrell, *A True Narration of the Strange and Grevous Vexation by the Devil, of 7 Persons in Lancashire, and William Somers of Nottingham* (London, 1600), pp. 1–2. See also Jonathan Lumby's comments on this case in his chapter in this volume and his *Lancashire Witch-Craze*.

41 LRO, QSB 1/78/49. Another healer, Thomas Hope of Aspull, Lancashire, was similarly suspected when he showed too much interest in the health of Margery Mullineux's family: LRO, QSB 1/202/33, 38, 89.

42 Briggs, *Witches and Neighbours*, p. 71, states that local healers often provided a free service as part of the community exchange of services, while Thomas, *Religion and the Decline of Magic*, pp. 244–5, 296–9, notes that the fees of cunning folk in his study varied, but were generally less than those of physicians.

43 LRO, QSB 1/139/81.

44 LRO, QSB 1/139/85. Macfarlane, *Witchcraft in Tudor and Stuart England*, pp. 120–1, refers to several cases of people travelling long distances to visit cunning folk.

45 This method of counter-magic was reportedly still used in the nineteenth century, a common Lancashire proverb being 'Draw blood of a witch, and she cannot harm you': Harland and Wilkinson, *Lancashire Folk-lore*, pp. 69, 164.

46 LRO, QSP 214/8.

47 Thomas, *Religion and the Decline of Magic*, pp. 252–9. Other popular forms of divination continued until the nineteenth century, including divination using a Bible and a key, and by suspending a wedding ring by a piece of hair as a pendulum: Harland and Wilkinson, *Lancashire Folk-lore*, pp. 7, 102–3.

48 LRO, QSB 1/255/38, 70–71.

49 Holmes, 'Popular culture?', p. 103; Briggs, *Witches and Neighbours*, p. 121. The late medieval Church recommended the use of prayers when healing or gathering herbs, and the belief in the efficacy of these appears to have continued despite the opprobrium of the Protestant elite: Thomas, *Religion and the Decline of Magic*, pp. 46–51. The appropriation of religious terms and symbols by healers and cunning folk was also evident in other countries: see A. Megged, 'Magic, popular medicine and gender in seventeenth-century Mexico: the case of Isabel de Montoya', *Social History* 19: 2 (May 1994), pp. 197–8.

50 LRO, QSB 1/139/81.

51 LRO, QSB 1/202/89.

52 LRO, DDX 412/66.

53 LRO, DDX/611/4/8, DDX 471/1; charms have also been found dating from the medieval period: Harland and Wilkinson, *Lancashire Folk-lore*, pp. 10, 62–9, 73, 75, 77–9.

54 Allen, *Sussex Folk Medicine*, pp. 12–15; K. Smith, 'The wiseman and his community', *Folklife* 15 (1977), pp. 24–35.

55 Harland and Wilkinson, *Lancashire Folk-lore*, p. 203.

56 Holmes, 'Popular culture?', pp. 85–111, notes how this activity almost became a replacement for formal action against witches after the repeal of the Witchcraft Act in 1736. See also Sharpe, *Instruments of Darkness*, pp. 71–5, 136–9, 163; Willis, *Malevolent Nurture*, pp. 88–9; O. Davies, *Witchcraft, Magic and Culture 1736–1951* (Manchester: Manchester University Press, 1999).

57 Allen, *Sussex Folk Medicine*, pp. 5, 43–6.

58 See Michael Mullett's chapter in this volume.

PART III

REWRITING THE
LANCASHIRE WITCHES

In a sense the fictionalising of the Lancashire witches began even before the trials. If the witches of 1612 were (as Stephen Pumfrey argues above) the first example in fact in England of an alleged devilish confederacy, the first example in fiction came six years earlier with the most famous witches of all: the 'weird sisters' in Shakespeare's 1606 play *Macbeth*. Richard Wilson here shows how far the connections extend, in a chapter rich in both historical and literary references. In the first part of the chapter, Wilson inspects the grisly contents of Macbeth's witches' cooking pot, finding the macabre relics of English Catholic priests, martyred under Elizabeth I. He goes on to tease out connections with the Gunpowder Plot of 1605, to which, as we have seen, the activities of the Lancashire witches were compared by Thomas Potts, and whose conspiratorial connections reached into Lancashire. Finally, he shows how Lancashire's gentry families were implicated in the underworld of persecuted Catholicism, particularly through the mission of the martyred Edmund Campion, and suggests that their mostly Protestant Jacobean descendants sought to demonstrate their loyalty to the state by seeking out witches. The background to all this work is the work of Richard Wilson and others on the 'Lancastrian Shakespeare' thesis, now the subject of much serious scholarly attention, that Shakespeare not only came from this same Catholic milieu but may well have sojourned at Hoghton Tower in Lancashire in 1580–81, not far from Lancashire witch country, perhaps arriving with Campion himself. It would be too much to say that Shakespeare's witches were Lancashire witches, for the play came years before the trial, but we can now see that they shared a common construction.

So too did the Lancashire witches of 1633–34 and those of Heywood and Brome's play *The Late Lancashire Witches*, also of 1634. This second major Lancashire witch trial is much less well known than that of 1612, but its fame spread further and faster at the time and the number initially condemned (and then reprieved) was even greater – up to nineteen. Alison Findlay's chapter sets out the main outlines of the 1634 case and shows how it came to be adapted for the London stage after some of the victims were brought to London for questioning that summer. The stories told against them were invented, but they were effective because they expressed common attitudes and drew on still-current memories of the events of 1612 – fictions which were again recirculated in the 1634 play. Here, Findlay shows, they were refashioned around themes such as disruptive women, transgressive sexual energy, and social inversion. Heywood and Brome also brought in the religious politics which (as we saw in Parts I and II) formed the background to the 1612 trials, but a generation later things had moved on. Not popery but Puritanism and the ritualistic high Anglicanism of the 1630s are the targets of its even-handed satire; and whilst the witches are still the object of real fears and fascinations they are beginning to become figures of fun.

With Jeffrey Richards's chapter, we move from contemporary stories about the Lancashire witches to those of later generations, in the form of W. Harrison Ainsworth's phenomenally popular novel of 1849, *The Lancashire Witches*. Ainsworth's novel followed the first publication of Potts's book for over two hundred years by his friend James Crossley, who also helped guide his researches in the landscape around Pendle. Between them, these two antiquarians – the rationalist Crossley and the Gothic novelist Ainsworth – brought the Lancashire witches to a modern audience, but there is no doubt whose interpretation was the more widely read. Richards's exposition of the complex plot explains how Ainsworth wove into the historical sources appealing material about Lancashire identity and 'merry England', adding ingenious sub-plots and Gothic motifs, and peopling the whole with memorably realised characters. Ainsworth's decision to expand his Gothic panorama to embrace the dissolution of Whalley Abbey at one end and the visit of James I to Hoghton Tower at the other was not only dramatically successful but, as the contributions to this book by Michael Mullett and Richard Wilson show, historically percipient. In the Victorian age, as in the Jacobean, the Lancashire witches were made to serve narrative purposes other than their own.

Finally, Joanne Pearson looks at the way in which modern-day Witches, Wiccans and Pagans have viewed the witch trials of the past. The idea that early modern witchcraft was a relic of an organised pre-Christian religion, consciously divorced from Christianity, remains remarkably prevalent despite having long ago been comprehensively discredited – and, as this volume shows, exhaustive research on the Lancashire trials has produced not a shred of evidence for it. Like all views of witchcraft, however, the point is to understand and explain it, and here (as so often) historical understanding of the recent past is much weaker than of the distant past. During the middle decades of the twentieth century the myth of the pagan witch was promoted by reputable historians, but as the pagan hypothesis crumbled before serious research it was taken up by parts of the emergent women's and pagan movements as a symbol of the historical persecution of women and religious dissidents, and also seized upon by some evangelical Christians as evidence that witchcraft was the product of anti-Christian forces. But this interpretation too is passing, and Pearson's research amongst the Wiccans and Pagans of present-day Lancashire reveals an interesting and reflective variety of views about the relationship (or lack of it) between modern paganism and the witches of the past. As the saga of the Pendle cross indicates, it is the evangelical critics of paganism who are more inclined to see in it an organised continuity with the past. In the twentieth century, as in the seventeenth, witchcraft was as much the creation of its enemies as of its practitioners.

8

The pilot's thumb:
Macbeth and the Jesuits

Richard Wilson

'When shall we three meet again? / In thunder, lightning, or in rain?' Editors point out that the satanic verses which open *Macbeth* make this non-natural-istic prologue unique in all Shakespearean drama, and that the 'drumming insistence' of their four-beat rhythm produces a musical effect which is irre-sistibly conspiratorial, 'hovering between a ritual and a threat'.[1] Like the first bars of Beethoven's Fifth Symphony, this diabolical tattoo fixes Shakespeare's witch scenes (unlike those added to the play by Middleton) as uncannily com-pelling, because so urgently repetitive. As the Porter later says, 'Here's a knocking indeed' (II, iii, 1) that raps like fate. For Terry Eagleton this repeti-tiveness is a signifier of the 'sisterly community' in which the witches exist, revolving around 'dance, the moon, pre-vision', and a co-operation that is the sororial opposite of Macbeth's male egomania.[2] And by reciprocating in rhyme, the 'weird sisters' do seem to accumulate a collective purpose that may, in fact, be Shakespeare's decisive contribution to the witch repertoire. For what is most striking about the riddle that both convokes and disperses 'we three' at the beginning of *Macbeth* is that this was the first time in an English drama when witches had ever been represented as congregating in a group. Though they have associations with those 'Sisters Three' or 'Furies fell' who shear the thread of life in *A Midsummer Night's Dream* (V, i, 274, 323), the source for this demonic trio was Holinshed's *Chronicles*, where Macbeth and Banquo encounter the three baleful women by chance. But it was in the opening of Shakespeare's play that the idea was introduced onto the London stage of witches convening deliberately for their own malign purposes, and with it a new paradigm of witchcraft as conspiracy centred on rituals of the witches' sabbat.

    Macbeth dates from August 1606, when it was staged at court for a visit of the King of Denmark.[3] All leaders of the English judiciary would have been in attendance at this state occasion, and this is significant, because just six years later the fantasy of a convention of 'the most dangerous, wicked and damnable witches in the country' would first appear in English law – at the trials of the witches of Lancashire.[4] There is a conceptual affinity, therefore, between these two key manifestations of the Jacobean witch-craze, and this might be more than a sheer coincidence. For *Macbeth* is, of course, a tragedy darkly aware of its own prophetic status:

> The weird sisters, hand in hand,
> Posters by the sea and land,
> Thus do go, about, about,
> Thrice to thine, and thrice to mine,
> And thrice again, to make up nine.
> Peace, the charm's wound up. (I, iii, 32–7)

Like Shakespeare's 'weird sisters', the Lancashire witches, it was alleged, had come together at 'a special meeting', and 'according to solemn appointment, solemnized this great festival day ... with great cheer, merry company, and much conference'.[5] Never before had it been alleged in England that witches gathered for ritual meetings, according to a recent study of the case by Jonathan Lumby;[6] yet it was precisely by weaving 'Thrice to thine, and thrice to mine' in tri-fold collusion that Macbeth's witches generated a compound malevolence that far exceeded the powers conjured by Shakespeare's earlier solitary sorceresses, Joan of Arc and Margaret of Gloucester.

According to the New Historicist critics, Shakespearean theatre 'shapes the fantasies by which it is shaped, begets that by which it is begotten'; and, if this is so, then 'the charm wound up' in these hypnotic verses was powerful enough to inaugurate an entire genre of witch dramas by writers such as Dekker, Marston and Jonson.[7] What has never been discussed, though, is how unprecedented Shakespeare's convocation of 'weird women' (III, i, 2) was to his London audience, and how his representation of a satanic confederacy may have influenced the contemporary criminalisation of witchcraft as a political conspiracy. For though, as James Sharpe confirms in his recent survey of English witchcraft, *Instruments of Darkness*, terror that a coven of witches might go 'hand in hand' in combination together was the essential incentive in mobilising all seventeenth-century witch-hunts, allegations of such a conspiratorial assembly were alien to English law before the acting of Shakespeare's tragedy. In fact, it was precisely the *absence* of a concept of conspiracy, Sharpe argues, that separated Elizabethan witch-beliefs from those of contemporary Europe, for not only is there 'absolutely no evidence that early modern English witches ever were organised' in collectives, 'there is very little trace in English records of the blasphemous orgiastic sabbat found in continental trial records'. Sharpe's research supports the view, therefore, that 'little or nothing of the black mass is to be traced' in early modern England, and that 'English witches showed no sign of co-operation'; so, wherever he does uncover accusations of collaboration or belief in communities of witches – as at Windsor in 1579, or with the three Throckmorton sisters of 1593 – he concludes that these were 'little more than suspicions of *ad hoc* co-operation and certainly nothing by way of organised rituals'.[8] Editors who question the authenticity of the opening of *Macbeth*, on the ground that these witches have no function other than to meet to say they will meet again, underestimate, therefore, the malefic potential they acquire, simply, as the First Witch boasts, by assembling in such an unholy trinity together. For by sealing their triple alliance, Macbeth's 'secret, black, and midnight hags' (IV, i, 63) became the first witches in English culture to pervert the words of the Book of Common Prayer: that prayers will be heard and requests granted 'When two or three are gathered together'.[9]

Summoned by Grey Malkin at the climactic moment of Christ's denial by St Peter, when 'Thrice the brinded cat hath mewed' (IV, i, 1), Macbeth's interceptors display by their league – 'thrice ... And thrice again, to make up nine' – how they multiply their powers so exponentially. And as the American journalist Gary Wills observes, 'No one in Shakespeare's time would have been in doubt' about 'what brought all three together on this battlefield', when it offered such rich pickings of 'the most vital ingredients of witches' work: dead body parts'.[10] In fact, it was not until the Lancaster trials that English law incorporated the French idea that the aim of witches was to exhume dead bodies, 'carry them to their synagogue and college, and offer them to the Prince of Devils'.[11] Then, it was claimed, one set of accused smuggled human teeth dug from corpses to their meeting-place at Malkin Tower in Pendle Forest, while the other disinterred a dead baby from Salmesbury churchyard, stewed it in a casserole, ate the flesh, 'and with the fat that came from the bones', anointed themselves, so as to copulate with Satan.[12] These were standard fantasies in continental demonology, but historians are at a loss to explain why they were imported into Lancashire;[13] so it cannot be chance that *Macbeth* had given credibility to just such a phantasmagoria, with the irruption onto stage of a coven whose entire conclave is founded on scavenging ingredients for the cauldron from gallows, graveyards and shipwrecks.

Whether 'Liver of blaspheming Jew ... Nose of Turk ... Tartar's lips ... grease that's sweaten / From the murderer's gibbet', or 'Finger of birth-strangled babe / Ditch-delivered by a drab' (IV, i, 26–36), what gives these *objets trouvés*, culled from corpses of condemned religious and sexual heretics, sensationalism is their human origin (in contrast to the banal animal extracts, such as 'juice of toad' or 'oil of adder' (55), dreamed up by Middleton). The 1604 Witchcraft Act had specifically decreed death for those who 'take up any dead man, woman, or child out of his, her, or their grave, or any other place where the dead body resteth – or the skin, bone, or any other part of any dead person – to be employed or used in any manner of witchcraft, sorcery, charm, or enchantment';[14] but it was not until Shakespeare's tragedy was performed for the courtiers and lawyers at Hampton Court that the full repertoire of the black mass was witnessed in England, complete with the pact, infanticide, cannibalism, and necromancy that would all soon be projected onto the accused of Lancashire.

'Double, double' (IV, i, 20): Macbeth's 'weird sisters' were the first stage characters to confront the Jacobean authorities with the nightmare of a witches' sworn combination that had haunted European elites since printing of the persecutorial *Malleus Maleficarum* by the Dominicans in 1486. But whereas, as Stuart Clark notes in his account of 'the idea of witchcraft in early modern Europe', *Thinking With Demons*, continental demonologists were obsessed with the powers raised through rituals of *inversion* (a fixation reflected by Jonson in his 1609 *Masque of Queens*, where the devilish antimasquers 'do all things contrary'), nothing suggests these 'weird women' derive pleasure from things 'That befall preposterously' (*Midsummer Night's Dream*, III, ii, 121). Their unprecedented 'double trouble' is generated by the *duplication*, rather than reversal, of liturgical ceremonies, for they seem, in contrast to French or Italian satanists who were reported to 'say the Mass upside-down',[15] to accumulate their horrific morsels with something like a popish adoration. And the fact that they collaborate to collect and preserve such gallows carrion does link their necrophilia to Protestant suspicions, like those in Samuel Harsnett's *Declaration of Egregious Popish Impostures*, that likened the abuse of dead bodies in witchcraft to the worship of body parts by Catholic congregations.

Editors have fretted over Shakespeare's cue for his witches' brew, but his itemisation of 'poisoned entrails' or 'ounces of a red-haired wench' (IV, i, 5, 58) resembles nothing so much as those nauseated inventories compiled by Tudor commissioners of the contents of monastic reliquaries, which rather than containing 'hair of the Blessed Virgin ... parings of St. Edmund's nails', or 'the finger of St. Stephen', as claimed, they denigrated as compacted of 'stinking boots, mucky combs, rotten girdles, filthy rags, and gobbets of wood under the names of parcels of the holy cross'.[16] 'I think you have heard of St. Blaise's heart at Malvern, and St Algar's bones', sneered Latimer, 'how long they deluded people' into reverencing at 'their solemn and nocturnal bacchanals ... pigs' bones instead of saints' relics';[17] and in *Macbeth* the recipe to make 'a hell-broth boil and bubble' (IV, i, 19) seems to tap the same discourse of reformist disgust. More specifically, Shakespeare's staging of a witches' sabbat looks like a demonisation of the torchlit vigils at which papist women embalmed the debris of martyrs in Stuart London, on behalf of collectors such as the Hapsburg Ambassador, Count Egmont, whose catalogue avidly listed the macabre fruits of their 'diligence and devotion' as a provocation to revenge:

Of the venerable William Ward, his heart, drawn from the fire wherein it had laid, and the handkerchief he had in his hand when he died ... Of Father Bartholemew Roe, a thumb, a piece of burnt lung, a kidney burned to a cinder, and a towel dipped in his blood; of Mr Arnold Green, a thumb, a piece of burnt liver, and the apron of his torturer. Of the venerable John Morgan ... pieces of burnt flesh, three pieces of his *praecordia*, some hair, four towels dipped in his blood, the straw on which he was disembowelled, some papers greased with his fat. Of the venerable Paul ... a toe, three small bones, a piece of windpipe, some burnt flesh, four napkins dipped in his blood. Of the venerable Francis Bell, a right-hand quarter of his body, six pieces of flesh and fat, three napkins dipped into his melted fat, with remains of flesh, two fingers, and his *thyrotheca*. Of the venerable Thomas Holland, a bone, some pieces of skin, a nail, a little box of fat, the shirt in which he suffered ... Of Mr Duckett, the right hand, a piece of his neck, one vertebra and a half. Of Father Corby, a tooth, a few napkins stained with his blood, two handkerchiefs that he used at his martyrdom, his girdle and his hat, some remains of burnt viscera. Of the venerable Henry Morse, his liver pulled out of the fire, a handkerchief stained with his blood, ashes of his burnt intestines, the rope wherewith he was hanged ...[18]

'Fire burn and cauldron bubble': if their mummy, tooth, stomach, gullet, liver, gall, nose, lips, blood, and entrails (22–37) do align Shakespeare's midnight hags with the 'pious Catholics' who 'came back to the gallows' after the executions of the English martyrs, 'and scraped up the ashes where the bowels had been burnt', to 'search for some lump of flesh all parched and singed by the embers',[19] then it is no wonder their spells are so strong. For ever since the regime had obliterated each remnant after the beheading of Mary Queen of Scots, salvage of these grisly remains had become an act of collective resistance, as 'Catholics vied in taking away handkerchiefs dipped in dismembered bodies, or bloodstained straw from the ground; while some snatched intestines thrown in the cauldron'.[20]

Arthur Marotti speculates that this fetishism was prompted by the rediscovery of the Roman catacombs in 1578; but the Catholic ideologue Robert Bellarmine put it into sectarian context, when he wrote that 'There is nothing [Protestants] shudder at more than veneration of relics', and the Tridentine church took his lead by enjoining relic-worship expressly to inspire a new crusade.[21] It was reviving, that is to say, the medieval cultic procession of relics for political purposes, and from Mexico to Manila its missions paraded the rags and bones of martyrs as signs of suicidal militancy.[22] As Sharpe comments, the question of how the witch-panic related to 'concerns of the upper echelons of the Church of England' over this ecstatic cult is therefore moot;[23] but what is certain is that by the time of *Macbeth*, English witch-specialists regularly asserted that the miracles attributed to relics were 'mere Satanical wonders', and that, just as witches were supposed to raise demons from the organs of the dead, so the Jesuits 'do cog and coin devils, spirits, and *souls departed this life'* in exorcisms.[24] We know one such scandalised outburst by Harsnett caught Shakespeare's attention, because he quoted it extensively in *King Lear*. Its fascination for him was that it retailed the grotesque uses put in 1586 by his townsman (and possible cousin) Robert Debdale, when exorcising the young Williams sisters of Denham in Buckinghamshire, to relics of priests he may also have known: Alexander Briant, Edmund Campion, and the brother of the Stratford schoolmaster Thomas Cottam. And when his three witches stirred fingers and noses into their boiling cauldron, it would have been difficult for a Jacobean audience not to think of such 'home-bread relics' as 'the thumbs, bones, and joints' of these 'three champions sent for fire-work in England', who in Harsnett's scathing report had been 'executed at Tyburn, canonised at Rome, and sainted by the devils':

> We never read in all the miracle book that the devil trembled at the name of our blessed Saviour; but Bryant's bone being applied and St. Cottam being called upon, the devil answered in a trembling, quivering voice, 'Thou shalt not have thy prayer.' And he was scarcely to be understood, the poor devil chattered his teeth so sore. What then should I tell you of Campion's thumb put into Fid's mouth, Bryant's bone pinched hard to Sarah's bare leg, as hard as a priest could hold it, the great old rusty nail crammed into Fid's mouth amongst an handful of other choking relics, what wonders they wrought with these poor she-devils: how these made them to vomit, screech and quack like geese that had swallowed down a gag?[25]

'Here I have a pilot's thumb, / Wrack'd as homeward he did come' (I, iii, 28). Like the martyrs' bones used at Denham, in Shakespeare's text the witches' trophies are what Harsnett calls 'fresh green new relics, that were not antiquated or out of date'. But the one that cements their conspiracy when the First Witch puts it on show, since it instantly cues Macbeth's drum, seems to be nothing less than a relic of 'The pilot of the Galilean lake', and keeper of the keys of heaven,[26] Saint Peter. Or, rather, it is the hallowed thumb of his representative and the Pied Piper of his mission, notoriously *racked* in the Tower of London to confess treason on returning in 1580 from Prague: the thumb of Edmund Campion himself. If 'thumb' rhymes with 'drum' in *Macbeth*, then that is because this grisly remainder was both a physical cause and effect of sectarian war in Shakespeare's England. By far the most celebrated relic of the Catholic martyrs, it had been hacked from one of the quarters of Campion's body in the mêlée at Tyburn, when the crowd rushed to dip handkerchiefs in his blood, in an incident to which Shakespeare may be alluding when Caesar's killers learn how 'great men press / For tinctures, stains, relics and cognizance' at scenes of martyrdom, as the Romans 'dip their napkins in his sacred blood' (*Julius Caesar*, II, ii, 89; III, ii, 135). According to the Jesuit Robert Parsons, 'the loss was quickly discovered, but the thief could never be found', and since the hangman 'reluctantly refused twenty pounds for another joint', the digit became the sole piece of the martyr preserved.[27]

Later, it was divided, and the two halves were enshrined in Rome and Roehampton; but its immediate fate was to become the member that, as Harsnett exclaimed, was 'applied to such a diabolical service as the devil himself without such a relic could never have accomplished', when the exorcists inserted it in 'the most secret part' of the girl Sarah Williams, to confound 'the devil that did reside in that place' while she menstruated.[28]

So, it may be that the obscene glee with which Macbeth's witches flaunt the 'pilot's thumb' reflects the lengths to which the authorities went to prevent papists acquiring any further relics after the mass-hysteria at Campion's execution, when, as the author of *A Yorkshire Recusant's Relation* grieved, 'they used singular diligence that no part of blood, or flesh, or garment, or anything belonging to the martyr be unburnt or escape their hands', and even 'the apparel the murderers take and disperse, the pins, points, buttons, and all, lest Catholics get them and use them for relics'.[29] But the lurid pornographic reputation of the thumb also suggests that in *Macbeth* the prop was introduced at the opening of the play as a symbol of religious fanaticism, affiliating the witches immediately with what Harsnett condemned as 'the most impious and unnatural villainy' in the Denham exorcisms, and placing the entire action under the sign of this 'devil's dildo':

> Good God, what do we here? Or is it but a dream? St. Campion or sainting devil help us out with this, for I am at a stand. Relics to that place? It is able to possess a man with fury to cry out, *Earth gape and hell swallow* such devil-saints, such devil-relics, such devil-priests and all. Was it ever heard that any heathen durst ever abuse the vilest thing consecrated to their idol-devils in such execrable manner? Holy saints, holy relics, holy priests, holy devil that made them and moved them to this! It was no marvel they made so fast with the devil to Saint their Champions, Campion and his crew from hell, and to deify and hellify their relics, since they were to be applied to such a diabolical purpose.[30]

Devil's dildo, or sacred relic: if the stump paraded by Macbeth's witches like a god in their cultic procession was indeed a fragment of the martyr's relic, there could be no more apt instrument to initiate a drama about assassination. For the reason why Campion's thumb had acquired veridical importance is that the priest made it his witness at his trial, when 'with his hands folden in linen cloth' Campion demonstrated such feebleness that 'he was neither able to pluck off his own mitten, nor lift a cup to his mouth', and this was claimed as proof that, after the rack, he could never have signed a confession of treason.[31] According to Parsons, Thomas Norton, the rackmaster and author of *Gorboduc*, liked to jest how he had pulled one priest a 'foot longer than God made him' before he confessed;[32] but though Campion was tortured until his nails were torn out, he swore he 'never declared any secrets', and would not, 'come rack, come rope'.[33] His silence ensured he never saw 'paper, ink, and pen', rejoiced one poem, for he won glory with 'every wrench'.[34] Yet Campion did crack under 'the intolerable torment'.[35] And so the thumb that signed the paper, and from which he was strung, became a symbol of his slipperiness on the 'Bloody Question' of conspiracy; as Shakespeare recalled in an earlier parodic inquisition, Feste, pretending to be 'parson' Parsons, taunts Malvolio with the tale of how 'the old Hermit of Prague, that never saw pen and ink, very wittily said to a niece of King Gorboduc, "That is, that is"' (*Twelfth Night*, IV, ii, 11–13). This caricature of the rackmaster as a 'Goneril, with a white beard' reminds us how much in Shakespeare's rewriting of *Gorboduc*, 'He hates him / That would on the rack of this tough world / Stretch him out longer' (*King Lear*, IV, vi, 95; V, iii, 313–15), and implies that the witches who severed the hermit's thumb could be identified with prosecutors as well as priests. Hagiographers always did insist that horror attached not to the victims, 'but the brutes who presided over their butchery', with blood splashing the judges or bowels staining the hangmen;[36] but in *Macbeth*, the effect of flaunting Campion's thumb at a witches' sabbat must have been to taint all who found a meaning in martyrdom, whether of treason or truth. Indeed, Elizabeth Hanson relates how, during his ordeal, Campion withdrew into 'a kind of conceptual pun' of deniability, that thwarted his interrogators and still baffles historians.[37] So, when Macbeth's temptresses enter brandishing what looks to be the relic of this 'pilot' of the Jesuit invasion, the bloody baton – which would travel from Tyburn to Tiber *via* the devils of Denham, and on which detractors and idolators would look with fanaticism – generates similar anxiety. This gory fetish associates the witches directly with the 'prattling, juggling, Jesuits' whose theatricality made them into the 'divine sorcerers' of the exorcisms, but whose equivocation and fireworks also made them, to Protestant eyes, a suicide squad of crazed assassins.[38]

Stephen Greenblatt remarks that when they first meet the witches, 'So wither'd and so wild in their attire' that they 'look not like th'inhabitants o'th'earth', Banquo and Macbeth are plunged into a perceptual quandary, and the latter sets the scene for the epistemological 'queasiness' of the plot when he admits, 'You should be women, / And yet your beards forbid me to interpret / That you are so' (I, iii, 38–44). For Greenblatt, 'What is happening here is that Shakespeare is staging the ontological dilemmas that in the deeply contradictory situation of the time haunted all attempts to determine the status of witchcraft';[39] but there is a more acute context for this enigma, and this is made explicit in the contemporary witch play by Dekker, *The Whore of Babylon*, where it is Campeius – or Campion – and his Jesuits who are ordered to 'unsex' themselves (I, vi, 39) to slip undetected into England: 'Have change of hairs, of eye-brows ... Be shaven and be old women, take all shapes / To escape taking'.[40] As often with this writer, Dekker's text reads like an X-ray of Shakespeare's intentions, and with Marston's *Sophonisba* and Barnabe Barnes's *The Devil's Charter*, also dating from 1606, confirms that what happens when Macbeth confronts these bearded ladies is part of a concerted campaign, equating Jesuits with witches, and their equivocation with the treachery of 'juggling fiends' (V, x, 19). Such was the theme of a sermon delivered at court by Lancelot Andrewes two days before *Macbeth*, which condemned the missionaries as creatures with 'a man's face, women's hair, but lion's teeth';[41] and editors have noticed how Shakespeare's play contributes to the manoeuvre, as it slides from martyrs to devils, with the entry into the Porter's scene of the ghost of the executed Jesuit Henry Garnet, alias 'Farmer', carrying his own relics in Limbo. Limbo was the name given 'Death Row' by priest-hunters; and in this interlude the Charon-like keeper of Hell-gate mocks the hanged man as 'an equivocator ... who committed treason enough for God's sake, yet could not equivocate to heaven' (II, iii, 9), as courtiers joked Garnet would 'equivocate to the gallows, but be hanged without equivocation'.[42] The scene is a dark judgement, then, on the holy war inspired by the 'pilot's thumb'; though when Garnet's head was impaled on London Bridge, its uncorrupted flesh was seen as a proof of his innocence.[43] But in *Macbeth*, a play which opens by defiling Campion's remains wastes no tears on those who dipped 'napkins' in Garnet's corpse, or the 'English tailor' who stole a miraculous husk of blood-stained corn 'out of a French hose' worn to the scaffold by the priest:

> PORTER: Knock, knock, knock. Who's there i'th'name of Beelzebub –
> Here's a farmer, that hang'd himself on th'expectation of plenty; come in
> time-pleaser; have napkins enough about you. Here you'll sweat for it. (II, iii,
> 3–6)

Henry Garnet was executed on 3 May 1606 for alleged involvement in the Gunpowder Plot, and the Porter's gallows humour has therefore been read as a gesture towards *Macbeth*'s historical occasion. But the question this topicality begs is why its author should collude with the Puritan discourse that made Catholicism equivalent to witchcraft, drafting an entire drama around the fact that just as 'Catholics sought relics from the scaffold', so 'witches took body parts from the gallows'.[44] What prompted this transfer of guilt from the Gunpowder assassins to Macbeth's witches, and why were the weird sisters presented, like Garnet's Jesuits, as an organised political conspiracy? Why, indeed, did Shakespeare write a tragedy about witches at all, when he might have written one expressly (like Jonson's *Catiline*) on 'Roman' nobles? For while it comes as no surprise that this 'royal play' of 1606 speaks of the traumatic events of 1605, the mystery is why *Macbeth* itself *equivocates* about Macbeth's crime, by invoking the 'black legend' of international Jesuit terrorism?

The answer lies, of course, in the author's own compromising proximity to the Gunpowder conspirators. For, as Antonia Fraser reminds us in her study of the Plot, the epicentre of the Gunpowder treason was Shakespeare's world, since 'the great arc of Plotter's houses that spread across the Midlands' converged around Stratford-upon-Avon: on the homes of Robert Catesby, at Lapworth Park, and the dramatist's own relative, John Grant, at Norbrook. It was at Lapworth in 1580 that Shakespeare's father probably received a copy of the Catholic Testament of Faith brought by Campion from Milan; and at Norbrook in 1583 that his kinsmen, Edward Arden and John Somerville, planned their suicidal mission to shoot the Queen. Both here and at the Mermaid Tavern, where Catesby conferred, the Plot was laid, as Fraser says, in 'Shakespeare country'.[45] So, as Leslie Hotson concluded, 'when we consider he had known Catesby and Grant from childhood; that Francis Tresham and the Winters were connected by marriage with his daughter ... and that his friend Jonson dined with Catesby and Winter just a few days before the explosion' was due, it is 'far from impossible' that *Macbeth* was provoked by Shakespeare's inside knowledge of the Plot, and that its anti-hero was inspired by Catesby: 'this daring, able and magnetic gentleman, who turned fanatic king-killer and bloody butcher, and like Macbeth died fighting'.[46] Rumours of 'a huge conspiracy among local Catholics' had, in fact, been rife in Stratford for a year before the event;[47] so, it is closeness to the plans that may explain the dramatist's need to formulate, with a near-anagram of the surname, the same extenuation as the excuse offered by Catesby's neighbours and kin: that this 'valiant cousin [and] worthy gentleman' (I, ii, 24) was nothing but 'an idiot, full of sound and fury' (V, v, 26), betrayed by the Jesuitical 'equivocation of the fiend' (V, v, 41):

> ... oftentimes, to win us to our harm,
> The instruments of darkness tell us truths,
> Win us with honest trifles to betray's
> In deepest consequence. (I, iii, 121–4)

'Shakespeare makes us pity Macbeth', it is said, when 'meeting with the Witches', this 'brave and loyal soldier is seduced by their equivocation'; and critics have registered how, by empathising with his villain, the dramatist creates a disconcertingly evasive tragedy, in which a traitor whose face 'is as a book' (I, v, 62), and so 'does not deceive anyone for very long', is himself 'undone by treason's amphibolic tongue'.[48] Such exculpation extends, they point out, to the imagery of the play itself, which is dominated by an opposition between hand and heart, figuring Macbeth's inability to make the 'firstlings of [his] heart ... The firstlings of [his] hand' (IV, ii, 163). The effect of this exoneration is to objectify the protagonist's hand, as if 'the murderous hand detaches itself from the murderer', when Macbeth bids 'the eye wink at the hand' (I, iv, 52); his 'hangman's hands' bear 'filthy witness' to his deed (II, ii, 25, 45); his hands return to 'pluck out' his eye; 'all great Neptune's ocean' will not wash 'blood / Clean' from his hand (57–60); and lastly, he feels 'His secret murders sticking on his hands' (V, ii, 17).[49] Macbeth's weirdly dissociated hand becomes, in other words, a metonym for the deniability of his own acts, and, as such, an eerie correlative of the rush, in the wake of the Plot, to displace guilt from English Catholics onto the Jesuits, whose mission had been fired by that peripatetic relic of Campion's thumb. It is the symbolic equivalent of the arms-length strategy adopted by court Catholics such as the Howard family, three of whose members sat on the Bench at Garnet's trial; or by tame clerics like the Archpriest George Blackwell, who urged the laity to take the Oath of Allegiance, imposed in 1606 deliberately to prise 'his Majesty's subjects that adhere in their hearts to the popish religion' away from 'the devilish counsel of Jesuits'.[50] In its anathematising of the Jesuits as witches, *Macbeth* conforms, in fact, to the tactics of the English Benedictines, who 'hedged their bets' over the Oath because the rival Jesuits opposed it, with the result that their leader, Thomas Preston, was lodged at public expense, and had the freedom 'to go out to the theatre with priests who shared his views'.[51] This tragedy, famed for the feverishness of its punning, condenses 'The panic-striken dismay of leading Catholic activists when the Oath was formulated',[52] but, above all, the shifty opportunism of Catesby's co-religionists, frantic to deflect the blame for his conspiracy onto fanatical zealots, with their 'supernatural' and supranational 'soliciting' (I, iii, 129).

Gunpowder Plot would always be called 'the Jesuit treason', opined Sir Edward Coke, the Attorney General, in which 'Garnet ... as *author*, was more to blame than all the *actors*';[53] but what is striking about popular culture is how it failed to follow this line, burning instead the Catholic gentry, in the effigy of Guy Fawkes. As Richard Hardin observes, the unofficial reaction to the Plot focused unmercifully on the knot of provincial aristocrats, and was 'much closer to the story told by modern historians than to the mythic version' (followed by Milton), which vilified 'Satan, in friar's disguise'. In *Traitorous Percies and Catesbies*, for instance, the schoolboy poet Edward Hawes abused Catesby and Thomas Percy as 'Atheists' driven by 'Envy and hope of gain'; while 'the most influential of all the early poems', Francis Herring's *Pietas Pontificia*, had Fawkes take the rap as the eternal terrorist bogeyman. By 1610, Hardin shows, the 'Guy' of 5 November was well on the way to becoming a perennial 'focus of the culture's hatreds and fears', in a story 'propelling into history a ready scapegoat for collective failure' in the guise of the Catholic cavalier.

In the 'demon-haunted atmosphere' of post-Plot politics, the hunt for the villain fixed on Fawkes as the archetypal 'enemy within', who looked like any English nobleman, 'with an English family, education, and tongue', yet with a 'foxy' foreign name.[54] Much of this class hatred, which lingers on modern Guy Fawkes Night, flared up in the Midland Rising of 1607, when it was Catholic landlords, notably the Catesbys and Treshams, who were targeted by the rioters;[55] but what was absent from all such popular anti-popery was what makes *Macbeth* problematic: namely, the offloading of culpability onto a transvestite clerical foe. That the execution of priests was restarted, therefore, in 1607, could owe something to the seriousness with which Shakespeare took Coke's theatre metaphor, and depicted the aristocratic assassin as but 'a poor player / That struts and frets his hour upon the stage' (V, v, 23) under the wicked direction of the Jesuits' thumb. As John Bossy contends, the attitude to the missionaries of their patriarchal hosts was always one of latent hostility, since gentry like the Northamptonshire magnate Sir Thomas Tresham could never concede 'clerical pretensions' to leadership. Thus, though he was prosecuted for harbouring Campion, Tresham could still greet the accession of James I by offering to expel the Jesuits in return for Catholic emancipation. To such grandees, 'The idea that priests might be counselling them to abandon allegiance was fantastic';[56] but when in 1605 Tresham's heir, Francis, incriminated Garnet to save his own neck, the tragedy written by their Midland neighbour betrayed the bad faith of the entire cabal of Ardens, Throckmortons and Catesbys, as it had its conspirator likewise blame the 'filthy hags' (IV, i, 131) for leading him astray:

> And be these juggling fiends no more believed,
> That palter with us in a double sense,
> That keep the word of promise to our ear
> And break it to our hope. (V, x, 19–22)

Whether or not Macbeth's recrimination against 'these juggling fiends' expresses the sense of betrayal felt by recusants at the Jesuit failure to sustain the 'Enterprise of England', from the day Campion came to Stratford the Catholic *fronde* to which Shakespeare was tied was far more deeply steeped in terrorism, concludes a recent study of the Treshams, than its protestations of 'mouth-honour' (V, iii, 28) would ever suggest.[57] But it was their ability to 'lie like truth' (V, v, 40), and evade the consequences of this collusion, even when 'old Sir Fulke Greville raised the militia against the papists' in the aftermath of the Gunpowder Plot,[58] that made a text like *Macbeth* their blueprint for escape. Meanwhile, the poet's *politique* aloofness from martyrdom was deployed in his most obfuscating smokescreen, Sonnet 124, which taxes 'our fashion' as too apt to be drawn into 'thralled discontent', and contrasts premature 'fools of time, / Which die for goodness, who have lived for crime', with the faith that outlasts 'the child of state ... fortune's bastard ... that heretic' (presumably Elizabeth), because it stands 'all alone' and 'hugely politic'. And here the metaphor of a tall secluded house, 'builded far from accident', was revealing, for it was indeed as a quietist sect in seigneurial retreat that Jacobean Catholics would learn to survive in the decades after 1605.[59] To do so, however, they had first to repeat the symbolic substitution effected in Shakespeare's play, and shift responsibility for treason onto a demonised extreme.

It cannot, then, be chance that the testing-ground for *Macbeth* should have been in the north-west, the only region visited by Campion's crusade to share with Warwickshire a similar religious community, under 'a cohesive, much inter-married Catholic group' whose domination of the county ensured that 'recusancy flourished in all ranks'.[60] For in 1580 it was to Lancashire that the missionaries rode from Stratford, and at Hoghton Tower that the 'pilot' of the mission, Edmund Campion, pitched his headquarters, during a fervent six months when the household may have included the boy Shakespeare. From Hoghton, Campion made recruiting drives through adjoining estates, staying with the Allens at Rossall, Heskeths at Rufford, Listers at Westby, Sherburns at Stoneyhurst, Southworths at Salmesbury, Tempests at Bracewell, Towneleys at Towneley Hall, and Worthingtons at Standish.[61] This itinerary would yield a rich harvest, for aside from the Allens, who had already produced Cardinal William Allen, and the Heskeths, who would soon be lured into a calamitous plot, the Hoghton, Lister, Sherburn, Southworth, Tempest, Towneley and Worthington families would all send sons to Douai and receive them back as priests. Yet a generation later, it was the same network, Lumby relates, that was the core of a different mania, when as a fall-out of the Gunpowder conspiracy, the now-Protestant Hoghtons and Towneleys mimicked Shakespearean drama, to dissociate from terrorist attacks by projecting onto their Catholic neighbours the satanic nightmare of *Macbeth*.[62]

The myth of the witches' sabbat, insists Robert Muchembled, is 'simply and solely a figment created by the elite classes of Europe', who 'revived stereotypes that had no popular basis in order to demonstrate the existence of a huge satanic plot ... Their imaginary sabbat was a copy of the Mass, a dark, morbid parody of the original.'[63] If this analysis holds, then *Macbeth* may be its classic instance. For in this play Shakespeare tapped into the force-field of early modern persecution, located by historians on the interface between rival confessional extremes. A Catholic gentry divided against itself, and a magistracy primed to reawaken the Inquisition fear of some demonic sect, were all the elements required to ignite a conflagration. For 'where those who promoted conformity met resistance, there dissidents would be created. Scapegoated and marginalised, they were charged with the same crimes as the deviants of the middle ages. It was said that they boiled babies and met in unspeakable sabbaths.'[64] Lumby's summing-up of the 1612 witch-hunt suggests that one answer to the riddle in *Macbeth* is that, while Shakespeare's coven may have been modelled on secret masses in Midland mansions, when the 'hellish and devilish band of witches'[65] did 'meet again' it would be on Good Friday at Malkin Tower in Pendle. There may have been, Lumby infers, some Catholic ritual behind this Good Friday feast of so-called witches, but what is telling is how their accusers belonged to families that hosted Campion, and now stood guilty by association. None more so than that of Thomas Lister, whose allegations instigated the Lancastrian pogrom. A great-nephew of Alexander Hoghton, who died in gaol for aiding the 1580 mission, as well as of Allen, Lister counted two Jesuits among kin: John Lister, who suffered years of imprisonment; and Thomas Lister, a neurotic hothead Garnet 'kept at his side', until he put them all in danger by refusing to obey. Convinced he was deranged, Garnet sent Lister home to Lancashire in 1602, hoping 'visits to his family will make him completely healthy'.[66] In fact, it is easy to see in Lister's disloyalty to superiors the blame-calling which would divide the English Catholics and lead, in the after-shock of the Plot, to the accusations of witchcraft that fell first upon a group that had never disowned its priests: the family of John Nutter, hanged in 1584, and Robert Nutter, martyred in 1600 at Lancaster and the one member of Garnet's inner cell whose hanging and dismemberment had actually taken place in the locality.[67]

'The County of Lancashire may now be said to abound as much in Witches', declared the Clerk of the Court, Thomas Potts, in his 'Discovery' of the 1612 trials, 'as Seminaries, Jesuits, and Papists'. With this parallel in mind, it was logical he should dedicate the book to Thomas Knyvet, Lord Escrick, the 'discoverer' of Guy Fawkes in the cellars of Westminster, and allege that the Malkin meeting was another powder conspiracy, 'to blow up the Castle' at Lancaster.[68] Paranoia over 'dire combustion, and confus'd events, / New hatch'd to th'woeful time' (II, iii, 57) followed *Macbeth* in mixing witches with Jesuits and gunpowder; and the trail of suspicion led inevitably to Lancashire, where the 1605 plotters had been racing before they blew themselves up, and to the tightly knit Lancastrian gentry from which they had hoped for aid. No wonder, then, that, beside Lister, fomentors of the Lancashire persecution included recusants like Robert Holden, who may have sparked the inquiry at Salmesbury Hall to smoke out its Jesuit chaplain, Christopher Southworth; and Sir Thomas Gerard, brother of the 'most wanted' priest in England, John Gerard, who in fact escaped to France on the day that Garnet died. As historians point out, a magistrate such as Sir Thomas, 'with a suspect family to live down', needed to look zealous, and since 'he could hardly attack his own Catholic relations', it was by searching for witches that he could prove himself both 'loyal and religious'.[69] With his brother-in-law, Sir Richard Hoghton, Gerard had displayed tangible loyalty in 1611, when the two crypto-Catholics each paid £1,000 to be the very first of the baronets created to fund Protestants in Ulster. But it was by witch-hunting that these suspected fifth-columnists were relegitimated, when their *epuration* signalled what Shakespeare staged with his Scottish play: that in the far north 'the time' was now 'free' (V, ix, 21) from treason.

Macbeth's impaled head may be the ghoulish symbol of this disassociation, a debasement of all those papist relics that had haunted the dramatist, ever since he had been traumatised at sixteen by his proximity to Campion at Hoghton. And though Lancashire Catholicism would long remain a cult of saints' heads in secret shrines, Shakespeare might well have intimidated the

Hoghton circle with his boiling cauldron of religious violence. For whether or not Gerard and Hoghton were present, beside the judges, when *Macbeth* was first performed, 'The works of Mr Shakespeare' stood, we know, in Sir Richard's library.[70] And as the poet John Weever reported, when he placed the dramatist with them in his Lancastrian *Epigrams*, 'honey-tongued Shakespeare' – who was once, perhaps, among the Jesuit recruits who received 'entertainment and great maintenance' in their houses – had created with his plays new 'saints' to whom these converts could safely transfer their 'subjective duty'.[71]

On 15 August 1617 James I was welcomed to Hoghton with a masque, in which 'the Landlord of this ancient Tower, / Thrice fortunate to see this happy hour', offered the King a 'trembling heart', which had been 'set on fire' by the royal visit to this 'heart of all the shire'. 'This Knight is thine, he is thy Ward', proclaimed a 'Household God', in punning allusion to the fact that Sir Richard had been adopted as a royal ward and forcibly educated in the state religion. Yet the baronet had indeed proved the difference of his heart from those ripped out of papist martyrs, by his part in the 1612 show-trials of his neighbours. Three times, the 'burning heart' recalled, Lancashire gentry had flirted with rebellion, in 1569, 1580 and 1605. But now James reacted to their homage by 'knighting' Sir Richard's sirloin of beef, and declaring, with his Book of Sports, a coded edict of Catholic toleration. In the north, as in the Midlands, the lesson of *Macbeth* was learned, and an elite stained with blood was rehabilitated when, in the words of the masque, it put the King before its faith: 'seeing that thy Majesty we see / Greater than Country Gods, more good than we'.[72]

The 'guilt of religious schism' felt by this clan was a prime cause, historians believe, of the Lancashire witch-craze;[73] but, if so, Shakespeare's tragedy had taught these Hoghtons that the way to clear themselves was to demonise outsiders in their midst. As Greenblatt admits, this play 'may not be reducible to its consequences', but by imagining witches as a 'monstrous threat to civilisation ... it cannot escape having a direct effect on lives'.[74] James summoned the surviving 'Lancashire witches' to Hoghton, where, to avoid the evil eye, the King observed the old women from behind a screen. But Shakespeare apparently had no doubt that 'the horrid deed' of Gunpowder treason had been blown back into the eyes of its perpetrators by Christ: 'like a naked new-born babe, / Striding the blast' (I, vii, 21). The reference may be to the playwright's kinsman, the Plotter Grant, blinded by his own explosives; but the verdict falls on all who followed Campion, as the retort is to a famous poem by the martyr Southwell, whose 'babe all burning bright / Did in the air appear' like an incendiary device.[75] To the end, then, Shakespeare associated martyrdom with conspiracy; and in *The Tempest* even draped Caliban's plot in the 'trumpery' left hanging by 'Mistress Line'. Anne Line was the Jesuits' aged landlady, hanged for hiding priests; but when these plotters garb themselves in the 'trash' from her 'line', she is roped into their crime, and the 'saintly widow' becomes a witch, as assassins reduce to a 'frippery', or rag-and-bone shop (IV, i, 186, 222–4), the spectacle of 'the noble and heroic Mistress Line suspended upon the gallows', where Father Garnet had 'cut the sleeve from her gown, dipped it in blood, and obtained one of her stockings' to be ripped to pieces for relics:

> For she used to have bandages on her legs, and thus her stockings were very large, but her legs were as thin as the rope on which she was hanged.[76]

Notes

1 G. K. Hunter (ed.), in the New Penguin Shakespeare edition of *Macbeth* (London: Penguin, 1967), pp. 42–3. See also Nicholas Brooke's similar comments in the Oxford edition (Oxford: Oxford University Press, 1990), p. 1.

2 Terry Eagleton, *William Shakespeare* (Oxford: Blackwell, 1986), pp. 2–4.

3 For the state visit as the occasion of the first performance, see the Arden edition of *Macbeth*, ed. Kenneth Muir (London: Methuen, 1951), p. xxiv; Alvin Kernan, *Shakespeare, The King's Playwright: Theater in the Stuart Court, 1603–1613* (New Haven: Yale University Press, 1995), pp. 71–7; and Henry Paul, *The Royal Play of 'Macbeth'* (New York: Macmillan, 1950).

4 Thomas Potts, *The Wonderfull Discoverie of Witches in the Countie of Lancaster* (London, 1613), C3.

5 Potts, *Wonderfull Discoverie*, C3.

6 Jonathan Lumby, *The Lancashire Witch-Craze: Jennet Preston and the Lancashire Witches* (Preston: Carnegie, 1995), p. 57. See also Stephen Pumfrey's chapter in this volume.

7 Louis Montrose, '*A Midsummer Night's Dream* and the shaping fantasies of Elizabethan culture', in Richard Wilson and Richard Dutton (eds), *New Historicism and Renaissance Drama* (Harlow: Longman, 1992), p. 130. John Marston's *Sophonisba*, Thomas Dekker's *The Whore of Babylon*, and Barnabe Barnes's *The Devil's Charter* all date from late in 1606; Ben Jonson's *Masque of Queens* from 1609.

8 James Sharpe, *Instruments of Darkness: Witchcraft in England 1550–1750* (1996; London: Penguin, 1997), p. 76; C. L'Estrange Ewen, *Witchcraft and Demonianism: A Concise Account Derived from Sworn Depositions and Confessions Obtained in the Courts of England and Wales* (London: Heath Cranton, 1933), p. 57; G. R. Quaife, *Godly Zeal and Furious Rage: The Witch in Early Modern Europe* (London: Croom Helm, 1987), p. 59.

9 Prayer of St Chrysostom.

10 Gary Wills, *Witches and Jesuits: Shakespeare's 'Macbeth'* (Oxford: Oxford University Press, 1995), p. 38.

11 Sebastian Michaelis, *Pneumalogie* (Avignon, 1587), trans. E. A. Ashwin; quoted in Lumby, *Lancashire Witch-Craze*, p. 59.

12 Lumby, *Lancashire Witch-Craze*, pp. 42, 139–40.

13 Sharpe, *Instruments of Darkness*, p. 99.

14 1 James I, c. 12.

15 Stuart Clark, *Thinking with Demons: The Idea of Witchcraft in Early Modern Europe* (Oxford: Clarendon Press, 1997), p. 15.

16 Quoted in Eamonn Duffy, *The Stripping of the Altars: Traditional Religion in England, 1400–1580* (New Haven and London: Yale University Press, 1992), pp. 164, 384, 414–15.

17 Duffy, *Stripping of the Altars*, p. 390.

18 Quoted in Richard Simpson (ed.), *Rambler*, new series, viii (1857), p. 114.

19 Quoted in Dom. Bede Camm, *Forgotten Shrines: An Account of Some Old Catholic Halls and Families in England and of Relics and Memorials of the English Martyrs* (London: Macdonald and Evans, 1910), p. 361.

20 Camm, *Forgotten Shrines*, p. 362.

21 Arthur Marotti, 'Southwell's remains: Catholicism and anti-Catholicism in early modern England', in Cedric Brown and Arthur Marotti (eds), *Texts and Cultural Change in Early Modern England* (London: Macmillan, 1997), p. 63, n. 47; Robert Bellarmine, *De controversiis christianae fidei* (Ingolstadt, 1601), ii, p. 826, quoted in Simon Ditchfield, 'Martyrs on the move: relics as vindicators of local diversity in the Tridentine Church', in Diana Wood (ed.), *Martyrs and Martyrologies* (Oxford: Blackwell, 1993), p. 283.

22 For the popular cultic procession of relics, see, in particular, Michael Goodich, *Violence and Miracle in the Fourteenth Century: Private Grief and Public Salvation* (Chicago: Chicago University Press, 1995), pp. 14–21, 36–7, 110–23, 153–5. For the Tridentine revival of the tradition, see John O'Malley, Gauvin Bailey, Steven Harris and Frank Kennedy (eds), *The Jesuits: Cultures, Sciences, and the Arts, 1540–1773* (Toronto: University of Toronto Press, 1999), pp. 262, 391, 588, 662, 682: among objects discussed are blood samples taken by surgeons (Quebec), mechanical birds (Akbar), bones (Manila), wax effigies (Mexico City), and the toga of Ignatius Loyala (Cologne). For a politicised English cult, see Claire Cross, 'An Elizabethan martyrologist and his martyr: John Mush and Margaret Clitherow', in Wood (ed.), *Martyrs and Martyrologies*, pp. 271–94.

23 Sharpe, *Instruments of Darkness*, p. 209.

24 William Perkins, *A Discourse of the Damned Art of Witchcraft*, 'Epistle Dedicatory' (Cambridge, 1608), quoted in Clark, *Thinking with Demons*, p. 533; Samuel Harsnett, *A Declaration of Egregious Popish Impostures* (London, 1603), reprinted in Frank Brownlow, *Shakespeare, Harsnett, and the Devils of Denham* (Newark: University of Delaware Press, 1993), p. 294.

25 Harsnett, *A Declaration*, pp. 294–5.

26 John Milton, 'Lycidas', l. 109, in C. A. Patrides (ed.), *Milton's 'Lycidas': The Tradition and the Poem* (Missouri: University of Missouri Press, 1983), p. 8. The allusion is to Matthew 16:19, 'but is by some readers said to be to Christ, and by others to be a composite portrait' of the 'mitred' (l. 112) – i.e. Roman – priest.

27 Quoted in Richard Simpson, *Edmund Campion* (London: John Hodges, 1896), p. 455. For the later history of the relic, see Camm, *Forgotten Shrines*, pp. 363, 377–8.

28 Harsnett, *A Declaration*, p. 297.

29 In John Morris (ed.), *The Troubles of Our Catholic Forefathers*, 3 vols (London: Burns and Oates, 1877), iii, pp. 98–9.

30 Harsnett, *A Declaration*, p. 297.

31 Robert Parsons, *A Defence of the Censure Given upon Two Books of William Charke and Meredith Hanmer, Which They Wrote Against Mr Edmund Campion* (Rouen, 1582), p. 8, quoted in Michael Graves, *Thomas Norton: Parliament Man* (Oxford: Blackwell, 1994), p. 273.

32 Robert Parsons, *An Epistle of the Persecution of Catholics in England* (Douai, 1582), quoted in Graves, *Thomas Norton*, p. 272.

33 Quoted in Elizabeth Hanson, *Discovering the Subject in Renaissance England* (Cambridge: Cambridge University Press, 1998), p. 48.

34 Evelyn Waugh, *Edmund Campion* (London: Longmans and Green, 1935), p. 216; 'Verses made by a Catholic in praise of Campion that was executed at Tyburn for treason', in Emrys Jones (ed.), *The New Oxford Book of Sixteenth Century Verse* (Oxford: Oxford University Press, 1991), pp. 332–7, ll. 1 and 148. The poem is now generally attributed to Henry Walpole.

35 Quoted in Hanson, *Discovering the Subject*, p. 51.

36 Richard Simpson, quoted in Camm, *Forgotten Shrines*, p. 361.
37 Hanson, *Discovering the Subject*, pp. 48, 53. For the debate about the degree of Jesuit complicity in assassination plots against Elizabeth, see, in particular, John Bossy, 'The heart of Robert Parsons', in Thomas McCoog (ed.), *The Reckoned Expense: Edmund Campion and the Early English Jesuits* (Woodbridge: Boydell Press, 1996), pp. 141–58.
38 Dominique Deslandres, 'The French Jesuits' missionary world', and Gauvin Bailey, 'Jesuit catechism and the arts', in O'Malley *et al.* (eds), *The Jesuits*, pp. 262, 391; Thomas Middleton, *A Game at Chess*, III, i, 330, cited in Robert Watson, '*Othello* as Protestant propaganda', in Claire McEachern and Debora Shuger (eds), *Religion and Culture in Renaissance England* (Cambridge: Cambridge University Press, 1997), p. 247.
39 Stephen Greenblatt, 'Shakespeare bewitched', in *New Historical Literary Study* (Princeton: Princeton University Press, 1992), pp. 108–35.
40 Thomas Dekker, *The Whore of Babylon*, in *The Dramatic Works of Thomas Dekker*, ed. Fredson Bowers , 4 vols (Cambridge: Cambridge University Press, 1953–61), ii: III, i, 162–4.
41 Quoted in Kernan, *Shakespeare, The King's Playwright*, p. 75.
42 Henry Foley (ed.), *Records of the English Province of the Society of Jesus*, 6 vols (London: Burns and Oates, 1877), i, p. 364; Sir Dudley Carleton reported in *Calendar of State Papers Domestic*, 1603–10, p. 315.
43 Philip Caraman, *Henry Garnet and the Gunpowder Plot* (London: Longman, 1964), pp. 442–3.
44 Wills, *Witches and Jesuits*, p. 102.
45 Antonia Fraser, *The Gunpowder Plot: Terror and Faith in 1605* (London: Weidenfeld and Nicolson, 1996), pp. 114–15. For the Stratford nucleus of the Plot, see also David Mosler, 'Warwickshire Catholics in the Civil War', *Recusant History* 15 (1979–81), p. 259; R. G. Abrahams, 'The Gunpowder Plot in Warwickshire' (unpublished typescript, Birmingham Archaeological Society, Birmingham Reference Library, 1951); E. A. Barnard, *A Seventeenth Century Country Gentleman: Sir Francis Throckmorton* (Cambridge: Cambridge University Press, 1948), p. 2; and Alice Fairfax-Lucy, *Charlecote and the Lucys* (London: Jonathan Cape, 1958), pp. 117–18.
46 Leslie Hotson, *I, William Shakespeare* (London: Jonathan Cape, 1937), pp. 197–8.
47 Sandeep Kaushik, 'Resistance, loyalty and recusant politics: Sir Thomas Tresham and the Elizabethan state', *Midland History* 21 (1996), pp. 48–9.
48 Frank Huntley, '*Macbeth* and the background of Jesuitical equivocation', *Proceedings of the Modern Language Association* 79 (1964), p. 397; Camille Wells Slights, *The Casuistical Tradition in Shakespeare, Donne, Herbert, and Milton* (Princeton: Princeton University Press, 1981), p. 109; and Steven Mullaney, *The Place of the Stage: License, Play, and Power in Renaissance England* (Chicago: Chicago University Press, 1988), p. 128. For the debate on Shakespeare and Jesuit theory, see also G. I. Duthie, 'Antithesis in *Macbeth*', *Shakespeare Survey* 19 (1966), pp. 25–33; David Kaula, '*Hamlet* and the *Sparing Discovery*', *Shakespeare Survey* 24 (1971), pp. 71–7; Steven Mullaney, 'Lying like truth: riddle, representation and treason in Renaissance England', *English Literary History* 47 (1980), pp. 320–47; and William Scott, '*Macbeth*'s – and our – self-equivocations', *Shakespeare Quarterly* 37 (1986), pp. 160–74.
49 Lawrence Danson, *Tragic Alphabet: Shakespeare's Drama of Language* (New Haven: Yale University Press, 1974), p. 129. See also Muir, *Macbeth*, p. xxiii; G. Wilson Knight, *The Imperial Theme* (London: Methuen, 1951), p. 153; and Stephen Greenblatt, *Hamlet in Purgatory* (Princeton: Princeton University Press, 2001), p. 188: 'a rhetorical effect produced again and again in *Macbeth*, an expression of psychic and social dissociation'.
50 3 Jac. I, c. 4 (1606), *An Act for the Better Discovering and Repressing of Popish Recusants*, quoted in Marvin Havran, *The Catholics in Caroline England* (Stanford: Stanford University Press, 1962), p. 13.

51 Quoted in Maurus Lunn, 'English Benedictines and the Oath of Allegiance, 1606–1647', *Recusant History* 10 (1969), p. 151.
52 Michael Questier, *Conversion, Politics and Religion in England, 1580–1625* (Cambridge: Cambridge University Press, 1996), pp. 106–7. For analysis of Catholic reaction to the Plot and the Oath of Allegiance, see also John LaRocca, '"Who can't pray with me, can't love me": toleration and the early Jacobean recusancy policy', *Journal of British Studies* 23: 2 (1984), pp. 22–36, esp. pp. 31–5; and Alexandra Walsham, *Church Papists: Catholicism, Conformity and Confessional Polemic in Early Modern England* (Woodbridge: Boydell and Brewer, 1993), pp. 84–5.
53 Quoted in Caraman, *Henry Garnet*, pp. 397–8.
54 Richard Hardin, 'The early poetry of the Gunpowder Plot: myth in the making', *English Literary Renaissance* 22: 1 (1992), pp. 62–79, esp. pp. 62–3.
55 Roger Manning, *Village Revolts: Social Protests and Popular Disturbances in England, 1509–1640* (Oxford: Oxford University Press, 1988), pp. 237–8.
56 John Bossy, *The English Catholic Community, 1570–1850* (London: Darton, Longman and Todd, 1975), pp. 37–8.
57 Kaushik, 'Resistance, loyalty and recusant politics', pp. 37–72.
58 Anne Hughes, 'Warwickshire on the eve of the Civil War: a "county community"?', *Midland History* 7 (1982), p. 51.
59 For a recent reading of Sonnet 124 as a critique of the Jesuit martyrs, see Richard McCoy, 'Love's martyrs: Shakespeare's *Phoenix and the Turtle* and the sacrificial sonnets', in McEachern and Shuger (eds), *Religion and Culture*, pp. 196–9.
60 McCoy, 'Love's martyrs', pp. 196–9. See also Anne Hughes, 'Religion and society in Stratford-upon-Avon, 1619–1638', *Midland History* 19 (1994), pp. 58–9; Anne Hughes, *Politics, Society and Civil War in Warwickshire, 1620–1660* (Cambridge: Cambridge University Press, 1991), pp. 61–4; and J. M. Martin, 'A Warwickshire market town in adversity: Stratford-upon-Avon in the sixteenth and seventeenth centuries', *Midland History* 7 (1982), pp. 26–41.
61 Simpson, *Edmund Campion*, pp. 265–6. On the 'Lancastrian Shakespeare' thesis, see E. A. J. Honigmann, *Shakespeare: The 'Lost Years'*, 2nd edn (Manchester: Manchester University Press, 1995); Richard Wilson, 'Shakespeare and the Jesuits', *Times Literary Supplement*, 19 December 1997; Park Honan, *Shakespeare: A Life* (Oxford: Oxford University Press, 1998), ch. 5; and R. Dutton, A. Findlay and R. Wilson (eds), *Lancastrian Shakespeare: Theatre and Religion* and *Lancastrian Shakespeare: Region, Religion and Patronage* (Manchester: Manchester University Press, forthcoming 2003).
62 For the Catholic context of the Lancashire trials, see Lumby, *Lancashire Witch-Craze*, esp. pp. 119–33, and the chapters by Lumby and Mullett in this volume.
63 Robert Muchembled, 'Satanic myths and cultural reality', in Bengt Ankarloo and Gustav Heningsen (eds), *Early Modern European Witchcraft: Centres and Peripheries* (Oxford: Clarendon Press, 1990), pp. 139–40.
64 Lumby, *Lancashire Witch-Craze*, p. 141.
65 Potts, *Wonderfull Discoverie*, K2.
66 Quoted Caraman, *Henry Garnet*, pp. 205, 296. For Thomas Lister's erratic career, see also pp. 91–2, 102, 115, 223–5, 233–4, 247, 296.
67 Caraman, *Henry Garnet*, p. 271. For the careers of John, Robert and Ellis Nutter, see Godfrey Anstruther, *The Seminary Priests: A Dictionary of Secular Clergy of England and Wales, 1558–1603* (Durham: Ushaw College, 1964), pp. 258–60.
68 Potts, *Wonderfull Discoverie*, T2, Y3. See also Stephen Pumfrey's chapter in this volume.
69 Rachel Hasted, *The Pendle Witch Trial 1612* (Preston: Lancashire County Books, 1987), p. 42.
70 Catalogue of the Cartmel Collection, University of Lancaster.

71 Potts, *Wonderfull Discoverie*; John Weever, 'Ad Gulielmum Shakespeare', repr. in Honigmann, *Shakespeare: The 'Lost Years'*, pp. 53–4. For the possibility that Shakespeare travelled to Hoghton in the company of Edmund Campion, as a potential Jesuit recruit, see Wilson, 'Shakespeare and the Jesuits', pp. 11–13.

72 'A Speech made to King James at his coming to Hoghton Tower', in John Nichols, *The Progresses ... of James the First* (London: Royal Society of Antiquaries, 1828), pp. 398–9. See also George C. Miller, *Hoghton Tower* (Preston: Guardian Press, 1948), pp. 83–7.

73 Lumby, *Lancashire Witch-Craze*, pp. 129–33.

74 Greenblatt, 'Shakespeare bewitched', pp. 114, 128.

75 'The Burning Babe', in Robert Southwell, *The Poems of Robert Southwell, S.J.*, ed. James McDonald and Nancy Pollard Brown (Oxford: Clarendon Press, 1967), p. 15.

76 Quoted in Caraman, *Henry Garnet*, p. 281; Foley, *Records of the English Province*, pp. 414–16, 497. Martyred in 1601, 'Mistress' Anne Line was canonised in 1970.

9

Sexual and spiritual politics
in the events of 1633–34 and
The Late Lancashire Witches

Alison Findlay

The prologue to Thomas Heywood and Richard Brome's *The Late Lancashire Witches* (1634) announces that the play will:

> *ground the Sceane that's now in agitation.*
> *The Project unto many here well knowne;*
> *Those Witches the fat Jaylor brought to Towne.*[1]

The '*Sceane*' in '*agitation*' was the case of four women confined in London and accused of witchcraft. Margaret Johnson, Mary Spencer, Frances Dicconson and Jennet Hargreaves already had a complex history behind them. They had been tried and condemned at the Lancashire Assizes on 24 March 1634, along with sixteen other people. One of these was Jennet Davies, who may have been that Jennet Device whose evidence in the earlier 1612 trial was instrumental in the condemnations of her mother, brother and sister to their deaths. In 1634 Jennet Davies found herself transformed from child witness to witch; the second Lancashire witchcraft trial clearly showed the potent legacy left by the first Lancashire witches. Although the presence of the second group of witches in London was current news, they were already part of a vivid cultural memory of Lancashire witchcraft.

Ten-year-old Edmund Robinson, the main accuser of the second generation of witches, stepped into the child-witness role previously occupied by the nine-year-old Jennet Device at the first trial. His testimony was imbued with memories and stories of what had gone before. He later admitted that 'he had heard neighbours talk of a witch feast that was kept at Mocking Tower in Pendle Forest about twenty years since and thereupon he framed those tales concerning the persons aforesaid'.[2] On 10 February 1633 he told two JPs for Lancaster that 'upon All-saints day past' he had been gathering wild plums when he spotted two greyhounds, one black and one brown, wearing shining golden leashes. When the dogs would not run after a hare, he beat them, and they changed into Dicconson's wife and a young boy.[3] According to Edmund Robinson, Frances Dicconson 'put her hand into her pocket, and pulled out a peace of silver much like to a faire shillinge and offered to give him to hould his tongue, and not to tell, whiche hee refused, saying, nay thou art a witch'. He went on to tell that she bridled her boy companion, who 'stood up a white horse' and then rode with Robinson to a witches' congregation at Hoare-stones House. Here Robinson claimed that he had seen meat roasting and 'other meate stirring in the house', that he had been served bread and meat and an ill-tasting drink which 'was nought'. He had then entered the adjoining barn to witness 'Sixe of them kneeling, and pulling at sixe severall roapes ... at or with which pullinge came then in this informers sight flesh smoakeing, butter in lumps, and milke as it were syleing [straining through] from the saide roapes'. Robinson also claimed that he had seen Jennet Davies 'at severall tymes in a croft or close adjoining to his fathers house, which put him in a great feare' and that 'upon Thursday after New Yeares day last past' he had seen Loynd's wife sitting on a 'crosse peece of wood' (either a cross or a beam) in his father's chimney, up which she disappeared. He alleged having witnessed Loynd's wife appear from a lantern, in another incident where he was fighting a boy with a cloven foot, and also claimed that she and two other women had taken down pictures pricked through with thorns. Robinson's description of the witches' feast perhaps recalls the Malkin Tower meeting of 1612, while his references to swift movement, haunting a building, transmutation, and the use of effigies are scraps drawn from popular witchcraft folklore and belief. When cross-examined in London by George Long, JP for Middlesex, Robinson admitted 'all that tale is false and feigned, and has no truth at all, but only as he has heard tales and reports made by women'.[4]

Robinson's allegations of witchcraft in Lancashire were supported by the confession of sixty-year-old Margaret Johnson, made on 2 March before the same justices. Although not mentioned by Robinson, she claimed the Devil had appeared to her as a spirit called Mamilion 'apparrelled in a suite of black, tyed about with silk points, who offered that if shee would give him her soule hee would supply all her wants'.[5] She too was familiar with the conventions of demonological practice as discussed in numerous European and British treatises on the subject, referring to transgressive sexual practices with the Devil ('committing wicked uncleannesse'), to the provision of incubi for female and succubi for male witches, and to the suckling of spirits or familiars at a special 'pappe or dugge'. Johnson claimed that spirits could transport humans to 'any place upon a sodaine' by animating a rod, dog or other means of conveyance. Her confession simultaneously tuned into more mundane, local explanations of witchcraft as *maleficium*, which typically blamed the suspect as the cause of some material disaster in the community, often a physical ailment in humans or animals. Johnson testified that covens 'can cause foule weather and storms' and that 'the end of their said meeting was to consult for the killing and hurting of men and beasts'.

Margaret Johnson appears to have internalised the folklore surrounding witchcraft as a means of (albeit temporary) empowerment. It may be that strong suspicions about the fabulous nature of her confession and Robinson's testimony were held by the judges of the Lancaster Assizes because although Sir George Vernon and Sir Francis Crawley[6] condemned all but one of the accused, they refused to pass the death sentences, and referred the matter to King Charles I. The condemned were held in Lancaster Castle.

On 16 May the Privy Council summoned 'some of the principall and most notorious offenders' to London at the King's command. Not having the names of the supposed malefactors caused a delay, and on 23 May the Lancaster judges were obliged to remind the King and Privy Council of the case. By the end of the month, more information had been supplied and the Council summoned Frances Dicconson, Margaret Johnson, Alice Higgin, Jennet Loynd, Jennet Hargreaves, Mary Spencer and John Spencer to London. Their accuser Robinson was also summoned for cross-examination. The Bishop of Chester, John Bridgeman, was directed to examine the principal suspects before their departure, for further information.[7] By the time he reached Lancaster to make his inspection, on 15 June 1634, Higgin, Loynd and John Spencer had died in gaol and Hargreaves was very ill, but his reports on the others uncovered inconsistencies and evidence of bribery. Margaret Johnson was found 'acknowledging that she was a witch, but more often faulting in the particulars of her actions, as one having a strong imagination of the former, but of too weak a memory to retain or relate the latter'. It was evidently the Bishop's opinion that Dicconson was the victim of malicious revenge by the Robinsons, who had been refused credit on a cow they bought from her husband, and had offered to drop the accusations if Mr Dicconson would pay them 40 shillings. Bridgeman pointed out that others would have been willing to testify to this act of blackmail and added 'conceit and malice are so powerful with many in those parts, that they will easily afford an oath to work revenge upon their neighbour'. Edmund Robinson senior was, in fact, arrested and held in the Gate House prison in London on 28 June.[8] Bridgeman also noted that the other witness against Dicconson had been accused of felony and was in dispute with her over some butter.

Bridgeman's examination of Mary Spencer exposed the workings of the folk process by which beliefs in the supernatural abilities of a suspect could grow via rumour, 'blown by surmises, Jealousy's conjectures'.[9] Mary 'utterly denie[d]' any knowledge of witchcraft, repeating the Creed and Lord's Prayer. She answered Nicholas Cunliffe's charge that she could make a pail move towards her of its own accord, with the story of a child's game:

> when she was a young girl and went to the pail for water she used to tumble
> or trundle the collock, or peal, down the hill and she would run along after it

to over take it, and did overye [over hie] it sometimes, and then might call it to come to her, but utterly denies that she ever could make it come to her by any witchcraft.

Bridgeman's sympathetic account of Mary Spencer's experience in court, where 'the throng' was 'so great that she could not hear the evidence against her', implicitly undermines the justice of the condemnations at Lancaster while carefully avoiding the presentation of 'such evidence' which would be 'as lawyers speak, against the King'.[10]

Bridgeman's scepticism was endorsed by the findings of a group of mid-wives, directed to 'inspect and search' the bodies of the four witches who were brought to London and lodged in the Ship Tavern in Greenwich. Under the supervision of William Harvey, the King's physician, these experts pro-nounced having found no unnatural marks on any of the women, save for two teat-like marks on the body of Margaret Johnson, the importance of which they dismissed.[11] The case against the women finally fell to pieces when Edmund Robinson admitted that 'he had framed the tale out of his own in-vention' in order to excuse his lateness in bringing his mother's cows home. He denied having seen the boy with the cloven foot, or the transformation of Loynd's wife, and claimed he 'told these tales to excuse himself when he had been at play'.[12]

Heywood and Brome's dramatisation of the witches' activities added another layer of fiction to the stories. The Epilogue assumed that the women were guilty, and *'must expect their due / By lawfull Iustice'* (ll. 2802–3), but recog-nised the provisional nature of that judgement: *'what their crime / May bring upon 'em, ripenes yet of time / Has not reveal'd'* (ll. 2805–6). This circumspect conclusion is appropriate to the liminal position occupied by the witches, who still awaited the King's judgement, just as the King's Men awaited the judge-ment of their audience. The currency of the play's subject and the expectations of spectators (in addition to details about its production) are revealed in a fascinating account by Nathaniel Tomkyns, discovered by Herbert Berry. In a letter of 16 August 1634, Tomkyns tells his friend Sir Robert Phelips of a visit to the Globe Theatre to see a performance of the play (I reproduce the account from Berry's fine article):

> Here hath bin lately a newe comedie at the globe called *The Witches of Lancasheir*, acted by reason of the great concourse of people 3 dayes togither: the 3ᵈ day I went with a friend to see it, and found a greater appear-ance of fine folke gentlemen and gentleweomen then I thought had bin in town in the vacation: The subject was of the slights and passages done or supposed to be done by these witches sent from thence hither and other witches and their Familiars; Of ther nightly meetings in severall places: their banqueting with all sorts of meat and drinke conveyed unto them by their familiars upon the pulling of a cord: the walking of pailes of milke by them-

selves and (as they say of children) a highlone [alone]: the transforming of men and weomen into the shapes of severall creatures and especially of horses by putting an inchaunted bridle into ther mouths: their posting to and from places farre distant in an incredible short time: the cutting off of a witch-gentlewoman's hand in the forme of a catt, by a soldier turned miller, known to her husband by a ring thereon, (the onely tragicall part of the storie:) the representing of wrong and putative fathers in the shape of meane persons to gentlemen by way of derision: the tying of a knott at a mariage (after the French manner) to cassate masculine abilitie, and the conveying away of the good cheere and bringing in a mock feast of bones and stones in steed thereof and the filling of pies with living birds and yong catts &c: And though there be not in it (to my understanding) any poeticall Genius, or art, or language, or judgement to state or tenet of witches (which I expected,) or application to vertue but full of ribaldrie and of things improbable and impossible; yet in respect of the newnesse of the subject (the witches being still visible and in prison here) and in regard it consisteth from the beginning to the ende of odd passages and fopperies to provoke laughter, and is mixed with divers songs and dances, it passeth for a merrie and excellent new play. *per acta est fabula. Vale.*[13]

Berry points out that Tomkyns calls the play *The Witches of Lancasheir* (rather than *The 'Late' Lancashire Witches* of the text printed after the event), and emphasises the 'newness' or currency of the subject.[14] The drama was, as A. M. Clark has called it, a piece of 'dramatic journalism'[15] and the King's Men (the theatre company of which Shakespeare had formerly been a member) certainly appreciated the value of a newsworthy scoop. On 20 July 1634 they petitioned the Lord Chamberlain to stop the performance of another play on witchcraft (*Dr Lambe and the Witches*) 'to the prejudice of their designed Comedy of the Lancashire witches, & desiring a prohibition of any other till theirs bee allowed and Acted'.[16] It probably opened on 11 or 12 August, and certainly no later than 13 August, three days before Tomkyns wrote his letter. His comments indicate that it was an immediate hit, attended by everyone who was anyone in London at the time, and played for three days in succession 'by reason of the great concourse of people'. The fictional play, as much as the 'real' witches, was an event, a place to learn the latest news about the 'state or tenet of witches'.

Many of the details Tomkyns recalls are familiar from the legal documents relating to the case. When we examine the play text, it is clear that Heywood and Brome knew Edmund Robinson's testimony of 10 February, Margaret Johnson's confession and examination by Bridgeman, and the accusations against Mary Spencer. Since this information was not public knowledge, Berry's theory that Heywood and Brome were commissioned to write the play by members of the Privy Council keen to condemn the women seems highly plausible. In return for exclusive rights to the source material, the King's Men were to produce a play presenting the case for the prosecution.

From the perspective of those who had seen all the evidence, the case was weak, especially after Robinson's confessions about the fanciful nature of his deposition. On 16 July Robinson admitted that 'Having heard the story of the meeting at Mocking Tower [Malkin Tower in the 1612 case], it came into his head to make the like tale of a meeting at Horestones' and that 'Nobody was ever acquainted with any part of his fiction or invention, nor did any body ever advise him, but it merely proceeded out of his own brain'.[17] Evidence for the prosecution had effectively collapsed before Heywood and Brome's play was presented. With no factual ground to stand on, the Council members wishing to sentence the witches did as Robinson had done before them, and turned to the power of the story. Apparently believing that fiction would be stronger, as well as stranger, than truth, they relied on the *fabula* (to quote Tomkyns) to promote their case.

Their faith was not misplaced. Margaret Johnson, Mary Spencer, Frances Dicconson and Jennet Hargreaves were duly pardoned, but, in spite of their innocence, they were taken back to Lancaster Castle and reimprisoned. In August 1636 they were still incarcerated as witches, along with Marie Shuttleworth, Alice Priestley, Jennet Cronkshaw, Agnes Rawsterne and Robert and Jennet Wilkinson. In autumn 1637, five women, one with a child, were still detained at His Majesty's pleasure.[18] Their fictional identity as a weird sisterhood outlived the evidence of their innocence. A performance of the play on 10 July 1635 in Oxford and exchanges of printed copies in 1637 and 1642 still called it 'The Witches of Lancasheire', as though the story retained its currency. Richard James's poem *Iter Lancastrense* (1636) candidly states 'I wonder much / If judges sentence with belief on such' and prays that for 'love of God they would give causes end / With equall justice'.[19]

Why did the folklore of witchcraft hold such fascination for the early modern imagination? Perhaps the first, most important point is that while narratives like Margaret Johnson's and Edmund Robinson's are easily recognisable as conventional stories of witchcraft, they are not easy to dismiss completely as fictions. For early modern people the existence of witchcraft, both good and bad, was, as James Sharpe observes, 'part of the fabric of everyday life, maybe something that you came across very rarely, but that was a known and recognized quantity when it did crop up'.[20] Like the sensational stories of today's media, witchcraft was a kind of news which drew attention to the newsmaking process: something with credibility which invited sharp critical evaluation. Readers, spectators and witnesses occupied an active role as interpreters of the evidence along the sliding scale of fact and fiction. Beliefs in the existence of witchcraft ranged across the social spectrum. In June 1634 Queen Elizabeth of Bohemia asked William Brereton, who was visiting her at The Hague, about the Lancashire witches, and responded with accounts of local witchcraft incidents:

after the queen had put me upon a discourse of the discovery of our Lancashire witches, she answered it with a relation of the discovery of witches in
Westphalia, where a whole village, all witches; and amongst them was the
Bishop of Wurzburg's chancellor and his page, all whom deservedly burned
... She also spoke (which Duke Bernard of Weimar averred unto her) that
some ministers being at supper together assembled together in a room of the
house of Duke William at Weimar, which was troubled w[ith] spirits; that
being at meat, all their stools upon a sudden [were] plucked from under
them. A gentelwoman sitting there at supper, feeling something under her
clothes, stabbing down suddenly w[ith] her knife, it came up all blood; her
garter was taken off her leg, and tied under all clothes upon her bare arm.[21]

Men from the medical and clerical professions also believed in the existence of
witchcraft. In the case of Anne Gunter, a range of Oxford dons were of the
opinion that she was the genuine victim of supernatural malevolence. When
brought to the Star Chamber in 1606, however, she admitted that her father
had obliged her to 'feign and counterfeit herself to be bewitched'.[22] Common
people like those of Anne Gunter's village, North Moreton, and like the populace of Lancashire, regularly consulted 'wise folk' with supposedly supernatural powers, as Kirsteen Macpherson Bardell's chapter in this volume explains.

The fate of the Lancashire women accused in 1634 tells us much about
the symbolic power of witchcraft. The fiction of demonic female activity
seems to have had a dangerous energy of its own, an electrical charge which
could not easily be diffused. Just because Edmund Robinson confessed that
the events did not actually happen did not mean that they could not happen.
Stories like Robinson's, constructed from standard elements, may not be reliable as evidence of what happened, but they are still historically valuable as
evidence of society's beliefs and anxieties. The reputation of the Lancashire
women, however unfounded, had momentum of its own because it provided a
focus for much wider disruptive energies in the kingdom. The close relationship between texts dealing with demonological beliefs and those dealing with
other forms of deviant behaviour has been convincingly demonstrated by
Stuart Clark, who argues that these literatures shared a common vocabulary
of misrule. The behaviour of witches was described according to the same
principle of inversion found in accounts of other types of rebellion. Witches,
like scolding women, disobedient children or subjects, turned the world up-
side down. In each case the inversion made an implicit validation of a rigidly
hierarchical society. Because all these types of disorderly behaviour used a
common discourse, witchcraft took on a significance far beyond its immediate
character. It worked intertextually with more overtly political writings to
warn of the dangers of a world of misrule.[23]

The Late Lancashire Witches exploits the repercussive power of witchcraft. It
uses the topical story of the witches to dramatise crises in the gender order and

in contemporary religious politics. Witchcraft fund
threats posed by unruly subjects whose actions cha
their paternal masters, both secular and spiritual. B
witches 'still visible' in London, to their fictional s
boy actors and displayed on the stage, we can explor
read as a projection of deviant extremism on the
women and religious dissidents.

The feminist critic Sandra Gilbert defines witchc
ised channel into which excess demonically flows – ex
excess creativity to be annihilated by society.[24] It seer
cess of female activity – actual and potential – is cha
the Lancashire witches. These women, whose behavic
ing surplus to the accepted gender norm, are like cult
outlets for a wider current of energy, physical and
ground by the dominant ideology in early-seven
Nicholas Breton's book of character types, *The Good*
scriptions of the Worthies, and Unworthies of this Age
of patriarchal ideology at work in its polarisations of
propriate female behaviour. Examples of the latter ar
the category of 'the badde' as examples of evil excess.
for example, is 'the misery of man, whose demeanour
but in extremities. Her voice is the screeching of an
unsupportable, her anger unquenchable, her will insat
unmatchable'. As another example of 'the badde', Bro
woman: 'A wanton woman is the figure of imperfection
quality a wagtail, in countenance a witch, and in condit
As Breton's text implies, the witch is a culturally moul
women's excess – that which is surplus to the officially
model – demonically flows. Women's mental and physica
tion constitute a subversive energy that threatens
homosocial market in which social and economic trans;
tween men to maintain the patriarchal status quo. Any
intervention by women needs to be siphoned off in orde
on that social and economic structure. It is concentratec
witch, a volcanic centre of disruptive energies who is de
tion. The witch can usefully be theorised as a human €
Bataille's economic category of the accursed surplus. Ac
the accursed surplus is that excess which society produces
for destruction: 'The victim is a surplus taken from the me;
... Once chosen [s]he is the accursed share, destined fo
tion.'[26]

Given the poverty and vulnerability of most people acc
the idea of the witch as surplus seems out of place. Howeve

;ued that witchcraft accusations were partly a symptom of socio-eco-
change, where an increasing gap between richer and poorer villagers
companied by inadequate official structures for dealing with the prob-
poverty and subsequent guilt on the part of substantial householders.
ling to Macfarlane, the guilt felt by richer villagers was transferred onto
ure of the witch, the accursed share of their own 'surplus' wealth. Their
responsibility to the poor within the community was displaced onto the
cium of the witch.[27] This socio-economic dimension of the Lancashire
s examined in John Swain's chapter in this volume. In the context of the
he witches are the demonised surplus of both the Lancashire community
ted on stage and the fashionable beau monde of London, the 'fine folke
men and gentleweomen' Tomkyns encounters at the Globe perform-
This social elite had been castigated by Charles I for neglecting their
isibilities to their provincial estates, and required to return by a 1632
proclamation.[28]

longside her symbolic role within the local economy, the figure of the
also represented a specifically female surplus, a portentous and sinister
s of unrestrained energy, chosen for sacrifice to preserve a fragile status
i which women were restricted to a subservient position because of their
>sedly weaker nature. Again it is vital to remember that the powerful
ist model of the witch is at odds with the material reality of most of the
is accused, who were vulnerable and poor. In that sense it exists only as
, but as the case of the Lancaster women demonstrates, the myth appears
ive had an autonomous reality. Christina Larner's work on Scottish
icraft prosecutions led her to the view that women would often 'fantasise
t the Devil to bring colour to their lives'.[29] It is now recognised that fan-
: ideas about witches' shape-changing abilities, deviant sexual practices
large-scale sabbats permeated English texts and folklore as well.[30]
und Robinson's and Margaret Johnson's testimonies are both made up of
elements. The details of shape-changing, image magic, sabbat meetings
familiar spirits are found in earlier testimonies, such as the confessions of
ibeth Stile of Windsor in 1579 or Agnes Pepwell of North Moreton in
shire in 1605.[31] Like these two elderly women, the accused Margaret
son probably drew on a deeply embedded set of witch-beliefs to fashion a
onic autobiography which would allow her to play the witch as a high-
is role, something very different from the reality of her life.
The play participates in the circulation of these narratives, using Edmund
inson's testimony to characterise the Lancashire witches as figures of ex-
, like Bataille's accursed surplus. They have an exaggerated freedom of
ement which defies both the strict controls on women's conduct, includ-
their confinement in the home, and the laws of logic. In fact the play
inates the geographical distance between Lancashire and London and, by
lication, erodes the difference between rural and urban communities. The

character Robin tells how Mal Spencer took him over three hundred miles in eight hours and claims that Mrs Generous could move over a hundred miles in a quarter of an hour (ll. 1210–11 and 1691–2). The London references suggest to the audience that such disruptive energies cannot be safely contained in the particular social context of a Lancashire village. The witches also cause an excess of noise. They frighten the miller and the soldier with 'such catterwawling, & such scratching and clawing' (ll. 801–2) as the men cannot endure.

The play's comic dramatisation of the wedding feast of two servants, Lawrence and Parnell, shows that the witches' superabundant energy re-animates the dead meat in the dishes. The mutton grows horns, the birds emerge from a pie and Joan reports that 'all the meat is flowne out o' the chimney top' and transformed into live snakes, bats, frogs, bees and hornets (ll. 1147–9). The spectator Tomkyns notes this inversion of festivity: 'the conveying away of the good cheere and bringing in a mock feast of bones and stones in steed thereof and the filling of pies with living birds and yong catts &c', a spectacle apparently effected on stage, with obvious novelty appeal. This is only one element of the chaos enacted by the witches. Following charivary traditions, they disrupt the 'house rites' promising 'joy and tranquility' (ll. 1033–4) by substituting bran for the wedding cake which was supposed to be broken over the bride's head on entering the house ('As they lift up the Cake, the Spirit snatches it, and powres down bran', l. 1075). The wedding entertainment proves no more successful; the bewitched musicians 'play the battle' (music designed to accompany battle scenes on stage), a signal of the disharmony which is to characterise the relationship between the married couple (l. 1071).

The parodic interruption of a wedding parade along these lines was a form of charivary in early modern England, as Tom Pettit has shown.[32] The play's nuptial charivary is somewhat different though. Normally the charivary was a stylised form of social criticism undertaken by villagers to signal the community's disapproval of the match (usually by casting aspersions on the bride's sexual continency). In contrast, the play's charivary is enacted by a group of women who have made metaphysical pacts which allow them to transcend social conventions. Isolated from the community's laws, the witches invert the charivary's usual function to destroy rather than restore social order, possibly as an expression of their rejection of the institution of marriage. While the wedding descends into chaos, order and 'jollitie' is found at their alternative, all-female 'bevy of beldames' (l. 1515) with its music and paired dancing (ll. 1558–73), and the service of the wedding dishes 'with all sorts of meate and drinke conveyed unto them by their familiars upon the pulling of a cord', as Tomkyns tells us. The play self-consciously comments on the failure of charivary as a social corrective through the behaviour of the bewitched Lawrence and Parnell. The couple present an exaggerated picture of gender disorder in Parnell's aggressive dominance over her impotent husband. A skimmington ride (a charivary ritual where figures representing the henpecked husband and the monstrously dominant wife ride past in mockery) is brought on stage but, far from taking their correction meekly, the bewitched bride and groom attack the performers. Parnell pulls the male Skimmington off his horse and fights him, and the charivary is driven off stage (ll. 1991–6).

Transgressive sexual energy, which stands in opposition to the fidelity and social containment symbolised by the marriage, is at the heart of the witches' activities. The play draws on the popular myth that associates witchcraft with an excess of passion, manifesting itself in the form of sexually deviant acts. Granny Peg Johnson, one of the coven, admits to an alliance with her familiar devil, saying that he never failed to give her satisfaction 'twice a weeke' and was a good bedfellow 'onely his flesh felt cold' (ll. 2749–56). Whetstone, a bastard, is a product of the sexual excess of a supposed witch (ll. 118–22) and promises to beget a bastard on Mal Spencer, a junior member of the coven (ll. 2058–9). He continually refers to Mrs Generous as his 'aunt' and the secondary meaning of 'whore' is used to imply that he has had sex with the other witches:

> Whetstone: Mine aunt's mine aunt, and shall be to her dying day.
> Doughty: ... O here comes more of your Naunts, Naunt Dickinson, Naunt Hargrave, ods fish, and Granny Johnson too.
> (ll. 2678–82)

Whetstone and the witches destabilise the male characters' virility, promoting female reproductive power in its place. Whetstone hints that their magic allows them to adopt both male and female shapes by transforming themselves into hares who are 'like Hermaphrodites, one while male and another female, and that which begets one yeare, brings young ones the next' (ll. 657–9). Under the suggestion of asexual reproduction is the implication that women can reproduce without men, or at least outside male control. Under the witches influence, Joan Seeley dresses up 'like one o' the Scottish wayward sisters' (l. 447) and sings a bawdy song about an unmarried woman who gets pregnant (ll. 452–60). By contrast, Lawrence is made impotent by means of a magical codpiece point (a ribbon to attach the codpiece to the breeches). 'Lusty Lawrence' was a figure popularised in ballads as the begetter of seventeen bastards in a year. Once the Lawrence of the play is married to Parnell, he finds himself unprovided of the proper instrument, in spite of his previous reputation as an 'over mickle man among the maids' (ll. 1900–1).

Common insecurities about female infidelity are exaggerated in the revenge plot involving Whetstone. The witches help him to punish the gallants Bantam, Shakstone and Arthur, who have made fun of his illegitimacy. Whetstone promises to let the gallants see their fathers and the witches' visions reveal that, far from being aristocratic lords, Bantam's father was his childhood tutor, Shakstone's was his mother's tailor, and Arthur's was a stable groom (ll. 2120–63). The trick unsettles the basis of all social hierarchy in the play, linking the gallants' mothers to the free-loving witches. Whetstone points out that illegitimacy has grown 'a great kindred in the Kingdome' (ll. 2175–6).[33]

Members of the audience certainly picked up on these disturbing elements of the witches' behaviour, as we can see from Tomkyns's account. He notes especially the witches' 'transforming of men and women into the shapes of severall creatures and especially of horses by putting an inchaunted bridle into ther mouths: their posting to and from places farre distant in an incredible short time'. At the end of the extract he also notes their trick of 'representing of wrong and putative fathers in the shape of meane persons to gentlemen by way of derision'.

Challenges to the gender order are highlighted in a plot involving Mrs Generous, the most fully characterised member of the coven. She inverts the image of the submissive wife by using a magical bridle to transform her serv-ant Robin into a horse – another aspect of the play noted by Tomkyns. The metamorphosis is a striking example of inversion since it parodies the picture of wifely subjection in William Whately's tract *A Bride Bush or A Wedding Sermon* (1617). Whateley claimed that the wife 'submits herself with quiet-ness, cheerfully, even as a wellbroken horse turns at the least turning, stands at the least check of the rider's bridle, readily going and standing as he wishes that sits upon his back'.[34] Far from submitting quietly, Mrs Generous disobeys her husband's commands against going out on horseback and takes the reins herself. She uses Robin to carry her to a sabbat where she and her 'Satanicall sisterhood' (l. 1507) cause a 'catterwalling' or noise which prevents the men from getting any sleep. The notorious punishment for the unquiet woman was, of course, the scold's bridle. It was a physical means of restraint as well as a metaphor of submission. When Mrs Generous bridles Robin, her actions therefore have another dimension: they are a wayward reversal of the persecutory powers used to silence women. She appropriates the instrument of torture and turns it back on its inventors. The magical bridle ties up Robin's tongue and liberates hers. Mrs Generous enacts a passionate fantasy of re-venge and makes a critical comment on the double standard on public speech. By punishing Robin and the husband for whom he speaks as scolds, she im-plies that men are as guilty as women when it comes to unseemly verbal out-bursts to impose their own will.

Heywood uses the plot to foreground an additional danger: the presence of female subversion beneath an apparent conformity to social and moral standards. When Generous accuses his wife of being a witch, she demon-strates supreme manipulative skill, promising to shed penitent tears until she is accepted back as a 'wife, sister and daughter' into a 'blest society' ruled by men (ll. 1826–30). This is not, as McLuskie implies, a scene of genuine repent-ance and reconciliation.[35] The next time we see Mrs Generous, she explains with pride how she managed to deceive her husband. The mock penitence was itself a form of witchcraft. She says:

> Some passionate words mixt with forc't tears
> Did so inchant his eyes and eares
> I made my peace, with promise never
> To doe the like; but once and ever
> A Witch thou know'st. Now understand
> New businesse wee tooke in hand.
> My Husband packt out of the towne
> Know that the house, and all's our owne. (ll. 2046–53)

Mrs Generous's conformity is no more than a mask to conceal her darker purpose to take over the household. In the denouement of the plot, Heywood shows how she is cut off from the wifely role in a grotesquely literal way. A soldier amputates the paw of one of the cat-like spirits and, to his horror, Mr Generous recognises it as the left hand of his wife: 'Is this the hand once plighted holy vowes, / And this the ring that bound then?' (ll. 2445–6). The hand with the wedding ring represents Mrs Generous's willingness to abide by the 'Homily on Matrimony' and 'cease from commanding and perform subjection' to her husband. The loss of that hand shows that her behaviour cannot be reconciled with the wifely role. However saintly she may have appeared, her irrepressible nature revolts against the duty of submission. The possibility of a gap between the ideal image and the reality is hinted at in the homily itself. It acknowledges that women 'must specially feel the grief and pains of their Matrimony, in that they relinquish the Liberty of their own Rule'.[36] In such circumstances, their co-operation in the unequal partnership may have been no more than skin deep. Some women, like Mrs Generous, literally 'performed subjection' rather than genuinely submitting themselves to their husbands' rule.

The Generous plot dramatises a widespread unease about gender hierarchy in the period, based on an awareness that the reality of marital relations rarely conformed to the patriarchal model.[37] That Tomkyns remembered the amputation and wedding ring detail in his account of the performance seems to confirm its importance as a projection of current insecurities. The play exposes a worrying discrepancy between the active energies of women – their intelligence, determination, qualities of leadership and organisation – and the social order into which they were supposed to fit.

The Late Lancashire Witches uses witch-hunting to investigate religious politics as well as gender issues, following in the tradition of Macbeth as explored in Richard Wilson's chapter in this volume. By considering the spiritual context of the 1630s we can see that the demonised women may represent other persecuted minorities whose beliefs were also extreme to the point of nonconformity. Lancashire was an appropriate setting for a play dealing with religious debate because it was a notorious centre of recusant activities. William Harrison, the King's Preacher, complained that different factions of believers in Lancashire included 'Popish recusants, Church Papists, prophane Atheists and Carnall Protestants which swarmed together like Hornets in those parts'. He pointed out that within the Church 'the constreyned union of Papists and Protestants' was in danger of breaking it up.[38] Puritans and quasi-Catholic believers hurled abuse at each other, grouping their so-called enemies of the faith along with the witches. In a side prosecution in the 1612 witch trials, a Jesuit priest had been responsible for mounting fraudulent accusations against three Protestant women, but was found out and accused of devilish activity himself. Puritan sympathisers regarded Lancashire as 'a nest of both Papists and witches'.[39] Lancashire was certainly a region in which old-style Catholic beliefs and practices still retained a strong hold. From the 1560s to the 1630s complaints were raised against parishes for celebrating saints' days and for using holy water, prayers for the dead and rosary beads in their services.[40]

Under the regime of William Laud, appointed Archbishop of Canterbury in 1633, the ritual and visual aspects of worship, previously identified with Catholic influence, were vigorously promoted, while godly Puritans were attacked as disturbers of the parish harmony. Laud exaggerated the dangers posed by Puritans and, in 1634, the High Commission ordered every JP to ferret out members of Puritan sects across the land.[41] Bishop Bridgeman, who examined the accused women, was brought before the Commission on charges of undue leniency towards non-conformists; as early as 1630, he had told the Puritan minister John Angier 'I have a good will to indulge you, but I cannot: for my Lord's Grace of Canterbury hath rebuked me for permitting two non-conforming ministers ... and I am likely to come into dishonour on this behalf'. Bridgeman was correct; he was cross-examined for a year by the High Commission between 1633 and 1634.[42]

Brome and Heywood are using the play to satirise the change of direction in spiritual politics instigated by Laud and the High Commission. The religious controversy may have had an additional local dimension for them if Herbert Berry's theory about the origin of the play is correct. He suggests that the Lancashire witch trial caused a split in the Privy Council between Puritan sympathisers (who wanted to condemn the witches) and others who followed Archbishop Laud and regarded witchcraft accusations as mere fictions created by over-zealous Puritans. If Berry's idea is correct, it is probable that Lord Pembroke would have headed the Puritan faction within the Privy Council. Pembroke (the estranged husband of the formidable Westmorland gentlewoman Lady Anne Clifford) was the only explicitly Puritan member of the Council, and had been in longstanding opposition to Laud and his policies, including contesting him in the election for the Chancellorship of Oxford University in 1630.[43] Since Pembroke was also the Lord Chamberlain, responsible for licensing plays, he would have been in an ideal position to commission a piece to further the interests of the would-be prosecutors.

How did Heywood and Brome respond to the task? In spite of the pressure to support the interests of those who commissioned the work, they seem to have steered an intriguingly ambiguous line. The play does show the witches condemned and sent off to their deaths, but its comic effects are made at the expense of both the witches *and* their persecutors. Furthermore Heywood and Brome complicate the representation of religious politics: instead of depicting the godly community of witch-hunters as Puritans (like Pembroke and his faction in the Privy Council), it is the witches themselves who are linked to radical Protestant ideas. The play's god-fearing Lancashire community is associated with the rituals and practice associated with old-style Catholicism and the new style of worship encouraged by Laud. Brome and Heywood give the witches the subversive social characteristics attributed to Puritans by their more mainstream opponents, a characterisation which seems to align the playwrights with the conservative, ritualistic ascendancy in Charles I's Church of England. However, the witches are the source of the play's dramatic energies, especially its humour, so probably drew audience sympathies, qualified in varying degrees by adherence to establishment ideas. The fictional community's reaction to the disorder provoked by the witches in the play could have been read by spectators as an over-zealous demonisation of all the anti-hierarchical forces associated with Protestantism on the part of the pro-Laudian establishment.

The practices of the witch coven can be linked to radical Protestant ideas. Their spells promote individual autonomy in opposition to traditional hierarchies. They bewitch the Seeley family so that 'The Sonne rebukes the Father old; / The Daughter at the mother Scold[s]', the wife chides her husband and the servants give orders to their master and mistress (ll. 559–67). Rebellions against the gerontocratic order had traditionally been attributed to the evils of Protestantism. Political commentator John Christopherson, author of *An Exhortacion to All Menne to Take Hede and Beware of Rebellion* (1554), complained that children would make 'a mery mockery of their parents', and in *Displaying of the Protestantes* (1555) he claimed that servants had 'in maner become masters themselves'.[44] Even though these texts were written well before *The Late Lancashire Witches*, the associations they made were still current. Laudian clerical inquisitors imposed their own prejudiced ideas about what Anabaptists or Familists ought to believe, just as they started with assumptions about what witches believed.[45] In the play, anxieties about the transformative power of Puritanism and its egalitarian principles are projected onto the bewitched Seeley household. They are mocked as a 'Family of love' (l. 1349) and Mr Seeley threatens to send them all to New England if they behave in such an unconventional way again (l. 1357). Lawrence and Parnell's attack on the skimmington carries Puritan overtones since they both call the male Skimmington figure 'an aydoll' (ll. 2002–3), as if linking it to icons allegedly worshipped by Catholics, a prominent feature of parades on saints' days.

The chaos caused by the witches at Lawrence and Parnell's wedding feast can be seen as an attack on the ritualised church ceremonies now sanctioned under Laud. They make the church bells ring backwards, the procession up to the bride table parodies the procession up to the altar, and the transformation of dishes of food into live animals is a travesty of the doctrine of transubstantiation. When the dance, traditionally a symbol of divine harmony, breaks down, the play makes the religious connotations of such a collapse explicit, as though commenting on the failure of Laudian reforms to make a new beginning in the English Church. When asked to play a tune called 'the beginning of the world', the fiddlers produce a cacophony of different tunes resembling primeval Chaos rather than divine Creation (ll. 1386–96). Another important detail links the godly community with the Catholics and the witches' *maleficium* with their Puritan opponents: Mr Generous has fallen in love with a wine from London, a divine liquor available only from a pub called The Mitre. There are several references to this wine. For example, Robin tells Mal that 'since he was last at London and tasted the Divinitie of the Miter, scarce any liquor in Lancashire will go downe with him, sure, sure, he will never be a Puritaine, he holds so well with the Miter' (ll. 978–81). The London reference connects the Lancashire plot with religious agitation in the capital. In April 1634 Laud launched an attack on French and Dutch Protestant communities living in London and Canterbury.[46] Individuals were also identified for persecution and in *The Late Lancashire Witches* Brome and Heywood may be caricaturing the fates of militant Puritans such as Willian Prynne, Henry Burton and John Bastwick. The years 1633–34 saw proceedings, instigated by Laud, against Bastwick and Prynne. Prynne's anti-theatrical tract *Histriomastix* was condemned as a seditious libel. He was sentenced to life imprisonment, a huge fine, the loss of his university degrees and two appearances in the pillory where he had his ears cropped.

The Late Lancashire Witches was certainly in touch with this topical event. In the second act, there is an allusion to Prynne's treatment in the pillory (ll. 897–8) so it is possible that the authors were drawing attention to a parallel between the cases of the witches and the religious dissenters. Records of Prynne's trial in the Star Chamber show how, like the women accused of witchcraft, his overtly non-conformist behaviour was seen as diabolically inspired. Lord Cottingham was of the opinion that 'Mr Pryn did not invent this booke alone, but was assisted by the devill himselfe, and it is not the first booke of this nature hee made, for hee made one booke against the due reverence of our Saviour, which none but a devill would doe'.[47] Writing against the 'due reverence' demanded by the Laudian Church made Prynne the Devil incarnate.

Neither Heywood nor Brome were sympathetic to Puritan extremists but the play seems to suggest that the excesses of the witches (and, by implication, of figures like Burton, Prynne and Bastwick) are a reaction against excessive paternal intervention. They are the product of laws which restrict female behaviour and religious belief to an unnaturally rigid model promoted by the paternal state. It is tempting to draw similarities between non-conforming Puritans and women. We should not assume that they shared the same values or ideals as persecuted minorities, however. Even though Puritanism may have enhanced the role of women as the spiritual equals of men, it simultaneously declared that the wife should be submissive to her husband. The Puritan accused of devilish practices against the State and the woman charged with witchcraft did not exist in a relationship of radical solidarity, as we can see from a strangely appropriate example. By a curious twist of fate, the Puritan Henry Burton found himself in prison at Lancaster Castle, where the Lancashire witches were also sent after their trial. His account of the witches demonstrates how the State was successful in dividing the forces opposing it:

> There was a darke room under mine, where they put five witches with one of their children, which made such a hellish noise night and day, that I seemed then to be in hell, or at least in some Popish Purgatory, the Region next above hell ... And their malice herein appeared the more, that they had roome enough elsewhere in the Castle to bestow these witches in, who had continued a long time there.[48]

Witch-hunting may be another name for religious persecution in the play, but in England in the 1630s the ruling ideology set its victims against one another. The view that a virtuous woman has to be chaste, quiet and subservient leads Burton to regard his fellow prisoners as devils. It is they rather than Laud who are the makers of a popish purgatory. He displaces his anger at the powers which have incarcerated him onto a group of women below him who make a noise. This episode encapsulates the means by which the Lancashire women were overmastered by the stories that surrounded them. Burton accuses those who lodge him near the witches of 'malice', but sees the female prisoners as evil itself. They are the first cause, the darkness and 'hell' from which there is no escape. This is an extraordinary view of a group of captive women, with power only to give birth to children and noise.

What the events of 1633–34 show, and what Heywood and Brome's fictional dramatisation emphasised, is the double-edged nature of witchcraft stories. No matter how thin their basis in fact, tales of the Lancashire witches exerted a fascination for authors and listeners. The witches became a locus of outlawed desires and energies and the bewitching narratives took on a life of their own. As the play's epilogue tellingly put it, '*What of their storie further shall ensue / We must referre to time*' (ll. 2819–20). Time showed how the Lancashire witch narrative could easily be co-opted by men in authority (whether boys of ten, members of the Privy Council, playwrights, or religious non-conformists). The Lancashire women became the victims of a discourse which may have given them a temporary illusion of power as Satan's agents but ultimately confined them as the scapegoats of an anxious patriarchal society.

Notes

1 Thomas Heywood and Richard Brome, *The Late Lancashire Witches* (1634; ed. Laird H. Barber, New York and London: Garland Publishing, 1979), Prologue, ll. 5–7. All references to the play will be to line numbers in this edition.

2 'Re-examination of Edmund Robinson the younger, taken before George Long, 16 July 1634', *Calendar of State Papers Domestic* (hereafter *CSPD*), 1634–35, pp. 152–3.

3 'The Examination of Edmund Robinson, Son of *Edm. Robinson*, of *Pendle* forest, mason, taken at *Padiham* before *Richard Shuttleworth* and John Starkie, Esqs.' This testament appears along with that of Margaret Johnson in several manuscript copies: Dodsworth 61 (fols 45–7) and Rawlinson D 399 (fols 211–12), both at the Bodleian Library, are derived from the original via one route, although Rawlinson is rougher. Harleian 6,854 (fols 22–9) and Additional 36,674 (fols 193, 196) (the Londesborough MS), both at the British Library, come via a different route. John Webster's *The Displaying of Supposed Witchcraft* (London, 1677) also prints a version of Robinson's testament (sigs. Yy2–Yy3), which according to Berry (see below) is superior to any of the manuscripts. Quotations here are taken from the version of Webster in the introduction to Thomas Potts, *The Wonderfull Discoverie of Witches in the Countie of Lancaster* (London, 1613; ed. James Crossley, Manchester: Chetham Society publications vi, 1845), pp. lix–lxx.

4 'Examination of Edmund Robinson the younger, of Newchurch, co. Lancaster, aged ten years or thereabouts, taken by George Long, Justice of the Peace for Middlesex, by command of Sec. Windebank, 10 July 1634', *CSPD*, 1634–35, p. 141.

5 Potts, *Wonderfull Discoverie*, pp. lxxii–lxxv.

6 Heywood and Brome, *The Late Lancashire Witches*, p. 220.

7 PC 2/43, pp. 652, 656, 657–8, and 2/44, pp. 56, 73. All in *CSPD*, 1634–35, pp. 77–9, 98, 129–30 141, 144, 152–3, and cited in Herbert Berry, 'The Globe bewitched and *El hombre fiel*', *Medieval and Renaissance Drama in England* 1 (1984), pp. 211–30, p. 215.

8 Bishop Bridgeman of Chester to Secs. Coke and Windebank, 15 June 1634, in *CSPD*, 1634–35, pp. 77–8; Petition of Edmund Robinson to Sec. Windebank, 16 July 1634, *ibid.*, p. 152.

9 *Henry IV Part II*, Induction, 16.

10 Bridgeman to Coke and Windebank, 15 June 1634, *CSPD*, 1634–35, pp. 77–8.

11 The Council to Alexander Baker and Sergeant William Clowes, His Majesty's surgeons, 29 June 1634, *CSPD*, 1634–35, p. 98.

12 *CSPD*, 1634–35, p. 141.

13 Berry, 'The Globe bewitched', pp. 212–13 (abbreviations expanded).

14 A performance of the play on 10 July 1635 in Oxford and exchange of printed copies in 1637 and 1642 still called it 'The Witches of Lancasheire', as though the story retained its currency. See G. E. Bentley, *The Jacobean and Caroline Stage*, 6 vols (Oxford: Clarendon Press, 1941–68), iii, p. 74.

15 A. M. Clark, *Thomas Heywood: Playwright and Miscellanist* (Oxford: Blackwell, 1931), p. 120.

16 N. W. Bawcutt (ed.), *The Control and Censorship of Caroline Drama: The Records of Sir Henry Herbert, Master of the Revels* (Oxford: Clarendon Press, 1995), p. 189.

17 *CSPD*, 1634–35, 16 July 1634, item 96.

18 *The Farrington Papers*, ed. Edward Hawkins (Manchester: Chetham Society publications xxxvi, 1856), and *A Narration of the Life of Mr Henry Burton* (London, 1643), pp. 16–17, cited by Barber (ed.) in Heywood and Brome, *The Late Lancashire Witches*, p. 68.

19 Richard James, *Iter Lancastrense*, ed. Thomas Corser (Manchester: Chetham Society publications vii, 1845), pp. 10–11, cited by Barber (ed.) in Heywood and Brome, *The Late Lancashire Witches*, pp. 230–1.

20 James Sharpe, *The Bewitching of Anne Gunter: A Horrible and True Story of Football, Witchcraft, Murder, and the King of England* (London: Profile Books, 1999), p. 89.

21 William Brereton, *Travels in Holland 1634–5*, ed. Edward Hawkins (Manchester: Chetham Society publications i, 1844), pp. 33–4.

22 Sharpe, *Bewitching of Anne Gunter*, pp. 5, 98–106.

23 S. Clark, 'Inversion, misrule and the meaning of witchcraft', *Past and Present* 87 (1980), pp. 98–127.

24 Sandra Gilbert, 'Introduction' to Hélène Cixous and Catherine Clément, *The Newly Born Woman*, trans. Betsy Wing (Manchester: Manchester University Press, 1986), p. xii.

25 Nicholas Breton, *The Good and the Badde, or Descriptions of the Worthies, and Unworthies of this Age* (London, 1616), cited in N. H. Keeble (ed.), *The Cultural Identity of Seventeenth Century Woman: A Reader* (London and New York: Routledge, 1994), p. 80.

26 Georges Bataille, *The Accursed Share: An Essay on General Economy*, trans. Robert Hurley (New York: Zone Books, 1988), p. 85.

27 Alan Macfarlane, *Witchcraft in Tudor and Stuart England: A Regional and Comparative Study* (London: Routledge and Kegan Paul, 1970).

28 Martin Butler, *Theatre and Crisis 1632–1642* (Cambridge: Cambridge University Press, 1984), p. 118.

29 Christina Larner, *Enemies of God* (Oxford: Blackwell, 1983), p. 96.

30 James Sharpe, *Instruments of Darkness: Witchcraft in England 1550–1750* (London: Hamish Hamilton, 1996), pp. 70–9.

31 Sharpe, *Bewitching of Anne Gunter*, pp. 81–8.

32 Tom Pettitt, 'Protesting inversions: charivary as folk pageantry and folk-law', *Medieval English Theatre* 21 (1999), pp. 21–51, at pp. 30–3. Pettitt deliberately uses the archaic spelling 'charivary' to identify specifically those performances which constitute customary expressions of disapproval of the personal behaviour of particular and specified members of the community, and I have followed his model.

33 On the role of illegitimacy in the play, see Alison Findlay, *Illegitimate Power: Bastards in Renaissance Drama* (Manchester: Manchester University Press, 1994), pp. 14, 60–2.

34 William Whateley, *A Bride Bush, or A Wedding Sermon* (London, 1617; reprinted Amsterdam: Theatrum Orbis Terrarum / Norwood, N.J.: Walter Johnson Inc., 1975), p. 43.

35 Kathleen McLuskie, *Renaissance Dramatists* (New York and London: Harvester Wheatsheaf, 1989), p. 82.

36 'Homily on Matrimony' (1547) in *Main Sermons or Homilies Appointed to be Read in Churches in the Time of Queen Elizabeth of Famous Memory and Now Thought Fit to be Reprinted by Authority from the Kings Excellent Majesty* (Oxford, 1683), pp. 322, 323.

37 Susan Dwyer Amussen, *An Ordered Society: Gender and Class in Early Modern England* (Oxford: Blackwell, 1983).

38 Cited in Alexandra Walsham, *Church Papists: Catholicism, Conformity and Confessional Polemic in Early Modern England* (London: Boydell and Brewer, 1993), p. 113.

39 H. R. Trevor-Roper, *Religion, the Reformation and Social Change* (London: Macmillan, 1967), p. 188.

40 Barry Reay, 'Popular religion', in Barry Reay (ed.), *Popular Culture in Seventeenth Century England* (London: Routledge, 1985), pp. 91–128, at p. 109. See also Eamon Duffy, *The Stripping of the Altars: Traditional Religion in England, 1400–1580* (New Haven: Yale University Press, 1992).

41 Charles Carlton, *Archbishop William Laud* (London: Routledge, 1987), p. 122.
42 H. R. Trevor-Roper, *Archbishop Laud* (London: Macmillan, 1940), pp. 173–4.
43 Trevor-Roper, *Archbishop Laud*, pp. 113–14.
44 John Christopherson, *An Exhortacion to All Menne to Take Hede and Beware of Rebellion* (London, 1554), sig. Tiiv, and Miles Huggarde, *Displaying of the Protestantes* (London, 1555), sig. Lvii, both cited in Susan Brigden, 'Youth and the English Reformation', *Past and Present 95* (1982), pp. 37–67, at p. 39.
45 Christopher Hill, *Religion and Politics in Seventeenth Century England* (Brighton: Harvester, 1986), p. 98.
46 Trevor-Roper, *Archbishop Laud*, pp. 198–9.
47 S. R. Gardiner (ed.), *Documents Relating to Proceedings Against William Prynne* (London: Camden Society, new series 18, 1877), p. 16.
48 *A Narration of the Life of Mr Henry Burton* (London, 1643), pp. 15–17, cited by Barber (ed.) in Heywood and Brome, *The Late Lancashire Witches*, pp. 60–1.

10

The 'Lancashire novelist' and the Lancashire witches

Jeffrey Richards

They called him 'the Lancashire novelist'. In his day, he was hailed as the successor of Sir Walter Scott as Britain's premier historical novelist. Early Victorian England spoke of him in the same breath as Thackeray and Dickens. Yet while Thackeray and Dickens retain their places in the literary canon, few nowadays remember William Harrison Ainsworth. Although most of his novels languish unread today, his legacy as a mythmaker remains. For it was Ainsworth who made the nineteenth century's most substantial contribution to the mythologisation of Dick Turpin (in his novel *Rookwood*, 1833) and Jack Sheppard (in his novel *Jack Sheppard*, 1838) and who gave new life to the legend of Herne the Hunter (in *Windsor Castle*, 1843). But significantly the only one of his forty novels to remain continuously in print to this day is *The Lancashire Witches* (1849), in which he turned his mythmaking talents to the subject of the 1612 Pendle witch trials.

The Lancashire Witches was in many ways a labour of love, a celebration of his native county, its landscape, its people and its traditions. For William Harrison Ainsworth was the scion of an old-established Lancashire family. Born in Manchester in 1805, he attended Manchester Grammar School from 1817 to 1822, remaining devoted to his old school for the rest of his life and dramatising his time there in his semi-autobiographical novel *Mervyn Clitheroe* (1858). Ainsworth was brought up in a 'strict atmosphere of Whiggism and Nonconformity', but, perhaps in reaction against this, developed in his youth a romantic attachment to Jacobitism, and later identified himself with 'Tory principles' and the Church of England.[1] He began training for the law when he left school and qualified as a solicitor in London in 1826. But he soon abandoned the law for the world of letters. While still in his teens he had been a prolific author of plays, poems and articles and by the time he was eighteen he had had essays and reviews published in literary journals.

When *Rookwood* was published in 1833, it was a sensation and Ainsworth became a literary celebrity almost overnight. His house at Willesden became one of the most glittering salons in London. Some of Ainsworth's most eminent contemporaries, Thackeray, Dickens, Disraeli, Bulwer-Lytton and Cruikshank, became friends and regular dinner companions. His portrait was painted at the age of thirty-one by Daniel Maclise, at thirty-four by R. J. Lane, at thirty-six by H. W. Pickersgill, and at thirty-nine by Maclise again.

Ainsworth was at the height of his fame in the 1840s. Indeed for a short while Ainsworth's fame overshadowed even Dickens's, when in 1839 *Jack Sheppard* and *Oliver Twist* came out at the same time. In 1840–41 he was simultaneously planning, researching and writing three of his best-known and most popular novels, *Guy Fawkes, The Tower of London* and *Old St Pauls*. In 1842 he founded *Ainsworth's Magazine*, one of the most notable mid-Victorian journals.

But in the 1860s, as Dickens went from strength to strength, Ainsworth's celebrity declined. Although he continued to publish several novels a year, he was forced to move from publisher to publisher, travelling ever down-market, as he became less and less of a draw. Several of his later novels appeared in paper covers only, a far cry from the handsomely produced three-volume hardbacks of the 1830s and 1840s with their Cruikshank engravings. In 1837 Ainsworth was one of the few novelists to command £1,000 for a novel. During the 1860s, as Dickens was earning £10,000 per novel, Ainsworth's value steadily declined from £400 per novel to £100.[2] He moved to Brighton, closed *Ainsworth's Magazine*, gradually sold off his Manchester family properties and became a forgotten figure in late Victorian literary London, even though he carried on writing until his death in 1882.

Although his popularity had waned elsewhere, he was remembered with affection in his home town and on 15 September 1881 a dinner in his honour was held at Manchester Town Hall, hosted by the Mayor and attended by the leading literary figures in Manchester. The Mayor, Thomas Baker, described him as the greatest living Manchester writer, and was applauded when he said that Ainsworth had earned the gratitude of all Lancastrians 'by introducing into his works the legends and the characters of past times in this county and by making the folklore and speech of Lancashire a distinctive literature'.[3] The mayor also announced that there were 250 copies of Ainsworth's novels in Manchester's free public libraries and during the previous twelve months had been borrowed 7,660 times. The six most popular titles were *The Tower of London, The Lancashire Witches, Old St Pauls, Windsor Castle, The Miser's Daughter* and *The Manchester Rebels*. Significantly all of them apart from *The Manchester Rebels* (1873) dated from before 1850. Ainsworth's biographer ascertained that in 1909 the Manchester public libraries contained 457 copies of Ainsworth and they had been issued 6,000 times. The most popular titles were *The Tower of London, Guy Fawkes, Windsor Castle* and *The Lancashire Witches.*

Ainsworth replied to the Mayor's speech, saying that nothing had delighted him more than to be styled 'the Lancashire novelist' and that his desire had been 'to write a Lancashire novel, a novel that should please the whole county, and I don't care whether it pleased anybody else'. His thoughts had turned more and more to the scenes of his childhood in the latter part of his career. *The Manchester Rebels* (1873) dealt with the occupation of the city by the Jacobite rebels of 1745; *Preston Fight* (1875) chronicled the events of the 1715 Jacobite rebellion in Lancashire; *The Leaguer of Lathom* (1876) dealt with Lancashire in the English Civil War and detailed the siege of Manchester, the capture of Warrington and the storming of Bolton; *Beatrice Tyldesley* (1878) covered the Jacobite trials in Manchester in 1694.[4]

But Ainsworth's greatest contribution to the literature of Lancashire was undoubtedly *The Lancashire Witches.* It was his life-long friend James Crossley, the Manchester bibliophile and antiquarian and a partner in Ainsworth's father's legal practice, who suggested the subject of the Pendle witch trials, the memory of which had been preserved in seventeenth- and eighteenth-century ballads and chapbooks.[5] Crossley had edited Thomas Potts's *Wonderfull Discoverie of Witches* (1613) for the Chetham Society in 1845. The Society itself, dedicated to the study of the history, topography and archaeology of Lancashire, had been founded in Crossley's house in 1843 and he became its second president in 1848. Another Chetham Society publication, *Nicholas Assheton's Journal,* covering the years 1617 and 1618 and edited in 1848 by Rev. F. R. Raines, the Rural Dean of Rochdale, was a further major source used by Ainsworth. In addition, he drew on John Nichols's *Progresses of James I* (1828) and James I's *Daemonologie* (1597/1604) and *Book of Sports* (1618).

The literary sources were supplemented by a series of visits to Lancashire during which Ainsworth, accompanied by Crossley, went repeatedly to all the principal sites of the story – Pendle Hill, Whalley, Hoghton Tower, Malkin Tower, the Gorge of Cliviger – to ensure precise topographical accuracy and to absorb local colour. Researching the book in 1846 and 1847, he spent the whole of 1848 writing it. Fittingly Ainsworth dedicated the book: 'To James Crossley Esq. (Of Manchester), President of the Chetham Society, and the learned editor of *The Discoverie of Witches in the County of Lancaster* – the Groundwork of the Following Pages – This Romance, undertaken at his suggestion, is inscribed by his old and sincerely attached friend, the Author'.[6]

The Lancashire Witches first appeared in serial form in the *Sunday Times* in 1848. A volume for private circulation only was printed from the type used for the *Sunday Times* in 1849. The author received £1,000 with the copyright reverting to him on completion of the serialisation. It was properly published by Henry Colburn in book form also in 1849 in three volumes with the subtitle *A Romance of Pendle Forest*; the first illustrated edition, with twelve plates by John Gilbert, was published by Routledge in 1854, and reissued in 1878 and 1884. Ainsworth's biographer S. M. Ellis considers it his best work, a view with which a modern critic of the Gothic, David Punter, agrees.[7] From the time of Sir Walter Scott to the 1880s, the standard form of novel publication was the three-volume work, popularly known as the 'three-decker'. It was prohibitively expensive at 31s 6d (a week's wages for a skilled worker). But there were four ways in which a novel could reach a mass public: serialisation, cheap single-volume reprints, borrowing from the many circulating libraries, and the practice of producing a cheap collected edition of a living author at a shilling a volume. *The Lancashire Witches* became available in all four ways.

The book is a combination of the antiquarian picturesque and the Gothic. In it Ainsworth is doing three things at the same time: celebrating 'Merry England', chronicling the landscape, buildings, traditions and dialect of Lancashire, and providing a Gothic version of an actual historical event. So, it is a potent combination of fact and fancy, of history and romance, of chronicle and melodrama.

One of the key characteristics of Romanticism, as Stephen Bann has argued, was 'the desire for History'. History permeated literature and painting, and the representation of history became the function of the new modes of popular spectacle such as the panorama and the diorama. Bann writes:

> An irreversible shift had occurred, and history – from being a localised and specific practice within the cultural topology – became a flood that overrode all disciplinary barriers and, finally, when the barriers were no longer easy to perceive, became a substratum to almost every type of cultural activity.[8]

This meant that the historical novelist as well as the historian had a prime role to play in interpreting the past. The eighteenth-century cult of the picturesque influenced the rise of a new kind of history prominent in the 1830s and 1840s. It was strongly influenced by Sir Walter Scott, represented a fusion of the picturesque and the antiquarian, and, as characterised by Rosemary Mitchell, concentrated on the medieval and early modern periods, was particularist and localised, highlighted rebels, outsiders and underdogs, stressed the accumulation of detail, and displayed empathy, authenticity and a strongly visual sense.[9] This describes the novels of Ainsworth to perfection.

Ainsworth was writing at precisely the period in the 1840s and 1850s when antiquarian history was flourishing and antiquarian societies were mushrooming. The antiquarians, tireless and industrious, published antique documents, undertook archaeological excavations, collected coins, manuscripts, relics and artefacts, published learned journals, compiled local histories and guide-books, charted the evolution and iconographic significance of churches, castles and cathedrals, drew up family genealogies, studied and interpreted heraldry, collected folktales and superstitions. The imprint of such activities is to be found in Ainsworth's novels.

The antiquarians' interests were omnivorous. Charles Dellheim says of them: 'It was antiquity itself, not just one era, that preoccupied them'.[10] Their aim was 'to marry the literary and material evidence of past ages'.[11] Their method was one of collection, description and classification. Their activities were characterised by a strong sense of place and a strong sense of the visual. Again, this applies directly to Ainsworth.

Much of the work of the antiquarians was directly stimulated by the impact on British society, culture and landscape of the Industrial Revolution. Historical sites were under attack by the railways. When the railways began to spread, there was no protection for landscape or historical antiquities and there were many examples of 'vandalism', such as the demolition of Trinity Hospital in Edinburgh and Northampton Castle, and the breaching of the ancient city walls of York, Chester and Newcastle to make way for the railways. The first building to get statutory protection from railway development was Berkhamsted Castle in 1833. It was the threat from the railways to the landscape of the Lake District that later led to the foundation of the National Trust.[12] The movement to preserve, protect and in some cases restore the buildings of the past and to protect the landscape in its pristine state developed in those decades when Ainsworth was writing.

Linked to concern about the destruction of buildings and environment by industrialisation was concern about the disruption of old patterns of life, old traditions, customs and celebrations which had bound together the community. This was linked to the growth of a class society marked by class consciousness, class divisions and class antagonism. Antiquarians sought to combat both these trends by recuperating a lost or disappearing past in all its colourful detail to emphasise the continuity of the industrial present with the pre-industrial past and to stress a shared national historical heritage and a tradition of community that transcended class. As Dellheim suggests: 'The myth of historical continuity was a psychological necessity for Victorians in pioneering communities, who were anxious to find sources of orientation and stability after the initial phase of expansion was complete'.[13] It was a means of combating 'the existential insecurity' that was the product of rapid social, economic, demographic and cultural change.[14]

Antiquarian research was a manifestation of provincial pride and regional consciousness. It established the newly emerged and transformed industrial north as historically as significant as the more secure and dominant south-east. The recuperation and preservation of the old helped to offset the shock of the new. One of the effects of the Industrial Revolution had been the economic differentiation of the towns of the north and each was anxious to establish its own particular history. Lancashire was as keen as anywhere to do this, hence the creation of the Chetham Society in 1843, the Historical Society of Lancashire and Cheshire in 1848 and the Lancashire and Cheshire Antiquarian Society in 1883.

But the dominance of picturesque antiquarian history was short-lived. From the 1850s onwards a major split developed between historians and antiquarians, between professionals and amateurs. Influenced by intellectual developments in Germany, a class of professional historians emerged in England. Their methods were critical, scientific and analytical, their approach professedly objective. They were committed to archival research, they were increasingly specialised, and they concentrated in particular on the political and constitutional history of the nation. They disparaged and marginalised the antiquarians, deriding them as 'picturesque compilers'.[15] So 'picturesque', which had been a term of approbation in the Romantic era, became a term of disapproval in the late Victorian world of the professional historian.

This emerging split was already clear to Lord Macaulay, who wrote in 1828:

> To make the past present, to bring the distant near ... To invest with the reality of human flesh and blood ... to call up our ancestors before us in all their peculiarities of language, manners, and garb, to show us over their houses, to seat us at their tables, to rummage their old-fashioned wardrobes, these parts of the duty which properly belongs to the historian, have been appropriated by the historical novelist.[16]

It was the growing split between the professionals and the amateurs which led to the appointment of the historical novelist Charles Kingsley as Regius Professor of History at Cambridge in 1860 being greeted with derision by professional historians.

The split can properly be seen as one between academic and popular history. For the antiquarian picturesque which fulfilled Macaulay's dictum extended from the work of historians to the work of novelists, dramatists and painters. As a historical novelist Ainsworth was integral to the school of the antiquarian picturesque and his works fulfilled many of the objectives and aims and responded to many of the impulses of the antiquarians proper, and very precisely conformed to Macaulay's description of the work of the historical novelist, not least in *The Lancashire Witches*.[17]

Ainsworth makes no secret of his Lancastrian loyalties in *The Lancashire Witches*. Describing the May Day celebrations in the early seventeeth century, Ainsworth declares:

> For, with pride, I speak it, there were no lads who, in running, vaulting, wrestling, dancing, or, in any other manly exercise, could compare with the Lancashire lads. In archery, above all, none could match them; for were not their ancestors the stout bowmen and billmen, whose cloth-yard shafts, and

trenchant weapons, won the day at Flodden. And were they not true sons of their fathers? And then, I speak it with yet greater pride, there were few, if any lasses who could compare in comeliness with the rosy-cheeked, dark-haired, bright-eyed lasses of Lancashire.[18]

And Squire Nicholas Assheton might well have been speaking for the author when he declared:

> I love Pendle Hill ... and from whatever side I view it – whether from this place where I see it from end to end, from its lowest point to its highest; from Padiham where it frowns upon me; from Clitheroe where it smiles; or from Downham, where it rises in full majesty before me – from all points and under all aspects, whether robed in mist or radiant with sunshine, I delight in it. Born beneath its giant shadow, I look on it with filial regard. Some folks say Pendle Hill wants grandeur and sublimity, but they themselves must be wanting in taste. Its broad, round, smooth mass is better than the roughest, craggiest, shaggiest, most sharply splintered mountain of them all. And then what a view it commands! – Lancaster with its grey old castle on one hand; York with its reverend minster on the other – the Irish Sea and its wild coast – fell, forest, moor and valley, watered by the Ribble, the Hodder, the Calder and the Lime – rivers not to be matched for beauty ... There is no hill in England like Pendle Hill.[19]

Throughout the narrative the peasants, the countryfolk, the lower classes and most of the witches speak in a phonetically rendered Lancashire dialect: '"Oh, he's a feaw teyke – a verra feaw tyke", replied Ashbead; "wi' a feace as black as a boggart, sooty, shiny hewr loike a mowdywarp, an' een loike a stanniel"'.[20] The gentry, heroes and heroines, all speak standard English of a suitably archaic kind. This has narrative significance in that Alizon Device, daughter of one of the witches who is suspected of not being lower-class, and during the course of the novel is discovered to be the daughter of upper-class Alice Nutter, speaks throughout in standard English, unlike her presumed sister and brother, thus demonstrating linguistically her innate superiority.

The landscape of Lancashire is precisely described topographically and on the basis, as we know, of first-hand observation of the locales. But it is also imbued with the appropriate Romantic atmosphere. The book opens on Pendle Hill, with a detailed description of its geographical location and the views from its summit, but then Ainsworth begins to add the evocative atmosphere: 'Dreary was the prospect on all sides. Black moor, bleak fell, straggling forest, intersected with sullen streams as black as ink, with here and there a small tarn, or moss-pool, with waters of the same hue – these constituted the chief features of the scene.'[21] Similarly there are lyrical descriptions of the Calder Valley and an extended and cumulatively sinister one of the Boggart's Glen.[22]

The various manor houses in the area, all of which figure in the action of the narrative, are described with a combination of antiquarian accuracy and romantic atmosphere: Wiswell Hall, Whalley Abbey, Read Hall, Rough Lee, Downham Manor House and Middleton Hall. Ainsworth eloquently laments the decay of Hoghton Tower, the setting of the novel's climax.[23] There is a long and loving account of Whalley parish church, 'a picturesque and beautiful structure'. Ainsworth also gives a vivid and wholly imagined account of the ruined conventual church of Whalley Abbey, which was in fact demolished in the middle of the seventeenth century but which he evokes as an archetypal romantic ruin, 'more picturesque, indeed than in the days of its pride and splendour': the tower a roost for jackdaws, ivy entwined round the pillars, rain falling through the open rood-loft, the high altar stripped of its ornaments, trees taking root in the crevices of the masonry. 'Beautiful at all times were these magnificent ruins; but never as beautiful as when seen by the witching light of the moon – the hour according to the best authority, when all ruins should be viewed'.[24] When he describes Whalley Abbey itself in 1537, now desecrated and despoiled, he reflects in a manner reminiscent of Carlyle and Pugin on the virtues of the old medieval monastic system:

> A sad, sad change hath come over Whalley Abbey. The libraries, well stored with reverend tomes, have been pillaged and their contents cast to the flames; and thus long laboured manuscript, the fruit of years of patient industry, with gloriously illuminated missal, are irrevocably lost. The large infirmary no longer receiveth the sick; in the locutory sitteth no more the guest. No longer in the mighty kitchens are prepared the prodigious supply of meats destined for the support of the poor or the entertainment of the traveller. No kindly porter stands at the gate, to bid the stranger enter and partake of the munificent abbot's hospitality ... Closed are the buttery-hatches and the pantries; and the daily dole of bread hath ceased.[25]

Fulfilling to the letter Macaulay's definition of the remit of the historical novelist, Ainsworth describes in very precise detail and vivid colour the costumes of the leading characters.[26] He revels in the descriptions of the banquet at Whalley Abbey and lavish breakfasts.[27] He describes a midnight mass at Whalley Abbey in dreamlike, almost cinematic terms ('The whole scene appeared like a vision') and gives a historical account of the perambulation of the boundaries of Pendle Forest complete with etymological disquisitions (vaccary, purlieu).[28] He describes the various dances at the feast, seeing their modern counterparts as a definite retrogression and commenting of the pavane that he would like to see it supersede the modern polka.[29] He describes hunting dogs and hunting birds.[30]

Book 3 of the novel is replete with factual detail. Ainsworth brings James I's visit to Hoghton Tower forward from 1617 to 1612 to provide the antiquarian picturesque climax of the story. He assembles all the leading characters for the festivities and traces their respective fates amid the detailed reconstruction of the royal visit, describing the King's procession with his nobles, the preparations for and conduct of the hunt in Hoghton Park, the banquet with the food described in mouth-watering detail and the famous etymological folk-tale of the King knighting a side of Lancashire beef and dubbing it 'Sir-Loin of Beef'.[31]

Ainsworth was a prime exponent of the potent concept of 'merry England'. The term seems originally to have been coined in 1552 by Dr John Caius, who was lamenting the destruction of the 'old world when the country was called "Merry England"'.[32] He was referring to the way in which in a comparatively short time many though not all of the secular and religious festivals which constituted the ritual year of old medieval Catholic England had been swept away by the Protestant Reformation. Some of the old secular festivals which were the occasion for communal merry-making survived, new ones developed, but in the late eighteenth and early nineteenth centuries the same laments were to be heard with many of the same refrains. The causes of the threat to merry England this time were not the Puritans of the Protestant Reformation but the processes of industrialisation and urbanisation, and in particular the desire of industrialists, capitalist entrepreneurs and moral reformers to produce a sober, disciplined and serious-minded workforce. The laments focused in particular on Christmas, which was depicted as being in terminal decline. This decline was exaggerated, as Mark Connelly has shown, but there was a large literature generated which associated Christmas with the lost world of Tudor and Stuart England and the myth of the society of contented peasants, generous landlords and communal solidarity which was seen to have preceded the social and cultural upheavals of the Industrial Revolution.[33]

Sir Walter Scott embodied this feeling of nostalgia in the much-quoted introduction to canto 6 of his epic poem *Marmion* (1808), a tale of intrigue and romance set at the time of the Battle of Flodden:

> England was merry England when
> Old Christmas brought his sports again,
> 'Twas Christmas broached the mightiest ale;
> 'Twas Christmas told the merriest tale;
> A Christmas gambol oft could cheer
> The poor man's heart through half the year.[34]

But Christmas was only one of the traditions whose decline was regretted. The idea of the rituals and traditions, particularly in sports and games, which were based in the countryside and highlighted the paternalistic relationship of the country squirearchy and the rural peasantry, sharing a common love of England, beer, hunting and good sportsmanship, was particularly powerful among Tory writers, who used it as a reproach to the emerging industrial society with its class divisions and tensions, the elimination of the old rural ways and by implication the social harmony of hierarchy.[35]

In 1841 William Howitt wrote:

What a revolution in taste has taken place in the English people ... the times, and the spirit of the times, are changed – we are become a sober people. England is no longer merry England, but busy England; England full of wealth and poverty – extravagance and care. There has been no small lamentation over this change.[36]

Ainsworth himself gave the title *Merry England* to his 1874 novel set in fourteenth-century England, dealing with Wat Tyler's Rebellion and featuring among its characters that iconic figure of merry England, Geoffrey Chaucer. But the concept is explored elsewhere in his work, notably in *The Lancashire Witches*.

Next to Christmas, the other focus of nostalgia was May Day. Where Christmas was seen as enshrining the spirit of the family, May Day was seen as the embodiment of community feeling. It is May Day that features in *The Lancashire Witches*. Chapter 1 of Book 1 of the novel, entitled *The May Queen*, celebrates the cross-class nature of the occasion:

On a May-day in the early part of the seventeenth century, and a most lovely May-day too, admirably adapted to usher in the merriest month of the year, and seemingly made expressly for the occasion, a wake was held at Whalley, to which all the neighbouring country folk resorted, and indeed many of the gentry as well, for in the good old times, when England was still merry England, a wake had attractions for all classes alike, and especially in Lancashire ... Assemblages of this kind, therefore, where the best specimens of either sex were to be met with, were sure to be well attended, and in spite of an enactment passed in the preceding reign of Elizabeth, prohibiting 'piping, playing, bear-baiting and bull-baiting on the Sabbath-days, or on any other days, and also superstitious ringing of bells, wakes and common feasts', they were not only not interfered with, but rather encouraged by the higher orders.[37]

Ainsworth suggests that King James I, by contrast with his predecessor,

desirous of checking the growing spirit of Puritanism throughout his kingdom, had openly expressed himself in favour of honest recreation after evening prayers and upon holidays; and furthermore, had declared that he liked well the spirit of his good subjects in Lancashire and would not see them punished for indulging in lawful exercises.

The result:

This expression of royal opinion removed every restriction and the old sports and pastimes, May-games, Whitsun-ales, and morris-dances, with rush-bearings, bell-ringings, wakes and feasts, were as much practised as before the passing of the obnoxious enactment of Elizabeth.[38]

Ainsworth's history is faulty here. The parliamentary bill to ban Sunday sports and revels had been vetoed by Elizabeth in 1584 but had been enacted by James I by royal decree soon after his accession in 1603. But he later repented and because Ainsworth is merging the story of the Lancashire witches of 1612 and the visit to Hoghton Tower in 1617, he is able to elide events. In 1616 Lancashire JPs banned piping, dancing and other 'profanation' on a Sunday. It was in response to the reaction against this ban that James, having enjoyed the dancing, feasting, rush-bearing, masquing and merry-making at Hoghton, had a royal decree for Lancashire drawn up allowing piping, dancing, archery, athletics and rush-bearing on Sundays after evening service, though banning bowling, plays and animal-baiting. It was reissued in 1618 from Greenwich Palace with application to the whole country, adding permission for Whitsun ales, May games, morris dancing and the maypole. It became known as *The Book of Sports*.[39]

In *The Lancashire Witches* Ainsworth merges the May Day festivities with the distinctive north-western custom of rush-bearing, attested at Whalley as early as 1617, to create a joyous and colourful folk fesival.[40] Flowers and greenery are collected by the young people, the rush cart is decorated, the bells peal. The rush cart, the morris dancers, the hobby horse, the masquers dressed as Robin Hood and his merry men, all pass in procession, the maypole is erected, the rush cart goes to the church, ale is distributed, and the May Queen is hailed and venerated. The May Queen is Alizon Device, thus weaving the May Day events directly into the narrative of the Lancashire witches. The rustics entertain their friends to dinner, strangers throw themselves upon the general hospitality, the squire and his guests mingle with the commonality in the inns: 'such was the invariable practice in the northern counties in the reign of James the First', writes Ainsworth approvingly.[41] Inspired by the scenes he has described, Ainsworth editorialises:

> Laugh on, my merry lads, you are made of good old English stuff, loyal to church and king, and while you, and such as you, last, our land will be in no danger from foreign foe! Laugh on, and praise your sweethearts how you will. Laugh on, and blessings on your honest hearts![42]

He returns regularly to his theme of the mutual respect and harmony within the social hierarchy. Sir Ralph Assheton of Whalley Abbey is depicted as the ideal landlord:

> Between Sir Ralph Assheton of the Abbey and the inhabitants of Whalley ... the best possible feeling subsisted ... he was very hospitable to his friends, very bountiful to the poor, a good landlord, and a humane man ... Among Sir Ralph's other good qualities, for such it was esteemed by his friends and retainers, and they were of course, the best judges, was a strong love of the chase.[43]

Ainsworth also celebrates the inn Bess's O' Th' Booth, run by the forthright Bess Whitaker, noting 'it was the custom of all classes in the northern counties, men and women, to resort to the alehouses to drink, and the hostel at Goldshaw was the general rendezvous of the neighbourhood'.[44]

The issuing of the declaration on sports figures notably during the account of the visit to Hoghton Tower, with James I declaring: 'Honest mirth is not only tolerable but praise-worthy, and the prohibition of it likely to breed discontent, and this our enemies ken fu'weel ... for when shall the common people have leave to exercise if not upon Sundays and holidays, seeing they must labour and win their living upon all other days'.[45] The visit to Hoghton culminates again in the entertainment lovingly described by Ainsworth: after various sports (wrestling, cudgelling, etc.) comes the rush-cart procession, the morris dancers, 'the fool and his five sons' drollery, the plough and sword dance, the mock tourney.[46] In the evening there is a court masque on the theme of the hunt and after that various dances and satirical drolleries. So the novel reaches its climax as it began with a celebration of the games and sports and revels of merry England. Interestingly support for the May games and May festival grew during the nineteenth century and from the 1840s onwards May Day festivities were consciously revived in various parts of the country.[47]

For all its antiquarian and historical detail, *The Lancashire Witches* was first and foremost a Gothic Romance. Ainsworth, a Tory, an Anglican and an arch-Romantic, had consciously sought to revive the Gothic novel. He admitted in a preface to *Rookwood*:

> Romance, if I am not mistaken, is destined shortly to undergo an important change. Modified by the German and French writers – by Hoffman, Tieck, Hugo, Dumas, Balzac and Paul Lacroix – the structure, commenced in our own land by Horace Walpole, Monk Lewis, Mrs. Radcliffe and Maturin, but left imperfect and inharmonious, requires, now that the rubbish which choked up its approach is removed, only the hand of the skilful architect to its entire renovation and perfection.[48]

This was the form he chose in which to tell the story of the Lancashire witches.

Belief in witchcraft continued to flourish among the lower orders of England into the mid and later nineteenth century. Among their educated betters it had collapsed by the early eighteenth century. The English and Scottish witchcraft laws were repealed in 1736, the result of the rise of science, the growth of judicial scepticism and the valuing of reason over superstition. Popular superstition was deemed irrelevant and doomed to disappear. But by the end of the eighteenth century, stimulated in part by the rise of Methodism and the increasing interest in the spiritual and moral health of the labouring poor, it was once again perceived to be a serious social and moral problem. James Crossley reported in his introduction to Potts's *Discoverie* that witchcraft superstitions still lingered in the Pendle region.

Renewed attempts to control popular practices and beliefs in the early nineteenth century led not only to assaults on superstition but the suppression or transformation of wakes, May Day revels and harvest celebrations. It is fascinating therefore to find Ainsworth's literal interpretation of witchcraft sitting alongside a full-hearted affirmation of the old unreconstructed traditions and festivities. As Owen Davies has shown, both in town and country witchcraft beliefs continued throughout the nineteenth century. Witch-swimmings and witch-mobbings were still being instigated within local communities; astrologers, fortune-tellers, folk healers, charmers and 'wise women' flourished; and the rise of cheap literature spread the old superstitions, myths and folk beliefs just as much as it disseminated rational and useful knowledge. There may very well have been among the readers of the cheap editions of Ainsworth working-class readers who believed firmly in the literal truth of his witchcraft accounts.[49]

Among writers, painters and poets the Age of Reason had provoked its own reaction in the rise of Romanticism, bold, individualist and unconventional. In the place of reason, science, classical equilibrium, it exalted the imagination, the emotions, dreams and fantasies, everything that was alien and abhorrent to the world of the rational, the balanced and the intellectual. At its root, Romanticism had a desire for freedom from rules and restraints, and the unshackling of imagination. It had certain basic fascinations: the past, particularly the medieval past, individualism and the occult. The Gothic novel was one of its primary products and in the later eighteenth and early nineteenth centuries Horace Walpole, Ann Radcliffe, Matthew Gregory Lewis and Charles Robert Maturin evolved the form whose characteristics David Punter defined as: 'an emphasis on portraying the terrifying, a common insistence on archaic settings, a prominent use of the supernatural, the presence of highly stereotyped characters and the attempt to deploy and perfect techniques of literary suspense'.[50]

The recurrent themes of the Gothic were outlined by Eino Railo as gloomy castles, picturesque ruins, deep dungeons, dark forests, graveyards, ghosts, skulls, skeletons, caves, sinister portraits, ruthless bandits, doppelgängers, demons, prophecies, mysterious voices and corrupt monks. Every one of these ingredients is to be found in The Lancashire Witches. The key motifs of the Gothic are said to be paranoia, the notion of the barbaric, political and psychological borderlands, concern with nature and the sublime, social, religious and psychological persecution. Once again all these ideas run through the novel.[51]

The Lancashire Witches, 492 pages long in its 1884 edition, has a 62-page prologue, The Last Abbot of Whalley, and is then divided into three books: Alizon Device, Pendle Forest and Hoghton Tower. The cast of characters is drawn from both Thomas Potts's Discoverie and Nicholas Assheton's Journal: the Demdike and Chattox families, Alice Nutter and the Asshetons. Both Thomas Potts and Nicholas Assheton appear as characters. Potts is depicted as a bustling, comically pompous London lawyer, constantly quoting the Daemonologie of King James I (as indeed he does in his book). He is subject to a succession of indignities: thrown into the river after the witch-swimming, thrown by his horse into a swamp, and horse-whipped by the forthright, dialect-speaking Lancashire lass Bess Whitaker. But Ainsworth sees his humiliations as entirely justified by his proclaimed hatred of Pendle ('I hate your bleak Lancashire hills ... Highgate Hill is quite mountain enough for me, and Hampstead Heath wild enough for any civilized purpose').[52] Assheton appears as an amiable, easy-going, hard-drinking, womanising country squire. But there are several changes made in the nature and status of participants in the witch trials. Alizon Device, in reality hanged as a self-confessed witch, becomes the beautiful tragic heroine of Ainsworth's romance, dying before she can reach the scaffold. Christopher Howgate, son of Mother Demdike, becomes bold, bad Christopher Demdike, leader of a gang of bandits terrorising the area. Alice Nutter, in reality a rich widow aged seventy with five children and also hanged as a witch, becomes an apparently childless, handsome widow in her forties who discovers that she is Alizon's mother and also dies before reaching the scaffold.

The *Discoverie* provides Ainsworth not just with characters but reported events which he turns into action sequences. Whatever historians now make of the witchcraft tales told at the trial, Ainsworth takes many of them literally for the purposes of his novel. He recounts the witchcraft activities and the feud between the families of Mothers Demdike and Chattox, their familiars, their visitations by the Devil, and their bewitching of the pedlar John Law, of the daughter of Richard Baldwyn, and of the hero Richard Assheton, all of whom die following their witchery. The night-flying, the burial of clay models of victims, the gathering of skulls and teeth from graveyards, the witch-gathering at Malkin Tower, all reported in the trial evidence, are all to be found in Ainsworth's narrative, faithfully recreated.

The *Journal of Nicholas Assheton* provided a further set of characters and incidents. Nicholas Assheton (1590–1625), although by avocation a Puritan, was also a roisterer: huntsman, gamester and ladies' man. His journal records sixteen fox chases, ten stag hunts, two hunts each of buck, otter and hare, one badger hunt, four days of grouse-shooting and fishing, and two days of hawking. Ainsworth duly describes an otter hunt with Nicholas. Nicholas's cousin, Richard Assheton, Ainsworth's handsome 22-year-old romantic hero, who dies at Hoghton Tower of witchcraft, is a composite figure. The real Richard Assheton, son of Sir Richard Assheton of Middleton, and known as a man of 'great piety, prudence and learning', died in 1618 at 41, having been married to Mary Venables. Ainsworth merges him with Nicholas's elder brother, also called Richard Assheton, who died in 1597 and was believed to have been killed by witchcraft. Ainsworth's Richard falls in love with Alizon Device and they are buried together when both die at the end of the book.

The *Journal* records Nicholas's presence at Hoghton during the King's visit and mentions the rush-bearing, banquet and masque. Also mentioned in the *Journal* and featured in the novel as characters are Nicholas's brother-in-law Richard Sherborne, his confidential agent Fogg (whom Ainsworth makes Christopher Demdike in disguise) and the fiery Sir Thomas Metcalfe. Nicholas records that Metcalfe and forty men besieged Raydale House in Wensleydale, the home of Nicholas's Aunt Robinson, in some property dispute. Nicholas and his men relieve the siege. Ainsworth has Metcalfe and his gang on their way to attack Raydale House stopping off to besiege Rough Lee and assist in the arrest of Alice Nutter.

Ainsworth provides the events of 1612 with a backstory, which allows him to establish the basic Gothic motifs. He begins his narrative in 1536 during the Pilgrimage of Grace, the rebellion of the northern Catholics against the Protestant reforms initiated by Henry VIII and in particular the Dissolution of the Monasteries. A leading role in the rebellion was taken by Abbot John Paslew of Whalley.

Paslew and some of his followers wait on Pendle Hill for news of the progress of the rising. But the wizard Nicholas Demdike appears, accompanied by his black hound ('The aspect of the wizard was dark and forbidding, and, seen by the beacon light, his savage features, blazing eyes, tall, gaunt frame and fantastic garb, made him look like something unearthly'). He warns them that the rebellion has collapsed and royal troops under John Bradyll and Richard Assheton are on their way to arrest them. Paslew has previously excommunicated Demdike and his wife Bess Blackburn as witches and refused to baptise their infant daughter. Demdike now offers to rescue Paslew if he will reverse his judgement. He summons up a flash flood to wash the soldiers away. But the abbot rejects his offer, rescues Bradyll and Assheton from the flood and, unconscious after his efforts, is arrested and conveyed to the Abbey where he finds that Demdike is his gaoler.

Demdike again urges Paslew to reverse his judgement and instead the abbot pronounces a curse on the Demdike child and all its descendants. Hearing of this, Bess dies of shock. Paslew and two of his monastic brothers are tried and condemned to death by the Earl of Derby. Paslew is permitted a final confession. A strange monk arrives to hear his confession. Paslew, haunted by guilt, reveals that in his ambition to become abbot, he had disposed of an ecclesiastical rival, Borlace Alvetham, by charging him with witchcraft. Found guilty, Borlace was walled up alive in a cell. The monk then reveals that he is Borlace. He describes his torments in the cell and how he eventually prayed to the Dark Powers, was freed by a demon, wandered abroad for years and returned as Nicholas Demdike and married Bess Blackburn. It is their child that Paslew has cursed. Again Paslew refuses to recall the curse. He is duly hanged with Demdike acting as executioner.

After the execution, as Demdike gloats over the body of Paslew in the convent church, the loyal Catholic Hal O'Nabs pushes the statue of St Gregory de Northbury down on him and he is crushed to death. Nicholas is interred with his wife Bess. Thereafter the ghost of Paslew haunts Whalley

Abbey and Demdike's child and her progeny become the Lancashire witches. So already in the prologue, we get the classic Gothic themes of the gloomy abbey, the corrupt monk, curses, prophecies, demons and ghosts. The novel proper will recount the working out of the curse with the ghost of Paslew appearing repeatedly to aid the forces of good.

The action of the story proper begins with the May Day festivities and the gathering of all the leading characters. Book 1 established the rivalry between the Demdike and Chattox families and the love of Richard Assheton for Alizon, the supposed daughter of Elizabeth Device. But Alice Nutter learns that Alizon is in reality her long-lost daughter Millicent, switched in childhood with another child who was then killed by her jealous husband who believed Millicent to be the child of Alice's lover. This discovery begins the battle for Alice's soul, which is a continuing theme of the book. Hitherto the leader of the witches, she seeks to abandon her evil life and this begins as she prevents her daughter being enlisted in the coven.

In Book 2, Mother Demdike lures Alizon away and imprisons her in Malkin Tower. Mother Chattox, inspired by her hatred of Demdike, comes to Alice's aid. They fly on Chattox's broomstick to Pendle Hill where Demdike is preparing to sacrifice Alizon to the Devil. They find themselves powerless but Richard and Nicholas Assheton and their men arrive in the nick of time to save Alizon and the two old women are burned.

Book 3 brings all the narrative threads to a conclusion during the visit of King James I to Hoghton Tower. The witches are rounded up. Alizon refuses her sister Jennet's demands that she help get Jem and Elizabeth out of prison. So Jennet touches Richard Assheton with her witch's hand and he dies; she then betrays to Thomas Potts the hiding place of Alice Nutter, who is being protected by Nicholas Assheton, and Alice is arrested. Alizon dies and is buried side by side with Richard. The Devices, Alice and Nan Redferne are taken to Lancaster Castle where they are tried and condemned. The trial is not described, since all the evidence given has already formed the basis of the narrative. Alice dies on her way to the stake, the Devices are executed but Jennet is freed – only to be executed years later as a witch.

The May Day celebrations at the start of the book culminate in the denunciation of Nance Redferne (sometimes also called Nan), the grand-daughter of Mother Chattox (in reality her daughter), as a witch. She is put to the ordeal by water on the orders of Potts and survives, thanks to the intervention of cousins Nicholas and Richard Assheton. What is interesting about this early section of the book is that Ainsworth lays out all the common sense reasons for not believing in witchcraft. Many of them are given to Alice Nutter to articulate. To rumours that witchcraft caused the death of her husband, she declares: 'Alas, poor man! He died from hard riding after hard drinking. That was the only witchcraft in his case.'[53] She says that Demdike and Chattox are harmless old women and that witch-hunts have increased to pander to the King, whose *Daemonologie* confirmed his belief in witchcraft. She declares the King's anti-witchcraft law 'a wicked and bloody statute ... and many an innocent life will be sacrificed thereby ... It will make more witches than it will find.'[54] Potts lists all the means of finding witches and quotes James I on why women are more susceptible than men to becoming witches, earning Nutter's scorn.[55] All her objections make perfect sense to modern ears. The only problem is that Alice Nutter turns out to be the leader of the witches and an expert in the practice of witchcraft.

Nicholas Assheton expresses his belief in witches but warns Potts: 'you must not put faith in all the idle tales told you, for the common folk hereabouts are blindly and foolishly superstitious, and fancy they discern witchcraft in every mischance, however slight, that befalls them'. He goes on to list all the natural occurrences commonly ascribed to witchcraft. Richard Assheton warns against believing the charges made against Mother Demdike:

> The prejudice existing against her is sure to convict and destroy her ... her great age, infirmities and poverty, will be proof against her. How can she or any old enfeebled creature like her, whose decrepitude and misery should move compassion rather than excite fear – how can such a person defend herself against charges easily made, and impossible to refute? I do not deny the possibility of witchcraft, even in our own days, though I think it a very unlikely occurrence; but I would determinedly resist giving credit to any tales told by the superstitious vulgar, who, naturally prone to cruelty, have so many motives for revenging imaginary wrongs ... So many undefined charges have been brought against Mother Demdike, that at last they have fixed a stigma on her name, and made her an object of dread and suspicion. She is endowed with mysterious power, which would have no effect if not believed in; and now must be burned because she is called a witch, and is doting and vain enough to accept the title.[56]

He says that Demdike and Chattox are 'two poor old creatures who, persuaded that they really possess the supernatural power accorded to them by the vulgar, strive to act up to their parts, and are mainly assisted in doing so by the credulity and fears of their audience'.[57] He later denounces the ordeal by water as 'iniquitous' and savouring of 'the barbarous ages'.[58] He insists that John Law's seizure, attributed by others to witchcraft, is the result of a stroke. He rejects the idea of the curse and ghost of Abbot Paslew. But Richard Assheton, the arch-sceptic, will later die as a result of witchcraft.

When Potts organises the 'swimming' of Nance Redferne, and she sinks and is pulled out of the water, Ainsworth editorialises:

> Neither her beauty, her youth, nor her sex, had any effect upon the ferocious crowd, who were too much accustomed to such brutal and debasing exhibitions, to feel anything but savage delight in the spectacle of a fellow-creature so scandalously treated and tormented, and the only excuse to be offered for their barbarity, is the firm belief they entertained that they were dealing with

a witch. And when even in our own day so many revolting scenes are enacted to gratify the brutal passions of the mob, while prize-fights are tolerated, and wretched animals goaded on to tear each other in pieces, it is not to be wondered at that, in times of less enlightenment, and refinement, greater cruelties should be practised. Indeed, it may be well to consider how far we have really advanced in civilization since then; for until cruelty, whether to man or beast, be wholly banished from out sports, we cannot justly reproach our ancestors, or congratulate ourselves in our improvement.[59]

The modern common-sense belief that witchcraft did not exist having been clearly put in the early part of the book, the rest of the narrative is concerned to show witchcraft in full operation in all its aspects.

Book 1, having begun with the arguments against belief in witchcraft, ends in riveting fashion with a full-blooded supernatural sequence. Dorothy Assheton, Richard's sister, and Alizon, having drunk a mysterious potion, witness a witches' sabbat in the conventual church ruins. Alice Nutter presides with Chattox, Demdike and Redferne all present. They invoke the shades of Abbot Paslew and the votaress Isole de Heton who abandoned her vows to serve the Devil. Little Jennet Device, Alizon's sister, is inducted as a witch, although Alizon intervenes to save her. Elizabeth Device insists Alizon be baptised as a witch. Alice Nutter offers Dorothy instead. Alizon prays for Dorothy, the witches flee and thereafter Dorothy, recovering, denounces Alizon for bewitching her. The witchcraft rituals, the storm, the sinister voice (the Devil) and the ghosts all combine to fashion a climax of memorable diablerie.

After this, Ainsworth leaves his readers in little doubt about the reality and power of witchcraft. Book 2 opens with Dorothy repeating her accusation against Alizon. But Alice Nutter puts a spell on Dorothy, causing her to retract her accusations and become reconciled with Alizon. To resolve a legal dispute between Alice Nutter and Roger Nowell, the boundaries are ridden – but they are altered by witchcraft in Alice's favour. Nowell plans to arrest Alice as a witch. But Nicholas and Richard Assheton, believing her innocent, join forces with her to defend Rough Lee against attack. They succeed in capturing Nowell, Thomas Potts and their men, who are later freed by Sir Thomas Metcalfe.

When Alice learns that Mother Demdike has captured Alizon, she gives Richard Assheton a protective talisman and sends him to the rescue. He rides through a storm, assailed by magic creatures. But when he reaches Malkin Tower, he is tricked by Demdike and thrown insensible to the ground. Alice and Mother Chattox fly by broomstick to Pendle Hill after witnessing in Alice's cauldron Demdike's bid to tempt Alizon. As the witches gather, Alice and Chattox try to defend Alizon. But Chattox is stabbed and Alice, having renounced the Devil, has lost her magical powers. Book 2 ends just as spectacularly as Book 1. Richard, arriving in the nick of time, rescues Alizon and lights the beacon. The beacon reveals Nicholas Assheton, Thomas Metcalfe and their men arriving. Demdike and Chattox are seized and hurled into the beacon fire and burned alive. In reality, Demdike died in prison and Chattox was hanged at Lancaster. But Ainsworth sacrifices the historical truth for Gothic theatricality and bravura spectacle.

In Book 3, both Alice and Alizon resist the attempts on their souls but both die. At this point, Ainsworth injects into the action that classic figure of Romantic fiction – the bandit. Nicholas Assheton is warned by Nance Redferne that he is to be robbed by his confidential agent Laurence Fogg, in reality Christopher Demdike who had been terrorising the Scottish border with his robber band until he heard of his mother's death and returned. The bandits ambush Nicholas but he escapes. Malkin Tower is captured by the bandits, who hold Alice Nutter prisoner there. Nicholas rescues Alice after fighting Demdike. Nance Redferne blows up Malkin Tower, destroying the robber band, apart from Christopher Demdike who escapes, only to be found later fatally gored by the wild cattle in Hoghton Park. The novel ends with the deaths of the witches, the hero and the heroine.

In penning his novel, Ainsworth was parting company with the rationalist interpretation of his old friend Crossley. Ainsworth throughout the novel deploys malevolent and beneficent supernatural forces, embodied respectively in Alice Nutter's demon familiar and the ghost of Abbot Paslew. In his introduction to Potts, by contrast, Crossley wrote from the position of a total sceptic on the subject of witchcraft. He praised at some length those few sixteenth- and seventeenth-century figures who exposed the fallacy and fraudulence of witchcraft: Reginald Scot, Sir Robert Filmer, John Wagstaffe and John Webster. He denounced the beliefs of the people of Pendle as mere superstition, but intriguingly reported that they lingered on still in his own time.[60] But Ainsworth, temperamentally attracted to the romantic and the supernatural, preferred to take the events literally and interpret them in recognisably Gothic terms.

Ainsworth has been regularly disparaged by latter-day critics. Andrew Sanders is typical. He calls Ainsworth's success 'inexplicable' and the author 'unimaginative', his work characterised by sensationalism, stereotyped characters, ramshackle plots, stilted dialogue, Gothic clichés and the indiscriminate mixing of history and fiction. His work is, says Sanders, devoid of moral teaching and 'destructive of the real potential of historical fiction' in its absence of social and psychological complexity.[61] But Sanders is judging Ainsworth by a particular set of criteria: realism, accuracy, dialectic, progressive values, moral and social teaching. There was a split within the genre of historical fiction between the novel, embracing the values of which Sanders approves and represented by the work of Thackeray, George Eliot, Mrs Gaskell and Thomas Hardy, and the romance which embodies Gothic values.

By the criteria and approach of the Gothic Romance, it could be argued that Ainsworth's characters are archetypes, his dialogue stylised, his plots multi-layered, his mixture of history and fiction extremely adroit, his manipulation of the Gothic elements confident and effective and his construction and exposition of an intricate and complex plot admirable. It is Ainsworth's particular strengths (a strong visual imagination, a vividly theatrical sense of drama, a powerful and engaging narrative drive) that ensured that his best novels continued to be read until well into the twentieth century. While it is true that his hero and heroine are conventional, they conform to the Romantic archetypes defined by Eino Railo: 'he is the romanticist's symbol of young, pure and idealistic heroism; she, a rosy embodiment of womanly beauty and virtue'.[62] And there are strong and compelling characterisations of some historical personalities: Alice Nutter, the handsome strong-minded widow who repents of her witchcraft, recants, is tormented by fears for her daughter and fights for her soul against the forces of darkness; Jennet Device, the small, deformed, malicious child who testifies against her family and contrives the death of the hero; and Nicholas Assheton, the roistering, good-natured, country squire.

The Lancashire Witches remains a remarkable achievement, successfully blending descriptions of the historical topography of Lancashire with an antiquarian love of buildings, customs and costume, then using both to bring to life the events and characters of the Pendle witch trial in a narrative which deploys all the themes, atmosphere and ethos of the Gothic Romance. Ainsworth scrupulously sets out all the rational objections to the existence of witchcraft before negating them with a full-blooded literal account of the diabolical goings on which are finally terminated in good Tory fashion by the King and the Law. Reason may not have prevailed but Order has, bringing a satisfying closure to the events.

Notes

1 S. M. Ellis, *William Harrison Ainsworth and His Friends*, 2 vols (London: Bodley Head, 1911), i, p. 24. This remains the definitive biography and the source of biographical information.
2 John Sutherland, *Victorian Novelists and Publishers* (London: Athlone Press, 1976), p. 160.
3 Ellis, *Ainsworth*, ii, pp. 321–5.
4 Ellis, *Ainsworth*, ii, p. 326.
5 J. O. Halliwell, *The Palatine Anthology/The Palatine Garland* (London, 1850); Samuel Bamford, *Early Days* (Manchester: John Heywood, 1849), p. 90.
6 Quoted in S. M. Ellis, 'A great bibliophile: James Crossley', in *Wilkie Collins, La Fanu and Others* (1931; reprinted Freeport, N.Y.: Books for Libraries Press, 1968), pp. 239–40.
7 Ellis, *Ainsworth*, ii, p. 140; David Punter, *Literature of Terror* (London: Longman, 1908), p. 180.
8 Stephen Bann, *Romanticism and the Rise of History* (New York: Twayne, 1995), pp. 6–7.
9 Rosemary Mitchell, *Picturing the Past: English History in Text and Image,1800–1870* (Oxford: Clarendon Press, 2000), p. 15.

10 Charles Dellheim, *The Face of the Past: The Preservation of the Medieval Inheritance in Victorian England* (Cambridge: Cambridge University Press, 1982), p. 56.
11 Philippa Levine, *The Amateur and the Professional: Antiquarians, Historians and Archaeologists in Victorian England, 1838–1886* (Cambridge: Cambridge University Press, 1986), p. 70.
12 Jack Simmons, *The Victorian Railway* (London: Thames and Hudson, 1991), pp. 155–73.
13 Dellheim, *Face of the Past*, p. 66.
14 Dellheim, *Face of the Past*, p. 75.
15 Levine, *Amateur and Professional*, p. 30.
16 Thomas Babington Macaulay, *Critical and Historical Essays*, i (London: Methuen, 1903), pp. 115–16.
17 Mitchell, *Picturing the Past*, illuminatingly discusses Ainsworth's work in this context, though she does not include *The Lancashire Witches* in her discussion.
18 W. Harrison Ainsworth, *The Lancashire Witches* (London: Routledge, 1884), p. 63.
19 Ainsworth, *Lancashire Witches*, p. 220.
20 Ainsworth, *Lancashire Witches*, p. 7.
21 Ainsworth, *Lancashire Witches*, p. 1.
22 Ainsworth, *Lancashire Witches*, pp. 121, 208, 224–5.
23 Wiswell Hall (pp. 56–7), Whalley Abbey (p. 142), Read Hall (p. 221), Rough Lee (p. 266), Downham Manor House (p. 364), Middleton Hall (p. 389), and Hoghton Tower (p. 428).
24 Ainsworth, *Lancashire Witches*, p. 130.
25 Ainsworth, *Lancashire Witches*, pp. 18–19.
26 Ainsworth, *Lancashire Witches*, pp. 21, 66, 78, 80.
27 Ainsworth, *Lancashire Witches*, pp. 160–1, 214, 370.
28 Ainsworth, *Lancashire Witches*, pp. 32–5, 258–74.
29 Ainsworth, *Lancashire Witches*, pp. 176–7, 186.
30 Ainsworth, *Lancashire Witches*, p. 368.
31 Ainsworth, *Lancashire Witches*, pp. 436 (procession), 442–3 (hunt), 459 (banquet).
32 Ronald Hutton, *The Rise and Fall of Merry England: The Ritual Year 1400–1700* (Oxford: Oxford University Press, 1994), p. 89. Hutton gives a detailed account of the phenomenon.
33 Mark Connelly, *Christmas: A Social History* (London: I. B. Tauris, 1999).
34 Sir Walter Scott, *Poems* (London: Cassell, n.d.), p. 213.
35 R. W. Malcolmson, *Popular Recreations in English Society 1700–1850* (Cambridge: Cambridge University Press, 1973); Bob Bushaway, *By Rite: Custom, Ceremony and Community in England 1700–1880* (London: Junction Books, 1982).
36 William Howitt, *The Rural Life of England* (London, 1841), p. 351, quoted in Bushaway, *By Rite*, p. 239.
37 Ainsworth, *Lancashire Witches*, p. 63.
38 Ainsworth, *Lancashire Witches*, p. 64.
39 Hutton, *Merry England*, pp. 154, 168.
40 Ronald Hutton, *The Stations of the Sun* (Oxford: Oxford University Press, 1996), p. 325.
41 Ainsworth, *Lancashire Witches*, pp. 64–6, 69–72, 105.
42 Ainsworth, *Lancashire Witches*, pp. 76–7.
43 Ainsworth, *Lancashire Witches*, p. 77.
44 Ainsworth, *Lancashire Witches*, p. 238.
45 Ainsworth, *Lancashire Witches*, p. 444.
46 Ainsworth, *Lancashire Witches*, pp. 463–6.
47 Hutton, *Stations of the Sun*, pp. 295–303.
48 Quoted in Ellis, *Ainsworth*, i, pp. 286–7.
49 James Sharpe, *Instruments of Darkness: Witchcraft in England 1550–1750* (1996; London: Penguin, 1997), pp. 284–95; Owen Davies, *Witchcraft, Magic and Culture 1736–1951* (Manchester: Manchester University Press, 1999).

50 Punter, *Literature of Terror*, p. 1.
51 Eino Railo, *The Haunted Castle* (London: Routledge, 1927).
52 Ainsworth, *Lancashire Witches*, p. 220.
53 Ainsworth, *Lancashire Witches*, p. 95.
54 Ainsworth, *Lancashire Witches*, p. 97.
55 Ainsworth, *Lancashire Witches*, p. 98.
56 Ainsworth, *Lancashire Witches*, p. 108.
57 Ainsworth, *Lancashire Witches*, p. 109.
58 Ainsworth, *Lancashire Witches*, p. 115.
59 Ainsworth, *Lancashire Witches*, p. 119.
60 Thomas Potts, *The Wonderfull Discoverie of Witchcraft in the Countie of Lancaster* (London, 1613; ed. James Crossley, Manchester: Chetham Society publications vi, 1845), Introduction, pp. iii–lxxix.
61 Andrew Sanders, *The Victorian Historical Novel 1840–1880* (London: Macmillan, 1978), pp. 32–46.
62 Railo, *Haunted Castle*, p. 283.

11

Wicca, Paganism and history: contemporary witchcraft and the Lancashire witches

Joanne Pearson

During the 1940s, a form of contemporary spirituality known as Wicca emerged. It drew on the cultural impulses of the nineteenth-century *fin de siècle*, and included initiation, passwords and secrecy influenced by Freemasonry, ideas about ritual magic drawn from the Hermetic Order of the Golden Dawn, and concepts common to the mystery religions[1] of the ancient world. Additionally, the retired colonial civil servant who was most prominent in the revival of Wicca, Gerald Gardner, drew heavily on images of witches and witchcraft throughout history, including the early modern period which witnessed what was labelled 'the Great Witch Hunt'. Of particular importance were the writings of the classicist Sir James Frazer on folklore and fertility rites and, even more so, the theories of the egyptologist Margaret Murray on the witch-cult.

Murray's *Witch Cult in Western Europe* (1921) and *The God of the Witches* (1933) wove together ideas of rural fertility religion as popularised by Frazer, the witch-cult as described in Jules Michelet's *La Sorcière* (1862) and Charles Leland's *Aradia* (1899), and folk customs to assert her theory that the witch-cult contained the vestigial remnants of a pre-Christian European fertility religion perhaps first developed in Egypt, which she called 'Dianic'.[2] Murray used the Lancashire witch trials as part of her evidence, arranging the witches into three covens of thirteen (i.e. thirty-nine persons)[3] and characterising the meeting at the Malkin Tower as a sabbat. She also made explicit links between age-old practices and witchcraft, which Gardner believed 'was directly descended from the Northern European culture of the Stone Age', uninfluenced by anything except 'the Greek and Roman mysteries which [he says] originally may have come from Egypt'.[4] Britain's repositioning of itself after two World Wars and the beginning of the loss of Empire elicited an urge for national identity among some sections of the population, which may have lent greater attractiveness to Murray's idea of ancient religious practices indigenous to Britain. Both this, and the freedom provided by the practice of naturism, further influenced Gardner's ideas for the revival of Wicca as he creatively wove together all these threads.

Early views of the history of Wicca thus incorporated efforts to produce historical legitimisation through claims of an unbroken lineage of witchcraft going back to the dawn of time. Gardner's books *Witchcraft Today* (1954) and *The Meaning of Witchcraft* (1959) perpetuated the Murrayite theory and made use of Murray's scholastic weight to provide Wicca with a history and tradition which would defy accusations that Gardner had invented it.[5] An apparent historical context for Gardner's Wicca had been found and given academic credibility, despite the fact that Murray's theory was never fully accepted in academic circles.[6] Nevertheless, Murray's favourable reassessment of witchcraft provided the impetus for a surge of interest in this 'Dianic cult', just as Gardner had hoped. Perhaps, as Nancy Ramsey has argued, Murray's work remains important in this small part of the field of religious studies because sometimes, 'as Mircea Eliade stated, what remains important is the effect an idea had on popular culture, not its validity'.[7]

During the 1970s, however, historians produced the first specific studies of 'the Great Witch Hunt' and overturned Murray's theory. Her sources and her use of them were proved to be defective, with Cohn observing that her argument 'is seen to be just as fanciful as the argument which Michelet had propounded, with far greater poetic power, some sixty years earlier'.[8] We may therefore quite legitimately ask how her book managed to convince so many people that one scholar, in 1962, was moved to lament, 'The Murrayites seem to hold ... an almost undisputed sway at the higher intellectual levels. There is, amongst educated people, a very widespread impression that Professor Margaret Murray has discovered the true answer to the problem of the history of European witchcraft and has proved her theory.'[9] Of course, she had done nothing of the sort, but, as Ronald Hutton points out, nobody in 1921 'knew anything about the reality of the Great Witch Hunt, no systematic local study having been made'[10] and so, despite earlier criticisms, it was not until the 1970s that Murray's theory was effectively challenged. Keith Thomas's celebrated study of *Religion and the Decline of Magic* (1971) and Norman Cohn's *Europe's Inner Demons* (1975) fractured Murray's thesis and provided alternative explanations for the Great Witch Hunt. It has become generally accepted within Wicca that the Great Witch Hunt (as we will continue to call it, with these reservations) has to be understood as a phenomenon produced by a whole matrix of factors, including delusion and the imagination (Cohn), and social and political forces (Trevor-Roper), rather than as a campaign launched to combat a surviving pre-Christian pagan religion.

The Murrayite thesis having collapsed, then, modern Witches, Wiccans and Pagans[11] had to come to terms with strong arguments against the survival of a pre-Christian religion indigenous to Britain and Europe: although charms and spells, folk customs, magic, and the ancient mysteries were pagan survivals, 'paganism had not survived with them, for they were the work of Christians who had detached them from any previous religious context'.[12] One option open to practitioners was to do as sociologist Ken Rees suggests, and act 'as if' the myth were true.[13] The other, more widespread (though by no means universal) reaction was to embrace the historical facts as they became apparent and trust to the efficacy of modern-day Witchcraft, Wicca, and Paganism for legitimisation rather than rely on pseudo-history.

This short sketch of the development of Wicca by Gerald Gardner reflects his use of history, and his attempts to claim an unbroken tradition not just back to the Great Witch Hunt of early modern Europe but to the Stone Age. His belief in an underground pagan nature/fertility cult which survived from pre-Christian times is a powerfully romanticised fiction based on Michelet, Leland and Murray with the purpose of making Wicca attractive to newcomers so that it would not die out. Undoubtedly, then, these myths have formed a subtext in the development of Wicca, Witchcraft and Paganism over the past fifty years – the myths of continuity of pagan religion throughout the era of Christianity, protecting the under-class of women and peasants and representing a level of religious tolerance and liberty barely visible even today.

As a result, modern Wiccans, Witches and Pagans have often been regarded by scholars as manipulators of history, clinging stubbornly to narratives long since proven false by historians, archaeologists and the hard-headed objectivism of academe. According to historians such as Robin Briggs,[14] the 'modern pseudo-religion of witchcraft' is a syncretic construct which cobbles together elements of genuine pagan belief and ritual on the foundation of a false genealogy of descent from medieval witches who followed a pre-Christian nature religion indigenous to the British Isles. However, to the scholar of religion, contemporary Wicca, Witchcraft, and Paganism are not 'pseudo' religions, and their practitioners are often well aware that 'the witches of the past were not adherents of surviving pagan cults or guardians of secret knowledge'.[15]

Nevertheless, many of the popular books[16] on modern Witchcraft, Wicca and Paganism reveal surprisingly limited knowledge of the historical investigations of the past thirty years or so, and the resulting distortions of the history of the witch-hunt can have a tendency to mar what are otherwise well-written and informative volumes. Yet the writers of such volumes are not historians, the sources and specialised literature are largely unknown to them, and they, just like the historian, have their own agenda which can lead to misinterpretation. Thus on the one hand Briggs, as a historian, bemoans the picking out and exaggeration of details by the non-specialists to fit their own narrative, but remains unaware of the fact that there has been a marked revision of historical narrative within Wicca in Britain during the past ten years.[17] On the other hand, some practitioners of Wicca, Witchcraft and Paganism resent what they see as the ownership of history by academia and the perceived continued lack of respect shown by historians whose own agenda seems to be to dismiss the validity of contemporary Wicca to its practitioners because of its earlier ahistoricism.[18]

In such readings of Wicca, what might be missed is a willingness by practitioners to experiment with history, mythology and archetypal imagery, all of which are the stalwarts of the origins of religions. The ways in which history is used by people other than historians is perhaps ignored or mentioned only for the purposes of derision. The power of historical and mythical undercurrents which inform to a greater or lesser extent the identity, imagery and practice of religion can easily be left unexplored, and the point of view of the practitioner, or the amount of historical factual information known and accepted by practitioners, dismissed as unworthy of consideration.

This chapter therefore comments on the use of history in modern Wicca, Witchcraft and Paganism, rather than on the history of Witchcraft or Wicca *per se*. The actual history of Wicca, which is relatively well-documented and researched,[19] stands in contrast to the mythic undercurrents which influenced its development, and which historians and other scholars still tend to believe inform the identity of all Wiccans, Witches and Pagans. As Rees points out, the use of foundation myths creates 'the need to keep the historicity of modern Paganism (a complex enough area on its own) clearly defined in distinction to its more mythic undercurrents'.[20] As explored in the following section, despite the historical inaccuracy of the early Wiccan view of its history, there are reasons for its deployment which are perfectly valid. In addition, it would be unfair to summarily dismiss a community's use of history as devious simply because that history was incorrect, and as wilfully ignorant when such ignorance was, until the 1970s, entirely in line with the current knowledge of the academy itself in an area of research which has only recently started to come of age.

But as the study of the Great Witch Hunt has come of age, so have Wicca, Witchcraft and Paganism. This chapter is concerned with the evidence of Wiccans' and Pagans' attitudes towards the Witch Hunt today, now, rather than with Gardner's belief in an unbroken lineage. What do Pagans today think of the Great Witch Hunt? What connections, if any, do Witches feel they have with those accused of witchcraft in the early modern period? And, more importantly to this volume, how do Wiccans in Lancashire relate to the trial of the Lancashire witches?

The time of the Great Witch Hunt of early modern Europe, still commonly known as 'the burning times' despite the fact that witches were hanged rather than burned in England, is perhaps the most important epoch with which contemporary Wiccans, Witches and Pagans have identified. An exaggerated nine million women were said to have been put to death during the persecution, and this 'myth of nine million' until recently constituted a substantial mythic thread. It was computed in the late eighteenth century through the false extrapolation of local records by an antiquarian at Quedlinburg, Germany,[21] and was then repeated by various German historians. The feminist writer Matilda Jocelyn Gage then made use of the number in *Women, Church and State* in 1893 in order to emphasise the crimes of the Church against women. It is from Gage that the number entered Wiccan mythology: the Museum of Witchcraft and Magic on the Isle of Man, owned by Cecil Williamson with Gerald Gardner as 'resident Witch', sported a plaque commemorating the nine million witches who died in the Great Witch Hunt, and Mary Daly's use of the figure in *Gyn-Ecology* (1978) introduced the myth to feminist Witches. It was not until the late 1980s, however, that estimates of the death toll were produced based on solid evidence, with current scholarly estimates ranging from 40,000 to 60,000.[22] It is therefore not so surprising that an exaggerated death toll was popular prior to the production of these estimates.

This later figure of 40,000–60,000 remains large enough to instil a sense of horror in its own right, despite the fact that the individuals comprising this figure were executed over a long period of time which included only a few instances of intense persecution; for most communities over most of that period, the execution of a witch remained a rare and sensational event. Nevertheless, despite the production of verifiable and academically acceptable figures, the myth retained its hold on Wicca, acting as a mechanism of legitimisation, relating the persecution of witches to the Jewish Holocaust of the Nazi era and demanding respect through the use of an enormous number[23] – witches (and women) were assimilated to persecuted minorities in a general distortion of history in order to suit the political aims of feminist witchcraft in particular.[24]

The persecution and execution of witches in the Great Witch Hunt has thus been reinterpreted as a holocaust against women, a repackaging of history which implies conscious victimisation and the appropriation of 'holocaust' as a badge of honour[25] – 'gendercide rather than genocide'.[26] The Holocaust set the standard for enormous persecutions, and by comparing the witch trials to the Holocaust modern Witches were demanding that the same level of respect be given to it. The death toll thus became a matter of fundamental importance, and any attempt to lower the number was perceived as a direct attack on modern Witches.[27] An elective affinity with the image of the witch during the time of the persecutions is commonly regarded as part of the reclamation of female power, a psychological link which aids modern feminist Witches in their struggle for freedom from patriarchal oppression. The past is thus focused on as a central source of meaning, where the 'burning times' is used as a rallying symbol, and the witch is regarded both as a martyr and as a symbol of repressed female power.

Apart from the use of the witch figure as an image of female power, however, there was another reason for forging affinities with the 'nine million' persecuted witches of the 'burning times'. Even though witchcraft was no longer illegal after 1951, many modern Witches still feared, and still do fear, the 'subtle' persecution of being forced out of jobs or losing their children through trumped-up charges if they are publicly known as a Witch. Thus, on the one hand thirty-six of the Wiccan respondents to a survey conducted in 1995[28] reported that they kept their identity as a Witch secret precisely because of fears of persecution for themselves and their families, claiming 'fear of misunderstanding from employers, family, friends, teachers, social workers i.e. children may be taken away' and stating the necessity of remaining secret 'lest I should be criticised and/or labelled/judged/discriminated against'. On the other hand, however, seventy-one respondents stated that they were open about their Witchcraft, believing that only by providing accurate information about modern Wicca and standing up for Witchcraft could the misconceptions be erased and, along with them, the fear that leads to persecution. Many said that they were open because they had 'nothing to hide' or 'nothing to be ashamed of – I'm proud of being a Witch', 'I am proud of my religion and I want to dispel misconceptions about it'. One person said she was open because, 'though this can lead to persecution and/or mickey-taking, I feel it is only by being open that one can get people to accept the authenticity of Pagan religion and ethics', and another added, 'people can't ignore us if we're "out"'. Others said they were open but only because they knew it would not be detrimental to their careers if people knew they were Witches. For one man, the myth of continuity informed his choice to be open about being a Witch, since

> misinformation and false stereotypes/fears about 'witches' and what they do/ believe has been perpetuated for centuries ... I strongly argue that if practising witches/Pagans want to have an end to being misjudged and victimised/ ridiculed and persecuted *the only effective way to deal with this is to be open*! Counter misinformation and false stereotypes with true and accurate information. If people are not denied knowledge of what is 'going on', then they will not have to fall back on age-old falsities (their only other source of knowledge!) for forming their opinions, and consequently their attitudes towards people who hold these beliefs.[29]

In these attitudes of being 'open', we can perhaps see another way in which history plays its role in Wicca, for not only do Wiccans remember early modern European witchcraft, the general public does too. People in general have, according to the last respondent, been fed misinformation, or false memories – they fall back on 'knowledge' gleaned from 'age-old falsities'. Part of the Wiccan reading of witchcraft from earlier times is, then, valued for its attempts to reclaim the witch figure and present 'her' as good and wise – a 'true' history rather than the 'false' history of the witch as evil, constructed (in

Wicca's view) by the Christian Church.

In addition, history has a role to play in differentiating Wicca from early modern witchcraft and in providing evidence against commonly held perceptions. Briggs[30] asserts in his conclusion the importance of further work on the witch-hunts because the human imagination will continue to see the witch as 'other': 'just as rabbits have a "hawk detector" in their retina, so human beings have a "witch detector" somewhere in their consciousness, and derive excitement from having it activated'. He says, in relation to the satanic ritual abuse claims of the late 1980s which were linked to witchcraft by the popular media, that 'the descriptions of rituals are like identikit pictures, slightly varied combinations of precisely the same elements found in the charges against heretics, Jews, witches and other scapegoats in the past. To anyone who recognises their antecedents it is incredible that this tawdry collection of recycled fantasies can be mistaken for anything but inventions.'[31] Given the 'misguided and dangerous thinking' which allowed the ritual abuse panic to occur, it is perhaps not so surprising that modern Witches at times do feel persecuted and identify with the witches of the past – in cases like this, one might be forgiven for agreeing with them that nothing has changed. In such situations, the role of the historian as well as scholars of religion and practitioners themselves thus takes on a very real importance. Whilst it seems strange that Briggs dismisses modern Wicca and its 'persecution complex' earlier in his book, given his comment about the importance of further study to avoid future satanic abuse scares, it might also seem strange that people still choose to identify themselves as Witches. The first part of this chapter has looked in general terms at the relationship of modern Wicca, Witchcraft and Paganism to the Great Witch Hunt, and examined the way in which history has been used. The remaining sections focus on the image of the witch and on the more localised response of contemporary Wiccans, Pagans and Witches to the Lancashire witches.

Knowledge of historical facts and evidence, as we have seen, does not preclude the use of historical narrative, and the eclectic nature of Witchcraft, Wicca and Paganism means that practitioners borrow from history as well as from other sources. The representation of the early modern witch in history and literature has been an important part of the development of Wicca, and remains relevant to the heritage of Wiccans, Witches and Pagans in the twenty-first century. It is a representation open to manipulation by Witches and non-Witches alike, and as such it evolves with the human imagination according to the specifics of cultural influences. Thus, in 1604 a witch was (according to Peel and Southern):

> a woman, or man, who had abandoned Christianity and renounced her baptism, who worshipped Satan as her God and had made a definite act of surrendering herself to him, body and soul, offering herself as an instrument for

the evil work he could only perform through a human agent. In exchange she had been promised anything she desired to have.[32]

It is this promise which brings people to witchcraft, for according to James VI's *Daemonologie* of 1597, people sought to become witches for two reasons: the lure of food and wealth for the poverty-stricken, and the promise of power and revenge on their enemies for the wealthy.[33] Elizabeth Southerns ('Demdike') is clearly of the former category, and has been described by Peel and Southern as 'a witch of the classic fairytale mould, old, lame and blind'.[34]

There would seem to be little reason for people today to identify with such images. But if the witch can be identified with as a victim, she can also be identified with as a symbol of strength and power. A feminist reclaiming of the witch as an image of woman victimised, persecuted, and derided as evil because of her sexuality and control over the processes of life and death, enables some women to reclaim their own power. The powerful imagery of the witch thus remains attractive because she lives her own life, and is strong and independent. As Ronald Hutton recounts,

> the advantage of the label 'witch' is that it has all the exciting connotations of a figure who flouts the conventions of normal society and is possessed of powers unavailable to it, at once feared and persecuted. It is a marvellous rallying point for a counter-culture, and also one of the few images of independent female power in early modern European civilization.[35]

The witch thus becomes a trump card in the 'war of the sexes', and woman becomes not only another persecuted minority but also a source of strength. Her power, once thought to originate from those 'hidden and potent forces' imbuing the world which ultimately stemmed from either God or the Devil,[36] is now regarded as residing in nature or within a person rather than stemming from God or the Devil.

Some Witches, such as Leo Martello, see the image of the historical witch as important precisely because 'in Medieval times "the only liberated woman was the witch"',[37] and indeed this image of the witch as a free woman has maintained its hold. But whilst historical images to a certain extent inform the caricature of the witch which has continued into the present century, 'she' is now an altogether different character. In the second half of the twentieth century, in Wicca and feminist witchcraft, the witch has been reclaimed from her early modern association with 'evil'. No longer allied with Satan except by those religious groups which see the work of the Devil everywhere, she instead gains her power from the forces of nature. She has become that mythic figure of our urban age imagined as close to nature, dealing in magic and spellcraft and worshipping the old pagan deities. She is the reclaimer of the lost power of woman, and of the image of the Goddess. And 'she' is just as likely to be 'he'. The witch has been incorporated into the priesthood of Wicca as the religion of Witchcraft, or has become the activist, or remains the isolated individual whose connection to religion is neither here nor there. The thread thus continues, reminding us 'how easily the pliable figure of the witch can be manipulated to fit the spirit of each age'.[38]

Undoubtedly, then, the image of the witch still haunts the human imagination, and retains strong connections to areas such as Essex and Lancashire for Witches and non-Witches alike. In the documentary *Lucifer Over Lancashire*, broadcast by the BBC in the era of the satanic/ritual abuse panic in 1987, we are told by the Reverend Kevin Logan, vicar of St John's Church, Great Harwood, that 'Pendle Hill speaks for itself, casting a dark shadow over the land', it is a 'magnet which draws witchcraft to it', the 'traditional haunt of witches', and is 'the witchcraft capital of England', despite the fact that Pendle Hill is not mentioned in Thomas Potts's account of the witch trials.[39] But Logan goes on to tell us that there are thirty covens in the area of Pendle Hill, twenty in Preston, and another ten to fifteen in the Rossendale Valley. That is a total of between sixty and seventy-five covens, yet fieldwork in the north-west from 1994 to 1999 revealed between fifteen and twenty Wiccan covens in the region as a whole, involved in the worship of nature rather than that of the Devil. The Devil is regarded by Wiccans as a Christian invention, and as such one must be a Christian to believe in him and thus also to worship him. Wiccans are not Devil worshippers or Satanists but worship old pagan gods and goddesses such as Herne, Pan, Diana and Isis. Wiccan beliefs and practices, like those of medieval Jews, tend to be the opposite of Christianity's caricature of them.

Such an image of Pendle and the exaggeration of the scale of witchcraft in Lancashire seems to suggest that the witchcraft heritage of Lancashire has had an effect on Logan's Christian community. Indeed, in 1986 they had decided to erect a 20-foot cross on Pendle Hill on Hallowe'en 'as a symbol of Christ rather than of Satan': the old association of witches with the Devil clearly continues for the Christians living in 'the Devil's domain', fighting for control of the 'spiritual wasteland' of north-east Lancashire. Unfortunately for Logan, the local planning committee rejected his plan to erect the 20-foot cross, saying it would constitute a 'new development', but as recently as Hallowe'en 1998 Christians planned a walk-in on Pendle Hill, allegedly to cleanse it from the evil created by local Witches, and have used strategies such as outdoor tea, sermons, and hymns to try and prevent people from celebrating Pagan festivals on the hill. In recent years, the hill has been closed off by police anxious to avert public disorder.

The effect of the Lancashire witches on some Christian groups thus seems clear. What is the effect on modern Witches? This is more difficult to determine. In general, the mythic history outlined in this chapter is more of a subtext in British Wicca, and Wiccans, Pagans and Witches rarely discuss the Great Witch Hunt, focusing instead on the modern history of Wicca: that is, the past century. A passing comment from a Wiccan in a coven in Lancaster revealed a dislike of Lancaster Castle and its immediate surroundings, which was felt to have an oppressive, almost evil aura. This feeling was thought to be connected with the imprisonment and presumed execution of the witches there. Yet whereas in Exeter modern Wiccans campaigned to have a memorial plaque erected for the Devon witches Temperance Lloyd, Susannah Edwards, Mary Trembles and Alice Molland, the last people to be executed for witch-craft,[40] no such feeling seems to have been stirred in Lancaster until very re-cently, despite Peel and Southern's assertion that the Lancashire witches are 'undoubtedly the most famous witches in English history'.[41]

However, the year 2001 saw the fiftieth anniversary of the repeal of the 1736 Witchcraft Act, and this event was celebrated by many Wiccans, Witches and Pagans. This is despite the fact that the repeal of this Act was brought about by Spiritualists and their supporters rather than by Witches, since as Mr Monslow, Labour MP for Barrow-in-Furness, argued, 'for over half a century the spiritualist movement had been seeking to have accorded to it what was accorded to other religious denominations – religious freedom', whilst a Mr Ede remarked that the passing of the bill marked recognition that in religious matters, England needed 'not uniformity but unity'.[42] According to the Labour MP for Normanton, Mr T. Brooks, the replacement of the 1736 Witchcraft Act with the Fraudulent Mediums Act 'would help to remove a real grievance and indignity which the spiritualists had suffered for many years'.[43]

The bill went through on a nod, along with such esteemed legislation as the Pet Animals Act, in June 1951, just a few months before the general elec-tion of October that year swept aside Attlee's Labour government.[44] It was, then, hardly a momentous occasion, warranting only a small report in *The Times* of April 1951, and inclusion in a list of assents in *The Times* of June 1951. And yet to Gerald Gardner, as mentioned earlier in this chapter, the repeal signified that the time was ripe for the regeneration of Wicca and he set about writing his *Witchcraft Today*, subsequently published in 1954. For those who had read Gardner's earlier works, particularly *High Magic's Aid* (1949), and those who were inspired by *Witchcraft Today* and *The Meaning of Witchcraft* (1959) to establish covens and initiate witches, the 1951 repeal was of the utmost importance. But this importance did not lie in a nostalgia for traditional witchcraft, which is certainly prevalent in today's spiritual milieu, or in the opportunity to forge more fictional connections with the witches of the past. Rather, the repeal offered a chance for unity rather than uniformity and, more importantly, a celebration of religious freedom.

In the year of the fiftieth anniversary of the repeal, the journal of the Pagan Federation, *Pagan Dawn*, included an article on the Lancashire witches in its spring 2001 issue, and in this and previous issues appealed to its reader-ship to prepare events to celebrate and remember the repeal of the Witchcraft

Act. Pagans in East Anglia, for example, set about compiling a register of those persecuted for witchcraft in that area, and in Lancashire the Lancashire Witch Project[45] was established by those interested in the history of the witch trials, as a means of remembering this anniversary. The project includes a museum exhibition,[46] the majority of which concentrates on the seventeenth-century trials of the Lancashire witches, with other sections on old pagan religion and the witchcraft revival of the past half-century. A plaque has been placed on the Golden Lion pub in Lancaster by the north-west branch of the Pagan Federation, listing the names of the executed witches, plus Demdike as 'died in gaol', with the legend, 'In memory of all those who suffered through prejudice and intolerance'. The pub also carries another plaque from the brewery, recording that it was founded in about 1612 and was traditionally the last drinking stop for the condemned. The plaque hints that this included the Lancashire witches, although the last drink can hardly have been a tradition at this time, nor is it likely to have been started by the witches themselves.

Involvement in such projects does not, however, indicate any particular celebration of the Lancashire witches themselves. Jez, a one-time member of the project, who runs Daemon Books in Lancaster, told me that:

> Despite having visited [Pendle] hill and read a little about the witches, the topic never really appealed to me. There is so much that is hard to establish about them. I guess at base it is the fact that the records we have were not written by the witches. 16th century magic is so much richer in texts by its practitioners that it seems possible to gain access to their mindset, whereas I feel unable to link with the Pendle group in this way.

Visitors to his bookshop tend to have a historical interest in the witches, but they are a different group of people from those interested in being Witches now.

For those who are Witches now, attitudes towards the Lancashire witches and their story appear to be quite consistent: the Lancashire witches do not inform contemporary Witchcraft, and those persecuted are remembered as human beings who suffered horrifically rather than as witches, whilst attempts to sensationalise the story in fiction and tourism are met with disappointment. One Lancashire Witch, born almost within sight of Pendle but now living elsewhere in the UK, remembered primary school outings to Lancaster Castle 'where we were regaled with tales of the witch trials, among other horrors'. She recently returned to the area for a visit and explored the Pendle area using the Tourist Board's Witch Trail map; she recalls Pendle Hill being used as a place for a walk and picnic or school trips to look at the geology and botany of the place, and was surprised to see it marketed as a tourist attraction, although reflected that the Tourist Board could hardly ignore the only distinctive story about its area. She told me:

We did visit a tourist office, and I looked at their collection of books about the Lancashire witches, but I didn't buy any. To be honest, I think it is such a horrible story that I did not want to be made to think about it too closely. But I was intrigued to see how it has become a subject of interest and research in recent years.

She was also less than happy with the dummies dressed as witches to be found outside shops, a 'tradition' observed by Peel and Southern in the 1960s when 'witches galore still abound for visitors to Newchurch and the district. Made from pipe-cleaners, cork and scraps of material, they hang in their dozens in a shop in the village street and sit astride their tiny broomsticks in practically every bar in every pub for miles around.'[47] Another witch told me that Lancashire bookshops are stocked with 'ridiculous novels like *Mist Over Pendle*' (by Robert Neill, 1951) and 'fairly ghastly touristy books which sensationalize (and awfulize!) the accused witches'. Thus, when she visited Pendle Hill, she found herself very aware of the baggage she was carrying: 'historical evidence and interpretations, feminist theories of witchhunting, myth and mystery (and rubbish) surrounding the Pendle witches' story(ies)'. As Peel and Southern noted over thirty years ago, notions of the Lancashire witches are largely 'based on fiction, legend and occasional articles in the papers [which are] so vague and inaccurate as to make the serious student wince ... Nowhere ... are they more firmly held than among those who live within the shadow of Pendle Hill.'[48]

There are, then, Witches who have knowledge of Pendle Hill and may even make use of Tourist Board trails, and there are undoubtedly Pagans who are drawn to Pendle Hill at various times of the year, as well as to Arbor Lowe and other historic/pre-historic sites. But this is not evidence of a desire on the part of twenty-first-century Witches to identify with the Lancashire witches of 1612. Rather, as another Lancashire Witch said,

> I remember them every year at Samhain [Hallowe'en], the misfit Demdikes and Devizes and the rest of them, not because I think they are witches, I don't, but because they were named and punished and perished as witches and someone has to remember them as human beings. As it is, their memory has become distorted into a cipher for contemporary fantasies about witches ... I remember them as flawed human beings who became and informed the stereotype that still stigmatises witches today.

If 'historical European witchcraft is quite simply a fiction',[49] as Briggs assures us, then modern Witches are free to construct their own fiction, to use their imagination to affirm a positive image of the witch. The 'slippery' status of witchcraft 'as a logical and linguistic construct whose boundaries are both arbitrary and insecure'[50] can be seen to aid this ongoing process of reinvention, as can the images of witchcraft during the Great Witch Hunt.

Thus, the witch appears as an active and powerful figure, culturally constructed throughout history and easily manipulated to fit each age: that people today are happy to call themselves witches is just one more example of this process.

By identifying themselves as Witches, modern practitioners do have to come to terms with the connotations of the word 'witch' from previous eras, many of which continue into the present. This includes an identification with the so-called witches who were persecuted in the early modern period. Witches exist in history as real people, as the doers of both good and evil but also as the victims of horrific persecution at the hands of the Christian Church. Although certain elements of the Christian Church, not to mention the British tabloid press, continue to conflate witchcraft with Satanism, the re-emergence of the witch in Wicca, Witchcraft and Paganism sees her as the guardian of the secret powers of nature and of woman, as the priestess of the Goddess, as the herbalist, and as the practitioner of magic. Modern Wicca and Witchcraft thus offer a critical synthesis of the polarities and ambiguities of the witch figure to produce a 'witch' who is both modern and timeless. Perhaps most importantly, the witch has not died but has remained within the human imagination throughout the course of history, and the call of the witch from four hundred years ago still echoes for some in Lancashire today:

> the folk esotericism and sorcerous lore of the northern shires are presently being recovered, explored and elucidated as a living experiential pathway, a work being undertaken beneath the aegis of the arcane association known as 'The Demdike Club'. For mysteries and passwords which bind together all Elvish Blood into a timeless unity are spoken in lonely and concealed places, secretly uttered as the moon rises over the brow of Pendle Hill and the coiling wraiths of the Witch-Dead call out to the Faithful at the noon of night.[51]

Notes

1 Based on and attempting to emulate the secret religious rites honouring various deities which flourished during the Hellenistic period, such as the mysteries of Demeter and Persephone at Eleusis, the mysteries of Isis, and the Orphic mysteries.

2 It is an obvious point, but nevertheless worth noting, that 'Dianic' has been the name of a feminist branch of witchcraft for the past thirty years, though named after the virgin goddess Diana (Artemis), whom Charles Godfrey Leland characterised as the witches' goddess in *Aradia or The Gospel of the Witches* (1899; reprinted Washington: Phoenix, 1990), rather than after Murray's Roman god Dianus.

3 Margaret Alice Murray, *The Witch Cult in Western Europe: A Study in Anthropology* (Oxford: Clarendon Press, 1921), p. 192.

4 Gerald Gardner, *Witchcraft Today* (London: Rider, 1954), p. 54.

5 Indeed Norman Cohn, in *Europe's Inner Demons* (New York: Basic Books, 1975), p. 108, appears to blame Murray for the very existence of modern witchcraft: 'the *Witch Cult* and its progeny have stimulated the extraordinary proliferation of "witches' covens" in Western Europe and the United States during the past decade [i.e. the 1960s]'. See also the preface to

Cohn's work, pp. x–xi.

6   Murray's thesis received criticism from the time of its publication: see G. L. Burr, 'A review of M. A. Murray's *Witch Cult in Western Europe*', *American Historical Review* 27 (1921–2), pp. 780–3; C. L'Estrange Ewen, *Some Witchcraft Criticisms: A Plea for the Blue Pencil* (London: printed for the author, 1938); R. H. Robbins, *Encyclopedia of Witchcraft and Demonology* (London: Peter Nevill, 1959), pp. 116–17; E. E. Rose, *A Razor for a Goat: Witchcraft and Diabolism* (Toronto: University of Toronto Press, 1962).

7   Nancy Ramsey, 'The myth of historical narrative in M. Murray's *The God of the Witches*', *The Pomegranate: A New Journal of Neo-Pagan Thought* 3 (1998), p. 11.

8   Cohn, *Europe's Inner Demons*, p. 115. See also Caroline Oates and Juliette Wood, *A Coven of Scholars: Margaret Murray and her Working Methods* (London: Folklore Society, 1998).

9   Rose, *A Razor for a Goat*, pp. 14–15, and see also Edgar Peel and Pat Southern, *The Trial of the Lancashire Witches: A Study in Seventeenth-Century Witchcraft* (Newton Abbot: David and Charles, 1969), p. 148.

10 Ronald Hutton, *The Pagan Religions of the Ancient British Isles: Their Nature and Legacy* (Oxford: Blackwell, 1991), p. 304.

11 In this essay the terms 'Wicca', 'Witch', 'Pagan', etc. when capitalised refer to specific, modern-day religions and their practitioners, whereas 'witchcraft', 'witch', 'pagan', etc. when not capitalised refer to general historical phenomena. Despite their commonalities, Wicca, Paganism and Witchcraft are not synonymous; however, the common perception among scholars has been to treat these different entities as if they were one and the same. The growing popularity of these religions over the last three decades has seen the development of a variety of forms of Witchcraft and Paganism which have fanned out from classical Wicca. For further information, see J. Pearson 'Demarcating the field: Paganism, Wicca and Witchcraft', in G. Harvey and M. Bowman (eds), *Pagan Identities*, special issue of DISKUS (2000) [www.uni-marburg.de/fb03/religionswissenschaft/journal/diskus/#6], and J. Pearson, *A Popular Dictionary of Paganism* (London: Routledge Curzon, 2002).

12 Hutton, *Pagan Religions*, p. 293.

13 Ken Rees, 'The tangled skein: the role of myth in paganism', in Graham Harvey and Charlotte Hardman (eds), *Paganism Today: Wiccans, Druids, the Goddess and Ancient Earth Traditions for the Twenty-First Century* (London: Thorsons, 1996), p. 26.

14 Robin Briggs, *Witches and Neighbours: The Social and Cultural Context of European Witchcraft* (London: Harper Collins, 1996), p. 5.

15 Briggs, *Witches and Neighbours*, p. 5.

16 See for example Vivianne Crowley, *Wicca: The Old Religion in the New Millennium* (1989; London: Thorsons, 1996) and Janet and Stewart Farrar, *Eight Sabbats for Witches* (London: Hale, 1981). See also Starhawk, *The Spiral Dance: A Rebirth of the Ancient Religion of the Great Goddess* (1979; New York: Harper Collins, 1989), pp. 16–22, and Ann Moura, *The Origins of Modern Witchcraft: The Evolution of a World Religion* (St Pauls, Minn.: Llewellyn, 2000).

17 As Hutton points out in the introduction to the 1993 edition of *Pagan Religions*, p. xiii, Wicca 'has proved capable of re-evaluating its own claims with a genuine scholarly rigour'. Nevertheless, there remain many Witches and Pagans who do assume an unbroken line of descent from prehistory to the present day, including the author of the passage quoted at the end of this chapter.

18 Cohn, *Europe's Inner Demons*, pp. x–xi, for example, mentions contemporary Witchcraft only in order to dismiss it as anti-historical.

19 Most recently by Ronald Hutton in *Triumph of the Moon: A History of Modern Pagan Witchcraft* (Oxford: Oxford University Press, 1999). See also Philip Heselton, *Wiccan Roots: Gerald Gardner and the Modern Witchcraft Revival* (Berkshire: Capall Bann, 2000), for a recent insider perspective on Wiccan history.

20 Rees, 'The tangled skein', p. 30. This is not to devalue the mythic undercurrents, since foundational myths are often used to validate a religious tradition and to provide practitioners with roots embedded in tradition. See also Margot Adler, *Drawing Down the Moon: Witches, Druids, Goddess-Worshippers, and Other Pagans in America Today* (Boston: Beacon Press, 1986), p. 45, for a discussion of the myths of Wicca.

21 I am grateful to Ronald Hutton for pointing out the origins of the figure of nine million, which was established by the German historian Wolfgang Behringer.

22 Hutton, *Pagan Religions*, pp. 306, 370, has suggested a figure of 40,000, whilst 60,000 is favoured by Brian Levack, *The Witch-Hunt in Early Modern Europe* (London: Longman, 1987), pp. 21–7. Briggs, *Witches and Neighbours*, pp. 8, 260, suggests 40,000–50,000.

23 See Diane Purkiss, *The Witch in History: Early Modern and Twentieth-Century Representations* (London: Routledge, 1996), who entitles one of her chapters 'A Holocaust of one's own: the myth of the Burning Times'.

24 Briggs, *Witches and Neighbours*, p. 8.

25 Stjepan G. Meštrovic, *Postemotional Society* (London: Sage, 1997), p. 11.

26 Briggs, *Witches and Neighbours*, p. 8.

27 As one American academic reported, 'If your estimate is "too low", you are dishonoring the ancestors and trivializing the Burning Times (as if there was some quota of deaths we had to meet in order to be a bona fide atrocity)': J. Gibbons, pers. comm. to Nature Religion Scholars' List (natrel-l@uscolo.edu), 12 March 1999.

28 This survey constituted part of the author's doctoral research, 'Religion and the return of magic: Wicca as esoteric spirituality' (unpublished Ph.D. thesis, Lancaster University, 2000), revised and published as: *Wicca: Magic, Spirituality and the 'Mystic Other'* (London: Routledge, forthcoming 2003).

29 Compare Kirsteen Macpherson Bardell's chapter in this volume. It is interesting to note that today, as in the past, witches are still linked only with *maleficia* in the public imagination, rather than with any forms of beneficial magic such as healing.

30 Briggs, *Witches and Neighbours*, p. 410.

31 Briggs, *Witches and Neighbours*, pp. 410–11.

32 Peel and Southern, *Trials of the Lancashire Witches*, p. 54.

33 Peel and Southern, *Trials of the Lancashire Witches*, p. 35.

34 Peel and Southern, *Trials of the Lancashire Witches*, p. 26. See also Jeffrey Richards's chapter in this volume, where in Harrison Ainsworth's novel Demdike is sure to be convicted since her 'great age, infirmities and poverty, will be proof against her'. Of course, the reverse is also true, and those with beauty and youth on their side are also condemned as witches.

35 Hutton, *Pagan Religions*, p. 335.

36 Briggs, *Witches and Neighbours*, p. 4.

37 Adler, *Drawing Down the Moon*, p. 213. It is a common misconception that the Great Witch Hunt dates from the medieval era rather than the early modern.

38 Briggs, *Witches and Neighbours*, p. 5.

39 As Peel and Southern point out in *The Trials of the Lancashire Witches*, p. 149, 'the picture of a coven of hags astride their broomsticks sweeping silently across the bleak expanse of Pendle is an intriguing one' given that the Hill is not mentioned by Potts. It is also interesting to note that, far from lingering only throughout the eighteenth and nineteenth centuries, as Richards suggests in this volume, witchcraft superstitions appear to have been alive and well in the Pendle region at the end of the twentieth century.

40 *Pagan Dawn* 124, Lammas 1997.

41 Peel and Southern, *Trials of the Lancashire Witches*, p. 11. One correspondent told me that 'no-one I have met in the south has ever heard of the Lancashire witches at all'.

42 'Rights of Spiritualists', *The Times*, 21 April 1951, p. 5.

43 'Rights of Spiritualists', *The Times*, 21 April 1951, p. 5.

44 Thanks are due to Dr Nick Freeman of the University of the West of England, who supplied copies of the relevant *Times* articles and discussed their importance with me.

45 My thanks to Jez Green of the Lancashire Witch Project, with whom I communicated extensively, and to Ann-Marie Gallagher of the University of Central Lancashire for sharing her thoughts on the Lancashire witches. I would also like to thank the Witches and Wiccans who spoke to me about the Lancashire witches but wish to remain anonymous.

46 The exhibition has the backing of the Lancashire County Museums Service, and opened in the main county museum at Preston in November 2001 for six months. It was then intended to tour several smaller museums such as Clitheroe Castle and The Judges Lodgings in Lancaster.

47 Peel and Southern, *Trials of the Lancashire Witches*, p. 159.

48 Peel and Southern, *Trials of the Lancashire Witches*, p. 10.

49 Briggs, *Witches and Neighbours*, p. 6.

50 Briggs, *Witches and Neighbours*, p. 7.

51 Nigel Aldcroft Jackson, 'Witch-fire over Lancashire: the wysard craft of north west England', *The Cauldron* 91 (1999), p. 25. Compare the descriptions of Pendle Hill in Richards's chapter in this volume.

Bibliography

The bibiliography includes all works cited in the references, together with a small selection of other relevant works, under two headings: contemporary sources (sixteenth- and seventeenth-century material, including modern editions) and later works (first published after 1700).

Contemporary sources

Acts of the Privy Council of England.

Anon., *The Examination and Confession of Certaine Wytches* (London, 1566).

Anon., *A Detection of Damnable Driftes* (London, 1579).

Anon., *The Most Strange and Admirable Discoverie of the Three Witches of Warboys, (Arraigned, Convicted and Executed at the Last Assizes at Huntington)* (London, 1593).

Anon., *The Triall of Maist. Dorrell: A Collection of Defences* (London, 1599).

Anon., *The Witches of Northamptonshire* (London, 1612).

Bernard, Richard, *A Guide to Grand Jury Men: Divided into Two Bookes* (London, 1627).

Brereton, William, *Travels in Holland 1634–5*, ed. Edward Hawkins (Manchester: Chetham Society publications i, 1844).

Brinley, J., *A Discovery of the Impostures of Witches and Astrologers* (London, 1680).

Calendar of State Papers Domestic.

Dalton, Michael, *The Countrey Justice, Containing the Practice of the Justices of the Peace out of their Sessions* (London, 1618, 1630).

Darrell, J., *A True Narration of the Strange and Grevous Vexation by the Devil, of 7 Persons in Lancashire, and William Somers of Nottingham* (London, 1600).

Dekker, Thomas, *The Dramatic Works of Thomas Dekker*, ed. Fredson Bowers, 4 vols (Cambridge: Cambridge University Press, 1953–61).

Dugdale, William, *Monasticon Anglicanum: A History of the Abbies and Other Monasteries, Hospitals, Frieries, and Cathedral and Collegiate Churches, with their Dependencies in England and Wales* (London, 1655–73; London: James Bohn, 6 vols, 1846).

Fairfax, Edward, *Daemonologia: A Discourse on Witchcraft as it was Acted in the Family of Mr Edward Fairfax of Fuyston, in the County of York in the Year 1621*, ed. William Grainge (Harrogate, 1882).

Goodcole, Henry, *The Wonderfull Discoverie of Elizabeth Sawyer a Witch Late of Edmonton, her Conviction and Condemnation and Death* (London, 1621).

Harsnett, Samuel, *A Discovery of the Fraudulent Practices of John Darrel* (London, 1599).

Harsnett, Samuel, *A Declaration of Egregious Popish Impostures* (London, 1603).

Hawkins, Edward (ed.), *The Farrington Papers* (Manchester: Chetham Society publications xxxvi, 1856).

Heywood, Thomas, and Brome, Richard, *The Late Lancashire Witches* (London, 1634; ed. Laird H. Barber, New York and London: Garland, 1979).

James I, *Daemonologie* (Edinburgh, 1597; ed. G. B. Harrison, London: Bodley Head, 1924; reprinted New York: Barnes and Noble / Edinburgh: Edinburgh University Press, 1966). Also reprinted in Lawrence Normand and Gareth Roberts, *Witchcraft in Early Modern Scotland: James VI's Demonology and the North Berwick Witches* (Exeter: Exeter University Press, 2000).

James, Richard, *Iter Lancastrense*, ed. Thomas Corser (Manchester: Chetham Society publications vii, 1845).

Jonson, Ben, *The Divell is an Asse*, in Ben Jonson, *Works*, ed. C. H. Herford (Oxford: Oxford University Press, 1938).

Main Sermons or Homilies Appointed to be Read in Churches in the Time of Queen Elizabeth of Famous Memory and Now Thought Fit to be Reprinted by Authority from the Kings Excellent Majesty (Oxford, 1683).

More, George, *A True Discourse Concerning the Certaine Possession and Dispossession of 7 Persons in One Familie in Lancashire* (London, 1600).

Paracelsus, *The Archidoxes of Magic* (London, 1656).

Perkins, William, *A Discourse of the Damned Art of Witchcraft* (Cambridge, 1608).

Potts, Thomas, *The Wonderfull Discoverie of Witches in the Countie of Lancaster* (London, 1613; ed. James Crossley, Manchester: Chetham Society publications vi, 1845).

Scot, Reginald, *The Discovery of Witchcraft* (London, 1584; ed. Brinsley Nicholson, London, 1886).

Shadwell, Thomas, *The Lancashire Witches and Teague o'Divelly, the Irish Priest*, in *The Complete Works of Thomas Shadwell*, ed. Montague Summers, 7 vols (London, 1927), iv.

Shakespeare, William, *Macbeth*, Arden edition, ed. Kenneth Muir (London: Methuen, 1951); New Penguin Shakespeare edition, ed. G. K. Hunter (London: Penguin, 1967); Oxford edition, ed. Nicholas Brooke (Oxford: Oxford University Press, 1990).

Sidney, Philip, *An Apology for Poetry* (London, 1595; Manchester: Manchester University Press, 1973).

Smith, Thomas, *De Republica Anglorum* (London, 1583; ed. Mary Dewar, Cambridge: Cambridge University Press, 1982).

Southwell, Robert, *The Poems of Robert Southwell, S.J.*, ed. James McDonald and Nancy Pollard Brown (Oxford: Clarendon Press, 1967).

Sprenger, J., and Kramer, H., *Malleus Maleficarum* (1486; ed. Montague Summers,

London: John Rodker, 1928).

Stearne, J., *A Confirmation and Discovery of Witch Craft* (London, 1648).

Stow, John, *Annales, or a General Chronicle of England*, ed. E. Howes (London, 1631).

T. W., *The Clerk of Assize* (London, 1682).

W. W., *A True and Just Recorde, of the Information, Examination and Confession of All the Witches, Taken at S. Oses in the Countie of Essex* (London, 1582).

Webster, John, *The Displaying of Supposed Witchcraft* (London, 1677).

Whateley, William, *A Bride Bush, or A Wedding Sermon* (London, 1617; reprinted Amsterdam: Theatrum Orbis Terrarum / Norwood N.J.: Walter Johnson Inc., 1975).

Later works

Abrahams, R. G., 'The Gunpowder Plot in Warwickshire' (unpublished typescript, Birmingham Archaeological Society, Birmingham Reference Library, 1951).

Ackernecht, E. H., 'Midwives as experts in court', *Bulletin of the New York Academy of Medicine* 3 (1976), pp. 1224–8.

Adler, Margot, *Drawing Down the Moon: Witches, Druids, Goddess-Worshippers, and Other Pagans in America Today* (Boston: Beacon Press, 1996).

Ainsworth, W. Harrison, *The Lancashire Witches* (London: Routledge, 1884; reprinted Manchester: Aurora, n.d.).

Allen, A., *A Dictionary of Sussex Folk Medicine* (Newbury: Countryside Books, 1995).

Amussen, Susan Dwyer, *An Ordered Society: Gender and Class in Early Modern England* (Oxford: Blackwell, 1983).

Ankarloo, Bengt, and Henningsen, Gustav (eds), *Early Modern European Witchcraft: Centres and Peripheries* (Oxford: Oxford University Press, 1990).

Anstruther, Godfrey, *The Seminary Priests: A Dictionary of Secular Clergy of England and Wales, 1558–1603* (Durham: Ushaw College, 1964).

Bailey, Gauvin, 'Jesuit catechism and the arts', in John O'Malley *et al.* (eds), *The Jesuits: Cultures, Sciences, and the Arts, 1540–1773* (Toronto: University of Toronto Press, 1999).

Baines, Edward, *The History of the County Palatine of Lancaster*, 2 vols (London: Fisher, Son and Jackson, 1836).

Bamford, Samuel, *Early Days* (Manchester: John Heywood, 1849; ed. W. H. Chaloner, London: Frank Cass, 1967).

Bann, Stephen, *Romanticism and the Rise of History* (New York: Twayne, 1995).

Barnard, E. A., *A Seventeenth Century Country Gentleman: Sir Francis Throckmorton* (Cambridge: Cambridge University Press, 1948).

Barry, Jonathan, Hester, M., and Roberts, G. (eds), *Witchcraft in Early Modern Europe: Studies in Culture and Belief* (Cambridge: Cambridge University Press, 1996).

Barstow, A., *Witchcraze: A New History of the European Witch Hunts* (London: Harper Collins, 1995).

Baskerville, Geoffrey, *English Monks and the Suppression of the Monasteries* (London: Jonathan Cape, 1965).

Bataille, Georges, *The Accursed Share: An Essay on General Economy*, trans. Robert Hurley (New York: Zone Books, 1988).

Bawcutt, N. W. (ed.), *The Control and Censorship of Caroline Drama: The Records of Sir Henry Herbert, Master of the Revels* (Oxford: Clarendon Press, 1995).

Beier, Lucinda M., *Sufferers and Healers: The Experience of Illness in Seventeenth-Century England* (London: Routledge, 1987).

Behringer, Wolfgang, 'Witchcraft studies in Austria, Germany and Switzerland', in Jonathan Barry *et al.* (eds), *Witchcraft in Early Modern Europe: Studies in Culture and Belief* (Cambridge: Cambridge University Press, 1996).

Benjamin, W., 'The work of art in the age of mechanical reproduction', in *Illuminations* (1936; London: Fontana, 1992).

Bentley, G. E., *The Jacobean and Caroline Stage*, 6 vols (Oxford: Clarendon Press, 1941–68).

Berry, Herbert, 'The Globe bewitched and *El hombre fiel*', *Medieval and Renaissance Drama in England* 1 (1984), pp. 211–30.

Bossy, *The English Catholic Community, 1570–1850* (London: Darton, Longman and Todd, 1975).

Bossy, John, 'Moral arithmetic: seven sins to ten commandments', in E. Leites (ed.), *Conscience and Casuistry in Early Modern Europe* (Cambridge: Cambridge University Press, 1988).

Bossy, John, 'The heart of Robert Parsons', in Thomas McCoog (ed.), *The Reckoned Expense: Edmund Campion and the Early English Jesuits* (Woodbridge: Boydell Press, 1996).

Brigden, Susan, 'Youth and the English Reformation', *Past and Present* 95 (1982), pp. 37–67.

Briggs, R., *Witches and Neighbours: The Social and Cultural Context of European Witchcraft* (London: Harper Collins, 1996).

Brownlow, F. W., *Shakespeare, Harsnett, and the Devils of Denham* (Newark: University of Delaware Press, 1993).

Burr, G. L., 'A review of M. A. Murray's *Witch Cult in Western Europe*', *American Historical Review* 27 (1921–2), pp. 780–3.

Bushaway, Bob, *By Rite: Custom, Ceremony and Community in England 1700–1880* (London: Junction Books, 1982).

Butler, Martin, *Theatre and Crisis 1632–1642* (Cambridge: Cambridge University Press, 1984).

Camm, Dom. Bede, *Forgotten Shrines: An Account of Some Old Catholic Halls and Families in England and of Relics and Memorials of the English Martyrs* (London: Macdonald and Evans, 1910).

Caraman, Philip, *Henry Garnet and the Gunpowder Plot* (London: Longman, 1964).

Carlton, Charles, *Archbishop William Laud* (London: Routledge, 1987).

Cartwright, James J., *Chapters in the History of Yorkshire* (Wakefield: B. W. Allen, 1872).

Cixous, Hélène, and Clément, Catherine, *The Newly Born Woman*, trans. Betsy Wing (Manchester: Manchester University Press, 1986).

Clark, A. M., *Thomas Heywood: Playwright and Miscellanist* (Oxford: Blackwell, 1931).

Clark, Stuart, 'King James's *Daemonologie*: witchcraft and kingship', in Sydney Anglo (ed.), *The Damned Art: Essays in the Literature of Witchcraft* (London: Routledge, 1977).

Clark, Stuart, 'Inversion, misrule and the meaning of witchcraft', *Past and Present* 87 (1980), pp. 98–127.

Clark, Stuart, 'The rational witchfinder: conscience, demonological naturalism and popular superstitions', in S. Pumfrey *et al.* (eds), *Science, Culture and Popular Belief in Renaissance Europe* (Manchester: Manchester University Press, 1991).

Clark, Stuart, *Thinking with Demons: The Idea of Witchcraft in Early Modern Europe* (Oxford: Clarendon Press, 1997).

Clark, Stuart (ed.), *Languages of Witchcraft: Narrative, Ideology and Meaning in Early Modern Culture* (London: Macmillan, 2001).

Cockburn, J. S., *A History of English Assizes 1558–1714* (Cambridge: Cambridge University Press, 1972).

Cockburn, J. S., *Calendar of Assize Records: Home Circuit: Essex: Elizabeth I* (London: HMSO, 1978).

Cockburn, J. S., *Calendar of Assize Records: Home Circuit: Elizabeth I and James I* (London: HMSO, 1985).

Cockburn, J. S., and Green, T. A., (eds), *Twelve Good Men and True: The Criminal Trial Jury in England 1200–1800* (Princeton: Princeton University Press, 1988).

Cohn, Norman, *Europe's Inner Demons* (New York: Basic Books, 1975).

Collier, J. Paynes (ed.), *The Egerton Papers* (London: Camden Society publications xii, 1840).

Connelly, Mark, *Christmas: A Social History* (London: I. B. Tauris, 1999).

Cook, Alice M. (ed.), *Act Book of the Ecclesiastical Court of Whalley 1510–1538* (Manchester: Chetham Society publications, new series xliv, 1901).

Crawford, P., *Women and Religion in England 1500–1720* (London: Routledge, 1993).

Cressy, David, *Agnes Bowker's Cat: Travesties and Transgressions in Tudor and Stuart England* (Oxford: Oxford University Press, 2000).

Cross, Claire, 'An Elizabethan martyrologist and his martyr: John Mush and Margaret Clitherow', in Diana Wood (ed.), *Martyrs and Martyrologies* (Oxford: Blackwell, 1993).

Crowley, Vivianne, *Wicca: The Old Religion in the New Millennium* (1989; reprinted London: Thorsons, 1996).

Daly, Mary, *Gyn/Ecology: The Metaethics of Radical Feminism* (Boston: Beacon Press, 1978).

Danson, Lawrence, *Tragic Alphabet: Shakespeare's Drama of Language* (New Haven: Yale University Press, 1974).

Davies, Owen, *Witchcraft, Magic and Culture 1736–1951* (Manchester: Manchester University Press, 1999).

de Blecourt, W., 'Witch doctors, soothsayers and priests: on cunning folk in European historiography and tradition', *Social History* 19: 3 (Oct. 1994), pp. 285–303.

Dellheim, Charles, *The Face of the Past: The Preservation of the Medieval Inheritance in Victorian England* (Cambridge: Cambridge University Press, 1982).

Delumeau, Jean, *Catholicisme entre Luther et Voltaire* (Paris: Presses universitaires de France, 1971).

Deslandres, Dominique, 'The French Jesuits' missionary world', in John O'Malley *et al.* (eds), *The Jesuits: Cultures, Sciences, and the Arts, 1540–1773* (Toronto: University of Toronto Press, 1999).

Dietz, Frederick C., *English Public Finance 1558–1641* (1932; 2nd edn, London: Cass, 1964).

Ditchfield, Simon, 'Martyrs on the move: relics as vindicators of local diversity in the Tridentine Church', in Diana Wood (ed.), *Martyrs and Martyrologies* (Oxford: Blackwell, 1993).

Dolan, F. E., *Dangerous Familiars: Representations of Domestic Crime in England 1550–1700* (London: Cornell University Press, 1995).

Duffy, Eamon, *The Stripping of the Altars: Traditional Religion in England, 1400–1580* (New Haven and London: Yale University Press, 1992).

Durston, Christopher, and Eales, Jacqueline (eds), *The Culture of English Puritanism, 1560–1700* (London: Macmillan, 1996).

Duthie, G. I., 'Antithesis in *Macbeth*', *Shakespeare Survey* 19 (1966), pp. 25–33.

Dutton, Richard, Findlay, Alison, and Wilson, Richard (eds), *Lancastrian Shakespeare: Theatre and Religion* and *Lancastrian Shakespeare: Region, Religion and Patronage* (Manchester: Manchester University Press, forthcoming 2003).

Dworkin, Andrea, *Woman Hating* (New York: E. P. Dutton, 1975).

Eagleton, Terry, *William Shakespeare* (Oxford: Blackwell, 1986).

Ehrenreich, B., and English, D., *Witches, Midwives and Nurses: A History of Women Healers* (New York: Feminist Press, 1973).

Ellis, S. M., *William Harrison Ainsworth and His Friends*, 2 vols (London: Bodley Head, 1911).

Ellis, S. M., 'A great bibliophile: James Crossley', in *Wilkie Collins, La Fanu and Others* (1931; reprinted Freeport, N.Y.: Books for Libraries Press, 1968).

Elmer, Peter, 'Towards a politics of witchcraft in early modern England', in Stuart Clark (ed.), *Languages of Witchcraft: Narrative, Ideology and Meaning in Early Modern Culture* (London: Macmillan, 2001).

Ewen, C. L'Estrange, *Witch Hunting and Witch Trials: The Indictments for Witchcraft from the Records of 1373 Assizes Held for the Home Circuit A.D. 1559–1736* (London: Kegan Paul, 1929).

Ewen, C. L'Estrange, *Witchcraft and Demonianism: A Concise Account Derived From Sworn Depositions and Confessions Obtained in the Courts of England and Wales* (London: Heath Cranton, 1933).

Ewen, C. L'Estrange, *Some Witchcraft Criticisms: A Plea for the Blue Pencil* (London: printed for the author, 1938).

Fairfax-Lucy, Alice, *Charlecote and the Lucys* (London: Jonathan Cape, 1958).

Farrar, Janet, and Farrar, Stewart, *Eight Sabbats for Witches* (London: Hale, 1981).

Findlay, Alison, *Illegitimate Power: Bastards in Renaissance Drama* (Manchester: Manchester University Press, 1994).

Fletcher, Anthony, *Tudor Rebellions* (London: Longman, 1968).

Foley, Henry (ed.), *Records of the English Province of the Society of Jesus*, 6 vols (London: Burns and Oates, 1877).

Forbes, T. R., 'Midwifery and witchcraft', *Journal of the History of Medicine and Allied Sciences* 17 (1962), pp. 264–83.

Forbes, T. R., 'A jury of matrons', *Medical History* 32: 1 (1988), pp. 23–33.

Foster, Elizabeth Read (ed.), *Proceedings in Parliament 1610* (New Haven and London: Yale University Press, 1966).

Fraser, Antonia, *The Gunpowder Plot: Terror and Faith in 1605* (London: Weidenfeld and Nicolson, 1996).

Frazer, Sir James G., *The Golden Bough* (London: Macmillan, 1890).

Gage, Matilda Joscelyn, *Women, Church and State* (1893; reprinted New York: Arno Press, 1972).

Gardiner, S. R. (ed.), *Documents Relating to Proceedings Against William Prynne* (London: Camden Society publications, new series 18, 1877).

Gardner, Gerald, *Witchcraft Today* (London: Rider, 1954).

Gardner, Gerald, *The Meaning of Witchcraft* (London: Aquarian Press, 1959).

Gaskill, Malcolm, 'Attitudes to crime in early modern England, with special reference to witchcraft, coining and murder' (unpublished Ph.D. thesis, University of Cambridge, 1994).

Gaskill, Malcolm, 'Witchcraft and power in early modern England: the case of Margaret Moore', in J. Kermode and G. Walker (eds), *Women, Crime and the Courts in Early Modern England* (London: UCL Press, 1994).

Gaskill, Malcolm, 'The displacement of providence', *Continuity and Change* 11 (1996), pp. 341–74.

Gaskill, Malcolm, 'Witchcraft in early modern Kent: stereotypes and the background to accusations', in Jonathan Barry *et al.* (eds), *Witchcraft in Early Modern Europe: Studies in Culture and Belief* (Cambridge: Cambridge University Press, 1996).

Gerard, John, S.J., *What was the Gunpowder Plot? The Traditional Story Tested by Original Evidence* (London: Osgood and McIlvaine, 1897).

Gibson, Marion, *Reading Witchcraft: Stories of Early English Witches* (London: Routledge, 1999).

Gibson, Marion, *Early Modern Witches: Witchcraft Cases in Contemporary Writing* (London: Routledge, 2000).

Gibson, Marion, 'Understanding witchcraft? Accusers' stories in print in early modern England', in Stuart Clark (ed.), *Languages of Witchcraft: Narrative, Ideology and Meaning in Early Modern Culture* (London: Macmillan, 2001).

Ginzburg, Carlo, *Night Battles: Witchcraft and Agrarian Cults in the Sixteenth and Seventeenth Centuries*, trans. J. and A. Tedeschi (London: Routledge, 1983).

Godwin, Joscelyn, *The Theosophical Enlightenment* (New York: State University of New York Press, 1994).

Goodare, Julian (ed.), *The Scottish Witch Hunt in Context* (Manchester: Manchester University Press, 2002).

Goodich, Michael, *Violence and Miracle in the Fourteenth Century: Private Grief and Public Salvation* (Chicago: Chicago University Press, 1995).

Graves, Michael, *Thomas Norton: Parliament Man* (Oxford: Blackwell, 1994).

Green, M., 'Women's medical practice and health care in medieval Europe', *Signs* 14: 2 (1989), pp. 434–73.

Greenblatt, Stephen, 'Shakespeare bewitched', in *New Historical Literary Study* (Princeton: Princeton University Press, 1992).

Greenblatt, Stephen, *Hamlet in Purgatory* (Princeton: Princeton University Press, 2001).

Haigh, Christopher, *Reformation and Resistance in Tudor Lancashire* (Cambridge:

Cambridge University Press, 1975).

Haigh, Christopher, 'The continuity of Catholicism in the English Reformation', *Past and Present* 93 (1981), pp. 37–69.

Haigh, Christopher, *The English Reformation Revised* (Cambridge: Cambridge University Press, 1987).

Haigh, Christopher, *English Reformations: Religion, Politics and Society Under the Tudors* (Oxford: Clarendon Press, 1993).

Halliwell, J. O., *The Palatine Anthology/The Palatine Garland* (London, 1850).

Hanson, Elizabeth, *Discovering the Subject in Renaissance England* (Cambridge: Cambridge University Press, 1998).

Hardin, Richard, 'The early poetry of the Gunpowder Plot: myth in the making', *English Literary Renaissance* 22: 1 (1992), pp. 62–79.

Harland, J., and Wilkinson, T. T., *Lancashire Folk-lore* (1882; reprinted Wakefield: S. R. Publishers, 1972).

Harley, David, 'Historians as demonologists: the myth of the midwife witch', *Journal of the Society for the Social History of Medicine* 3 (1990), pp. 1–26.

Hasted, Rachel, 'The new myth of the witch', *Trouble and Strife* 2 (Spring 1982), pp. 9–17.

Hasted, Rachel, 'Mothers of invention', *Trouble and Strife* 7 (Winter 1985), pp. 17–25.

Hasted, Rachel, *The Pendle Witch-Trial 1612* (Preston: Lancashire County Books, 1987).

Havran, Marvin, *The Catholics in Caroline England* (Stanford: Stanford University Press, 1962).

Heinsohn, G., and Steiger, O., 'The elimination of medieval birth control and the witch trials of modern times', *International Journal of Women's Studies* 3 (1982), pp. 193–214.

Heselton, Philip, *Wiccan Roots: Gerald Gardner and the Modern Witchcraft Revival* (Berkshire: Capall Bann, 2000).

Hester, M., *Lewd Women and Wicked Witches: A Study of the Dynamics of Male Domination* (London: Routledge, 1992).

Hill, Christopher, *Religion and Politics in Seventeenth Century England* (Brighton: Harvester, 1986).

Hilton, J. A., *Catholic Lancashire from Reformation to Renewal 1559–1991* (Chichester: Phillimore, 1994).

Historical Manuscripts Commission, *Salisbury* Series 9 (reprinted London, 1970).

Holmes, C., 'Popular culture? Witches, magistrates, and divines in early modern England', in S. L. Kaplan (ed.), *Understanding Popular Culture: Europe from the Middle Ages to the Nineteenth Century* (Berlin: Mouton, 1984).

Holmes, Clive, 'Women: witnesses and witches', *Past and Present* 140 (1993), pp. 45–78.

Honan, Park, *Shakespeare: A Life* (Oxford: Oxford University Press, 1998).

Honigmann, Ernst, *Shakespeare: The 'Lost Years'* (Manchester: Manchester University Press, 1985).

Horsley, R. A., 'Who were the witches? The social roles of the accused in the European witch trials', *Journal of Interdisciplinary History* 9 (1979), pp. 689–715.

Hotson, Leslie, *I, William Shakespeare* (London: Jonathan Cape, 1937).

Hughes, Anne, 'Warwickshire on the eve of the Civil War: a "county community"?', *Midland History* 7 (1982), pp. 42–72.

Hughes, Anne, *Politics, Society and Civil War in Warwickshire, 1620–1660* (Cambridge: Cambridge University Press, 1991).

Hughes, Anne, 'Religion and society in Stratford-upon-Avon, 1619–1638', *Midland History* 19 (1994), pp. 58–84.

Hulton, W. A. (ed.), *The Coucher Book or Chartulary of Whalley Abbey*, iv (Manchester: Chetham Society publications xx, 1849).

Hume, Lynne, *Witchcraft and Paganism in Australia* (Melbourne: Melbourne University Press, 1997).

Huntley, Frank, '*Macbeth* and the background of Jesuitical equivocation', *Proceedings of the Modern Language Association* 79 (1964), pp. 390–400.

Hutton, Ronald, *The Pagan Religions of the Ancient British Isles: Their Nature and Legacy* (Oxford: Blackwell, 1991).

Hutton, Ronald, *The Rise and Fall of Merry England: The Ritual Year 1400–1700* (Oxford: Oxford University Press, 1994).

Hutton, Ronald, 'The English Reformation and the evidence of folklore', *Past and Present* 148 (1995), pp. 89–116.

Hutton, Ronald, 'The roots of modern paganism', in Graham Harvey and Charlotte Hardman (eds), *Paganism Today: Wiccans, Druids, the Goddess and Ancient Earth Traditions for the Twenty-First Century* (London: Thorsons, 1996).

Hutton, Ronald, *The Stations of the Sun* (Oxford: Oxford University Press, 1996).

Hutton, Ronald, 'The discovery of the modern goddess', in J. Pearson *et al.* (eds), *Nature Religion Today: Paganism in the Modern World* (Edinburgh: Edinburgh University Press, 1998).

Hutton, Ronald, *The Triumph of the Moon: A History of Modern Pagan Witchcraft* (Oxford: Oxford University Press, 1999).

Jackson, Nigel Aldcroft, 'Witch-fire over Lancashire: the wysard craft of north west England', *The Cauldron* 91 (1999), pp. 21–5.

Jones, Emrys (ed.), *The New Oxford Book of Sixteenth Century Verse* (Oxford: Oxford University Press: 1991).

Karle, Warren J., 'The devil in the vineyard: the role of seminary priests in the introduction of continental witchlore into England' (unpublished M.A. thesis, University of York, 1992).

Kaula, David, '*Hamlet* and the *Sparing Discovery*', *Shakespeare Survery* 24 (1971), pp. 71–7.

Kaushik, Sandeep, 'Resistance, loyalty and recusant politics: Sir Thomas Tresham and the Elizabethan state', *Midland History* 21 (1996), pp. 37–72.

Keeble, N. H. (ed.), *The Cultural Identity of Seventeenth Century Woman: A Reader* (London and New York: Routledge, 1994).

Kernan, Alvin, *Shakespeare, The King's Playwright: Theater in the Stuart Court, 1603–1613* (New Haven: Yale University Press, 1995).

Kittredge, G. L., *Witchcraft in Old and New England* (Cambridge, Mass.: Harvard University Press, 1929; reprinted New York, 1958).

Klaits, Joseph, *Servants of Satan: The Age of Witch Hunts* (Bloomington: Indiana University Press, 1985).

Knight, G. Wilson, *The Imperial Theme* (London: Methuen, 1951).

Larner, Christina, *Enemies of God* (Oxford: Blackwell, 1983).

Larner, Christina, *Witchcraft and Religion: The Politics of Popular Belief* (Oxford: Blackwell, 1984).

LaRocca, John, '"Who can't pray with me, can't love me": toleration and the early Jacobean recusancy policy', *Journal of British Studies* 23: 2 (1984), pp. 22–36.

Leatherbarrow, J. S., *The Lancashire Elizabethan Recusants* (Manchester: Chetham Society publications, new series lxxxx, 1947).

Leland, Charles G., *Aradia or The Gospel of the Witches* (1899; reprinted Washington: Phoenix, 1990).

Levack, Brian, *The Witch-Hunt in Early Modern Europe* (London: Longman, 1987; 2nd edn, 1995).

Levine, Philippa, *The Amateur and the Professional: Antiquarians, Historians and Archaeologists in Victorian England, 1838–1886* (Cambridge: Cambridge University Press, 1986).

Lucifer Over Lancashire, BBC Television, 1987.

Lumby, Jonathan, *The Lancashire Witch-Craze: Jennet Preston and the Lancashire Witches* (Preston: Carnegie, 1995).

Lunn, Maurus, 'English Benedictines and the Oath of Allegiance, 1606–1647', *Recusant History* 10 (1969–70), pp. 146–63.

Macaulay, Thomas Babington, *Critical and Historical Essays*, i (London: Methuen, 1903).

McCoy, Richard, 'Love's martyrs: Shakespeare's *Phoenix and the Turtle* and the sacrificial sonnets', in Claire McEachern and Debora Shuger (eds), *Religion and Culture in Renaissance England* (Cambridge: Cambridge University Press, 1997).

Macdonald, Malcolm, *Witchcraft and Hysteria in Elizabethan London: Edward Jorden and the Mary Glover Case* (London: Routledge, 1991).

Macfarlane, A., *Witchcraft in Tudor and Stuart England: A Regional and Comparative Study* (1970; 2nd edn, with an introduction by James Sharpe, London: Routledge, 1999).

Macfarlane, A., *The Origins of English Individualism: The Family, Property and Social Transition* (Oxford: Blackwell, 1978).

McLuskie, Kathleen, *Renaissance Dramatists* (New York and London: Harvester Wheatsheaf, 1989).

Macpherson Bardell, K., '"Death by divelishe demonstracion": witchcraft beliefs, gender and popular religion in the early modern midlands and north of England' (unpublished Ph.D. thesis, Nottingham Trent University, 1999).

Malcolmson, Robert, *Popular Recreations in English Society 1700–1850* (Cambridge: Cambridge University Press, 1973).

Manning, Roger, *Village Revolts: Social Protests and Popular Disturbances in England, 1509–1640* (Oxford: Oxford University Press, 1988).

Marcus, Leah S., *The Politics of Mirth* (Chicago and London: Chicago University Press, 1986).

Marotti, Arthur, 'Southwell's remains: Catholicism and anti-Catholicism in early nodern England', in Cedric Brown and Arthur Marotti (eds), *Texts and Cultural Change in Early Modern England* (London: Macmillan, 1997).

Martin, J. M., 'A Warwickshire market town in adversity: Stratford-upon-Avon in the sixteenth and seventeenth centuries', *Midland History* 7 (1982), pp. 26–41.

Maxwell-Stuart, P. G., *Witchcraft in Europe and the New World, 1400–1800* (Basingstoke: Palgrave, 2001).

Megged, A., 'Magic, popular medicine and gender in seventeenth-century Mexico: the case of Isabel de Montoya', *Social History* 19: 2 (May 1994), pp. 189–207.

Meštrovic, Stjepan G., *Postemotional Society* (London: Sage, 1997).

Michelet, Jules, *Satanism and Witchcraft: The Classic Study of Medieval Superstition* (1862; trans. A. R. Allinson, New York: Carol Publishing Group, 1992).

Miller, George C., *Hoghton Tower* (Preston: Guardian Press, 1948).

Mitchell, Rosemary, *Picturing the Past: English History in Text and Image,1800–1870* (Oxford: Clarendon Press, 2000).

Montrose, Louis, '*A Midsummer Night's Dream* and the shaping fantasies of Elizabethan culture', in Richard Wilson and Richard Dutton (eds), *New Historicism and Renaissance Drama* (Harlow: Longman, 1992).

Morrill, John, *Cheshire 1630–1660: County Government and Society during the English Revolution* (Oxford: Oxford University Press, 1974).

Morris, John (ed.), *The Troubles of Our Catholic Forefathers*, 3 vols (London: Burns and Oates, 1877).

Mosler, David, 'Warwickshire Catholics in the Civil War', *Recusant History* 15 (1979–81), pp. 259–64.

Moura, Ann, *The Origins of Modern Witchcraft: The Evolution of a World Religion* (St Pauls, Minn.: Llewellyn, 2000).

Muchembled, Robert, 'Satanic myths and cultural reality', in Bengt Ankarloo and Gustav Heningsen (eds), *Early Modern European Witchcraft: Centres and Peripheries* (Oxford: Oxford University Press, 1990).

Mullaney, Steven, 'Lying like truth: riddle, representation and treason in Renaissance England', *English Literary History* 47 (1980), pp. 320–47.

Mullaney, Steven, *The Place of the Stage: License, Play, and Power in Renaissance England* (Chicago: Chicago University Press, 1988).

Mullett, Michael A., *Catholics in Britain and Ireland, 1558–1829* (Basingstoke: Macmillan, 1998).

Murray, Margaret A., *The Witch Cult in Western Europe: A Study in Anthropology* (Oxford: Clarendon Press, 1921).

Murray, Margaret A., *The God of the Witches* (1933; 2nd edn, London: Faber and Faber, 1970).

Nagy, D. E., *Popular Medicine in Seventeenth-Century England* (Ohio: Bowling Green State University Press, 1988).

Neill, Robert, *Mist over Pendle* (London: Hutchinson, 1951).

Nichols, John, *The Progresses … of James the First* (London: Royal Society of Antiquaries, 1828).

Normand, Lawrence, and Roberts, Gareth, *Witchcraft in Early Modern Scotland: James VI's Demonology and the North Berwick Witches* (Exeter: Exeter University Press, 2000).

Notestein, Wallace, *A History of Witchcraft in England from 1558 to 1718* (Washington, DC: American Historical Association, 1911).

Oates, Caroline, and Wood, Juliette, *A Coven of Scholars: Margaret Murray and her Working Methods* (London: Folklore Society, 1998).

Oldridge, Darren, *The Devil in Early Modern England* (Stroud: Sutton, 2000).

O'Malley, John, Bailey, G., Harris, S., and Kennedy, F. (eds), *The Jesuits: Cultures, Sciences, and the Arts, 1540–1773* (Toronto: University of Toronto Press, 1999).

Pagan Dawn, Lammas 1997 and Spring 2001 (London: The Pagan Federation).

Parkinson, Anne C., *A History of Catholicism in the Furness Peninsula 1127–1997* (Lancaster: Lancaster University Centre for North West Regional Studies, 1998).

Patrides, C. A. (ed.), *Milton's 'Lycidas': The Tradition and the Poem* (Missouri: University of Missouri Press, 1983).

Paul, Henry, *The Royal Play of 'Macbeth'* (New York: Macmillan, 1950).

Pearson, Joanne, 'Demarcating the field: Paganism, Wicca, and Witchcraft', in G. Harvey and M. Bowman (eds), *Pagan Identities*, special issue of DISKUS (2000) (www.uni-marburg.de/fb03/religionswissenschaft/journal/diskus).

Pearson, Joanne (ed.), *A Popular Dictionary of Paganism* (London: Curzon/ Routledge, 2002).

Pearson, Joanne, Roberts, Richard H., and Samuels, Geoffrey (eds), *Nature Religion Today: Paganism in the Modern World* (Edinburgh: Edinburgh University Press, 1998).

Peck, Linda Levy, *Northampton: Patronage and Policy at the Court of James I* (London: Allen and Unwin, 1982).

Peel, Edgar, and Southern, Pat, *The Trials of the Lancashire Witches: A Study in Seventeenth-Century Witchcraft* (Newton Abbot: David and Charles, 1969; Nelson: Hendon, 1994).

Pettitt, Tom, 'Protesting inversions: charivary as folk pageantry and folk-law', *Medieval English Theatre* 21 (1999), pp. 21–51.

Plowden, A., *Tudor Women: Queens and Commoners* (Stroud: Sutton, 1979).

Punter, David, *Literature of Terror* (London: Longman, 1908).

Purkiss, Diane, *The Witch in History: Early Modern and Twentieth-Century Interpretations* (London: Routledge, 1996).

Quaife, G. R., *Godly Zeal and Furious Rage: The Witch in Early Modern Europe* (London: Croom Helm, 1987).

Questier, Michael, *Conversion, Politics and Religion in England, 1580–1625* (Cambridge: Cambridge University Press, 1996).

Railo, Eino, *The Haunted Castle* (London: Routledge, 1927).

Raines, F. R. (ed.), *The State, Civil and Ecclesiastical, of the County of Lancaster, about the Year 1590* (Manchester: Chetham Society publications xcvi, 1875).

Ramsey, Nancy, 'The myth of historical narrative in M. Murray's *The God of the Witches*', *The Pomegranate: A New Journal of Neo-Pagan Thought* 3 (1998), pp. 2–15.

Reay, Barry (ed.), *Popular Culture in Seventeenth Century England* (London: Routledge, 1985).

Rees, Kenneth, 'The tangled skein: the role of myth in paganism', in Graham Harvey and Charlotte Hardman (eds), *Paganism Today: Wiccans, Druids, the Goddess and Ancient Earth Traditions for the Twenty-First Century* (London: Thorsons, 1996), pp. 16–31.

Regardie, Israel, *The Golden Dawn: The Original Account of the Teachings, Rites and Ceremonies of the Hermetic Order of the Golden Dawn* (1941; reprinted St Pauls, Minn.: Llewellyn, 1989).

Rickert, Corinne Holt, *The Case of John Darrell: Minister and Exorcist* (Gainsville, Fla.: University of Florida Monographs, Humanities, 9, Winter 1962).

Robbins, R. H., *Encyclopedia of Witchcraft and Demonology* (London: Peter Nevill, 1959).

Rose, E. E., *A Razor for a Goat: Witchcraft and Diabolism* (Toronto: University of Toronto Press, 1962).

Rosen, Barbara, *Witchcraft* (London: Edward Arnold, 1969).

Rosen, Barbara, *Witchcraft in England 1558–1618* (Amherst: University of Massachusetts Press, 1991).

Rothenberg, E., 'The cunning folk in witchcraft trials, 1560–1700' (unpublished M.Stud. dissertation, University of Oxford, 1999).

Rowse, A. L., *The Elizabethan Renaissance: The Life of the Society* (London: Sphere Books, 1974).

Salgado, Gamini, *The Elizabethan Underworld* (Stroud: Sutton, 1997).

Sanders, Andrew, *The Victorian Historical Novel 1840–1880* (London: Macmillan, 1978).

Scarisbrick, J. J., *The Reformation and the English People* (Oxford: Blackwell, 1994).

Scarre, Geoffrey, *Witchcraft and Magic in Sixteenth- and Seventeenth-Century Europe* (London: Macmillan, 1987; 2nd edn, London: Palgrave, 2001).

Schofield, R. S., 'The geographical distribution of wealth in England, 1334–1649', *Economic History Review*, 2nd series, 18 (1965), pp. 483–510.

Scott, Walter, *Poems* (London: Cassell, n.d.).

Scott, William, 'Macbeth's – and our – self-equivocations', *Shakespeare Quarterly* 37 (1986), pp. 160–74.

Scully, S., 'Marriage or a career? Witchcraft as an alternative in seventeenth-century Venice', *Journal of Social History* 28 (1995), pp. 857–76.

Sharpe, James, 'Witchcraft and women in seventeenth-century England: some northern evidence', *Continuity and Change* 6 (1991), pp. 179–99.

Sharpe, James, *Witchcraft in Seventeenth-Century Yorkshire: Accusations and Counter-Measures* (York: Borthwick Institute, 1992).

Sharpe, James, *Instruments of Darkness: Witchcraft in England 1550–1750* (London: Hamish Hamilton, 1996; London: Penguin, 1997).

Sharpe, James, *The Bewitching of Anne Gunter: A Horrible and True Story of Football, Witchcraft, Murder, and the King of England* (London: Profile Books, 1999).

Sharpe, James, *Witchcraft in Early Modern England* (London: Longman, 2001).

Sim, A., *The Tudor Housewife* (Stroud: Sutton, 1996).

Simmons, Jack, *The Victorian Railway* (London: Thames and Hudson, 1991).

Simpson, Richard (ed.), *Rambler*, new series viii (1857).

Simpson, Richard, *Edmund Campion* (London: John Hodges, 1896).

Slights, Camille Wells, *The Casuistical Tradition in Shakespeare, Donne, Herbert, and Milton* (Princeton: Princeton University Press, 1981).

Smith, J., and Randall, T. (eds), *Kill or Cure: Medical Remedies of the Sixteenth and Seventeenth Centuries from the Staffordshire Record Office* (Stafford: Staffordshire Record Office, 1996).

Smith, K., 'The wiseman and his community', *Folklife* 15 (1977), pp. 24–35.

Snape, Michael, '"Oh happy reformation": Anglicanism and society in a northern parish, 1689–1789' (unpublished Ph.D. thesis, University of Birmingham, 1994).

Snape, Michael, '"The Surey imposter": demonic possession and religious conflict in seventeenth-century Lancashire', *Transactions of the Lancashire and Cheshire Antiquarian Society* 90 (1994), pp. 93–114.

Starhawk, *The Spiral Dance: A Rebirth of the Ancient Religion of the Great Goddess* (1979; New York: HarperCollins, 1989).

Starkey, David *et al.* (eds), *The English Court from the Wars of the Roses to the Civil War* (London: Longman, 1987).

Sutherland, John, *Victorian Novelists and Publishers* (London: Athlone Press, 1976).

Swain, John T., 'Industry and economy in north east Lancashire circa 1500–1640' (unpublished Ph.D. thesis, University of Cambridge, 1983).

Swain, John T., *Industry Before the Industrial Revolution: North-East Lancashire c. 1500–1640* (Manchester: Chetham Society publications, third series xxxii / Manchester University Press, 1986).

Swain, John T., 'The Lancashire witch trials of 1612 and 1634 and the economics of witchcraft', *Northern History* 30 (1994), pp. 64–85.

Szasz, Thomas S., *The Manufacture of Madness: A Comparative Study of the Inquisition and the Mental Health Movement* (London: Routledge, 1971).

Taylor-Taswell, S. T., *Whalley Church and Abbey* (Blackburn: Blackburn Times, n.d.).

Teall, J. L., 'Witchcraft and Calvinism in Elizabethan England: divine power and human will', *Journal of the History of Ideas* 23 (1962), pp. 21–36

Thomas, Keith, *Religion and the Decline of Magic: Studies in Popular Beliefs in Sixteenth- and Seventeenth-Century England* (1971; London: Penguin, 1973).

Trevor-Roper, Hugh, *Archbishop Laud* (London: Macmillan, 1940).

Trevor-Roper, Hugh, *Religion, the Reformation and Social Change* (London: Macmillan, 1967).

Trevor-Roper, Hugh, *The European Witch-Craze of the Sixteenth and Seventeenth Centuries* (London: Penguin, 1969).

Trevor-Roper, Hugh, 'The European witchcraze and social change', in Max Marwick (ed.), *Witchcraft and Sorcery* (London: Penguin, 1970).

Ussher, J., *Women's Madness: Misogyny or Mental Illness?* (Hemel Hempstead: Harvester Wheatsheaf, 1991).

Walker, D. P., *Unclean Spirits: Possession and Exorcism in France and England in the Late Sixteenth and Early Seventeenth Centuries* (London: Scolar Press, 1981).

Walsham, Alexandra, *Church Papists: Catholicism, Conformity and Confessional Polemic in Early Modern England* (Woodbridge: Boydell and Brewer, 1993).

Watson, Robert, '*Othello* as protestant propaganda', in Claire McEachern and Debora Shuger (eds), *Religion and Culture in Renaissance England* (Cambridge: Cambridge University Press, 1997).

Watts, Michael, *The Dissenters: From the Reformation to the French Revolution* (Oxford: Clarendon Press, 1978).

Waugh, Evelyn, *Edmund Campion* (London: Longmans and Green, 1935).

Webb, James, *The Flight From Reason: Volume 1 of the Age of the Irrational* (London: Macdonald, 1971).

Webb, James, *The Occult Establishment* (La Salle, Ill.: Open Court, 1976).

Whitaker, Thomas Dunham, *History of the Original Parish of Whalley* (Blackburn, 1801; 3rd edn, London, 1818; 4th edn, ed. J. G. Nichols and P. A. Lyons, 2 vols, London: Routledge, 1872–76).

Willis, D., *Malevolent Nurture: Witch-Hunting and Maternal Power in Early Modern England* (Ithaca and London: Cornell University Press, 1995).

Wills, Gary, *Witches and Jesuits: Shakespeare's 'Macbeth'* (Oxford: Oxford University Press, 1995).

Willson, D. H., *King James VI and I* (London: Cape, 1956).

Wilson, Richard, 'Shakespeare and the Jesuits', *Times Literary Supplement*, 19 December 1997.

Wood, Diana (ed.), *Martyrs and Martyrologies* (Oxford: Blackwell, 1993).

Youings, Joyce, *The Dissolution of the Monasteries* (London: Allen and Unwin / New York: Barnes and Noble, 1971).

Index